TROUBLED WATERS

An Unauthorised and Unofficial
Guide to *Dawson's Creek*

Scott Andrews

This edition first published in 2001 by
Virgin Books Ltd
Thames Wharf Studios
Rainville Road
London
W6 9HA

A catalogue record for this book is available from the British
Library.

ISBN 0 7535 0625 4

Typeset by TW Typesetting, Plymouth, Devon
Printed and bound in Great Britain by
Clays Ltd, St Ives PLC

Contents

Acknowledgements

Jims Sangster and Smith – for mentioning my name to the right people at the right time. Ta guys.

Eddie Robson – for *enormous* help getting the proposal together and for providing a far better title than my lame effort.

Ashley Rance – for lending me copies of all the episodes so I could see all of what I was talking about.

All those folks on the various Usenet groups who have answered my questions over the last few months.

My friends who have growled down the phone at me every time I've said 'I can't come out to play tonight, I've got to spend some time in Capeside.' You can start calling me again now. Please. Guys . . .?

Introduction

Welcome to Capeside, where everyone talks until they're blue in the face and angst is in the water supply. *Troubled Waters* is your guide to Capeside: it's not really designed to be read in one go – although you can if you have the stamina – but rather as a companion to watching *Dawson's Creek* or as a reference and *aide-mémoire*. Each episode will be dealt with individually and the commentary will be broken into the following categories:

The Ballad of Joey and Dawson: These two characters, and their relationship, sit at the heart of the show – pretty much everything revolves around it, reflects upon it, influences it or stems from it. This section will chronicle the ups and downs, the break-ups and make-ups (other ballads include Andie and Pacey, Jen and Henry, Pacey and Joey, Dawson and Gretchen, and Jack and Tobey).

Character Sections: Each of the central characters gets his or her own section showing how they develop during the series and drawing attention to lines of dialogue that define them:

The Movie Brat	Dawson Leery
The Tomboy	Joey Potter
The Clown	Pacey Witter
The Delinquent	Jen Lindley
The Basket Case	Andie McPhee
The Outsider	Jack McPhee
The Wicked Witch	Grams
The Puppy Dog	Henry Parker
The White-Bread, Country-Club	
Goody-Two-Shoes	Abby Morgan
The Dark Horse	Drue Valentine
The Big Sis	Gretchen Witter

Family Sucks!: It isn't easy living at home, and half the gang's problems stem from their families. This section looks at cases of parents, grandparents and siblings stepping all over their lives.

School Sucks!: And the rest of their problems come from here. Be fair, nobody likes school, and Capeside High is staffed by an erratic faculty.

That Three-Letter Word: Sex. It's tricky when you're still working out what it is and what you do with it. Watch the gang as they do just that.

Reality Bites: Self-awareness is the Capeside disease. Dawson, especially, seems to think that his whole life is either a movie or should be more like a movie. I note all the times this view of the world bumps up against the cold hard reality of life.

Metatextuality: This section points out all those moments when the world of the TV show meets the real world of TV production: all the in-jokes and the moments when the characters seem to know they're not real people – just impossibly good-looking characters in a teen soap, whose every word is scripted in advance.

All Things Spielberg: This show revels in references to other films, shows and general pop culture. This category will record every pastiche, homage, reference and rip-off employed.

All Things Freud: Psychiatrists, who needs them? Our heroes analyse each other for free, whether their advice is wanted or not. This presents their conclusions.

Grown-Up Stuff: One of the things that sets *Dawson's Creek* apart from most teen shows is the close focus on the adults in the story. Dawson's parents, Gale and Mitch, and their journey from bliss to divorce to remarriage, has been one of the show's strongest storylines.

Girl Talk: What the girls say about the guys when they aren't around, or when they're just not listening.

Guy Talk: Vice versa.

Kiss And Tell: Who's kissing whom, who wishes they were kissing someone and who wishes they hadn't.

Our Quips Are Wittier: The youngsters of Capeside are unfeasibly articulate, their dialogue is rich beyond the characters' years and they always have a witty quip ready for any circumstance. The best examples are chronicled here.

Ker-THUNK!: This category notes whenever reality is bent beyond plausibility simply because the story demands it, when writers write themselves out of corners in lame ways, adhere to clichés without sufficient explanation, or just drop huge chunks of unnecessary exposition and make characters explain the plot for the viewer when they wouldn't have to in real life.

Bloopers: When things go horribly wrong or the show contradicts itself, hoping no one will notice, I notice.

Guest Cast: Who's visiting town this week, and where you might have seen them before.

Contempo Pop Music: The soundtrack is an integral part of each episode. Every song will be identified.

Backstage: What was going on behind the scenes during this episode and how it affected what you see on screen.

The Big Issue: In which is identified the Moral of the Story, if there is one.

The Last Word: A brief, subjective review of the episode.

Season One

A head /

Created by Kevin Williamson
Executive Producers: Kevin Williamson, Paul Stupin,
Charles Rosin
Producers: Jon Harmon Feldman, Steve Miner,
Greg Prange
All episodes scored by Adam Fields

Regular Cast
James Van Der Beek (Dawson Leery)
Katie Holmes (Joey Potter)
Joshua Jackson (Pacey Witter)
Michelle Williams (Jen Lindley)
Mary-Margaret Humes (Gale Leery)
John Wesley Shipp (Mitch Leery)
Mary Beth Peil (Grams)
Nina Repeta (Bessie Potter)

Theme Music: The original choice of theme was Alanis Morissette's 'Hand In Pocket', and this can be heard on the unaired pilot. However, Morissette decided at the last minute not to allow its use when the pilot became a series. 'I Don't Want To Wait' was extensively used in the all-out media blitz that preceded the first season, but singer Paula Cole didn't give permission for the song to be used as the main theme until a few days before broadcast. Consequently, for Season One, the US and Canada heard 'I Don't Want To Wait', while the rest of the world heard a specially recorded and never released song by the Canadian singer Jann Arden. The song is sometimes called 'Run Like Mad' or 'Elsewhere'. From Season Two onwards the Paula Cole song was used worldwide.

Scheduling: The WB network was originally intending to show *Dawson's Creek* during the 'family hour' between 8 and 9 p.m., but instead it got cold feet at the last moment owing to the show's sexual content and moved it to 9 p.m. instead. *Buffy the Vampire Slayer*, the WB's highest-rated show, was moved mid-Season Two from Tuesdays (where it was getting trashed by *Ally McBeal*) to Wednesdays and scheduled as the *Dawson's Creek* lead-in at 8 p.m.

The Episodes

Originally, each episode was named after a popular movie, but owing to copyright issues the episodes were officially renamed. The original titles were:

100   Emotions In Motion

101   Dirty Dancing

102   Prelude To a Kiss

103   Carnal Knowledge

104   Blown Away

105   Look Who's Talking

106   Breakfast Club

107   Escape From New York

108   In the Company of Men

109   Modern Romance

110   Friday the 13th

111   Pretty Woman

112   Breaking Away

100
Pilot

1st US Transmission Date: 20 January 1998

Writer: Kevin Williamson
Director: Steve Miner
Guest Cast: Leann Hunley (Tamara Jacobs),
Mitchell Laurance (Mr Gold), Nicole Nieth (Nellie Olsen),
George Gaffney (Bodie Wells),
Ted King (Bob Collinsworth)

Joey and Dawson are in Dawson's room, watching *E.T.*
Joey normally sleeps over but today she doesn't want to
because she's worried about sex getting in the way of their
friendship. He persuades her to stay. Next day she,
Dawson and Pacey are filming a scene for Dawson's horror
movie when Jen, arriving from New York, interrupts them.
She will be in school with them and will be living with her
grandmother (Grams), Dawson's neighbour. Joey takes an
instant dislike to Jen, but Pacey and Dawson can't take
their eyes off her.

That evening Dawson meets Jen and shows her around
his Spielberg-shrine bedroom. At breakfast the next day
Grams warns Jen against Dawson and Joey, who she
thinks are bad influences. Grams is shocked when Jen
admits she is an atheist. At lunch Jen and Dawson
continue to get on very well while Joey sulks. Dawson
invites Jen to the cinema that night with him and Pacey
and then invites Joey to make up the numbers. Grams
agrees to let Jen go to the movies as long as she also comes
to church. Jen refuses.

The evening is a disaster – Joey starts grilling Jen about
her sex life, and ruins the evening. In the cinema, Dawson
takes Jen's hand. Joey freaks out so much that Dawson
takes her outside and demands to know what her problem
is. She tells him to grow up and goes home. Dawson walks
Jen home and she tells him how much she likes him. Back

in Dawson's room Joey has come to apologise. They talk and admit that their relationship is changing and they're both confused by it. To prove that there are things they can't talk about any more she asks how often he walks his dog (see **That Three-Letter Word**). He is embarrassed and she leaves in tears. When she is in her boat he shouts after her from his bedroom window that he does it in the morning, as he watches Katie Couric on the morning news. Joey laughs, the tension gone.

Dawson and Pacey work part-time in the local video store. Tamara, an attractive thirtysomething woman who is new in town, comes in to rent a video. She flirts with Pacey, who is smitten. She turns out to be Pacey's new English teacher. He tries to flirt with her as she eats lunch at her desk, and she tells him she is going to the cinema that night. Pacey thinks this is a hint and goes to the film, where he moves in on Tamara. She is horrified to see him because she is there with Mr Gold (Benji to his friends), Capeside High's film-studies teacher. Pacey gets punched by a guy when he accidentally spills Benji's popcorn on him. On his way home afterwards, with a big black eye, Pacey bumps into Tamara and they have a confrontation. She kisses him but then runs off, shocked by what she has done.

When we first meet Dawson's parents, Gale and Mitch, they are making out on the coffee table in their living room. Dawson later tells Joey that he thinks his mom, a newsreader on local TV, is having an affair with her co-anchor, Bob. At the end, as Joey rows away from Dawson's house, she sees Gale kissing Bob goodnight.

The Ballad of Dawson and Joey: It's clear from the opening scene that this relationship, and the changes it's going to go through, will be the emotional heart of the show. They have been friends for ever. She often sleeps in his bed. She's seen him 'burp, barf, pick his nose and scratch his butt'. They can say anything to each other, and their relationship is 'the only thing that makes sense' to Dawson. Joey, however, is aware that sex is soon going to be a problem and faces the issue head on, bringing it out into the open and ending the innocent younger relationship, forcing them to try to renegotiate a more mature one. It's not easy, especially since it's obvious that Joey is hopelessly in love with Dawson and he hasn't a clue.

The Movie Brat: The Dawson Leery credo: 'I believe that all of the mysteries of the universe, all of life's questions, can be found in a Spielberg movie.' Unfortunately for Dawson, this doesn't cover everything (see **That Three-Letter Word**).

The Tomboy: Joey is acerbic, sassy, difficult and sulks from the second Jen arrives on the scene. She oozes jealousy from every pore and gives attitude to everyone, even her sister, Bess. Finally, at the end of the episode, she gives a genuine, radiant smile and we see a flash of the girl underneath all the sexual confusion.

The Clown: Pacey appears for the first time in a monster costume, establishing his role as the goof of the bunch. He homes in on Jen before she's even walked five paces, even though he's still dressed in green rubber and slime. His hormones are way out of control. He responds to Tamara's flirting at first with the awkwardness of a teenager but later with astonishing maturity. He delivers a speech that sets up the real depths of the character, depths that none of his friends are really aware of yet: 'You fantasise about what it would be like to be with that young boy on the verge of manhood, 'cause it helps you stay feeling attractive, makes the ageing process a little more bearable. Well let me tell you something. You blew it, lady, 'cause I'm the best sex you'll never have.' Tamara is right when she says he's not a boy. Despite his outward goofiness he's already one of the most complex characters in the show because he's the only one not really struggling with the nature of his sexuality.

The Delinquent: What an entrance. Slo-mo, great music, awe-struck gazes from the guys. Everything about her first appearance screams love interest, siren, sex. She's very

tender with both her granddad and Grams, despite their
differences, and for a hellraiser and delinquent, which is
obviously what Grams thinks she is, she comes over as very
gentle. She claims to be 'substance-free', yet immediately
afterwards admits she used to smoke. She also claims to be
a virgin, but do we believe her? Jen is a confirmed atheist
and is very upfront about it, even though she promises to
tolerate and accept Grams's religious beliefs. There are lots
of hints that things went badly for her in New York,
although it's not yet clear what she's running from, or why
she was sent away by her parents.

The Wicked Witch: 'My grandmother presents a challenge
. . .' Grams gets a great entrance, silhouetted in the
doorway with the light behind her like some serial killer in
a slasher flick. It's a potent movie image and instantly
places her role in the narrative. She tosses out judgments
left, right and centre. She softens as the episode progresses
and when she's telling Jen to come home early you can see
she has genuine affection for her granddaughter.

Family Sucks!: Pacey has three (ugly?) sisters, although by
the end of Season Four we have met only two, so maybe
he's counting his brother Doug (see **104**, 'Hurricane'), who
may or may not be gay, as a sister!
     Joey's mother died of cancer. Her father is in prison for
'conspiracy to traffic marijuana in excess of ten thousand
pounds', and she seems grudgingly proud about that. She
lives with her pregnant sister Bess, and Bess's boyfriend,
Bodie. Bodie is black, and Grams and Joey always refer to
him as 'Bess's black boyfriend'. Although there is no overt
racism in the show, it is implied that the multiracial union
is considered outrageous and unacceptable by Capeside at
large, and by Grams in particular. Joey's relationship with
Bess seems pretty spiky and they argue about borrowing
each other's clothes. Later, however, Bess gives Joey
lipstick tips and we see the bond of affection between them.
     Jen's parents have remained at home in New York. Her
grandfather has recently had serious heart surgery and
appears to be in a coma.

Dawson is an only child. He lives with his father, who is planning an 'aquatic-themed restaurant', and his mother, who has big, big hair.

School Sucks!: The gang are just starting tenth grade, which makes them about fifteen. It's one of the rules of American TV that every high school needs its über-bitch, and Nellie Olsen, whose father owns the video store Dawson and Pacey work at, steps up to have a go at Jen before she's even got her locker sorted out. Dawson is refused entry to film class because he's a sophomore, and immediately gets on the wrong side of Benji, the one teacher he needs to butter up. By the end of the first day of term Pacey has started a romance with his English teacher. My hero.

That Three-Letter Word: All the young characters have hit the brick wall of their burgeoning sexuality and are flapping about trying to make sense of it all. It also seems that it may be the only thing Dawson's parents have in common any more.

Pacey's on a 'hormonal mission', determined to lose his virginity with his English teacher – it's all he seems to talk about.

Dawson is hung up about it, not sure where it fits into the scheme of things: 'What is it with the sex? That's all anybody thinks of any more, sex, sex, sex! I mean, what's the big deal?' After all, Spielberg never deals with sex: 'If sex is so important then how come Spielberg has never had a sex scene in one of his movies, hmm? He keeps it in it's proper place in film as we should in life.' Dawson's source of all wisdom has failed him in one crucial area: he is totally unprepared for the entrance of sex into his life, so when Jen arrives he doesn't know what to do.

Joey demands to know if Jen is a virgin, reveals that Dawson is, and claims to have lost her virginity years ago to a 'trucker named Bubba'. Then she takes it even further by discussing penis size with Jen and knowingly harping on Dawson's long fingers.

Jen says the word 'penis' in prime time. Twice. Network executives take a valium and go to lie down in a darkened room. Kevin Williamson wanted Joey to say 'masturbate' rather than the made-up phrase 'walk your dog'. Needless to say, network execs can take only so much strain, and it was changed.

Reality Bites: The opening scene after the credits is a movie within a movie, where we see our characters playing other characters in a movie Dawson is making. Five minutes in and already they're messing around with different levels of reality.

Dawson realises his mom is having an affair by watching her on TV. It's his skill as a deconstructor of TV/movie images that allows him to see the reality of the affair before anyone else does. So in a way his immersion in fiction and artifice has led him to a better understanding of reality.

Joey on Dawson's reality issues: 'You're so far removed from reality you can't see what's in front of you . . . your life, it's a freakin' fairy tale and you don't even know it. You just want conflict for that script of yours. Stop living in the movies, grow up.' Dawson is constantly dealing with the (un)reality of his life. He imagines himself as a character in a movie, which of course he is. Joey tells him, 'Everything's a potential script to you. Accept your perfect life, Dawson. It's reality.' But earlier Dawson has said, 'I reject reality' and 'Movies are my life'.

Metatextuality: The video store displays a poster for *I Know What You Did Last Summer* (Jim Gillespie, 1997), writer Williamson's second big horror film. The same poster is on the wall in Benji's film class. Capeside's cinema is called the Rialto, which was also the name of the cinema in the opening sequence of *Scream 2*. Jen jokes that Dawson has clear skin, drawing attention to the fact that none of the teenagers on this show have acne. With four teenage leads, you'd think one of them, just by the law of averages, would have problems with a pustulant face. Williamson deliberately draws attention to the fact that we are watching an idealised version of teenage years, and that the actors have all passed the age of Clearasil.

All Things Spielberg: The first line ever spoken in the show is an *E.T.* quote – Joey says, 'I'll be right here' – and we're not even ten seconds into the first episode before being given a discussion of Spielberg's Peter Pan syndrome and how *Gandhi* (Richard Attenborough, 1982) robbed *E.T.* (Steven Spielberg, 1982) of the Best Film Oscar. When Joey is angsting about their growing genitalia Dawson asks, 'What's with all this "When Harry Met Eighties" crap?' a reference to *When Harry Met Sally* (Rob Reiner, 1989), a film about whether men and women can just be friends without sex getting in the way.

Pacey and Tamara's flirtation is conducted in movie references. She rents *The Graduate* (Mike Nichols, 1967) from him, a film in which the older Mrs Robinson (Anne Bancroft) seduces the younger Benjamin Braddock (Dustin Hoffman). Later, Pacey offers her *Summer of '42* (Robert Mulligan, 1971), again about an older woman seducing a younger man. She admits it's a favourite.

Dawson shows Jen his room, basically a shrine to Spielberg, whom he 'worships in a godlike way'. The posters to all Spielberg's movies are arranged in receding box-office order, with the turkeys *Always* (Spielberg, 1989) and *1941* (Spielberg, 1979) hidden in the closet. His three rentals this week, research for his own movie, a creature feature about a mutant sea serpent, are *Creature from the Black Lagoon* (Jack Arnold, 1954), *Humanoids from the Deep* (Barbara Peters, 1980) and *Swamp Thing* (Wes Craven, 1982). When Dawson tries to persuade Benji to let him take film class they discuss *Psycho* (Alfred Hitchcock, 1960) trivia.

Nellie is named after a character in *Little House on the Prairie* – even people's names are TV or movie references in Capeside.

Grown-Up Stuff: Dawson's parents make out so passionately that they break the coffee table. It's bad enough that Mrs Leery calls her husband 'Mr Man-Meat', but in front of their son? *And* his best friend? Dawson suspects that his mom is having an affair with her co-anchor because she softens her Bs when she talks to him on air; Joey the anthropologist dismisses the idea. Mr Leery is still very attracted to his wife and always watches her on TV because 'watching her work is the best foreplay'.

Girl Talk: Joey tells Jen that she and Dawson arc just friends but then warns her not to mess with Dawson's emotions.

Guy Talk: Every time Pacey is alone with Dawson he initiates a conversation about sex. He's obsessed, that boy.

Kiss and Tell: Tamara and Pacey get passionate within a day of meeting each other. Jen doesn't kiss Dawson after the date because Grams materialises, but she tells him she's willing to pretend they did, just to let him know she would have. So that's all right.

Our Quips Are Wittier: From the very start these are the most mind-bogglingly articulate fifteen-year-olds TV has ever produced. Can you imagine yourself ever saying these lines when you were fifteen?

> *JOEY:* I just think our emerging hormones are destined to alter our relationship, and I'm trying to limit the fallout.
> *DAWSON:* We can still remain friends, despite any mounting sexual theoretics.
> *JEN:* Are you familiar with Obsessive Reality Disorder?
> *PACEY:* I have three menstrually diverse sisters, Cosmo is my saviour.

No? Thought not. Kevin Williamson explicitly states his priority when he has Dawson say, 'Wit, we like that around here'.

Blooper: Not really a blooper as such, but why is it that when people in TV shows go to the movies they never have to sit through adverts and trailers? Also, when Pacey meets Benji at the movies he doesn't recognise him from school, which seems a little strange. In one shot of the high school a sign says HOME OF THE WILDCATS, but in the next shot a different sign reads HOME OF THE MINUTEMEN. Two teams or a set dressing error? In time the Minutemen will be established as the genuine team. When Joey shrugs just before entering the Rialto her mike box can be seen sticking out of her back pocket.

Guest Cast: Leann Hunley has appeared in numerous TV shows, most notably *Days Of Our Lives* and *Dynasty*. Nicole Nieth has appeared on TV in *ER*, *Sabrina the Teenage Witch*, *The Love Boat – the Next Wave*, *The Magnificent Seven* and *Grosse Pointe* among others. Mitchell Laurance has appeared in *L.A. Law*, *Matlock*, *The Outer Limits* and many other TV films and series. George Gaffney plays Bodie in this episode and the original, unaired pilot but never appears again, replaced by Obi Ndefo.

Contempo Pop Music: Jen enters to 'Hey Pretty Girl' by the Bo-Deans, 'As I Lay Me Down' by Sophie B Hawkins, Chumbawumba's 'Tubthumping' punctuates all the school scenes, backing up the idea of school as somewhere that just keeps knocking you down, Bessie teaches Jen how to wear lipstick to Jann Arden's 'Good Mother', reinforcing her role as a surrogate mum and 'Stand By You' by the Pretenders.

The Unaired Pilot: When a TV series is created a pilot episode is produced and shown to various networks and studios in an attempt to get backing for a full set of episodes. Many pilots are made every year and very few ever get turned into series. As anyone lucky enough to see the unaired *Buffy* pilot knows, the pilot can differ drastically from the programme that is eventually broadcast.

In the original *Dawson's Creek* pilot there are some subtle differences and some major ones. Most significantly, Mitch is played by a different actor – Tim

Grimm rather than John Wesley Shipp. The discussion of the aquatic restaurant is cut, leaving Mitch sprawled on the sofa, less quirky than in the broadcast version. The video store set is much larger and when Tamara enters she is dressed more conservatively, in trousers and shirt. In the broadcast version her dress and slo-mo appearance explicitly mirror Jen's.

Dawson's bedroom set is different: the door faces the bed rather than being next to his cupboard. This makes the flow of movement through the room very undynamic; moving the door gives the set a much better range of shots and motion.

Although we hear Grams, and see her silhouette, she never appears in the pilot and all her scenes with Jen are missing. This has the added effect of reducing Jen's screen time. Jen's scene with Dawson at the start of school is also missing. Nellie doesn't appear at all. Also cut is the scene where Dawson tries to get into film class.

The conversation between Dawson and Pacey, where they discuss Tamara, plan their date for the evening and decide to invite Jen along, is missing, too. Dawson talks to his photo of Spielberg after Jen has left, describing her as having 'a bit of a Kate Capshaw thing happening' (Kate Capshaw is Spielberg's wife).

Finally, Dawson sees Gale kiss Bob at the end of the pilot, whereas in the broadcast version he doesn't. Although the shots in Dawson's room, and those featuring Mitch, were reshot for broadcast, and some new scenes added, those scenes that could be reused were.

Besides the different theme music (Alanis Morissette's 'Hand In Pocket') and a slightly different title sequence (obviously from the same day's filming but edited differently), the featured songs are almost entirely different as well.

The Big Issue: Peter Pan complexes and the difficulty of growing up. No one stays a child for ever. Sex screws you up.

The Last Word: This is a dynamite opening installment from Kevin Williamson. It works on multiple levels and crams so much character development into 42 minutes that it's almost a movie script. Storylines are set up to run and the main themes of the sho↑w – the relationship between reality and fiction, and the onset of adulthood – are clearly defined and established. The cast are all note-perfect and the show looks and sounds gorgeous. TV doesn't come much better than this.

101
Dance
1st US Transmission Date: 27 January 1998

Writer: Kevin Williamson
Director: Steve Miner
Guest Cast: Leann Hunley (Tamara Jacobs),
Mitchell Laurance (Mr Gold), Nicole Nieth (Nellie Olsen),
Scott Foley (Cliff Elliot)

At school there is a big football match coming up and a victory dance is planned for Friday in anticipation of a win. Dawson manages to get his study hall room (for his free periods) switched to Benji's film class, so he is allowed to sit in as long as he keeps his mouth shut. In film class they are making a film for the same festival Dawson plans to enter. *Helmets of Glory* is a sports film written by and starring Cliff Elliot, the schools star quarterback. It's a dismal film, and Dawson makes some suggestions for changes, which Nellie, as producer, dismisses.

Joey refuses to kiss Pacey for Dawson's movie, even though it is a crucial scene, so Dawson decides to kill Joey's character off and replace her with Jen, who will do the kiss. When they shoot his kiss with Jen, Pacey gets carried away and Dawson, very jealous, cuts the kiss entirely. Dawson is planning to kiss Jen and asks Mitch for advice, which Joey overhears. He has planned a movie night for him and Jen but she's accepted Cliff's invitation to the dance. She tells him to come along too, but he declines. Dawson moans to Joey about Cliff, eventually deciding to go to the dance after all. Cliff and Jen are dancing, so Dawson and Joey dance too and make small talk with them. Jen asks Dawson to dance, but he's so annoyed about Cliff that he makes her angry. Dawson then tries to cut in when Jen and Cliff are dancing, an argument ensues and Jen walks off.

Walking home with Joey, Dawson sees Jen at the waterfront and goes over to apologise. She eventually accepts his apology and admits she is interested in him, but she wants to take it slowly. Joey watches Jen and Dawson dancing on the dock, misery all over her face.

Pacey makes come-ons to Tamara before first class and also at the dance, but she's having none of it. After the dance she waits for Pacey at the site of their first kiss. She tries to end whatever it is they have going on, but Pacey is so persuasive that they end up kissing again.

Joey overhears Gale on the phone to Bob and tells her she knows about the affair.

The Ballad of Dawson and Joey: By the end of the episode it's clear they're a million miles apart – they're still friends but Joey is in love with Dawson and willing to put herself through hell just to be with him. She's just waiting for Dawson to get Jen out of his system and then she'll pounce, hopefully.

The Movie Brat: Dawson's reality problem threatens to overwhelm him completely when he decides he would rather rent videos of John Travolta dancing with beautiful girls than actually dance with a beautiful girl himself. He commits hara-kiri in spectacular fashion at the dance, running into romance like a bull in a china shop and making all the wrong moves in some desperate panicked attempt to regain script control of his life.

The Tomboy: Joey just can't resist torturing herself. She follows Dawson to the dance and forces herself to watch him try to pull Jen. She hangs around to watch them dance, too. Masochism as lifestyle choice.

The Clown: Pacey is really laying it on thick with Tamara, hounding her in class, flirting openly at the dance. His maturity really shows when he accepts equal responsibility for the kiss and takes his destiny in his hands.

The Delinquent: Jen is just trying to have a guilt-free, uncomplicated good time, but, when seriousness raises its head and Dawson tries to define what's going on, she doesn't handle it well. She's clearly running from some demons.

Family Sucks!: Jocy says her mother was the best, but her dad used to cheat on her mother all the time.

Reality Bites: The opening scene is two TV characters watching themselves on TV playing movie characters. The levels of reality are starting to make me dizzy. Dawson admits his horror movie, about a teenage boy who has an evil alter ego as a sea serpent, is a sustained metaphor. Of course the monster represents sex rearing its ugly head, and it isn't long before Joey throws this at Dawson: 'You're the sea creature from your own movie.' Eventually he admits that there's something in him he can't control. Yup, that'd be your hormones.

Metatextuality: When Dawson decides to kill Joey early in his movie he compares it to Janet Leigh in *Psycho* (Alfred Hitchcock, 1960). Pacey compares it to Drew Barrymore in *Scream* (Wes Craven, 1996) and Kevin Williamson has Joey call *Scream*, his own movie, a rip-off.

Everyone in this episode sees themselves as a character in their own movie. Dawson, especially, is scripting every move in his little plot and is constantly surprised when events don't go the way his movie logic dictates they should. Jen is becoming infected by the Capeside movie disease and responds to a particularly smooth line from

Cliff by saying that could 'have been my exit cue'. Instead of telling Dawson to act fast, Joey says 'Write something quick'; Dawson says 'Time for a rewrite'. Even Tamara succumbs, going for a retake of her kiss with Pacey so that she can change the ending. It must be something in the water at Capeside.

Dawson protests to Jen that he was worried he was being cast in the role of friend, and that's not the script he wants.

All Things Spielberg: Dawson's three rentals this week, for his non-dancing dance night, are *Saturday Night Fever* (John Badham, 1977), its sequel *Staying Alive* (Sylvester Stallone, 1983) and *Grease* (Randal Kleiser, 1978).

Mitch says kissing is easy: 'You just put your lips together and go.' This is a riff on Lauren Bacall's famous line to Humphrey Bogart in *To Have and Have Not* (Howard Hawks, 1944): 'You know how to whistle, don't you? You just put your lips together and blow.' He and Gale went to see *Ordinary People* (Robert Redford, 1980) on their second date. Gale remembers Mary Tyler being a terrible mother in it, so perhaps Joey's words are sinking in.

Pacey and Tamara continue their relationship by reference: this episode's set text is Emily Brontë's book *Wuthering Heights*. Tamara insists that Catherine would have been better off without Heathcliffe, and basically tells Pacey to get lost, in code, in front of an entire class.

Dawson sums up the dance as a *90210* evening.

Grown Up Stuff: Mitch and Gale remember their first kiss and how romantic it was. They then 'jumped each other', unsurprisingly. They've been using Dawson's camcorder for some private movie making of their own, much to Dawson's disgust. Joey delivers a stern warning to Gale: 'You know your reasons for doing what you're doing? They can't possibly outweigh the everlasting damage you're creating.' Joey doesn't, however, tell Dawson. Later, when Mitch and Gale are discussing their earliest dates, it's clear they still have a lot of love for each other, so why is Gale fooling around?

Girl Talk: In a nicely played scene Jen continues to try to make friends with Joey, helping her clean up after her death scene. They discuss their bodies. Jen is all compliments and admits that she hates her own body and thinks she looks like a duck. Joey disagrees and Jen is pleased that she's been able to get Joey to say something nice to her: 'I plan to make it really hard for you not to like me.' This echoes something Michelle said to *Entertainment Weekly* when the show launched: 'I know I'm going to get hate mail, but I'm going to be trying my damnedest to make people like me.'

Kiss and Tell: This whole episode is about kissing, wanting to kiss and failing to kiss. Joey gets the ball rolling by refusing to kiss Pacey for Dawson's movie, so Pacey gets to kiss Jen instead. To avoid retakes, Dawson actually cuts the kiss from his movie, which is what he effectively does in the real world later on. He drives Joey mad by going on about her 'kissing lips'; and her sly look when he suggests she kiss Pacey and think of someone else tells us exactly whom she would be thinking of. Later on Dawson tortures himself by imagining, in the most exhaustive detail, Cliff and Jen kissing at the dance. He finally spurs himself to action and tells Joey, 'I'm the one who should be kissing her, Joey . . . I'm going to kiss the girl.' Unfortunately, the only person he gets to kiss is his mother, on the cheek as he leaves. On the dance floor Joey and Dawson lock eyes in a perfect pre-kiss moment, but they are interrupted by Jen and Cliff, and Dawson seems to forget about it instantly. Finally, having built the first kiss with Jen into a huge thing, Dawson asks her to kiss him and she passes, afraid that if she kisses him she may lose her composure and fall back into her, as yet unspecified, bad old ways. In the end they just dance and she tells Dawson what he's been missing all along: 'The kiss is just the end result. It's not what's important. It's all about desire and wanting . . . and romance.'

Dawson and Mitch do some father–son bonding when Dawson asks for advice on the mechanics of kissing. Mitch gets Dawson to practise on the model head he's made of

Joey for the movie. Joey watches from the upstairs landing and closes her eyes as Dawson kisses her image, kissing him by proxy. In the end, concludes Mitch, 'it's all about romance' – the lips have to dance with each other.

Gale's kissy-kissy noises (and, by the way, yeuch!) down the phone to Bob give Joey more evidence of her infidelity. Mitch thinks his first kiss with Gale is 'the single most vivid moment of my life thus far'.

The fallout from the kiss between him and Tamara is driving Pacey mad, while she doesn't know how to get rid of him, or even whether she wants to. When she waits for him after the dance they discuss the kiss at length and, just when you think they've talked it to death, they decide on a repeat performance.

Our Quips Are Wittier: Pacey, when Tamara asks him how he feels: 'Confused, perplexed, bewildered, mystified. A thesaurus of emotion.'

Blooper: In **102**, 'Kiss', Benji tells Dawson that his movie class isn't open to sophomores. Nellie is in Dawson's English class, which makes her a sophomore, but she's in movie class, too.

Guest Cast: Scott Foley is a regular on *Felicity*, which follows Season Four of *Dawson's Creek* on the WB. He also appeared as Roman Bridger in *Scream 3*.

Contempo Pop Music: 'Am I Cool' by the Nowhere Blossoms, 'Flames of Truth' by Sarah Masen, 'I Want You' by Savage Garden, 'Happiness' by Abra Moore, 'Ooh, ahh . . . Just a Little Bit' by Gina G, 'Pretty Strange' and 'But You' by Paul Chiten and 'Apple' by the Autumns.

J. Crew: Naomi Klein's bestselling book *No Logo* talks about the merging of media and marketing in *Dawson's Creek*: 'Not only did the characters all wear J. Crew clothes, not only did the windswept, nautical set make them look as if they had stepped off the pages of a J. Crew catalog, and not only did the characters spout dialogue like "He looks like he stepped out of a J. Crew catalog" but the cast was also featured on the cover of the January J. Crew catalog.' Well this is the episode she's referring to, as Dawson says of Cliff and Jen, 'I should be the one kissing her, not some J. Crew ad.' Also in **203**, 'Alternative Lifestyles', Abby says that Joey 'does have that fresh-faced appeal in a very J. Crew catalog kind of way.' And if you read the end titles during Seasons One and Two very carefully you'll see the acknowledgement 'Wardrobe provided by J. Crew'.

The Big Issue: As Joey tries to say: 'The rewind on the remote of life does not work.'

The Last Word: A beautifully structured, multilayered episode that works on almost every level and is brave enough to make Dawson, who is the viewpoint character, almost unlikable at times.

102
Kiss

1st US Transmission Date: 3 February 1998

Writer: Rob Thomas
Director: Michael Uno
Guest Cast: Leann Hunley (Tamara Jacobs),
Mitchell Laurance (Mr Gold), Scott Foley (Cliff Elliot),
Ian Bohen (Anderson Crawford), Bodie (Obi Ndefo)

Joey, waiting tables at her sister's café, locks eyes with a young man she's never seen before, Anderson Crawford. Later she meets him on the docks. Joey lets him believe she is also passing through Capeside and tells him her name is

Deborah Carson. He asks her to come sailing with him and she agrees. On the boat she tells him she's from Manhattan and attends an expensive boarding school. They go ashore at a secluded beach to play Frisbee.

Joey tells him her dad runs a multinational corporation that sells tampons. He thinks she's dating someone because of her distant body language. Joey backs off when he tries to kiss her and they sail back to Capeside. Later, at the café, Jen and Dawson are having lunch, and Joey is serving, when Anderson comes in. Joey pretends to be a customer. Jen backs her up but Dawson is clueless. Bodie also covers for her and Anderson leaves, not having found out her secret identity.

She later visits him on the boat, he gives her his number and they kiss. She mentions a restaurant in New York to Anderson, but when Bodie and Bess pick her up she finds out she got her facts wrong and Anderson has probably realised she was lying. She drops his phone number out of the car window.

Tamara tells Pacey that she has heard he is failing classes. He says it is a deliberate ploy to get her to give him private tutoring. She tells him to come to her classroom after school, but when he does he can't stop flirting. She promises that if he gets all the answers right on a quiz she'll give him some 'positive reinforcement'. When he's finished the test Pacey comes on too strong for Tamara and she calls his bluff, proposing that they have sex on her desk. Pacey refuses. Tamara comes to her senses and insists their affair must end, and Pacey leaves. Next day he overhears Benji and Tamara talking intimately and he confronts Tamara, jealous, insisting he wants her even though she again tries to end their affair.

Dawson tells Pacey he is planning to film the closing shot of his movie at some ruins outside town, where he hopes to set the perfect scene for his first kiss with Jen. Trespassing at the ruins, Dawson constructs a romantic setting and films Jen's final scene. He then goes in for the kiss, but she notices that he's left the camera running. He apologises for trying to stage-manage everything and admits she makes him nervous. Jen admits she's nervous of disappointing him. A car pulls up and they hide. In their hiding place, they finally kiss. Dawson's camera is taping the occupants of the car having sex. It is Tamara and Pacey.

Benji lets Dawson work as a production assistant (PA) on *Helmets of Glory*, although he is still not a member of the film class. He meets Jen on the set and finds out she's been cast as a cheerleader by Cliff. He also gets told off by Nellie for dissing the awful script of *Helmets*. Cliff wants a tracking shot for the film and, after arguing with Nellie, Dawson persuades them to let him do it. Using a wheelchair, he gets a steady shot and Cliff is overjoyed.

The Ballad of Dawson and Joey: Dawson, still oblivious to Joey's feelings for him, tells her, 'One day you'll understand . . . what it's like to long for someone, to desire, to want to kiss them.'

The Movie Brat: Dawson insists that he can stage-manage his life, plan his future and turn his life into a series of scripted episodes. The scheme he comes up with to set the scene for his kiss with Jen is typical. He is scared and he tries to control that by orchestrating everything; he feels stupid, and tries even harder – it's a vicious circle. He is determined that he can storyboard the kiss because he believes you can have movie magic if you wish it. He has at least taken on the lesson of **101**, 'Dance': 'It's not about the kiss, Joey: it's about the journey.'

The Tomboy: Not so tomboyish when she goes to meet Anderson sporting lipstick and earrings – she looks stunning. Would Dawson still treat her the way he does if she unleashed that on him? She gives attitude and backs out of kissing Anderson at first because, as he correctly divines from her body language, she's in love with someone already. She tells Anderson she's a Pisces, but she could be lying.

The Clown: Pacey continues to pursue Tamara, and even gets jealous when she walks home with Benji. When she calls his bluff in the classroom he, surprise surprise, salvages dignity from embarrassment and states the Pacey creed: 'I'm a firm believer that sometimes it's right to do the wrong thing.' His maturity again wins over Tamara and eventually he gets lucky.

The Delinquent: Jen joins the cast of *Helmets of Glory* just because she knows Dawson will be there. Jen is *really* good at acting sadness and longing and admits that 'sadness is my specialty'. She is angry at Dawson for trying to video his first kiss. But even her annoyance at him, her previously stated fear of taking things too far too fast and her fear of disappointing him eventually give way.

Family Sucks!: Bodie and Bess run a diner, the SS Icehouse, where Bodie cooks and Joey waits tables. Bess gives Joey another speech about how she's responsible for her until she's eighteen or their father gets parole, but by the end she is being nice to Joey and thanking her for helping out so much.

School Sucks!: Dawson's impassioned speech in film class, listing all that's wrong with *Helmets of Glory*, seems to catch the attention of Benji. Can he be on his way to winning an official place in the class?

That Three-Letter Word: Pacey loses his virginity in a 'high-fantasy fashion', to his English teacher. It'll all end in tears, mark my words. At school he tells her to relax, that there is 'no film crew', but she obviously wants somewhere quieter where, unluckily for her, there *is* a film crew.

Reality Bites: Dawson and Joey are watching *From Here to Eternity* (Fred Zinnemann, 1953), which features a famous kiss between Burt Lancaster and Deborah Kerr, in the breaking surf of a beach. Dawson tells Joey that movies can be made real, that she can have that kiss, and she sets out to test the theory with Anderson. At the last moment she loses her nerve, still refusing to cross the boundary from her reality into the movie land that Dawson inhabits. Yet when discussing the assassination of

JFK with Anderson she uses knowledge garnered from the Oliver Stone film, whereas he has actually read the Warren Commission report. So who's living in the movies now?

Dawson continues trying to make his life a movie, and to make the movie of his life. Actually trying to video his first kiss is both audacious and amazingly stupid (and a little hypocritical given that he criticised his parents for videoing themselves in **101**, 'Dance'). It's almost as if the experience wouldn't be real for him unless it were on film. In the end she does kiss him, and the metaphorical beast in him is as slain as is the beast in his movie, already slain by Jen's character. Here endeth the three-episode monster/sexuality subtext.

Perversely enough Pacey, the only one not trying to stage a movie scene in this episode, is the only one who succeeds at being cast in a movie scene, unwittingly having his first sexual experience captured on video.

All Things Spielberg: Dawson protests at the script for *Helmets of Glory* and tells them there is a simple formula for sports movies, citing *Rocky* (John G Avildsen, 1976) and *The Karate Kid* (John G Avildsen, 1984) as examples. This week's Pacey/Tamara set text is *Ethan Frome* by Edith Wharton, about a poor Massachusetts farmer.

All Things Freud: Joey, still trying to get Dawson to live in the real world: 'This Peter Pan fantasy filmland you're living in ... it will be your downfall.' But Dawson thinks she's far too cynical. The man himself finally gets a mention: when Dawson asks, 'What does it mean when you keep doing dumb things around the same girl?' Jen replies, 'I'm sure something extremely Freudian.'

Girl Talk: Jen's campaign to make Joey like her gets a boost when she covers for Joey at the SS Icehouse.

Kiss and Tell: Joey kisses Anderson; Dawson finally kisses Jen.

Contempo Pop Music: 'First Time' by Billie Myers, 'Kingdom' by the Slugs, 'Too Many Times' by Wake Ooloo, 'The Right Place' by Eddie Reader, 'Pretty Deep' by Tanya

Donelly, 'All I Want' by Toad The Wet Sprocket, 'I'll Remember You' by Sophie Zelmani, 'What Would Happen' by Meredith Brooks.

The Big Issue: Don't try to force things: just let them happen. It's far easier, much less stressful and less likely to leave you looking like an ass.

The Last Word: Kevin Williamson passes the writing baton to Rob Thomas for this episode and the quality stays high, a good indication that the team on the show can maintain the high standard when Williamson isn't so hands-on. Joey's journey into movie fantasy, as she toys with life in Dawson's world, highlights the differences between her and the object of her affections well.

103
Discovery

1st US Transmission Date: 10 February 1998

Writer: Jon Harmon Feldman
Director: Steve Miner
Guest Cast: Leann Hunley (Tamara Jacobs),
Mitchell Laurance (Mr Gold),
Ric Reitz (Bob Collinsworth)

Dawson and Joey watch the tape of Pacey and Tamara and although it's clearly Tamara, they cannot make out who the guy is. They tell Pacey and Jen, and Pacey asks if he can see the tape. Dawson walks Jen home and they kiss in front of Grams, who disapproves. Dawson goes home and finds Pacey ransacking his room for the tape, which Dawson gives him. Pacey admits that it is him on the tape. He later sees Tamara having coffee and joins her. He tries to take her hand but she pulls it away. Next day he sees her with Benji at the coffee shop, and later at school. Pacey confronts Tamara, thinking she is seeing Benji, but she tells him that Benji is gay. He never tells her about the video.

Dawson and Joey go shopping to buy a present for Gale and Mitch's twentieth wedding anniversary. They bump into Bob and Gale. Later, Jen and Dawson are at Gale's TV station redubbing Jen's screams for Dawson's movie. They see Gale and Bob kissing. Dawson freaks out and runs to Joey to talk about it. He is very angry when he finds out that she knew all along. He goes to talk to Jen instead. She confesses that she lied to him: she is not a virgin.

At school the next day Dawson tries to avoid Jen as much as possible. Dawson resolves to tell Mitch about Gale's affair, but as they are getting ready to go out and celebrate their twentieth anniversary he chickens out. Jen tells Joey about her troubles with Dawson and Joey tells her to wait for Dawson to figure things out. The episode closes with Dawson alone on the waterfront, feeling sorry for himself.

The Ballad of Dawson and Joey: When Dawson finds out about Gale, Jen offers to be his shoulder to cry on, but, without a word, he runs to Joey. He feels totally betrayed when he finds out she knew already, and storms off, shouting that their friendship is over. Joey finds Dawson and they make up, again discussing the changing nature of their friendship and how confusing it is: 'We're not getting along the way we used to . . . are we more [than friends]? Are we less?' Joey is convinced that their relationship is fading and headed 'straight to the Smithsonian' museum. Jen admits that there's probably sexual tension between Dawson and Joey.

The Movie Brat: Joey, Jen and his mom – Dawson feels that all the women in his life let him down. In Jen's case he should just get over himself and take her confession for what it is, a compliment and a great trust. He appears to have learned 102 ('Kiss')'s lesson, though: 'it's about romance'.

The Tomboy: Joey softens to Jen, has an almost genuine conversation with Dawson at the end, and comes across as pretty sympathetic. Is she perhaps moving out of her phase of lurking, watching and torturing herself?

The Clown: Pacey gets the green-eyed monster but doesn't make too much of an ass of himself. He admits he really likes Tamara, 'not just the sex', and when we finally see him and Tamara together alone and in private at her house he seems happy with the state of things. Heading for a fall there, Pacey. Brace yourself.

The Delinquent: By the end of the day, Dawson and Grams both think Jen is, to use her own word, a slut. She feels isolated and cut off from Dawson and allies herself with Joey so she has someone sympathetic to talk to. We find out that her shady past is to do with sex, which she appears to have had often and with more people than just her boyfriend. She is clearly trying not to go down that path again and lets Dawson know that she's in no hurry to get beyond the kissing and hand-holding stage.

The Wicked Witch: Although the judgments and tight-lipped silences come thick and fast, there are moments when you can see that Grams really does care for Jen and is trying to do the right thing. She's pretty short with Dawson, though.

School Sucks!: Benji is gay, a fan of Barbra Streisand movies, and has a thing for Mel Gibson.

That Three-Letter Word: According to Pacey, Joey turns all her 'sexual repression into humour'. Jen and Dawson, meanwhile, are talking around the sex issue. Dawson says everyone who talks about it is probably really bad at it, and Jen jokes that she hangs around him so much because he doesn't talk about it at all. Later on he admits to Joey that he's jealous of his parents' sex life. He also assures Grams that he's not a 'sex-crazed teenager', but Jen's confession throws him totally out of whack and he can't deal with it.

Reality Bites: Dawson videos Jen and watches her in slow motion. Everything that matters to him he captures on film because only then does it seem real to him. Pacey asks Dawson to give a critical response to his motion-picture performance with Tamara. Dawson, ever the film critic, gives him two thumbs up. Dawson has seen Bob on TV and always thought him 'a tool', but when he meets him in person he quite likes him, proving once again that Dawson understands the world better when he sees it through a TV screen (although, to be fair, apart from the affair we never have any real evidence that Bob isn't a nice guy). Jen is falling ever deeper into Capeside movie-metaphor land when she tells Grams that her kiss with Dawson was 'the entire highlight reel'. When Dawson tells her about the censor's old rule that a couple in bed in the movies had to have one foot on the floor because they thought that meant nothing untoward was going on, she joins in, saying that they don't have to 'prove their censors wrong yet'. Pacey on Dawson and Jen: 'In your movies she can be whatever you like, but in real life your scripts get thrown out.' He and Dawson summarise all the current storylines and bemoan all the unexpected plot twists. In the final scene Dawson and Joey indulge in a little bit of storylining, scripting their imaginary wedding

All Things Spielberg: Joey sees the Pacey/Tamara tape and jokes that Dawson's now taking cinema cues from Russ Meyer, notorious maker of movies, such as *Faster Pussycat, Kill, Kill* (1965), about women with huge breasts. This week's Pacey/Tamara set texts are Shakespeare's *Romeo and Juliet*, *The Scarlet Letter* by Nathaniel Hawthorne, and Sophocles' *Oedipus*, all tales in which love and sex lead to the death, banishment or horrific mutilation of the main characters. For a change, Pacey just wants to read a book where a couple have sex and it all works out.

All Things Freud: Joey can't stop psychoanalysing Dawson: 'He's not exactly mature. He's the classic only child. He pouts when things don't go his way and only sees things in black and white. Anything else confuses him.' Pacey joins in, accusing Dawson of being 'cursed with self awareness'.

Grown-Up Stuff: Gale's affair is out in the open for Dawson, but he doesn't tell his dad because of the twentieth anniversary. Can't be too long, though, if Gale carries on kissing Bob in public all the time. She should take lessons in tact from Tamara.

Girl Talk: The girls bond at last when Jen asks Joey for advice about Dawson. Joey spills the beans, telling Jen how barren Dawson's sex life is, but pointing out that 'every guy that grows up to be one of the good ones was probably a dweeb with girls when he was fifteen, too'. She tells Jen to wait for him to grow up and admits she'd probably be stupid enough to wait for ever, tacitly admitting how she feels about Dawson. They decide to wait together. Later, Joey offers to pass messages between Dawson and Jen, so she must be thawing towards her at last.

Guy Talk: Pacey fesses up to Dawson about Tamara, and is honest about his reputation as the strike-out king. Later he insists that Jen's confession that she is not a virgin is her way of indicating that she wants to sleep with Dawson, who tells Pacey he has no idea of romance. Pacey insists that 'No guy's first time should be captured on video.' But that was exactly what Dawson tried to do in **102**, 'Kiss' – Dawson must be green with envy.

Kiss and Tell: Jen kisses Dawson in full view of Grams, who is worried because Jen's New York troubles started with a kiss. Gale cements her role as the dumbest adulterer in the world by snogging her boyfriend when she knows her son is in the building. Joey and Dawson share another perfect pre-kiss moment at the end, but he ruins the moment again, this time, though, perhaps aware of what nearly happened.

Contempo Pop Music: 'Beautiful Thing' by Kyf Brewer, 'Top of the Morning' by The Hang Ups, 'I Know' by the Barenaked Ladies, 'World Outside' by the Devlins, 'Stand By Me' by Say So, 'That's What I Can Do' by Tom Snow, Toad The Wet Sprocket's 'Amnesia' and 'Full of Grace' by Sarah McLachlan.

The Big Issue: Dawson: 'Secrets destroy. they hurt and wound and kill.'

The Last Word: Secrets are revealed: Jen's secret past damages her relationship with Dawson. Joey tacitly admits her secret love for Dawson to Jen and it draws them closer. Gale's secret affair destroys Dawson's respect for her. Pacey's secret affair is revealed to Dawson and he has no words to express his amazement. Another storming installment, which moves the characters forward and juggles all the plots and themes very nicely.

104
Hurricane

1st US Transmission Date: 17 February 1998

Writer: Kevin Williamson and Dana Baratta
Director: Lou Antonio
Guest Cast: Dylan Neal (Doug Witter),
Leann Hunley (Tamara Jacobs), Obi Ndefo (Bodie),
Ric Reitz (Bob Collinsworth)

A hurricane is coming to Capeside and school is cancelled. Pacey and his brother Doug spend the night at Tamara's, presumably to see that her house is secure. Doug tries to chat Tamara up, much to Pacey's horror.

Bodie, Bess, Joey, Jen and Grams all weather the storm at the Leerys'. As the wind blows Grams scowls her disapproval at pregnant, unmarried Bess and her black boyfriend, Bodie. Gale admits to Mitch that she has been having an affair. Jen and Dawson sort out their differences, as do Joey and Dawson.

The Ballad of Dawson and Joey: They used to re-enact the third act of *Jaws* (Steven Spielberg, 1977) in the closet. When they make up at the end they decide to stop being grown up for a while, and do it again. Lucky Jen didn't walk in.

The Movie Brat: Dawson finally gets to feel some real emotion, rather than his usual confusion and ennui, when he gets angry at his mom. His righteous wrath is a thing to behold as he lets Gale have it. In contrast to Pacey, who handles news of Tamara's previous relationships with aplomb, Dawson's freak-out continues and he is staggeringly rude to Jen. His apology to her later is lovely, though: 'My behaviour has been unredeemable and I don't deserve someone as impassionate and open and honest and beautiful as you are.'

The Tomboy: Joey gets bored with Dawson's self-pity and plays 'the mother card', saying that no matter what his mother is doing he should give thanks that he still has one. It seems a bit unfair that the one time she really lets him have it is the one time he genuinely has something to feel bad, even angry, about. She apologises later, though, admitting that it was a cheap shot.

The Clown: Pacey spends the whole episode forced to watch his brother make a pass at his girlfriend but powerless to do anything. The smug victory on his face when Tamara tells Doug she's seeing someone already is a picture. When he sneaks back later he again proves himself deceptively mature for his age, and a lot better balanced than Dawson, in his reaction to Tamara's previous life in NYC, from which she, like Jen, ran away.

The Delinquent: Jen tries to get close to Dawson but he continues to push her away. His outburst really makes her mad. Later, she tells Dawson the whole truth behind her exile from NYC. She lost her virginity at twelve to an older man who got her drunk and whose name she can't remember. She went on the pill after the 'first pregnancy scare', and didn't always use condoms. She drank a lot, had a lot of blackouts and similar stuff and was eventually caught having sex in her parents' bed. Her dad can no longer look her in the eye. 'I was sexualised way too young . . . sex at such a young age, more often than not, is a bad idea.' She still wants Dawson, though, and they get back together.

The Wicked Witch: Grams is a very interesting character in this episode. She won't even look at Bodie at first, does seem racist, and clearly disapproves of his and Bess's having a child. But later she says that her concerns are 'not a judgment, just an observation' and that what upsets her is when 'children raise children', a comment more on their age and maturity than their mixed race or unweddedness. Even more astonishingly, she makes the effort to comfort Dawson after his parents fight and she says, 'Forgiveness is one of the greatest gifts the Lord has given us. With it comes understanding'.

Family Sucks!: Pacey not only has three sisters, but has a previously unmentioned brother as well, Deputy Doug, local police officer. Their dad has apparently instilled in Doug a 'sense of duty and a belief in justice'. Pacey teases that Doug is a closet homosexual, saying his collection of Barbra Streisand and musical-soundtrack CDs is a dead giveaway. What is it with this show? Everyone who listens to Barbra Streisand is assumed to be gay! Pacey even tells Tamara that Doug is gay, leading Doug to pull a gun on Pacey to force him to recant. Doug calls Pacey in turn a 'punk ass', a 'goof' and a 'pinhead imbecile'. However, it's Doug who comes off looking dumb when he finds Pacey and Tamara on the floor, covered in food and giggling, yet doesn't immediately realise that there's some serious inappropriateness going on. And how did he miss the looks on Pacey's face throughout the night? He was like a big neon sign that blinked, 'I'm sleeping with this woman – back off, Doug.' With a police force of such honed deductive skill it's a wonder Capeside isn't crime capital of America.

That Three-Letter Word: Dawson has always used his parents' sex life as a barometer of their happiness, but now he finds out that their recent period of frantic shagging has masked their unhappiest time ever. Jen tells him that 'sex doesn't equal happiness', a lesson he says he has learned now.

Reality Bites: Jen starts singing Joey's song: 'We're not all as perfect as you, Dawson. Some of us aren't imaginary characters in a Spielberg film: some of us live in reality.'

All Things Spielberg: Dawson's three rentals this week, for his disaster-movie séance, are *Twister* (Jan De Bont, 1996), *Towering Inferno* (Irwin Allen and John Giullermin, 1974) and *The Poseidon Adventure* (Ronald Neame and Irwin Allen, 1972). He compares his dad to Tom Hanks or Harrison Ford. When Dawson tells his mom he knows about her affair he says, 'I've got a new award for you . . . it comes in the shape of an "A" and you stitch it right here' – a reference to *The Scarlet Letter*, when the adulteress Hester Prynne had to stitch a red 'A' on the chest of her dress. Grams is a fan of Frank Capra movies such as *It's a Wonderful Life* (1946), *Mr Smith Goes To Washington* (1939) and *Pocketful of Miracles* (1961). She and Dawson bond a little over similarities between Capra and Spielberg.

Grown-Up Stuff: The house is full of guests and it's very noisy so she may not hear someone coming, but Gale still sits on the stairs making kissy noises at Bob down the phone – worst adulteress in history. She goes all around the mulberry bush to tell Mitch, but in the end tell him she does, and he goes into shock. He fell in love at first sight and believes 'love is a choice you make'; but now he rescinds his love and he chooses to hate Gale instead. She tells him that she had the affair because she realised she had a perfect life and 'perfection obtained is a discomforting state'. She wanted to want again and so she destroyed her marriage, but she's succeeded because now she wants back everything that she's lost.

Girl Talk: The reluctant friendship between Jen and Joey continues to grow as they flee to the porch and talk about Dawson. Jen is starting to think that Dawson is trite, with his overreaction to her history, feeling that he can't measure up to her previous lovers. Joey is sure that Dawson is having a 'life-defining turning point in his life'. Then they once again return to Joey's favourite theme, which seems to get a mention only when Kevin Williamson is writing, as Jen asks Joey whether she thinks Dawson is packing a 'pistol or a rifle'. Joey thinks he's above average given his height and hand size. Is that *all* she ever thinks about?

Kiss and Tell: Not much kissing, just hugging (Jen and Dawson) and playing in a darkened closet (Joey and Dawson). Mitch and Gale's snogathon looks to have come to an abrupt end, too. Pacey saves the day, though, by snatching a swift kiss from Tamara when his brother is outside.

Our Quips Are Wittier: Pacey to Doug, teasing him about being gay: 'Answer me this: why did you choose a profession that requires you to dress like one of the Village People?'

Contempo Pop Music: 'Healing Hands' by Marc Cohn and REM's 'It's the End of the World As We Know It (And I Feel Fine)'.

Ker-THUNK!: Jen and Grams would never come over to the Leerys' and leave Grandpa alone in their house during a storm, but we need them at the Leerys' for the story to work. How to do that? I know, let's put in a throwaway line about his going back into hospital for tests.

The Big Issue: All the secrets you keep will come out into the open sooner or later.

The Last Word: This is a fantastic episode. The weather-induced havoc outside pales in comparison with the chaos indoors, as secrets are revealed, relationships redefined and real change effected. Mary-Margaret Humes and John Wesley Shipp finally get to really show their acting chops and they rise magnificently to the challenge in some very well-written scenes. Michelle Williams has never been better, and the whole cast seem to feel that they have to pull out all the stops for this one. In terms of sheer drama this is the best episode since the pilot.

105
Baby

1st US Transmission Date: 24 February 1998

Story: Joanne Walters
Teleplay: Jon Harmon Feldman
Director: Steve Miner
Guest Cast: Dylan Neal (Doug Witter),
Leann Hunley (Tamara Jacobs), Obi Ndefo (Bodie)

Bessie's baby arrives early and she can't make it to hospital, so she and Joey row to the Leerys' for help. All the local ambulances are busy elsewhere and she has to give birth in the Leerys' front room, with the help of Grams.

Pacey and Dawson are overheard, by a fellow student, Kenny Leaverton, discussing Pacey's relationship with Tamara. The school board finds out and a tribunal is called. Pacey tells the court that he made it all up and the action proceeds no further. Tamara, however, decides to resign and she and Pacey say a tearful farewell.

The Movie Brat: Dawson is the support character in this episode, backing up Pacey when he gets into trouble and standing helplessly by as the baby is born. As ever, his reaction to major life events is to want to get it all on camera, and so he films the birth for the absent Bodie.

The Tomboy: Joey rises to the challenge of her sister's pregnancy well. It is she who goes and begs Grams to come help deliver her nephew, which takes a lot of courage given Grams's behaviour towards Bess and Bodie in **104**, 'Hurricane'. When Bess is screaming in pain Joey has to leave because it reminds her too strongly of her mother's fatal illness. Dawson talks her back inside and her support is what helps Bess give the final push. We get a nice glimpse of the vulnerability underneath Joey's wisecracking exterior and for once it has nothing to do with her feelings for Dawson. Also, she finally gets a scene with Pacey where they are not biting each other's head off when she seeks him out and talks to him about how it feels to be the centre of gossip for a small town – something she knows a lot about given her father's incarceration and her sister's home life.

The Clown: Mr discreet asks his English teacher to go out with him right in front of the school building with students all over the place and then, since that didn't give the game away entirely, he talks to Dawson about it in the toilet, where he can be overheard. Nice one. Still, when he did ask her out he proved once again that he has more charm, and knows better how to pursue a relationship, than Dawson does. He comes across as far more self-aware than he likes to let on when describing the situation with Tamara: 'This is one of those rare milestone events that separates the first half of your life from everything that follows.' His big courtroom scene is a defining moment for Pacey, when he absolutely proves himself the most grown up of the four main leads by quite some distance, falling on his sword to save Tamara and telling the court that his stories were merely the fantasies of a pathetic teenage loser. They believe him and he's saved the day. His farewell scene with Tamara is a real gut-wrencher. As he walks along the beach at the end we can see how much the experience has forced him to grow up. Given that almost all his scenes so far have been about his relationship with Tamara, it is interesting to see how he now integrates into the lives of the three other regulars.

The Delinquent: Jen and Dawson have decided to take it slowly, although her unexpected presence at movie night causes tension with Joey. She is fighting with Grams about religion again, and admits that she doesn't even have much faith in *man* at the moment. But during the baby's delivery she manages to muster some faith in Grams, even going so far as to join in the recitation of the Lord's Prayer to help Bess, and by the end she's feeling a little more positive.

The Wicked Witch: This is another great episode for Grams as she saves the day, acting as midwife for Bess. As Dawson puts it, 'As frightening as Mrs Ryan is in daily life, I think she is incredibly capable when it comes to medical emergencies.' Again, she is a character of contradictions – perfectly happy with blood, afterbirth and all the biological messiness of childbirth, but outraged and a bit squeamish at pictures of naked men on a calendar. Her speech to Bess before the birth is marvellous: 'As your attending nurse you may feel an overwhelming outpouring of gratitude toward me when we're done here today, but I promise I will not take advantage of your post-partum bliss and I will resist any urge to bond with you over this shared experience . . . if you will just do me one small favour in return . . . shut up!'

Family Sucks!: Bodie is interviewing for a job as chef at a French restaurant in another town and so is away when Bess goes into labour.

Deputy Doug does not for one second believe that Pacey and Tamara are a couple and Pacey clearly feels betrayed when Doug just reports the town rumours to him and accuses him of making it up to cause trouble: 'Did it ever occur to you, for just a brief moment, to defend or support me . . . or does the Witter family credo prevent such emotions?' After the tribunal Doug tries to make another pass at Tamara, once again having a go at his younger brother in the process. Tamara sets Doug straight about Pacey: 'He's grown up from an unruly child to a sweet, sensitive, intelligent young man.'

School Sucks!: Kenny Leaverton spreads the gossip about Pacey and Tamara so quickly that we hardly have time to catch breath before it's all over school. Whispering in corridors, pointing at Pacey and making cracks in class, the students pounce on a scandal and within three scenes it's reached the teachers' room and the school board. Pacey is lucky not to get seriously disciplined.

That Three-Letter Word: Pacey about Tamara: 'This relationship is not all about sex . . . OK, luckily for me, some of it is.'

Reality Bites: Dawson, filming the birth, when Bess and Grams start to fight: 'Conflict . . . perfect!'

Joey to Pacey: 'Pray like hell for a better story to come along.'

Pacey on Tamara telling him she's moving to Rochester: 'Never in a million years would I have predicted Rochester to be a plot point in our little saga.'

Metatextuality: The poster for *I Know What You Did Last Summer* is now up in Dawson's room as well as the video shop and the film studies classroom where it was seen in **100**, 'Pilot'.

All Things Spielberg: Pacey and Tamara's set text is *Romeo And Juliet*, which provides opportunities for all sorts of snide comments from her English class when Pacey walks in. Grams calls Dawson 'Mr De Mille' when he's filming the birth, a reference to the great filmmaker, Cecil B De Mille.

All Things Freud: Jen analyses her relationship with Grams: 'Grams' way of dealing with my point of view is to pretend it doesn't exist, which of course infuriates me. It causes me to speak emotionally rather than rationally and I become rude and defensive and I give her even more of a reason to dismiss my viewpoints.'

Guy Talk: Pacey and Dawson discuss Tamara in the school toilets, which leads to all sorts of trouble. Later Pacey pours his heart out to Dawson, who gives him some pretty good advice – to try to play it down and not fuel the rumours.

Kiss and Tell: Poor old Pacey doesn't even get a proper goodbye kiss from Tamara, merely a kiss on the forehead because she doesn't think she could stand kissing him properly without becoming overemotional and saying things she might regret.

Blooper: Pacey checks under the toilet stalls but he misses a boy who is standing on the toilet smoking – what, he doesn't have a sense of smell? For some reason Dawson has stopped calling his parents Mom and Dad: they're Mitch and Gale now.

Contempo Pop Music: 'Sitting On Top of the World' by Amanda Marshall, 'Insecuriosity' by Andrew Dorff, 'All I Want' by Susanna Hoffs and 'Seven Shades of Blue' by Beth Nielsen Chapman.

Ker-THUNK!: Capeside, which is large enough to have a high school and a yacht club and a *hospital*, doesn't have a doctor for thirty miles? Our credulity is stretched to breaking point so the writers can wring every drop of drama from the baby's birth.

The Last Word: Although this episode really packs an emotional kick, there are some things that jar a little. At the end of the previous episode Dawson and Jen had patched up their differences and were going out again, but by the start of this one they've decided to take it easy. Why exactly? Also, Jen's religious battle with Grams feels like old territory, while Grams, who in the previous episode had seemed to soften towards Dawson, is back on the warpath. Those niggles aside, the birth is powerful stuff, as is the conclusion of the Pacey/Tamara storyline. Straight tie with **104**, 'The Hurricane' for most intense episode to date.

106
Detention

1st US Transmission Date: 3 March 1998

Writer: Mike White
Director: Allan Arkush
Guest Cast: Monica Keena (Abby Morgan),
Helen Baldwin (Mrs Tringle)

Dawson, annoyed at Pacey for telling Jen his old school nickname, and jealous because he feels threatened by Pacey's sexual experience, breaks Pacey's nose with a basketball; Joey beats up a jock; Jen swears in class. They, together with Pacey and a new character, Abby Morgan, are put in detention on Saturday. Throughout the day, as they're locked in a room together, all sorts of secrets emerge.

The Ballad of Dawson and Joey: This is a big episode for these two as Abby says out loud what we've known for ages: Joey is in love with Dawson. Jen looks stunned at this news, but if she's really surprised then she's up there with Deputy Doug in the perceptiveness stakes. At the end, Joey as good as admits how she feels about Dawson but refuses actually to say it out loud: 'I have all these feelings, these weird feelings, and I don't know how to say it and I can't say it. I mean, you know everything about me, everything, and I still can't say this . . . if I say these things I can't ever take them back, it'll change everything and I can't do that.' Dawson suggests that if she says them out loud then the feelings won't be as strong any more, but she just can't say it. No one, not even Dawson, can now pretend that they don't know the way she feels for him.

The Movie Brat: The obsession with sex that Dawson has been complaining about in everyone else finally hits him and he becomes a mess of angst, jealousy and insecurity. He feels threatened by Pacey because he's a better athlete, becomes jealous of his sexual experience and concludes that he's trying to steal Jen away. He apologises eventually. His nickname at school was Oompa Loompa, after the helpers in *Charlie and the Chocolate Factory* (Mel Stuart, 1971), and he hates it with a passion.

The Tomboy: As far as Joey is concerned, sometimes girls fall for guys for entirely superficial reasons, and yes she counts penis size high on that list – still obsessed, then. In her final speech to Dawson she admits that her feelings for him have left her really lonely, and as much as Dawson tries to assure her that she's not alone, she doesn't buy it.

The Clown: Pacey doesn't realise how sensitive Dawson is about his nickname, pushes him too far, and pays the price. Afterwards, the cheerleaders make quite a fuss of him. He gets 'excited' and is caught by coach 'relieving the tension' in the showers. As ever, sex is his downfall. He gets his own back on Dawson by asking Joey whom she is in love with, trying to force the issue between her and Dawson, and then he tries to whup Dawson's ass on the basketball court – without enormous success. Pacey: 'I'm a screw-up and everybody knows it.'

The Delinquent: Jen is still wild at heart. School is driving her crazy and she suggests river rafting or nude skydiving to Dawson. Later, she gets everyone to photocopy their backsides so they can play 'Guess My Butt'. Jen gets her most revealing speech yet: 'You're like a god to me, Dawson . . . This school hasn't exactly welcomed me with open arms. It seems like everybody here hates me and I don't know why. It seems like my life here is one big detention . . . but then I think of you and about how I've met a guy who is so romantic, so caring and who I like, and who I want so much. Dawson it's because of you that I get through the bad days.'

The White-Bread, Country-Club Goody-Two-Shoes: Please welcome to the stage Abby Morgan, 'the girl from hell'. She's bitchy, manipulative, a compulsive liar and terribly perceptive, dissecting the relationships of the others with unerring accuracy. She's taken the place of Nellie as school bitch.

School Sucks!: Mr Pickering, Jen's teacher, clearly hates her. When she puts up her hand to make a contribution, he asks someone who didn't have their hand up. Then, when she speaks, he tells her off for not putting her hand up! Also, he spouts his own opinions about a highly controversial subject (euthanasia) in a wholly inappropriate manner. Jen argues with him, and I was cheering her on.

As in every American high school on TV and in the movies, the jocks think they are kings of the castle. Two of them push in front of Joey at lunch, giving her a lecture on why they rule the roost. She punches the leader's lights out and brains his henchman. Yay, Joey!

That Three-Letter Word: Dawson is addled with worry because Jen won't sleep with him and he's starting to feel that she doesn't find him attractive. Joey doesn't exactly calm him down: 'If girls are so attracted to the romantic guy, why won't Jen have sex with you?' Dawson on Pacey: 'Ever since he lost his virginity he's been copping this attitude.' Confronting Jen about why she won't sleep with him, he admits he thinks about sleeping with her pretty much all the time.

All Things Spielberg: This whole episode is a riff on John Hughes's seminal eighties teen flick *The Breakfast Club* (1985). See box, *The Breakfast Club*.

Metatextuality: When discussing the subsequent careers of the cast of *The Breakfast Club* they mention Emilio Estevez and Pacey says 'he was in those Duck movies, remember? God, those were classics, so funny.' He's talking about *Mighty Ducks* (Stephen Herek, 1992), and its two sequels, all of which starred Joshua Jackson. Mrs Tringle sounds suspiciously like Mrs Tingle, the eponymous teacher in *Teaching Mrs Tingle* (written and directed by Kevin Williamson, 1999), which starred Katie Holmes.

Girl Talk: Jen and Joey, despite the thawing between them a few episodes back, are at loggerheads again. Joey's intrusive questioning about whether Jen lusts for Dawson leads Jen to retaliate: 'If you spent less time dwelling on me and Dawson maybe you'd have a boyfriend of your own.' As Pacey and Dawson battle it out on the basketball court, Jen finally snaps at Joey, 'I give up. I keep trying to get you to like me but there's nothing I can do is there . . .? All I've ever done is try to be your friend.' Joey replies, 'Why do you have to be like this? So nice. God, it would be so much easier if you were just a total wench.'

Kiss and Tell: When wrestling for the remote control on his bed, Dawson and Joey have their third pre-kiss silence that goes nowhere, but finally, during the game of 'Truth or Dare', Joey and Dawson kiss for the first time. It is, as Abby says, a 'kiss that could set the Atlantic Ocean on fire'. Pacey and Jen kiss also, and the look on Jen's face is worth a thousand words – she really dug it and no mistake.

Contempo Pop Music: 'Stupid' by Chickenpox, 'Saturday' and 'A Lot Like You' by Colony, 'Grace' by Michelle Malone and 'Will Tomorrow Ever Come' by the Dance Hall Crashers.

The Breakfast Club: Kevin Williamson is on record as saying he wants to make movies like John Hughes, who is his hero, and *The Breakfast Club* is both Hughes's best-loved film and the definitive eighties teen flick. Five high school students – a brain, an athlete, a basket case, a princess and a criminal – spend Saturday detention in the library at their school. During the day they share their secrets and become friends, finding that they all have things in common that they never would have suspected. This episode of *Dawson's Creek* adds an extra character, Abby, to the regulars, so there will be five students; casts Mrs Tringle as the headmaster from *The Breakfast Club*, Dick; and even riffs on whole scenes, particularly the jail break and the subsequent race back to avoid detection. Kevin Williamson later scripted *The Faculty* (Roberto Rodriguez, 1998), which is basically *The Breakfast Club vs the Bodysnatchers* in which, yes you guessed it, a brain, an athlete, a basket case, a princess and a criminal defend their high school from alien invasion. This film also parallels scenes from its predecessor, most notably a drug-taking scene that is given a horror-movie twist. Oh, and you can tell which one of the students is the alien – it's the only one not copied from *The Breakfast Club*.

The Big Issue: Jealousy destroys, trust your friends.

The Last Word: Taking the four regulars, locking them in a room and adding a fifth character whose sole purpose is to provoke them all to reveal their deepest secrets is a stroke of genius and works beautifully. This episode has real energy and wit, and the interplay between the cast is as complex and involving as it will ever be. A lovely homage to a great film.

107
Boyfriend

1st US Transmission Date: 10 March 1998

Story: Charles Rosin and Karen Rosin
Teleplay: Jon Harmon Feldman and Dana Barata
Director: Michael Fields
Guest Cast: Scott Foley (Cliff Elliot), Eion Bailey (Billy),
Jeremy Moore (Tyler)

Jen's ex-boyfriend, Billy, the one she was caught having sex with in her parents' bed (she told Dawson the sordid tale in **104**, 'Hurricane'), turns up in Capeside to take Jen back to the Big Apple. When he asks her to help him find somewhere to stay, she gets Dawson to put him up. Cliff invites Jen and Dawson to a barbecue at his house on the beach, but Dawson goes solo as Jen is with Billy, saying goodbye and telling him to leave. At the barbecue Dawson leaves Joey when Jen turns up, so Joey starts to get drunk. Billy turns up just as Jen is apologising to Dawson and an argument ensues, which ends with Jen storming off. Meanwhile, Pacey rescues Joey, who's by now very drunk, from a guy who's taking advantage of her. Dawson and Pacey take Joey home. Jen tells Billy to leave, and he does, but then she breaks up with Dawson.

The Ballad of Dawson and Joey: The traumatic semi-confessions of **106**, 'Detention', seem to have been forgotten. Dawson casually lets Joey sleep over for the first time in an age, and Pacey goes to lengths to confront both Joey and Dawson and try to get them to admit that something is going on between them, when all that was made crystal clear in **106**. When Joey is borderline unconscious and can't hear him, Dawson decides to pour his heart out to her: 'I realise how incredibly confusing things are between us. I can't even begin to explain our relationship . . . but I just want you to know that if you ever need me I'll always be here for you.' Great rehearsal, Dawson. Now try saying that when she's awake.

The Movie Brat: Dawson sees himself as a 'well-intentioned geek . . . the Gary Cooper type . . . likable but not too self-involved, smart without being arrogant'. He agrees to let Billy stay over, and trusts Jen enough not to pump Billy for information and scandal about her, but later he runs to Joey for help: 'My life is rapidly turning into some seriously disturbing joke.' Jen is his first and only girlfriend and he tries to lay down the law a bit, for the first time: 'I want things to go back to normal and I want Billy gone.' But his insecurity leads to more confrontations, harsh words and apologies. Finally, after Jen dumps him, he lets his bitterness out, and, even though he instantly regrets it, he can't bring himself to apologise again.

The Tomboy: Joey's passion for Dawson is really starting to get to her, and she finally lets off a little steam and gets totally wasted.

The Clown: In the video store Pacey comes flat out and says to Joey, 'You have some raging hormonal obsession with our friend Dawson,' he seems surprised when her reaction pretty much confirms it, but doesn't he remember detention? To Dawson he says, 'My fine oblivious friend . . . this girl is head-in-the-clouds, one-hundred-per-cent, ass-backwards in love with you.' He takes pity on Joey and drags her to the barbecue, both to get her out of work and because Dawson will be alone there. When it all goes wrong, he is the knight in shining armour, punching out some guy who's getting too friendly. His behaviour when he's looking after Bess's baby, Alexander, proves that he's good with babies, too.

The Delinquent: Jen is horrified to see Billy turn up and her first words to him are to ask him to leave, but he still has a hold over her and she agrees to cut school to talk to him although she tells him, 'I've changed . . . I'm not the same person you knew in New York.' But what, oh what, does she think she is doing asking Dawson to share his room with her ex-boyfriend? Is she *insane*? Given that she asked Dawson to display the restraint of a superhuman, she pretty much lost my sympathy at that point. The boy is a walking mass of insecurity. Did she really think he'd handle it well? This must count as the most spectacular own goal yet scored by a series regular. She clearly still has feelings for Billy, probably because he was the only person back in NYC who treated her decently, and her hesitation and indecision cost her dearly. When Dawson and Billy are arguing over her, she walks away, in an exact replay of the scene with Cliff at the dance weeks earlier. Finally, after eight episodes of 'will they, won't they?', Jen dumps Dawson. She has decided it's time she faced life on her own rather than trying to 'escape into a relationship'. She admits she'll miss him, and will probably come crawling back to him one day, but she stands firm despite Dawson's protests. By the end of the day she's pretty much isolated herself.

Family Sucks!: Joey's nephew, Alexander, 'the human alarm clock', is driving her nuts with his endless crying. She's not sleeping and her grade-point average is suffering.

Reality Bites: After Dawson lands one insult too many, Jen returns to an old theme: 'I may have made some mistakes but at least I don't live in a fantasy world.'

All Things Spielberg: Joey thinks Bess has given birth to Rosemary's Baby (from Roman Polanski's 1968 film of that name). Dawson is going through an American classic film phase and at the start he is watching *Meet John Doe*

(Frank Capra, 1941). Pacey is watching *Anaconda* (Luis Llosa, 1997) when Joey comes into the video store. The only thing that puts Alexander to sleep is *The English Patient* (Anthony Minghella, 1996) and in absence of a VCR Pacey acts out the film for him.

Grown-Up Stuff: Mitch and Gale are seeing a counsellor, Dr Keenan, who recommends that they find new activities to do together that will freshen up their relationship. They try scuba diving, which is, perhaps predictably, a disaster. Mitch tells Gale he still loves her and that he's 'willing to do whatever [he has] to do' and suggests that they should 'start with something simple'. They dance, but when Gale tries to kiss him he won't let her. Dawson is disturbed by their arguing and tells Joey how much he dreads a possible divorce. Mitch has a meeting with a big investor, presumably for his aquatic-themed restaurant, but we never hear how the meeting went. However, he makes a crack later about Gale being the breadwinner, so presumably not too well.

Guy Talk: Mitch and Dawson have a chat about relationships and it's never been clearer how completely Dawson is his father's son: 'Face it, Dad, we're a couple of nice guys, which stopped being a desirable trait about half a century ago.'

Kiss and Tell: Jen kisses Billy goodbye, barely, but he uses it as an excuse to stick around in **108**, 'Roadtrip'. Joey kisses Dawson, but how drunk is she and does she know what she's doing?

Guest Cast: Eion Bailey was one of the pack in the first season of *Buffy the Vampire Slayer* and appeared in *Fight Club* and *Almost Famous*.

Contempo Pop Music: 'We'll Get Through' by the Slugs, 'Being Right' by Cush, 'Dammit' by Blink-182, 'Elegantly Wasted' by INXS, 'Green Apples' by Chantal Kreviazuk and 'Evaporated' by the Ben Folds Five.

The Big Issue: Sometimes the past comes back to haunt you.

The Last Word: A bit of a disappointment. Dawson screws up and apologises. He fights another guy over Jen. Joey looks on in angsty silence, and it all feels a bit familiar. Having him put Billy up strains credulity way too far, although having Jen ask him in the first place is quite a leap. In the end the party, Joey's drunkenness and all the scenes with Pacey save the episode. The final scene, where Jen dumps Dawson, is so good it feels as if it had been lifted from another episode. Anyway, now the coast is clear for Joey and Dawson, how long before they sort themselves out? The shot at the foot of the bridge where Jen and Billy say goodbye is beautifully composed to make it look like Brooklyn Bridge in NYC, reminding us again what Jen is running away from.

108
Roadtrip

1st US Transmission Date: 17 March 1998

Writer: Rob Thomas
Director: Steve Robman
Guest Cast: Eric Balfour (Warren Gerry),
Eion Bailey (Billy), Monica Keena (Abby Morgan),
Melissa McBride (Nina)

Against her better judgment, Joey accepts a lift from a jock called Warren, who then spreads rumours around school that she slept with him. On Jen's advice Joey takes her revenge by spreading a counter-rumour that she is pregnant. Things get out of hand when Joey starts to get offers of counselling from staff. Jen hears that Warren's ex has told Abby that he is impotent. Warren agrees to back off and issue a full retraction as long as Joey does not spread a story that confirms the impotence tale.

Billy, who has decided to stick around after Jen's kiss in **107**, 'Boyfriend', invites Dawson to get over Jen by coming with him to a bar where they can pick up girls. Pacey tags along and they cut school and head out of town to Providence. On the boat to the mainland they play a practical joke on some guys who are drunkenly hassling people. Dawson ties a chain to their front axle and the back of Billy's truck. When they drive off they take the axle with them.

At the bar Pacey strikes out, but Dawson gets talking to an attractive film student called Nina. Although he could stay at hers for the night, he declines. Dawson then confronts Billy, saying he's known all along that his plan was to get Dawson to sleep with a stranger so he could go back, tell Jen and prove that Dawson was just like everyone else. Billy leaves the guys to catch a bus home.

The Ballad of Dawson and Joey: Jen tells Joey that Dawson is in love with her, that Jen is merely the 'object of his infatuation'. When Dawson returns and falls asleep, Joey tucks him in and, staring at him as he sleeps, says, 'Yeah, I can wait.'

The Movie Brat: Dawson proves to Pacey that he can misbehave and love it, crowing in triumph as he wrecks the car of the boors on the boat. However, his greatest moment is his chatting up of Nina, whom he singles out because she's wearing a film T-shirt. He is awkward and rambling yet somehow manages to turn that into a strength by, bizarrely, deconstructing his own chat-up strategy and listing his faults: 'hopeless optimism . . . reckless disregard for danger, my tiresome romanticism and . . . the way I keep on talking when the person I'm trying to impress has lost all interest.' Nina asks him to come home with her, platonically of course. When he refuses because he wants Jen back and it wouldn't be right, he single-handedly restores Nina's faith in the male sex.

The Tomboy: Joey's performance as the scorned, pregnant cast-off is Oscar-worthy and very inventive: 'One time he won this stuffed frog at Coney Island and he brought it back for me . . . when we made love he cried.' She doesn't like being the centre of attention but she shows that she can give as good as she gets any day of the week; she practically demolishes Warren.

The Clown: Pacey relishes the day out and, while Dawson is playing pool, Pacey is doing what they came there for: picking out girls. He totally strikes out, but that's probably his oh-so-lame choice of opening line: 'Hi, I'm the drummer for Pearl Jam.'

The Delinquent: Jen's efforts to make friends with Joey seem to pay off at last, and she's no slouch when it comes to scheming and revenge.

The Wicked Witch: Grams finds an unshaven, leather-jacketed youth in her granddaughter's bedroom and doesn't even blink, merely demands to know his name, and asks Jen to bring her a phone so she can call the National Guard. Quite the coolest cucumber in Capeside.

The White-Bread, Country-Club Goody-Two-Shoes: When you want gossip spread as fast as humanly possible, whom do you tell? If you're a boy, tell Kenny Leaverton, but if you're a girl it's got to be Abby Morgan. Abby is the gossip queen and she relishes every second of her scandal-mongering day, spreading Joey's retaliatory tale and then providing the impotence gossip that wins her the day.

School Sucks!: Dawson does the unthinkable and cuts class, but not before handing in his maths homework. Mrs Tingle recommends that Joey take the Family Living course, where Joey knows they make students 'carry around a sack of flour and pretend it's a baby'.

That Three-Letter Word: Warren, who we learn can't, ermm, perform to order, tells Joey it's obvious she's a virgin. She asks how he knows she and Dawson aren't working their way through the Kama Sutra, and says if she is a virgin it's because she chooses to be.

Reality Bites: Dawson tells Joey he's watching a movie but when she turns on the VCR he's watching the tape of Jen's arrival again. Dawson: 'Movies, by nature, are escape flicks. You want reality, look out the window.'

Metatextuality: Mrs Tringle, the librarian from **106** 'Detention' *has* changed her name to Mrs Tingle after all.

All Things Spielberg: Dawson's rental this week, for his I'm-so-pathetic mopeathon, is *Sid and Nancy* (Alex Cox, 1986), the story of the ill-fated relationship and deaths by suicide of the Sex Pistols' Sid Vicious and his girlfriend Nancy Spungen. Pacey likens Billy to the Fonz, and Dawson to Ritchie Cunningham, from the TV sitcom *Happy Days* (1974–84). Dawson replies that this makes Pacey Potsie. On the ferry Dawson pulls a stunt stolen from *American Graffiti* (George Lucas, 1973).

All Things Freud: Pacey deconstructs Dawson: 'You're just not the type of guy who does something bad just because it feels good . . . you're the nice Leery boy; you like being the nice Leery boy.'

Girl Talk: Jen makes a point of seeking Joey out, supporting her throughout the rumour saga and helping her plan revenge. Joey lets her, and they seem genuinely friendly. Later Joey, perhaps rightly, accuses Jen of using her to get back at men in general, and, perhaps wrongly, of treating Dawson badly for the same reason. Jen fights back: 'There's no more excuses . . . and now, when Dawson treats you like good ol' understanding Joey, just one of the guys, I'm not going to be around for you to hate.' In the end Joey goes over to Jen's with cookie-dough ice cream and they make up. Jen: 'So what do you think, Joey? Is there any way we can keep Dawson from coming between us?'

Guy Talk: Pacey tells Dawson that he is the good angel that pops up on his shoulder and tells him the right things to do but accuses him of being 'better at the verbiage than actual words' or, in layman's terms, 'all mouth, no trousers'. Pacey: 'Sometimes friendship means taking part in stupid stuff, no judgment, no questions asked, and no deconstruction of the event' – and that's precisely what they do in this episode. When Pacey realises Dawson kissed Nina the look on their faces, and the way Pacey punches Dawson's arm, is one of the closest moments the two characters have shared yet and it shows just how well Pacey and Dawson complement each other even though they are almost polar opposites.

Kiss and Tell: Dawson kisses Nina outside the nightclub and, although he doesn't want to admit it, the lipstick gives him away to Pacey.

Our Quips Are Wittier: Pacey, gleeful on being told Dawson is cutting school: 'Finally, Dawson's evil twin, this has been a much-anticipated pleasure.' Joey, being told about the Warren rumour: 'Yeah, right, I had sex with Warren Gerry, right after I gave a sponge bath to the navy pilots.'

Blooper: Dawson and Pacey have jackets on when they leave Capeside and when they're on the ferry, but when they leave the club and wait for the bus they are jacketless. Not a blooper, perhaps, but Billy keeps saying he heard Jen dumped Dawson, which is a bit unlikely given that he just got to town and doesn't know anyone there. Who would have told him?

Guest Cast: Eric Balfour played the ill-fated Jessie in the opening two-part episode of *Buffy*.

Contempo Pop Music: 'Truly, Madly, Deeply' by Savage Garden, 'Touch, Peel & Stand' by Days of the New, 'We Are the Supercool' by Space Monkeys, 'Requiem For a Lightweight' by the Slugs, 'Your Pleasure's Mine' by Super Deluxe, 'I'm Not Sleeping' by Nowhere Blossoms, 'Thinking Out Loud' by Ron Sexsmith, 'Carry Me' by Boom Hank, 'Nashville' and 'Monkey Mind' by Judge Nothing, 'The Step Inside' by Sounder and 'Right Today' by Swerve.

The Last Word: The dialogue sparkles in this wonderfully written episode, which shows us another side of Dawson, gives us real insight into his friendship with Pacey, and contains some excellent scenes between Jen and Joey. A great improvement on **107**, 'Boyfriend'.

109
Double Date

(The official *Dawson's Creek* website lists 'Double Date' as 110 and 'The Scare' as 109, which is supported by the *Best Of . . .* DVD. However, the episodes were not transmitted in that order and I have followed transmission order.)

1st US Transmission Date: 28 April 1998

Writer: Jon Harmon Feldman
Director: David Semel
Guest Cast: Scott Foley (Cliff Elliot),
Megahn Perry (Mary Beth)

Pacey convinces Dawson the best way to get Jen back is to pretend not to care and to date other girls. When Jen tells him she is going on a date with Cliff to the carnival, Dawson says he also has a date for that evening and asks why they don't make it a double. He asks Mary Beth, a girl from school, to go with him. The date is a disaster, and Mary Beth turns out to have the hots for Cliff as much as Dawson has the hots for Jen. They swap partners for the Ferris ride and, when the ride breaks down, Dawson and Jen argue.

Pacey is failing biology and is paired with Joey to do an extra credit project on snail mating. When he accidentally kills the snails, Pacey takes Joey to a tidal pool to get some more, but he forgets to tie up their boat and it drifts off. They wade back to Pacey's truck and get soaking wet. They don blankets and go home. Later they meet Dawson at the carnival and Pacey asks Dawson's permission to kiss Joey, which throws Dawson completely, but he says OK. Pacey does kiss Joey but she doesn't return his interest.

The Ballad of Dawson and Joey: In the opening scene, Dawson asks Joey, 'How could you simply be friends with someone when every time you look at them all you think about is how much more you really want them?' Joey tells him it's definitely doable and casts one of those oh-so-familiar guarded-but-longing looks at the dimwitted object of her desires. Dawson wrestles with the idea of Pacey kissing Joey and eventually decides he's not comfortable with it at all, but by then it's too late and Joey has given Pacey the brush-off.

The Movie Brat: Does Dawson not remember **100**, 'Pilot', and what happened last time he and Jen were part of a double date? Obviously not, because he suggests it again. A facility for lying and manipulation is emerging in our boy Dawson. He uses Mary Beth to get at Jen and when she rumbles him he constructs an even more elaborate lie to cover his tracks. The competitive streak that emerged in **106**, 'Detention', returns, as he takes on Cliff at carnival games and wins.

The Tomboy: Joey is doing an extra class for biology, not because her grades are down but because she needs them higher – she wants to go to college and her background and lack of money make it hard for her: 'When I apply I'd better have the grades not to give them a choice because a scholarship is about my only way out of Capeside.' She is understandably dissatisfied with her lot – sleeping in her sister's living room and waiting on table – so if she 'doesn't get out of here . . . it would be a sadder story than I can imagine'. Pacey thinks Joey is a 'repressed control freak'.

The Clown: He's been dimwitted before, but this week he outdoes himself. He fails a test, kills the snails, forgets to tie up the boat and then makes a pass at a girl he *knows* is in love with his best friend. Apart from being sympathetic when Joey talks, and asking Dawson's permission to kiss Joey, he doesn't do a thing right this week. Joey thinks Pacey is a 'remedial underachiever'.

The Delinquent: Jen makes the traditional post-break-up offer of friendship, which Dawson accepts. Later, after his mad double-date suggestion and behaviour at the carnival, she retracts the offer: 'I don't think a seamless transition to friendship is on the cards for us.' Dawson is angry that she is dating again because when she broke up with him she said it was because she needed time away from men. When they argue she starts to cry and never really answers Dawson's question about why she dumped him.

School Sucks!: Pacey is failing biology, even though his teacher says he has an aptitude for it. He's smart but doesn't apply himself to school at all.

That Three-Letter Word: Snails are having the only sex this week and, when Pacey adds a third snail to try to create a gastropod *ménage à trois*, the poor blighters get eaten. That'll teach 'em that sex in Capeside always has a consequence.

All Things Freud: Mary Beth likes Dawson, but she doesn't like-like him, mainly because he's 'too neurotic'. You got that right, sister.

Grown-Up Stuff: Bob phones Gale at home, ostensibly about work, and Mitch gets very angry. He asks Dawson, not too subtly, whether Bob has been phoning and Dawson says no. Later Gale and Mitch are dancing again and when the phone rings they let it. They seem pretty together by the end – the smile Gale gives Mitch speaks volumes.

Guy Talk: Pacey is the doctor of lurve this week, advising Dawson on strategies to get Jen back: 'The quicker you can fake some sort of indifference the less special she's going to feel, and the less special she feels the more she's going to want that very special feeling that comes from being Dawson Leery's girlfriend.' Pacey feels it is the honourable and proper thing to ask for Dawson's blessing because he knows the tension that could arise if he were to date Joey. Dawson says he doesn't mind: 'My two best friends kissing – what could be better than that?' He instantly changes his mind, however, and the look on Pacey's face as he turns and asks what they should do now hints that he would go ahead and do it anyway and that serious conflict would result. Dawson later seeks out Pacey and definitively says no, not aware that the kiss has already taken place. Luckily for him it didn't work out. Pacey asking permission to kiss Joey and Dawson's clear statement that he wouldn't be comfortable with it both foreshadow the events and the conflict in Seasons Three and Four. Pacey continues to play the confronter and insists that Dawson choose between Jen and Joey.

Kiss and Tell: Pacey, much to his surprise, finds himself 'confused, surprised and attracted' to Joey during their day together. After Joey's changed into her blanket, and given Pacey an unintentional eyeful, he says how much fun he's having and she's clearly very flattered and a little embarrassed. After the carnival he kisses Joey and she's not offended or angry, which we might have expected. Instead she actually seems flattered and apologetic that she doesn't feel interested in Pacey too. Pacey says that he can handle the brush-off easily, but as he's about to leave he says to Joey, 'If by some slim chance you had kissed me back you'd probably have been thinking about someone else, right?'

Our Quips Are Wittier: Joey to Dawson on Pacey: 'You're taking romantic advice from a guy who spent his evening trying to get three snails to sleep together?'

Guest Cast: Megahn Perry was killed by Angelus in an episode of *Buffy* and had a recurring role on a short-lived sci-fi show called *Prey*.

Contempo Pop Music: 'Come Back' by Vaporhead, 'She' by Louie Says, 'What's Going On' by Leslie King and Shelby Craft, 'I'm The Only One' by Melissa Etheridge and 'Hangin' By a Thread' by Jann Arden. 'She's The One' by World Party, later a No. 1 hit for Robbie Williams, plays out the episode.

Backstage: Katie Holmes and Josh Jackson were dating during the filming of Season One and the first part of Season Two. So their on-screen kiss mirrors offstage reality.

The Last Word: Joshua and Katie earn their pay this week, wading through a creek in cold water up to their necks. The double-date story works well in itself, but again Dawson is competing for Jen, and it doesn't feel that the storyline is any further forward than the previous two episodes. Pacey and Joey's scenes are far more engaging, unexpected and very well played and written. This development comes out of left field and takes two characters who've had little to do with each other till now and hothouses them. A nice character piece, but it's starting to feel as if the show is marking time till Joey and Dawson can kiss, finding ways to postpone it because the writers don't want to get there before the season ends.

110
The Scare

1st US Transmission Date: 5 May 1998

Writer: Mike White
Director: Rodman Flender
Guest Cast: Jennifer McComb (Ursula),
Justin Smith (Eddie), Scott Foley (Cliff Elliot),
Mitchell Laurance (Mr Gold),
David Blanchard (the Ladykiller)

A serial killer, 'the Ladykiller', is reported to be moving towards Capeside in search of his sixth victim – he works in 100-mile increments and taunts his victims with letters and phone calls before cutting out their hearts. Dawson assures Pacey that this Friday the 13th he will not play practical jokes on all his friends as he normally does. Pacey almost believes him until a plastic skull bursts out of his locker. Dawson invites everyone to a séance at his house.

Cliff awkwardly asks Jen out on a date and she accepts, with some reservations. Cliff asks Dawson's advice on what to do for the date. Dawson says he'll think about it. Jen opens her locker and finds a letter – from the

Ladykiller? At home she gets an anonymous phone call. At first she assumes it is Dawson, but the caller denies it so many times she gets really scared.

Pacey picks up Dawson and Joey. The guys go into the market to buy supplies for the party. In the market they witness a fight between a woman, Ursula, and her boyfriend, Eddie. It gets pretty violent but she sends him away and then chats up Pacey, who plays along. She shoplifts a bottle of wine and Pacey invites her to Dawson's séance.

Back in the jeep, Joey is surprised by a creepy man who asks her for directions. He starts to freak Joey out by asking if she's local and staring at her fixedly. As Pacey and Ursula leave the store, Eddie returns, eager to continue the fight. They race to the jeep and make a quick getaway.

Cliff picks up Jen and takes her to Dawson's party because he thinks it's unpredictable (rather than just plain weird) to take her to her ex's place. As the party gets going everyone, but especially Ursula, keeps falling for Dawson's practical jokes. As they gather round a table for the séance they each take their turns telling scary stories. Jen confronts Dawson over the phone call and letter but he protests his innocence. Ursula claims to be able to channel sprits and then freaks everyone out by telling a story about a woman who is picked up by a young boy in a store and who carries a knife in her bag for slitting throats. Just as they're all at their most spooked the power blows out. They split up into pairs to check power and phones. Dawson admits to Ursula that he set the power to cut out at 11 o'clock but it looks like someone's fused it so he can't turn it back on. Later, on the porch, Pacey is chatting Ursula up when Eddie bursts from the bushes. They run inside and barricade themselves in while Eddie smashes windows and tries to kick down doors to get in. They remember the ladder to Dawson's bedroom window and assume Eddie has used it and is inside. Pacey opens the front door to run for help but Eddie's out there and attacks him. Joey saves the day by repeatedly beating Eddie with a frying pan. Ursula saves Eddie and they leave, declaring their love for each other. Ursula dismisses Dawson and Co. as 'weird'.

Cliff walks Jen home and admits he made the calls and sent the letters to make himself seem interesting and fun. Joey and Dawson settle down for a sleepover and just before they go to sleep they see a news item – the Ladykiller has been caught, and it was the guy who asked Joey for directions outside the market!

The Ballad of Dawson and Joey: Ursula spots instantly that Joey is in love with Dawson and tells him he should forget Jen and go after Joey. She insists that Joey and he will end up together but Dawson dismisses the idea. Pacey again confronts Joey over her unrequited love for Dawson but she laughs it off too. Later, Dawson admits that if Joey were to die he'd be inconsolable; Joey admits the same would be true if their roles were reversed.

The Movie Brat: Finally admitting maybe he has a reality problem: 'I'm done trying to turn my life into some exciting movie, 'cause you know what? I only end up getting disappointed.'

The Tomboy: Joey comes over as the all-action hero, beating the living daylights out of Eddie with a frying pan. No wonder Ursula describes her as feisty.

The Clown: As soon as Ursula starts talking to Pacey he puts on his best Dean Martin smoothy voice, starts waggling his eyebrows for all he's worth and plasters a grin all over his face. As ever, his libido takes instant charge and bypasses his brain entirely. Joey insists that he has a 'bizarre mother complex' and, when he tries to chat up Ursula with the line 'I may look young but I have been with older women before', we can only agree.

The Delinquent: On the phone to her mystery caller, Jen admits that her heart is dented and that it's all her own fault. She hates being scared but still feels left out when no one tries to scare her, and even instigates a scare of her own to get back at Dawson.

The Wicked Witch: Grams just loves Cliff – he's in the football team, top of the honour roll, she's even seen him at the First Church of the Nazarene every Sunday: 'I really like that Clifford Elliot. Good stock.' Later, when she interrupts them on the porch, she is accommodation itself and says they should 'take as long as they want'. How's that for a change of tune?

Metatextuality: Dawson has posters for both *Scream* (Wes Craven, 1996) and *I Know What You Did Last Summer* (Jim Gillespie, 1997) on his bedroom wall. The phone call to Jen is a complete rerun of the opening scene from *Scream*, and the characters know it. At the start Joey and Dawson are watching Sarah Michelle Gellar, star of *Buffy* and a victim in Kevin Williamson's *Scream 2* (Wes Craven, 1997), die horribly in Williamson's other horror franchise, *I Know What You Did Last Summer*. Then Joey switches to *Jerry Maguire* (Cameron Crowe, 1996). In film class they are discussing the framing of shots in John Carpenter's seminal *Halloween* (1978), the latest installment of which, *Halloween H20* (Steve Miner, 1998), starred Michelle Williams.

All Things Spielberg: As you would expect from a series created by Kevin Williamson, the man who single-handedly revived the horror movie, this episode is one long list of horror-movie references. When Joey is giving directions to the Ladykiller she sends him to Elm Street. The presentation of the episode itself is full of visual clues. The handheld camera work and throbbing musical score is pure schlock horror; the sun goes ominously down to threatening music and the establishing shots of the house are pure *Halloween*.

Girl Talk: Jen admits that Dawson is 'probably the most original and imaginative date on the planet'. Thank heavens Dawson didn't hear her say that or she'd never be rid of him.

Guy Talk: Dawson to Pacey on his relationship with Jen: 'The characters were flawed and uninspired. The love scenes were, I dunno, amateurish to say the least, and the ending was definitely not happy.'

Kiss and Tell: Jen and Dawson kiss but then Jen backs off saying that it's a bad idea. Dawson doesn't look so sure. Although not wanting to kiss him, she still insists that he shouldn't cross her off any lists, which leaves poor old Dawson as confused as ever. Cliff tries to kiss Jen goodnight but she's not interested. In the end he does get a quick kiss, for which he should be grateful, given that the hapless schmuk scared her half to death earlier. She'd have been more than justified in punching his lights out.

Blooper: At the store Pacey asks Joey to stay in the jeep because it's a hassle to start it if he switches it off. But when he leaves Dawson's later on he just jumps in, turns the keys and he's away. On the video and DVD release the *Jerry Maguire* clip has been replaced by a clip from an old black-and-white Cary Grant film, presumably for copyright reasons, but the soundtrack is still *Jerry Maguire*.

Guest Cast: Jennifer McComb has appeared in *Sliders*, *ER* and *Saved By the Bell*. David Blanchard played a waiter in *Halloween H20* and was a series regular in Williamson's next TV series, *Wasteland*.

Contempo Pop Music: 'Nobody Cares' by Vaporhead, 'Will U Drive Me?' by the Rosenbergs, 'Do You Dream?' by Mary Thornton/Adam Castillo and 'Temptation' by the Tea Party.

The Big Issue: It's 'The Boy Who Cried Wolf', with knives.

The Last Word: One of the very best episodes of the season, justifiably one of the two episodes on the 'Best Of Season One' video release. It's funny, spooky and genuinely scary at times. It also manages to find time to move the relationships along, setting the scene for Dawson and Joey's inevitable kiss while establishing that there's still something between Jen and Dawson, even if they don't know exactly what. This is a cast and crew, and especially a writer, having the time of their lives.

·111
Beauty Contest
1st US Transmission Date: 12 May 1998

Writer: Dana Baratta
Director: Arvin Brown
Guest Cast: Lori Rom (Hannah Von Winning),
Cara Stoner (Roberta Crump),
Margueritte Lowell (Mrs Penmyer),
Robby Preddy (pageant sign-up lady)

It's time for the Capeside Yacht Club's Windjammer Days, when Miss Windjammer is elected. Jen persuades a reluctant Jocy to enter, while Pacey challenges convention and becomes the first man to enter the competition. Jen does an excellent job preparing Joey, who does really well despite almost quitting at one point after hearing rich snob girls calling her a charity case. She sings a song from *Les Miserables* and eventually comes second. Pacey is doing well, too, until he realises he can never win and goes out in a blaze of weirdness, dramatically reinterpreting a speech from *Braveheart*. Dawson sees Joey in a new light and when Jen asks him if they can get back together he declines, too confused by his sudden awareness of Joey's beauty.

The Ballad of Dawson and Joey: Dawson is openly disbelieving when Joey enters the contest and she's offended because it could seem he was insinuating she was not pretty enough, so they spend a lot of the episode not talking to each other. Joey on Dawson: he 'will always see me as the gawky little girl down the creek with Band Aids on her knee and one braid falling out'. Dawson on Joey: 'I've never thought of Joey in a romantic context: I've always thought of her as a sister. I just don't think I could ever get past that . . . it would be a little incestuous.' When Joey is about to quit the contest Dawson tells her he is proud of her and he thinks she has a lot of courage. After the show Dawson is speechless and sweaty-palmed, and tries to work out what he's feeling: 'You came completely out of your shell . . . this new-found confidence just seemed to burst out of you . . . it's like you transformed into this beautiful goddess . . . I feel like I'm seeing you for the first time tonight.' Joey is disturbed by this because 'it's only lipstick, it's only hairspray . . . I want you to look at me and see the person you've always known and realise that what we have is so much more incredible than just some passing physical attraction.' Dawson wants to talk it through and deconstruct their emotions till he understands them, but Joey leaves for home.

The Movie Brat: Dawson's getting bitter at Jen and at the start is throwing ill-disguised jibes her way. He just can't help it because 'winning her back has dissolved into some sort of bizarre hobby'. He films the pageant for a proposed news article on Pacey's entrance in the competition, which makes a small item on local news. So he's a reporter now. When did that happen?

The Tomboy: Joey's worries about getting into college, established in **109**, 'Double Date', rear their head again as the excuse to have her enter the contest. Her self-image is (perhaps unbelievably) bad – she thinks she's not pretty and keeps going on about being too tall until Jen says, 'We're going to have to work on your self-esteem issue.' She has no mentors or role models, which is a pretty sad thing for a fifteen-year-old girl to be able to say. In five years she wants to be as far away from Capeside as possible. Her competition speech is a moving and passionate plea for people not to judge each other by status, money or class.

The Clown: Pacey is so browbeaten at home that he wants to move out and get his own place but he can't afford it, so he enters the beauty contest to raise money. Pacey loves both the attention and the fact that he is breaking the rules in such a blatant and public fashion. Hannah Von Winning, high-class babe and top contender for the crown, once rejected Pacey's romantic overtures and calls him the 'class clown of Capeside High'. Mitch points out that

Pacey is becoming a political activist with this stunt, but he insists he's in it only for the cash. However, when he is told that he won't be allowed to win he really does act like an activist, and his rousing, if somewhat unhinged, performance in blue make-up is a pretty powerful statement after all, and you can't help feeling it's aimed squarely at his absent father. Gale likes him: 'You are funny, you are charming, the audience loves you.' Perhaps acting or stand-up is where Pacey should put his efforts. He is, as ever, the chorus commenting on the Jen/Joey/Dawson love triangle and he points out Jen's mistake in getting Joey to enter none too gently and perhaps a little gloatingly.

The Delinquent: Her mother used to enter her in 'disgusting Little Miss pageants'. When she was dating Dawson, Jen was always petrified that one day he would realise how gorgeous Joey was. So what does she do? She persuades Joey to enter a beauty contest, makes her look like every young man's dream, and comprehensively scuppers her own plans to get Dawson back. Second major own goal of the season for Miss Lindley.

Family Sucks!: We've already met Pacey's brother, Doug (**104**, 'Hurricane' and **105**, 'Baby'), but we finally get a bit of detail about his home life, and especially about his father, who sounds awful: 'I just spent the entire morning with my dad telling me what a scholastically inept, athletically challenged, underachieving loser I am . . . if I have to hear the words "why can't you be more like . . . Doug?" one more time my head is going to explode . . . he told me as soon as I want to become an emancipated minor to just show him where to sign.' In fact, it seems as if Pacey, whose home life is never really featured, has the roughest deal of all the gang, which makes it doubly curious that the writers haven't yet taken the story to Pacey's home and used that to generate even more drama.

Reality Bites: Just as Jen is making her play for Dawson, Joey walks on stage, looking a million dollars (even if she does keep doing that self-consciously gawky thing where she sticks her elbows out and kind of flaps them). Dawson is flabbergasted, for the first time seeing her as woman. And what does he do? He immediately goes to look at her through a camera! Only then, when he's mediated her through a screen, does he look back up at her with true realisation in his eyes. As ever, nothing is real for him; nothing registers till he sees it on film or through a lens.

Girl Talk: The Jen-and-Joey friendship leaps forward again this week, although it leaps from the place it's always been to the place it always is at the end of an episode. Jen makes the first move: 'Now that the proverbial wedge . . . is no longer between us we could actually be friends.' And Joey warily agrees, as long as they don't have to 'wash each other's hair or do each other's nails'. Jen tells Joey: 'You're one of the prettiest girls in school . . . how come every time I give you a compliment you look at me like I'm trying to hit on you?' They argue, analyse and reach an understanding and, lo, we've had the Jen-and-Joey-make-friends storyline for the third time (see **103**, 'Discovery' and **108**, 'Roadtrip').

Guy Talk: Dawson to Pacey: 'I think you've got testicles of steel for doing this!'

Kiss and Tell: Joey and Dawson have yet another pre-kiss moment on the pier after the contest, but no, not yet.

Our Quips Are Wittier: The Windjammer contest is the distillation of everything Joey hates and feels excluded from, so she swallows a dictionary and spits it out in disgust: 'It's a blue-blooded tradition that celebrates the grand tradition of being born rich, the culmination of which is an asinine formal dinner held at a yacht club . . . it's the most archaic form of ageism, racism and sexism known to man.'

Guest Cast: Lori Rom, who plays Hannah, was the original Phoebe in *Charmed*, played Laura in four episodes of *Party of Five*, Danielle in four episodes of *Providence* and Allison Hanau in four episodes of *Jack & Jill*. Robby Preddy appears in *The Gift*, which also starred Katie Holmes.

Contempo Pop Music: 'Small Town Trap' by Eve 6, 'The Girl With All the Goodbyes' by Susan Sandberg, 'Pretty Face' by Chickenpox plays at the meeting for the Miss Windjammer contestants, 'Superman' by Goldfinger and 'Surrounded' by Chantal Kreviazuk.

The Big Issue: Joey maintains that men are conditioned to fancy 'whatever supermodel the media decides is this week's perfect specimen' but Dawson stands up for 'pure animal instinct'. She pretty much proves her point because it's only when she dresses up and shows off on stage that he finally notices her; only when she fits all the stereotypes that she was berating earlier does Dawson realise what we've known all along: she's gorgeous.

The Last Word: The guide to this episode could go on a lot longer, it's so chock full of great lines and wonderful scenes. This is the other episode from the 'Best of Season One' video, and it's a beautifully written and played piece of TV drama. In their performance pieces Joshua Jackson and Katie Holmes get to strut their stuff and both are superb; Holmes singing 'On My Own' is one of the top moments of the whole season.

112
Decisions

1st US Transmission Date: 19 May 1998

Story: Jon Harmon Feldman
Teleplay: Mike White and Dana Baratta
Director: David Semel
Guest Cast: Dylan Neal (Doug Witter),
Gareth Williams (Mr Potter)

Joey is offered a scholarship to go and study in France but she is undecided whether to accept it. It is also her father's birthday and her turn to visit him in prison. She refuses but Bessie forces her, and Dawson escorts her for moral support. They miss visiting hours and have to spend the night together in a motel. Next day the meeting does not go well: Joey tells her dad she's leaving for France and storms out, leaving Dawson to tell Mr Potter about his daughter. Back in Capeside, Joey asks Dawson to give her one good reason not to go to France, and he can't. A meeting with Pacey prompts Joey to change her mind and return to the prison, where she talks to her dad and they patch things up somewhat. He tells her Dawson loves her.

Jen's grandfather wakes from his coma but the next day he suffers another stroke and dies. She takes comfort with Dawson and sleeps over, but in the morning Joey, coming back from prison to tell Dawson she loves him, finds them together and leaps to the wrong conclusion. Dawson chases after her but she has gone. He spends the whole day looking for her and eventually finds her in his closet that night. They talk and finally, after endless analysis, they kiss.

The Ballad of Dawson and Joey: This is the big one, folks, and they milk it for all it's worth. The opening scene has Joey refusing the temptations of movie night because they're in the same place they were three months ago and she thinks it's getting boring. Dawson admits he'd miss her if she went to France, but gallantly says that if it would make her happy he'd be happy for her. It is Dawson who suggests they get a motel room together (and what kind of motel rents a double room to two fifteen-year-olds?) and then he proceeds to rerun the opening scene of **100**, 'Pilot', coming over all awkward at sleeping in the same bed and offering to sleep on the floor. He seems about to make some statement, and Joey's face lights up, but then falls when she realises he's just analysing again. Joey gives Dawson an opportunity to keep her from going to France, but he fluffs it, not knowing what to say. It is Joey's father who finally settles it, telling her that Dawson loves her, getting her to admit she loves him and telling her that she must tell him. She runs to tell Dawson and enters at exactly the wrong moment. When Dawson spends a whole day looking for her, she spends a whole day moping and feeling sorry for herself, and they end up back in his room. By this point Joey's finally lost patience with him and he knows it: 'We spend all our time analysing our sad little adolescent lives ... but it doesn't get us forward. We're in the same place we were three months ago.' They both say they just want to be honest, and it's clear they're both still afraid of what will happen if they kiss, but eventually Dawson seizes the day and kisses her. Viewers across the world sigh with relief and cheer.

The Movie Brat: Dawson is paralysed by fear of what might happen if he seizes the day. Every time he and Joey get to the point of committing, he gets this terrified look on his face and his jaw locks. His speech to Mr Potter about Joey is the first time he's been honest about his feelings for her and he's very eloquent indeed, although it's typical of Capeside's most self-involved teenager that he ends up talking about her in relation to him, which is surely not something her dad needs to hear: 'She believes in me, and I'm a dreamer, so it's good to have somebody like that in my life.'

The Tomboy: Joey shows her vulnerable side in her second meeting with her father, where she says: 'I'm fifteen years old and I go through every day of my life thinking nobody loves me.' It must have taken a lot of courage to ask her father, flat out, 'Do you love me? Do you think about me?'

The Clown: Deputy Doug is really down on Pacey, calling him 'the leading contender for the title of official joke of Capeside ... one day ... you're going to wake up and realise you're a bad punchline nobody's laughing at.' Pacey obviously takes this to heart, no matter how much he tries to pretend otherwise, and he asks Joey, 'When was it I got designated town loser?' Still, with all his faults he comes riding to Joey's rescue yet again, driving her to see her dad and bribing the guard to make it happen.

The Delinquent: After her rebuttal in the previous episode, Jen is still trying to get Dawson back, asking him out for the night. When she says Joey should go to France the look on her face really gives away her ulterior motive – she wants the competition out of the way. She loves her grandfather very much and wishes he could come back and 'magically uncomplicate' her life as he used to. When she realises he's dying it's Dawson she turns to for solace, admitting that she blew their relationship, telling him how much she misses him, and as good as asking for a second chance. She asks if she can stay over and holds on to him, crying her eyes out. When she tries to kiss him in the morning and he runs after Joey instead, she seems to accept that she's finally lost him, and says goodbye.

The Wicked Witch: Grams is a bit of a gossip – when she's talking to her husband she's telling him all the scandals from the local church elders! She says that she and Jen are coexisting at last and, surprisingly, keeps him updated on Jen's love life, admitting that she thinks Jen misses Dawson. Her husband wakes up but, just when she thinks he's come back, he dies. As ever, she finds solace in her faith, solace that Jen can't share. Jen does visit Grams in church and we finally get to see her vulnerable side as she breaks down and weeps in her granddaughter's arms. Her transformation from bad guy to fully sympathetic character is complete.

Family Sucks!: Pacey: 'Fathers are weird creatures.' In an episode all about fathers we get a daughter (Joey) who doesn't want her father, and a father who doesn't want his son (Pacey), but strangely we don't get any interaction between the perfect father and his perfect son – Mitch and Dawson. Joey blames her dad, who cuts a pretty pathetic figure, for destroying her family. She spits at him, 'That family you miss, it doesn't exist any more. It's over.' But she still goes back to sort things out, telling him, 'You messed up because . . . I'm your daughter and you don't know me.' Pacey tells Joey how he once heard his dad, disappointed because Pacey had struck out in a little-league baseball game, tell Doug, 'At least I have you,' which must be one of the most hurtful things a son can hear. He feels like he's a 'walking embarrassment to my perfect family' and Doug seems to confirm that.

School Sucks!: Pacey has failed all his mid-terms and the principal has phoned his father to give the official failure warning.

Reality Bites: The opening scene is one of the best yet, as Dawson and Joey commentate on cliffhangers as an introduction to their own season ending. Joey doesn't like them – 'merely a manipulative TV standard designed to improve ratings' – but Dawson says they offer the possibility of real change. Joey scoffs: 'A cliffhanger's purpose is to keep people interested and keep them guessing what's going to happen in future episodes . . . the producers put the characters into some contrived situation hoping that the audience will think something is going to change. But you know what? It never does.' So we watch an episode in which there's a contrived situation – Joey's potential exit for Europe – and when Dawson demands finally to know if she's going or not she laments, 'Ah, the inevitable cliffhanger' mere moments before the season ends, leaving us guessing what's going to happen in future episodes and wondering if things really are going to change.

All Things Spielberg: The show comes full circle and we end where we began, in Dawson's bedroom, with Dawson telling Joey what she told him in the first scene of the pilot: 'Spielberg outgrew his Peter Pan syndrome.' The whole season has been about Dawson catching up with Joey: she told him that three months ago. It's taken him all this time to realise it, and now that they are finally on the same page they can be together at last.

Pacey calls his family 'the Stepford family', from a series of movies about a community that replaces its troublesome and individual members with androids; it began with *The Stepford Wives* (Bryan Forbes, 1975).

All Things Freud: Dawson analysing his tendency to analyse: 'I can analyse somebody else until the cows wander home but as soon as I turn all that adult perception on myself it's like I completely lose connection between my heart and my head.' Clearly he should abandon all hopes of becoming a filmmaker and pursue a career as a shrink.

Kiss And Tell: Jen tries to kiss Dawson after her sleepover, but judging by the mortified look on his face she wasn't going to get very far. Joey and Dawson finally, monumentally, and at first quite awkwardly, lock lips. The final shot of the season is of them silhouetted against the window of Dawson's bedroom kissing passionately.

Our Quips Are Wittier: Dawson admits his freakish articulateness: 'I know we know too many big words.'

Blooper: First it was Mrs Tringle, then Mrs Tingle, now it's Mrs Tringle again. Will someone *please* make up their mind?

Guest Cast: Gareth Williams, who plays Mr Potter, portrayed an abusive dad to a telekinetic girl in *Angel* and has also appeared in *Law and Order*, *Time of Your Life*, *JAG* and many other TV shows and films.

Contempo Pop Music: Much as I like the use of songs to narrate an episode – something *Dawson's Creek* does better than any other show – it would have been better if they'd not done it this week. The score by Adam Fields, who has scored all of Season One, is absolutely superb and his best work on the show to date, making a tangible contribution to the drama. He later returned to the show and did all the incidental music for Season Four.

'What Do You Do?' by Dog's Eye View, 'Angel' by Sarah McLachlan, 'I'll Be' by Edwin McCain, 'Broken Road' by Melodie Crittenden and 'Say Goodnight' by Beth Nielsen Chapman plays out the season.

The Big Issue: Family may let you down, but they're still family. Hold on to them before they're gone.

The Last Word: The music, the powerful emotional scenes, the acting, the dialogue, all come together beautifully in a clever, moving and entirely logical season finale that gets us to the point we always knew would close the season.

Season Two

Executive Producers: Kevin Williamson, Paul Stupin
Co-Executive Producer: Jon Harmon Feldman
Supervising Producer: Greg Prange
Producers: Mike White, David Semel
Co-Producers: Dana Baratta, Shelley Meals,
Darin Goldberg, David Blake Hartley,
Janice Cooke-Leonard

Regular Cast

James Van Der Beek (Dawson Leery)
Katie Holmes (Joey Potter)
Joshua Jackson (Pacey Witter)
Michelle Williams (Jen Lindley)
Mary-Margaret Humes (Gale Leery)
John Wesley Shipp (Mitch Leery)
Mary Beth Peil (Grams)
Nina Repeta (Bessie Potter)

(although they are credited as special guest stars, the following were
effectively series regulars this year, and were advertised as such in
publicity materials)

Meredith Monroe (Andie McPhee)
Kerr Smith (Jack McPhee)
Monica Keena (Abby Morgan)

Scheduling: When the expected controversy over sexual content in Season One failed to materialise WB decided to move *Dawson's Creek* back an hour to its originally intended timeslot of 8 p.m. This put it in direct competition with the reigning king of teen soaps, *Beverly Hills 90210*.

201
The Kiss

1st US Transmission Date: 7 October 1998

Writer: Jon Harmon Feldman
Director: David Semel
Guest Cast: Ali Larter (Kristy Livingstone)

The second season opens exactly where first season ended – same shot, same music, Joey and Dawson kissing in Dawson's bedroom. Next day Joey tells Bess, and Dawson tells Pacey.

Pacey, driving his dad's squad car, has a collision with Andie and he lets her think he's a police officer. He threatens to take her licence but lets her off with a caution. At school the next day Andie bumps into Pacey and makes him feel guilty for his little charade. However, she offers to set him up with Kristy Livingstone, head cheerleader and Pacey's latest object of desire. Following Andie's encouragement Pacey asks Kristy out and to his astonishment she agrees. When Pacey meets Kristy that night she is already on an anniversary date with her boyfriend. Andie told her Pacey had a deadly heart condition and she's just come to say how brave she thinks he is. Pacey meets Andie later at a store and they agree they're even.

At school Joey tells Dawson she has decided not to go to France and they make a date for Saturday to see the last film at the Rialto before it closes. Jen arrives at school, upset, tells them about her granddad dying and says she's going to take the rest of the day off. Dawson and Joey go to the cinema but Jen arrives, realises she's making things awkward and leaves. Dawson feels bad, goes to talk to her and finds Jen in the lobby, having a bit of a breakdown. They fight, and when he returns to his seat Joey has left. While Jen is being comforted by Grams, Dawson finds Joey and they kiss again.

The Ballad of Dawson and Joey: As soon as they have acted, their tendency towards 'gratuitous self-examination' comes crashing down and Dawson and Joey almost talk themselves out of its ever happening again. Dawson manages to save the day, just.

The Movie Brat: Turning up for his date with Joey, Dawson gets the speedboat-driving, slo-mo, wind-in-hair, rock-music-soundtrack entrance of a movie star. Dawson handles himself pretty well, for a change; the date goes well and he acts instead of just talking about it.

The Tomboy: Joey decides that in a toss-up between Dawson and France the boy with the big forehead wins hands down. She wears the shortest skirt ever to appear on the show for her date.

The Clown: Pacey decides to turn his life around and start dating a better class of girl, so he frosts his tips, which looks hideous – as Andie rightly points out – and asks out the senior cheerleader. Of course he crashes and burns, but the look he gives Andie in the store hints that maybe he has his eye on her now.

The Delinquent: Her granddad's death obviously hits Jen hard because she's a total mess this week. Feeling forlorn, she misinterprets Dawson's pep talk as an invitation to join him and Joey at the cinema and then, when she realises she's a third wheel and Dawson comes to find her, she unloads a whole heap of self-pity: 'It seems a little sad . . . I was the girl whose sole purpose was to allow you to figure out who you were really in love with.' She admits that she pushed him away and that she deserved to lose him, and asks him to promise not to sleep with Joey immediately because that might push Jen to razorblades. Grams talks to her after the film and finds her similarly pathetic: 'You may be the best friend I've got. I'm just not sure you like me.' When Grams says Jen is her whole world Jen replies, 'If I'm all you've got I pity you.'

The Basket Case: Andie's family have just moved from Rhode Island and are obviously well off, given the car she was driving. She's hyper and a little scatty, and when she confronts Pacey at school she says that she's been having 'major anxiety attacks, to the point of medication'. Her revenge is sweet – telling Kristy that Pacey has a life-threatening 'heart stripe' is creative and it works – although Pacey has to be the world's biggest idiot not to see it coming. A great introduction to a great character.

The Wicked Witch: Grams and her husband were married for forty-three years, but after the stroke she saw him waste away for two years and prayed that he would die. Her first date with him was at the Rialto, so she goes to see the last film there to remember that night. She tries to set depressed Jen straight: 'I know we may bicker from time to time but I love you and with your grandfather gone you're all I have.' Which makes you wonder: if she's mother to one of Jen's parents do they never call her, even to check up on their daughter?

Family Sucks!: Pacey's dad reportedly gives him a hell of a hard time for banging his squad car, but, fair enough. We discover what Pacey's dad does: he's the town sheriff!

That Three-Letter Word: Pacey and Bess immediately ask the question to Dawson and Joey respectively: how far did they go and are they going to have sex? Dawson surprises Joey, and us, by telling Joey, in the school corridor, that he's aroused and guaranteeing that he'll still be that way come Saturday. When Dawson picks her up for the date Joey says that they're now enduring the agony of whether to 'check into a motel and go at it like porn stars' and even tells him she knows a good motel, but he just wants to hold her hand. Altogether now: aaaaahhhhh.

Reality Bites: Reality finally eclipses the silver screen when Dawson admits his kiss with Joey was 'beyond any movie I could ever imagine'.

Metatextuality: Joey says she might stay in on Saturday and watch *Beverly Hills 90210* because Luke Perry's back. Luke Perry and *90210* were on the opposite channel as she said those very words.

All Things Spielberg: The last film showing at the Rialto is *The Last Picture Show* (Peter Bogdanovich, 1971). Pacey compares Dawson and Joey to Sam and Diane on *Cheers*, who didn't get together for four seasons, and Mulder and Scully on *The X-Files*, who hadn't even kissed when this episode was made.

Grown-Up Stuff: Gale comes on to Mitch in bed but he pushes her away and later that day he visits a divorce lawyer. He doesn't tell Gale but she finds a business card from the lawyers and confronts him about it, demanding that he either give her a proper second chance or get a divorce. Mitch can't decide what he wants to do. Things seemed on the mend with Gale and Mitch before they all but vanished for the last three episodes of Season One. Obviously things have changed while they've been off screen and Mitch is not sure that he wants to give the marriage a chance any more. Mitch is still running off to meetings left, right and centre but, apart from his restaurant plan, we still have no idea what he does for a living or what these meetings are about.

Kiss and Tell: Bess believes that the first kiss, the one that's all lust, isn't as good as the second kiss, the rational one. Joey and Dawson share their second kiss by the episode's end.

Blooper: The hair!! Dawson's hair in a scene that takes place seconds after the last scene of Season One is totally different. Obviously an effort has been made to brush it forward and make it look the same, but they just don't get away with it. Also, Joshua Jackson's bleached blond hairdo, which he sported in all the films he made between seasons, is almost gone, but his tips are still yellow – so Pacey decides to frost his tips and, *voilà*, a perfect excuse. When Pacey and Dawson start the next scene having their haircut it's a brilliant way around the problem and as good as winks at the audience and says, 'Yeah, we know we screwed up, but what could we do?'

Guest Cast: Ali Larter appeared alongside James Van Der Beek as a cheerleader in *Varsity Blues* (Brian Robbins,

1999). She later appeared alongside Kerr Smith in *Final Destination* (James Wong, 2000).

Contempo Pop Music: 'Say Goodnight' by Beth Nielsen Chapman opens this season as it closed the last. 'Out Of My Head' by Fastball, 'Birds of a Feather' by Phish, 'Swallow' by Nowhere Blossoms, 'London Rain' by Heather Nova and 'Have a Little Faith In Me' by John Hiatt.

Ker-THUNK!: Any season opener has to set new storylines in motion and introduce new characters and it's pretty hard to do it subtly. Andie literally crashes into the show, and Mitch's divorce thoughts come somewhat out of the blue, but compared with the clunker Season Three starts with, **301**, 'Like a Virgin', this is practically unnoticeable.

The Last Word: A superb season opener, laying the foundations for new storylines with minimum fuss and reintroducing us to old characters and storylines with aplomb. In large part this mirrors **100**, 'Pilot': we have a date at the Rialto that goes awry, a new blonde female character introduced to shake things up, and the beginning of a new downturn in Gale and Mitch's marriage. I suppose if it worked once it can work again. And it does.

202
Crossroads
1st US Transmission Date: 14 October 1998

Writer: Dana Baratta
Director: Dennie Gordon
Guest Cast: Tom Nowicki (Cole)

Dawson reads an entry in Joey's diary in which she says he is a hopeless filmmaker and his horror movie was terrible. He sulks, she finds out he read her diary and they fight, but they make it up in the end.

Dawson is so distracted by his fight with Joey that he forgets Pacey's birthday. Every time he tries to ask Pacey's advice, Pacey bites his head off and Dawson can't work out why. They fight but, of course, they make it up in the end.

Pacey throws a party for himself at the docks and Jen turns up with her unlikely new best friend, Abby Morgan.

The Ballad of Dawson and Joey: Dawson thinks his relationship with Joey is 'perfect . . . none of that pretentious getting-to-know-you crap. I already know all there is to know about you.' Joey counters: 'What you don't know about me, Dawson, could fill a book.' Later, when they've made up, Dawson says, 'I'm glad I don't know everything about you because every day you amaze me.'

The Ballad of Andie and Pacey: Andie is following Pacey around, and he's started calling her McPhee. He makes her mad, which beats nervous because 'New people make me nervous, I never know what to say and eventually I just clam up totally.' But with an outfit like the one she wears to his party it's a surprise half the guys there weren't beating a path to her door. She gives him a magic eight-ball, the only present he gets, but she drops it in the creek by accident. They're starting to warm to each other, even if Pacey does keep the little-rich-girl cracks coming.

The Movie Brat: Dawson is back to his old tricks, suffering bouts of insecurity, overreacting, crossing the wrong boundaries, getting it wrong and spending his day so preoccupied that he misses all of Pacey's hints. Will he ever learn? Pacey calls him 'self absorbed, self-centred, selfish' and tells him to 'get over yourself'. Joey, on the other hand, thinks he is 'the most extraordinary, talented person I've ever met'.

The Tomboy: Whenever Joey's feelings for Dawson drove her mad she would go and curse the world, and Dawson, in her diary, so when he reads it she feels violated and betrayed. Even when they've kissed and made up she won't let him off the hook (which is fair, because it was a really scummy thing to do).

The Clown: The Pacey tradition of awful birthdays gets off to an auspicious start when he fails his driving test. Then his best friend forgets his birthday altogether, and he throws a party to cheer himself up at which nobody speaks to him. Is it any wonder he's a walking bag of self-pity: 'I came to this dark realisation that everyone in Capcside has either written me off or deemed me unworthy of their time and their concern.' He also says he rides a 'fine line between insecurity and self-confidence'.

The Delinquent: Jen, still low after losing Dawson and a bit screwy since her granddad died, can't resist boasting. She gets throw-up drunk, kisses Dawson and then admits to Abby that she's in love with him and wants him back.

The Basket Case: Andie goes striding in where her shy brother fears to tread and sorts him out a job at the Icehouse. Could she *be* more different from Jack?

The Outsider: Jack gets a great introduction: unlike Andie he slips quietly into the show, as befits his character, and is instantly Mr Shy Empathic Sensitivity. He's working at the Icehouse, so while Andie gets lots of scenes with Pacey he should be featured a lot with Joey, allowing the siblings to come into the group through different routes.

The White-Bread, Country-Club Goody-Two-Shoes: Abby is back to stir things up, and thank heavens. Her pleasure at finding out that Jen had the kind of life Abby pretends she has is great. She makes a perfect foil for Jen, bringing out her bad side and promising an alliance to get Dawson back for her. Should be interesting! She stole some letter-headed paper from her doctor and uses it to get out of school activities.

That Three-Letter Word: Mitch and Gale decide it's time for the Sex Talk and go way overboard. Gale gives Joey a book called *Reproduction and Repercussion* while Mitch buttonholes Dawson in the kitchen and starts banging on about contraception and teenage pregnancy. Dawson: 'Joey and I are together a week and already my parents are shoving condoms in my pocket.'

Metatextuality: Grams tells Jen off for swearing, but Jen says that 'hell' is no longer a swearword because 'you can say it on network TV'. And she does. Pacey is 'sick and tired of being Dawson Leery's sidekick – I'm going to get my own storyline', unaware that his storyline for the year began last week when Andie drove into him.

All Things Spielberg: Pacey tells Jen he has a bad case of the Molly Ringwalds, referring to *Sixteen Candles* (John Hughes, 1984), the first of John Hughes's brat-pack teen comedies, in which everyone forgets Molly's sixteenth birthday. Mitch and Gale 'live for those coming-of-age *Wonder Years* moments'. *The Wonder Years* was a seemingly endless show in which Fred Savage took forever to grow up while his older self narrated life lessons for the week. Abby calls Dawson, Joey and Pacey 'Forrest Gump and company'.

Grown-Up Stuff: Mitch is still pushing Gale away when she tries to get frisky. After speaking to his best friend he suggests to Gale that they have an open marriage, which is a bit rich coming from the man who played responsible sex educator to his son earlier that day. What *is* he thinking? He's still looking for a restaurant location – is that all he ever does?

Girl Talk: Gale goes to Grams, of all people, for advice on saving her marriage, but her comments about 'cleaning out the marital-aids section of the pleasure palace' are just a little too much for Grams to handle.

Guy Talk: Mitch goes to talk with Cole, his best friend from high school, and we have a glimpse of a possible older Pacey and Dawson. Mitch is as clueless as his son and his Doctor of Lurve, Cole, is worldly wise and knowing, dispensing sex tips as if he'd been born to it.

Pacey admits he'll miss certain things about his friendship with Dawson now Dawson has Joey. Dawson replies, 'Just because everything is complicated and everything is changing . . . nothing is ever going to change so much that you're not going to be my best friend.'

Our Quips Are Wittier: Jen on Dawson and Joey: 'They're like brother and sister, Dawson told me himself.' Abby, watching Dawson and Joey kissing: 'Maybe they're pretending like they're in Kentucky.'

Guest Cast: Tom Nowicki has appeared in numerous TV shows, including *ER*, *The Cape* and *Matlock*; he has also featured in such films as *Remember The Titans* and *The Waterboy*.

Contempo Pop Music: 'Good Intentions' and 'Dear Mary' by Aryana, 'Sway' by Bic Runga, 'Killers' by Feeding Like Butterflies, 'Get 'Em Outta Here' by Sprung Monkey, 'Always' by the Sterlings, 'Kiss the Rain' by Billie Myers, 'Luckiest Guy' by the MacAnanys and 'Save Tonight' by Eagle Eye Cherry.

The Big Issue: No matter how well you think you know someone, you're an idiot if you think you know everything that goes on in their head.

The Last Word: Nothing spectacular happens this week, and Pacey's party seems a contrived way of getting everyone together in a charged atmosphere, but Abby's return is welcome, as is Jack's introduction. The scenes where Pacey gets angry at Dawson, who just looks confused (as always), add some nice conflict to a relationship that's normally plain sailing. Mitch gets the best scenes of the episode, though, showing that, no matter how awkward kids may be about sex, adults are just as clueless.

203
Alternative Lifestyles

1st US Transmission Date: 21 October 1998

Writer: Mike White
Director: David Semel
Guest Cast: Tamara Taylor (Laura Weston),
Colin Fickes (Kenny Reiling)

Pacey is paired with Andie, while Jen is paired with Dawson, for an Economics project on household budgeting. Jen carries through her plan to win back Dawson, and Pacey continues to tease Andie about being rich. Joey, meanwhile, does the project on her own as a single mother, which makes her think about her future.

Mitch takes down the ladder to Dawson's room, concerned about Joey sleeping over.

The Ballad of Dawson and Joey: No big crises this week, their biggest problem is getting enough privacy so they can make out.

The Ballad of Andie and Pacey: Andie begs Pacey to help her with notes for class and although he tries to escape she's not letting him get away. When they are paired together for the project she drags him around flat hunting and then complains that he's lazy and self-destructive, which just makes him lose his temper with her: 'You've never had a problem in your life . . . you basically throw your money away . . . you're rich and spoiled.' Andie runs off crying and Jack sets Pacey straight, hinting at dark family secrets. So Pacey comes up with another of his noble gestures, handing in a full project in both their names. By the end they are arguing like friends rather than enemies.

The Movie Brat: The Dawson of ten episodes previously would have dissolved into a quivering heap before Jen's attempts to win him back, but now he's got Joey he stays stoic throughout.

The Tomboy: Joey can't imagine what her future will be like, but doing the research for the project makes her realise that she could own her own business one day, and that maybe she does have prospects after all.

The Clown: Pacey's one priority for adult life is the immediate possession of a Dodge Viper. He does the 'broken record' bit again, giving Andie his black-sheep speech. He really has a self-esteem problem and his tendency to blame his underachievement on his family is not helping things.

The Delinquent: The 'old, naughty Jen' is back in full effect. She flashes cleavage, offers massages, strokes Dawson's hair and asks to sleep over. She accepts he is with Joey but she won't let that stop her making a play for him, and she 'puts the final nail in my coffin of shame' by letting him know he can have her back whenever he wants.

The Basket Case: Pacey finally hurts Andie's feelings for real and her reaction prompts Pacey to ask Jack if she's on medication, the second time that word's been used regarding her (see **201**, 'The Kiss') – signposting the future a bit. She says, 'My life is like a movie of the week.'

The Outsider: Jack practises his little-lost-puppy-dog look a lot, and he thinks that the way to mop is to pour a bucket of water over the floor and clean it up.

The White-Bread, Country-Club Goody-Two-Shoes: Abby is egging Jen on for all she's worth, telling her she's a 'sex kitten' and urging her to throw herself at Dawson whenever possible. She's a bad influence, but she's so much *fun*!

Family Sucks!: Joey is feeling the pressure of juggling school, babysitting for Bessie and working at the Icehouse, especially as a health inspection is imminent and she has to pull extra work hours for clean-up. She storms out but she can't sleep. Bessie fires her, saying that Joey is missing out on 'the fun of being young'. But Joey won't accept that: 'You and I are a team . . . I'm not going anywhere and I won't be fired . . . and I love you . . . and I don't ever want you to feel like you're alone.' The economics project has helped Joey realise the pressure Bess is under and she tells her how amazing she thinks she is.

School Sucks!: Mr Mattocks telling the two jocks that they're a gay couple is priceless. Whenever Pacey is asked a question in class he answers, 'Pass'.

That Three-Letter Word: Dawson is finally awake to the fact that he's a 'sexual being' and he thinks Mitch is in denial about it: 'One day, down the road, I am going to have sex . . . the sooner you accept that the sooner you and

I will have an honest relationship.' Dawson runs rings round Mitch the next morning, getting him to admit that fooling around with girls is more fun when you're fifteen if there's a danger of getting caught, and concluding that by 'restricting my access to Joey you're really trying to liven up my sex life'.

All Things Freud: Mitch to Dawson: 'You can psychologically deconstruct me all you want but here's the deal: parent me, child you.'

Grown-Up Stuff: Gale really doesn't like this open-marriage idea but Mitch insists on it because he hopes that 'by taking away the rules I can take away the need to trust you and we can get back some of what we lost'. He designates Thursday nights 'date night' and takes off on his own even though Gale has cooked dinner and got the candles out. She gives in, goes out on her own, too, and they each have a lonely, miserable evening that they then lie about to each other.

Girl Talk: Abby and Jen are best friends now, partners in crime, and Abby has a passion for gossip that's inspiring. She wants Jen to bed Dawson as quickly as possible. Abby thinks Dawson 'goes to sleep every night jerkin' the gherkin and wakes up every morning humping his mattress', but she's wrong – we know all about his Katie Couric fantasy, see **100**, 'Pilot'!

Our Quips Are Wittier: What fifteen-year-old kid ever says this to their dad: 'Whenever your parental authority is in question you just start barking out orders'?

Guest Cast: Leann Hunley's surprise appearance as Tamara is not mentioned in the opening credits, so when she turns up it's quite a shock. Tamara Taylor has had recurring roles on *City of Angels* and *Party of Five*. Colin Fickes appears in *Cherry Falls* and *Carrie 2 – The Rage*.

Contempo Pop Music: 'Anything You Say' by Chickenpox, Harvey Danger's 'Flagpole Sitta', 'Mary Be Merry' by Say-So, 'Four Eyes' by Sozzi, 'Swan Song' by Bruce

Hornsby, 'The Party's Over' by Catie Curtis and 'WooHoo' by Newsboys.

The Last Word: The economics project is a contrived way of forcing the characters together, but it's executed very well and the episode works nicely. Jack and Andie are being integrated into the show at a comfortable pace and Tamara's brief appearance promises high drama next week. Mitch and Gale's storyline continues to be a highlight.

204
Tamara's Return

1st US Transmission Date: 28 October 1998

Writer: Mike White
Director: Jesús Treviño
Guest Cast: Leann Hunley (Tamara Jacobs),
Joe Flanigan (Vince), Tamara Taylor (Laura)

Tamara's back in town, trying to sell a warehouse she owns to Mitch. Her arrival hits Pacey like a truck but they resist the temptation to get together again.

Joey develops a passion for art, which Dawson doesn't share, so when he teases her about it she plunges their relationship into uncertainty.

Abby and Jen continue their bad-girl trip with a shopping binge that ends with Abby chatting up a sailor, Vince. They later track him to the docks but he blows off Abby and offers to take Jen out any time.

Andie tells Dawson she likes Pacey, Dawson tells Pacey, Pacey finds he kind of likes the idea.

The Ballad of Dawson and Joey: Their relationship is in trouble. They've found a solution to Mitch and Gale's overreaction about sex – they're making out outside and Joey finds Dawson's romantic scene painting 'unbearably sexy'. Pacey sums up every Dawson-and-Joey crisis ('Joey is being sarcastic and overbearing and you, my friend, are being self-absorbed and suffocating') just in time for the crisis that breaks the mould. Dawson does make fun of Joey's art, but not maliciously or insensitively, and when she freaks out he's at a loss; even his perfect apologies don't work. Joey is scared: 'You've been everything to me and I have been your confidante, your sidekick, your other half for so long . . . that's how our relationship works . . . it's scary because I realised that apart from you I don't have anything. My entire life is attached to you, Dawson.' When Jack tells her to draw what she loves all she can think of to draw is Dawson, who's really moved by the drawing. Joey is so dependent on him that she's terrified of losing him, which in turn makes her feel she needs to be more independent. The situation remains unresolved.

The Ballad of Andie and Pacey: Andie's locker is now next to Pacey's. They bond over a shared love of *Dumbo* and even though he calls her a freak he asks her if she wants them to spend the afternoon together, much to his own surprise it seems, and Andie is delighted to be asked. Later that day, though, she's telling Dawson that Pacey is 'a pig' and 'obnoxious', which Dawson says is his way of flirting. It's strange after seeing Pacey in a reasonably mature relationship last season to see him involved in a second-grade kindergarten light, basically teasing the girl he likes in order to show interest. You half expect him to pull her pigtails and run off giggling at any moment.

The Movie Brat: Abstract art doesn't do it for Dawson: he likes art 'with a verdict . . . specific, coherent and to the point'.

The Tomboy: Joey practises her drawing in every spare moment – could this be the direction she's been after?

The Clown: Tamara's appearance floors Pacey. He's speechless and can't help but follow and talk to her; he's lucky Andie hasn't heard all the old gossip about him yet. He tells Tamara he's grown up, he's over her and he's moved on, but he's not entirely convincing and eventually he admits that he misses her 'teaching'.

The Delinquent: Jen's self-pity continues as she nurses her 'narcissistic wounds' and pines for Dawson. If Abby weren't around to liven her up she'd be the dullest character on the show; as it is she's the most unlikable. She's happy to be slipping back into her old ways: 'I left New York because I couldn't handle being a bad girl any more, but ... if being the bad girl means not walking around in a perpetual state of loneliness and depression, then bad girl it is.'

The Outsider: Jack's reputation as the world's worst waiter is confirmed when Joey, good-naturedly, sums up his abilities: 'Since we hired you it's been nothing but a slapstick comedy ... you're a walking sight gag.' But at the art show he blossoms, raving about expressionism, revealing all sorts of depth and coming out of his shell in a lovely scene with Joey where we can see a real friendship being forged and a real character emerging at last.

The White-Bread, Country-Club Goody-Two-Shoes: Abby is a shopaholic. She goads Jen into going with her and then throws herself at Vince in as nakedly lustful a manner as possible, but she overplays her hand and Vince calls her an 'oversexed, condescending teenybopper'. When Vince prefers Jen she is really hurt and rounds on Jen, all her insecurity pouring out.

Family Sucks!: Dawson was beginning to think that Mitch's restaurant plans were all pie in the sky; weren't we all?

That Three-Letter Word: Abby talks a good fight (but do we believe her?): 'I need a real man with chest hair and body odour and illegitimate children scattered across the country.'

Metatextuality: The scene between Tamara and Pacey where they share a 'Pinter moment' is lovely, narrating the way the writer, Mike White, is constructing the scene. It explicitly harks back to the way they conducted their relationship through set texts, a habit they fall back into effortlessly. Pacey: 'Harold Pinter, king of subtext: you say one thing but you mean another. We're big on that in Capeside.' Pinter is one of the best English playwrights of the twentieth century, famous for writing dialogue that contains lots of meaningful pauses, and has written plays such as *The Birthday Party*, and films such as *The French Lieutenant's Woman* and *The Go-Between*.

All Things Spielberg: Joey calls Jack 'Inspector Clouseau' after the bumbling French detective played by Peter Sellers in the Pink Panther movies. Andie's got the Dawson habit, and her three rentals are *Ghost* (Jerry Zucker, 1990), *The Way We Were* (Sydney Pollack, 1976) and *Dumbo* (Ben Sharpsteen, 1941), which Pacey thinks is 'one of the saddest movies ever'. Dawson says that Joey went *Sybil* on him, after the TV movie (Daniel Petrie, 1976) about a girl with multiple personality disorder.

All Things Freud: Dawson to Pacey: 'When a girl hates you the way Andie hates you, it really means she likes you. That's basic kindergarten psychology.'

Grown-Up Stuff: Mitch's eyes as good as come out on stalks when he meets Tamara in the street. He looks as if he's about to ask what she's doing next Thursday, but he never does.

Guest Cast: Joe Flanigan has featured in *Profiler*, *Providence* and *Cupid*.

Contempo Pop Music: 'Harvest Moon' by Donna Lewis, 'Breathe' by Colony, 'Half As Good' by Zoe, 'Northern Lad' by Tori Amos, 'And On a Rainy Night' by Shawn Mullins and 'Each Little Mystery' by Seven Mary Three.

Ker-THUNK!: Reintroducing Tamara was not a bad idea, and a good way to help Pacey move on to Andie. But having her own a warehouse is just silly – she was in town for only a few months and she was an English teacher – what would she want with abandoned warehouse space?

It's nice that Andie has a scene with Dawson, but we've never seen them introduced and here she is suddenly asking

him if Pacey likes her and confiding that she likes him.
Even if she admits she hardly knows Dawson, this is a little
too much to swallow.

There's a major exhibition of works by a world-
renowned painter – in Capeside??

The Big Issue: Tamara: 'The more complicated life becomes the more important it is to learn to say nothing' –
a skill Dawson and Joey will just never, ever learn.

The Last Word: Jesús Treviño composes some lovely shots
in the warehouse, using shadow and light to frame the
actors in a moody *X Files* way not usually seen in this
sunniest of shows. Joey's sudden worries about the relationship with Dawson come out of the blue, as does her
passion for art, giving the episode a rushed feel, – it's
trying to do too much too soon. But Jack gets a great
scene; Tamara's return, if contrived, yields two superb
scenes; and Andie is really endearing when she's twisting
Dawson's boxers and baring her soul.

205
Full Moon Rising
1st US Transmission Date: 4 November 1998

Writer: Dana Baratta
Director: David Semel
Guest Cast: Leann Hunley (Tamara Jacobs),
Joe Flanigan (Vince), Caroline Kava (Mrs McPhee)

It's full moon over Capeside and people are acting
strangely.

Pacey asks Andie out on a date and she accepts, but they
get confused where they're meeting and he goes to pick her
up at home, where he meets her mother. He discovers that
Andie's older brother Tim was killed in a car crash some
years before and her mother is gradually going mad.

The Icehouse is empty except for Joey, Jack and one guy drinking coffee, who helps them when the power goes out and leaves a $100 tip and a poem, which spurs Jack to kiss Joey.

Gale has a male colleague over for dinner, which annoys Mitch; Tamara comes to visit Mitch, which annoys Gale. When Dawson confronts them about their open marriage all hell breaks loose and the couple decide to go their separate ways.

Jen and Vince get better acquainted. This drives Abby so nuts that she breaks into Dawson's bedroom to spy on them. Jen and Vince are caught by Grams making out on the living room table.

The Ballad of Dawson and Joey: Dawson is relying on Joey more than ever as his parents' marriage breaks up, but the unresolved questions from **204**, 'Tamara's Return', are still around, and at one point Joey tries to pull away from him when he's kissing her; she relents when she sees how upset he is. She also doesn't tell him about Jack's kiss, although she seems to try to at one point. As the episode closes, and she cradles a weeping Dawson on the roof, her face makes it clear that she's not sure she ought to be there with him at all.

The Ballad of Andie and Pacey: 'You know, McPhee, we really should bite the bullet . . . all this verbal sparring is getting a little dangerous so we should just go out on a date before somebody gets hurt.' And so begins one of the show's great romances. But, as ever in Capeside, a first date can never go smoothly: it has to be a disaster. So they both go to the wrong place and the evening ends with Andie, in tears, telling Pacey her tragic life story. A genuine crisis always brings out the best in Pacey, and we fade out on him holding her and telling her that everything's going to be all right.

The Tomboy: Joey is still drawing in her spare moments. Jack wants to know why she's always angry, and correctly guesses that she hates being a waitress because she loathes the customers.

The Clown: Pacey whiles away his video store day with *Jacuzzi Floozies* and other assorted porn classics. At first his low self-esteem leads him to think that Andie's eagerness for him to leave her house is because she's embarrassed to be seen with him, until he understands it's because she's embarrassed for her mother.

The Delinquent: Jen moves fast with Vince, assured, flirtatious, in control, at least up to the point where she has to tell him she's sixteen to get him to stop. She's sailing very close to the wind. How much further can she slip back into her old ways without losing it entirely? And when is she going to have some scenes with the rest of the gang again? She talks only to Abby these days and is starting to feel like a marginal character, although that, of course, is the point.

The Basket Case: Jack doesn't talk about his family problems and it seems as if all the strain is being placed on Andie, which explains her slightly hyper attitude to things – she must be under a lot of pressure.

The Wicked Witch: Grams may have taken Billy's presence in her stride (**107**, 'Boyfriend'), but Vince on top of Jen on the dining table finally breaks her cool: 'Not even God will be able to save you if you don't get your hands off my granddaughter this instant.' Vince runs away, and so would I. In her speech to Jen afterwards she wisely avoids playing the God card, and instead she tells Jen to have some respect for herself and not to slide back into her old ways.

The Outsider: Jack waxes poetic about his job: 'At what other time in your life are you going to be exposed to so many different walks of life, so many different people that just randomly cross your path, each with a different story, different set of hopes, different set of dreams?' He's deep, that one – probably writes poetry. This dark horse of Capeside makes a move on Joey and spends a lot of time looking sullen, which he does very well.

The White-Bread, Country-Club Goody-Two-Shoes: Abby has finally flipped, changing from friendly to vicious in a heartbeat. Jen slaps her when she call her an 'easy lay'. She even tries to seduce Dawson to get back at Jen!

Family Sucks!: Andie and Jack used to have an older brother, Tim, who died in a car accident when their mother failed to see an oncoming truck. Their dad left and now lives in Rochester with his failing business, though he drops in once a week. Their mother is delusional and unbalanced, believing sometimes that Tim is still alive.

Grown-Up Stuff: Finally we find out what Mitch does for a living: nothing! Gale taunts him about his lack of work and complains about bankrolling his endless pipe dreams. He says he's got a loan, although we don't find out if he's going to buy Tamara's warehouse or not. The arrival of Gale's male guest, followed by Tamara, brings things to a head as the Leerys fight so everybody can hear. Dawson is scared stiff by his parents' fighting and really tries to take control. He's as astonished by the open-marriage idea as Gale was and asks: 'What were you thinking? . . . have you two completely lost your minds?' Mitch admits it was a mistake and breaks down crying after Gale walks out. Later he and Gale agree it's time to end things and he says he will go.

Girl Talk: The risqué bonding of Abby and Jen turns nasty: 'Let's never let a guy come between us again . . . we're kindred spirits . . . rebels bound together by the common need to break out of this small-town abyss.' By the time that conversation's over Jen's been called a bitch, slapped Abby and told her never to speak to her again.

Guy Talk: After Dawson confronts his parents we get the most powerful scene between him and Mitch to date. Dawson tells his dad to 'let her off the hook . . . you've got to get beyond your own ego . . . commit, forgive her and then go in there and fix this family'. Mitch can only reply, 'My dad had answers, man, to every question. He taught me so much . . . but, you know, he never told me what to do if my wife cheated on me. I didn't know to ask.'

Kiss and Tell: Jack, the shy, quiet one finally takes action and kisses Joey, out of nowhere.

Our Quips Are Wittier: Andie to Pacey regarding the titles of porn films: 'I don't know why they bother being clever . . . they should all be called the same thing, *Women Pacey Will Never Do.*'

Guest Cast: Caroline Kava has been in *Snow Falling On Cedars* and *Born on the Fourth of July* as well as the TV series *The Practice*.

Contempo Pop Music: 'Catch the Moon' by Marc Jordan, 'Secret Smile' by Semisonic and 'Hands' by Jewel.

Ker-THUNK!: The ladder, which they made such a big deal of removing, is back and no word is said about its reappearance. Obviously the writers needed it so that Abby could break into Dawson's room unannounced, and hoped no one would notice.

The Big Issue: Everybody goes a little crazy sometimes.

The Last Word: Things haven't been this overwrought since the storm hit Capeside (**104**, 'Hurricane'), and by the end everyone is either crying or looking mournfully at the moon. The highlight is the fight between the Leerys, as Dawson tries everything to get his parents talking and fails, revealing the real pain that Mitch has been hiding. But there are surprises, too: Jack kissing Joey is a shock; Abby's behaviour is off the wall even for this show; and the revelations about Andie's family add a lot of much-needed depth to the character.

206
The Dance
1st US Transmission Date: 11 November 1998

Writer: Jon Harmon Feldman
Director: Lou Antonio
Guest Cast: Ali Larter (Kristy Livingstone)

Andie persuades the gang to attend the homecoming dance. Jen and Jack are both invited and set up with each other. When Jack and Joey argue about their kiss, Dawson overhears and punches Jack. Jen walks Jack home and they get on very well. Later, at home, Joey breaks up with Dawson.

Pacey almost blows it with Andie by dancing with Kristy, but they make up and he dances with her instead and they kiss at last.

Mitch and Gale begin their trial separation when Mitch moves out to a nearby motel.

The Ballad of Dawson and Joey: The tension that's been building in Joey for weeks finally explodes. Dawson finds out about the kiss with Jack (**205**, 'Full Moon Rising') and, although she admits it was an 'error of judgment', she doesn't seem to understand why he's so upset by it. He protests, 'There is no justifiable reason why a girl who spent fifteen years of her life pretending that I was the only thing she wanted ended up kissing some other guy and lying about it.' She insists that it's not about him or them but about her, and she explains what's been bothering her: 'I got my dream and now I feel like I don't have anything else . . . I don't even know who I am, let alone who I want to be or accomplish and I need to figure that out. I need to find my something . . . it can't include you, Dawson.' She tells him he makes her 'so happy . . . but I have to make myself happy first,' and so she breaks up with him. He tells her he loves her and she says she loves him too, but still she leaves, to Dawson's amazement: 'We can't just say I love you for the first time and have it be over!' He kicks away the ladder to his window, symbolically cutting off any way for Joey to return.

The Ballad of Andie and Pacey: The 'passive-aggressive banter' between Andie and Pacey is getting better and better: she calls him 'beyond immature', she thinks he's boring, vulgar, deluded and an 'oafish clod'; he thinks she's overbearing and hypersensitive and even helps her out by calling himself a 'major cad' and a 'witless boor'. It must be love! Andie doesn't believe he doesn't dance and thinks he's only refusing as some sort of power manoeuvre. After he dances with Kristy he finds Andie and apologises, but his low self-esteem makes him amazed that he should have to: 'Why do you like me? I'm a screw-up, I'm thoughtless, I'm insecure . . . I can't understand why a woman like you would bother to care about me.' Andie responds by calling him as many good adjectives as she did bad ones earlier: funny, kind, smart, sharp, witty, brilliant. When they finally dance and kiss it's a great moment.

The Movie Brat: Dawson almost never *acts*, he simply *reacts* to those around him – Jen, his parents, Joey, Jack. So when he does show a little fire, like confronting his parents (**205**, 'Full Moon Rising'), or punching Jack, it's a shock to see him taking the initiative.

The Tomboy: Joey surprises Dawson by being concerned about Jen and the bad influence of Abby, which is pretty much the first notice Joey has paid to Jen since their various bonding moments in Season One. However she does later call Jen a 'barracuda'. She also calls Jack a 'nice, sweet guy', which implies that she isn't quite as mad at him as she makes out.

The Clown: Pacey doesn't dance, but when Kristy asks him to, after he's comforted her over Abby's poaching of her boyfriend, he agrees. He is nuzzling her neck and swaying to the music when Andie sees them. Despite his minor crash he is still driving his dad's squad car around town, without a driver's licence! His approach to life is displayed in his driving: 'If a light's turning red it's like an invitation to hit the gas.'

The Delinquent: Jen's reintegration into the lives of the others begins with her invitation to the party and the start of her friendship with Jack.

The Basket Case: Andie's integration into the main cast is complete when she joins Pacey, Dawson and Joey in

Dawson's bedroom for movie night, although with her hyperactivity and woeful dancing it's a wonder they don't just toss her out of the window and bolt all the doors.

The Outsider: Andie says Jack has always been a loner but this shy guy distinguishes himself by refusing to back down in the face of Dawson's righteous anger, and he gets whacked for it. 'I'm not going to apologise for it . . . truth is I'd do it again.'

The White-Bread, Country-Club Goody-Two-Shoes: Abby has a type – stupid men with good bodies. Her guidance counsellor told her to set goals for herself, so she sets out to steal Kristy's boyfriend, and when we last see her at the dance, in one hell of a red dress, snuggled up to him and complimenting him on his muscle groups, she seems to have achieved that goal.

That Three-Letter Word: It's the idea of dancing as foreplay that allows Andie to lure the gang to the dance by convincing them that 'dancing always ends in tawdry smut action'. Dawson is surprised when Joey mentions sex – when they were friends they talked about it all the time, but not at all since they've been a couple (although on their first date they were talking about going at it 'like porn stars' see **201**, 'The Kiss'), but the subject has been off limits to ease 'the transition from friend to lover'.

Reality Bites: The Capeside creed is laid out for an astonished Andie: 'You mean you'd rather watch a movie about something than doing it yourselves?' Dawson and Joey answer, 'Correct.'

All Things Spielberg: This week's movie rental is *Footloose* (Herbert Ross, 1984), a movie about a small town that bans dancing.

Grown-Up Stuff: Gale and Mitch tell Dawson they're separating on a trial basis and he, understandably, resists their conclusion, but they won't even discuss it with him. Mitch moves out, leaving Gale alone and crying in a house

that soon seems very big with just her in it. Mitch phones
her, and then later he drives by the house to watch her
through the window, but can't bring himself to come home
again.

Girl Talk: Joey tells Bess about Jack's kiss and she thinks
it's hilarious. Abby and Jen are talking again, although
relations seem a little frostier than before. Andie is
surprised when Jen leaves the dance because they were just
getting to know each other.

Kiss and Tell: Jack apologises for kissing Joey and admits
he was out of order, but he thinks she's angrier with
herself, for kissing him back, than she is with him for
kissing her. She thinks he was 'rude and inappropriate'.

Contempo Pop Music: 'Kiss Me' by Sixpence None The
Richer, 'Less Of Me' by Grammatrain, 'Sell Out' by Reel
Big Fish, 'She's So High' and 'If You Sleep' by Tal
Bachman, 'Did You Ever Love Somebody?' by Jessica
Simpson, 'Special' by Garbage, 'Cinnamon Waits' by
Nowhere Blossoms and 'Man On a Mast' by Wine Field.

The Last Word: It's a watershed episode: after thirteen
episodes of build-up the Dawson–Joey relationship lasts
six episodes before collapsing and I for one don't buy it. I
feel cheated and disappointed by a relationship I as a
viewer had invested in and don't think the break-up is
necessary or the reason for it convincing. When dumping
Dawson, Joey tells him, 'You're what I'm going to want,'
which implies that she has to find her own way now but
knows she will return to him eventually.

On the plus side the Pacey–Andie relationship progresses
beautifully, and the start of Jack's friendship with Jen adds
a new dimension to things. Dawson gets to show a little
passion rather than his usual passivity, but it's too little too
late. Also, the Mitch-and-Gale storyline continues to be
clear, focused and affecting – the writers haven't put a foot
wrong in that respect yet.

207
The All-Nighter

1st US Transmission Date: 18 November 1998

Writer: Greg Berlanti
Director: David Semel
Guest Cast: Jason Behr (Chris Wolfe),
Brighton Hereford (Dina Wolfe),
Edmund Kearney (Mr Peterson)

The mid-term exams are tomorrow but the teacher is absent and study period is cancelled. A local rich boy, Chris Wolfe, invites everyone over to his house for a study evening. Pacey persuades Andie and Dawson to come along because Chris is rich and he wants to see the house. Jen persuades Joey to come as well, much to her and Dawson's surprise. Nobody gets much studying done, but they do all take a sexual purity test, which reveals Pacey's affair with Tamara to Andie. Dawson and Joey argue about whether they can be friends. Jen, despite Dawson's attempts to prevent it, sleeps with Chris. Chris's young sister Dina develops a crush on Dawson and causes much mischief by stealing Joey's test answers and showing them to Dawson in return for a kiss. When morning comes they cram as much studying as possible into two hours and then race to school, only to find that the teacher is still absent and the test has been postponed. They all fall asleep on the football field.

The Ballad of Dawson and Joey: At first when Joey tries to talk to Dawson it's clear he doesn't want to be around her, at least until he is sure what she wants from him. She tells him that she 'asked for time . . . just time', but she's having selective memory loss because she dumped him clear and simple (**206**, 'The Dance'). She's messing with his mind and losing my sympathy pretty fast; poor Dawson's just going nuts trying to work out what she's about. Dina tells Dawson that Joey wrote she'd been in love twice in her purity test. Dawson confronts Joey, hurt and angry. She again says she just wants to go back to being friends but he says, 'If you don't understand why that can't happen . . . you don't get me.' In the end Dawson calms down and tells Joey that although he's been wishing he could have taken back the kiss that changed their relationship, he wouldn't, because it's brought so much that's new into his life, and to look at her and know she was feeling the same makes all the pain worth it: 'I want to regret kissing you, Joey, but . . . it was the smartest decision I ever made.' Joey tells him that both times she fell in love it was with him, and they resolve to try to remain friends.

The Ballad of Andie and Pacey: Pacey laughs at the purity test and Andie thinks it's because he's inexperienced and doesn't want it known, whereas of course it's the exact opposite. He lets her think that he's 'embarrassingly pure'. After Pacey has admitted he slept with Tamara, Andie goes off to be alone, but Pacey finds her. She wishes he'd told her, but he points out it was hardly an easy thing to admit. She thinks the purity test was innocent fun but Pacey's not having that, and gives quite a little speech about the reality of sex: 'I'm a sexual creature, Andie, so are you. Why do you think we talk about it so much . . . sex is never innocent! It's intense, it's passionate and sometimes it can be life-altering, but it's never innocent . . . if things are going to continue between us I think you're just going to have to accept that.' In the end she does, admitting she was just intimidated by the experience that he has. Pacey tells her she is 'the girl I love to hate' and Andie retorts, 'I love to hate you, too.'

The Movie Brat: Dawson has finally noticed how badly Jen has behaved recently and has started keeping tabs on her, warning her off Chris straightaway and later telling Chris that Jen is 'in a really weird vulnerable state right now'.

The Tomboy: In this talkiest of shows Joey doesn't want to talk about anything any more: 'I'm so sick of talking all the time. I just want to follow my feelings and not discuss it. We run it into the ground and . . . don't you just want to have something left to experience?'

The Clown: Put Pacey in a big rich man's house with lots of people, a Jacuzzi and a swimming pool and what does he want to do? Watch *The Three Stooges* in Cantonese. But, when time is short and they need to cram, he takes instant control and saves the day, which even he admits is becoming something of a habit.

The Delinquent: Jen thinks Chris is cute, and allows herself to be seduced by him, despite Dawson's warning that he has an agenda. She joins him in the bath and then in bed, and, judging by the condom wrappers on the bedside table, neither of them gets much rest.

The Basket Case: Andie reveals a whole new control-freak side to her as she keeps shouting, 'I'm in complete control here.' As soon as possible the others order pizza, grab the distraction of the purity test and head off for the hot tub.

School Sucks!: The English teacher is an evil genius, delivering a speech that mixes just the right amounts of contempt, loathing and uninterest: 'Your impending failure is but hours away ... unless of course your parents have dedicated at least a wing or two to an Ivy League institution, in which case your tragic, East Coast aristocratic, social-alcoholic fate has already been sealed.'

That Three-Letter Word: The month's *Jane* magazine contains a purity test – 100 questions designed to 'gauge your level of sexual experience'. The questions don't pull any punches: 'Have you ever caught your parents having sex?' (hands up, Dawson); 'Have you ever fantasised about a friend's significant other?' (hands up, Pacey, Jen and Joey); and most importantly for Pacey, 'Have you ever had sex with someone twice your age?' Surprisingly, Jen (69 per cent), despite all her delinquent stories, comes second to Chris (66 per cent). Dawson and Joey both get 85 per cent and Andie has a snow-white 92 per cent. We never find out Pacey's score. Chris is honest about his intentions, he just wants to sleep with Jen, nothing more. He won't force himself on her in any way but he can't resist rubbing Dawson's nose in it a bit.

All Things Spielberg: Dawson and Gale have a Shakespeare movie night and are watching Richard Burton and Elizabeth Taylor in *The Taming of the Shrew* (Franco Zeffirelli, 1967).

All Things Freud: In the wonderful opening scene (the first ever scene between Gale and Dawson in which they've been relaxed and friendly with each other) Gale is concerned about Dawson's 'perpetual state of melancholy'. She thinks he should enjoy the few good things about being dumped, such as listening to country music and writing bad poetry.

Girl Talk: Jen tries to talk to Joey for the first time in a while but Joey's not interested and refuses to believe that Jen is sorry she and Dawson have broken up. Jen: 'I used to think it was our mutual feeling for Dawson that kept us apart. I never really considered the fact that maybe you were just a bitch.'

Guy Talk: Pacey gets quite serious with Dawson for a change and when Dawson says, 'I seem to be having a lot of trouble saying a lot of things lately', he just replies, 'Try harder' and walks off.

Kiss and Tell: Chris's young sister, Dina, tries to bribe Dawson to kiss her, but he refuses. After once again having Joey mess with his head Dawson rounds on poor little Dina and lectures her: 'You wanted a kiss . . . are you prepared for everything that comes with that kiss? 'Cause it doesn't just end with a fade-out: there are repercussions. Hearts get broken. Friendships get ruined. Your entire life could fall apart because of one kiss.'

Our Quips Are Wittier: Pacey describes the study group as 'a true meeting of intellectuals in a highly moderated studious environment'.

Guest Cast: Jason Behr appeared as Buffy's ex-boyfriend in *Buffy* and then went on to head the cast of *Roswell*, which has more than once been described as '*Dawson's Creek* with aliens'.

Contempo Pop Music: 'Hold Onto Me' by the Cowboy Junkies, Swirl 360's 'Candy In the Sun', 'Push Me Over' by Bob Mair, 'You' by Switchfoot, 'Losering' by Whiskytown, 'Who Needs Sleep?' by Barenaked Ladies and 'Nobody But Me' by Save Ferris.

The Big Issue: Gale delivers a précis of the series premise: 'Every inch of pain that touches you makes you a deeper, more real individual.'

The Last Word: Like **106**, 'Detention', this takes all the regulars, locks them in one location, adds a new character to spice things up and *voilà*: one superb, character-driven episode chock full of dramatic moments. The best episode of Season Two so far.

208
The Reluctant Hero

1st US Transmission Date: 25 November 1998

Writers: Shelley Meals and Darin Goldberg
Director: Joe Napolitano
Guest Cast: Jason Behr (Chris Wolfe),
Richard K Olsen (Mr Milo), Rasool J'Han (Manager),
Caroline Kava (Mrs McPhee)

Mitch moves into his own place and tries to renegotiate his relationship with Dawson, which proves difficult. Andie's mother deteriorates and Pacey has to help out when she has an episode in the supermarket. Pacey's grades are off the rails and Andie tries to put him back on track.

Dawson wins a prize for the horror film he made at the start of Season One. He uses his half of the prize money to start work on a romance movie and gives the other half to Joey, who was producer. Joey begins dating Jack. Dawson attends a party with Jen but drags her away when she gets drunk and gets herself in a little too deep.

The Ballad of Dawson and Joey: Winning the film festival means Joey and Dawson have a budget of $2,500 for their next film, but Joey won't work on it with Dawson and he's disappointed. When he gives her half the money for art classes she again asks if they can go back to being friends and Dawson says that's fine, but without much conviction. Then, as he's leaving, he bumps into Jack, who is picking Joey up for a date. He realises she's falling for Jack and there's nothing he can do about it. After the date, Joey climbs the ladder to Dawson's room, presumably to tell him about it, but he's not there and that's probably for the best.

The Ballad of Andie and Pacey: Andie makes it her mission to save Pacey from academic ruin. She takes control, draws up a study plan and gives him pep talks: 'I don't think you're a joke . . . if you act like a joke people are going to treat you like a joke.' Pacey returns the favour by talking Mrs McPhee back to her senses in the supermarket and persuading her to come home. Is there ever going to be an episode where Pacey *doesn't* save the day? Andie tells him she's proud of him and he replies, 'I'm not really used to hearing those words . . . at least not when they're directed at me.'

The Movie Brat: The plotline that time forgot reappears when Dawson's horror flick wins the jurors' prize for best short film in the Junior Division of the Boston Film Festival. Dawson's started to realise that all he ever does is react: 'All I ever do is respect other people's wishes . . . I'm sick of that, it makes everybody else feel better but it makes me feel like hell.' So he goes to the party with Jen, even though she says he's 'way too far gone as a rebound case for me to be even remotely interested'.

The Tomboy: What is Joey doing? She's broken up with Dawson and now she's dating Jack, allowing herself to be charmed and kissed by him, even though she told Dawson she loved him only a few weeks ago. She's one mixed-up girl.

The Clown: Pacey's quite happy being below average. Dawson just thinks he's having another bout of low self-esteem and, when Pacey tells Andie that 'there's no hero here, I'm a joke', it looks like Dawson's right. And there's more: 'I've spent too long being a screw-up; I'm past the proverbial point of no return ... I'm not Luke Skywalker, I'm not even Luke Perry.'

The Delinquent: Jen appears drunk in Dawson's bedroom three times in this episode and Dawson knows she's spiralling out of control. Chris Wolfe is still in the picture, and when Jen agrees to go to a party with him Dawson's disapproval prompts a defence of her actions: 'I'm finally enjoying myself. You don't have to treat me like I've been lost to the other side. And I'm not out of control: all I'm doing is having fun.' When Dawson finds her making out with both Chris and one of his friends, he acts the hero, throws her over his shoulder and drags her away. He accuses her of 'hiding ... avoiding the fact that you're unhappy' and he takes her to his father's to sleep it off. Jen replies that she just wants someone to accept her. Later, she says, 'Dawson Leery, you're my hero.'

The Basket Case: Andie's bedroom contains a bookcase full of prizes and trophies. When Pacey asks her how she manages to win all those awards and take time to help him she says she has no choice. We get a glimpse of just how much pressure she is under and how much her peppy, hyperactive exterior is covering up her loneliness and fear.

The Wicked Witch: Grams hasn't appeared for ages, but with Jen spending more and more nights away from home, getting drunk and sleeping around, you've got to wonder how she's dealing with all this.

The Outsider: Jack tries to make things right with Joey. His persistence and charm pay off and she goes out on a date with him.

Family Sucks!: Mrs McPhee is on new medication and although Andie wants to believe she's getting better she has another episode in the supermarket, clearly not sure where she is or what she's doing, rambling about Tim and her husband and refusing to go home with a distraught Andie.

School Sucks!: We get another shining example of Capeside's faculty, the guidance counsellor, who tries to motivate Pacey thus: 'I didn't realise it was possible to fail an aptitude test . . . most people with your academic record can't walk upright . . . I'm really disappointed in you.' He then rounds it off by saying Pacey has 'no future that doesn't involve the fast-food industry'. That's going to do wonders for Low Self-Esteem Boy. Andie delivers a rousing and outraged speech in response, citing Einstein as an example of a brilliant man who failed school: 'just because a student doesn't fit into some cookie-cutter mould . . . that the public-school system deems acceptable they're ready to write 'em off . . . if someone had taken just two seconds to notice, to care, they would have noticed that you need to be rescued, not ridiculed.' The cafeteria gives her a round of applause.

That Three-Letter Word: At the party Jen gets to work seriously lowering her purity test score (**207**, 'The All-Nighter') by answering the *ménage-à-trois* question.

Reality Bites: Pacey thinks Dawson's love of old movies is killing him softly by reinforcing his James Stewart hero-who-helps-old-ladies complex. Dawson is 'the last of a dying breed', the old-style Hollywood hero: decent, kind, gentle and clean-living. Pacey, meanwhile, casts himself as the hero's best friend, 'born to walk in the shadows of greater men'. Dawson's relationship with Joey hasn't delivered a happy ending so he's making another movie, a 'boy-meets-girl, boy-gets-girl, boy-loses-girl, boy-gets-girl-back' romance with a happy ending, into which he can retreat. But Jen tells him not to give it a happy ending because they're totally unrealistic. Joey on Dawson: 'Life is a movie to him and in the movie the hero always punches the bad guy.' Jack, being the punchee, found himself being drawn into Dawson's movie world, as everyone who comes to Capeside must at some point: 'He made me feel like I was in the middle of a Western and he was John Wayne challenging me to a duel at sunset.'

All Things Spielberg: Pacey is outraged that Dawson wants to watch *Mr Smith Goes To Washington* (Frank Capra, 1939) because everyone in the film is dead. He's strictly a new-releases guy and hates black-and-white films. His loss, because *Mr Smith . . .'* is a classic. *Sybil* (referenced in **204**) is obviously the writers' main point of reference for madness – Jack uses it again to describe his mother.

Grown-Up Stuff: Mitch moves out for good and into a warehouse apartment. Presumably this means he bought the property from Tamara (**205**, 'Full Moon Rising'). He's struggling to redefine his relationship with Dawson, awkwardly pitching himself as more friend than father. Dawson isn't buying it because he wants a father, not a buddy. Dawson tells Mitch he's always been this 'larger-than-life Harrison Ford ideal' and Mitch replies that 'no one could live up to that . . . not even Harrison Ford', and they reach an understanding.

Kiss and Tell: Jack kisses Joey at the end of their date and this time she doesn't mind at all.

Guest Cast: Rasool J'Han played Deb in *I Know What You Did Last Summer*. Richard K Olsen has appeared in *Matlock* and *The Young Indiana Jones Chronicles*.

Contempo Pop Music: 'Sitting With an Angel' by Dana Mase, 'This is Who I Am' by Shooter, 'Hope' by REM, 'Celebrity Skin' by Hole, 'Got You (Where I Want You)' by the Flys and 'Acoustic #3' by Goo Goo Dolls.

The Big Issue: Everyone's a hero this week: Dawson saves Jen; Pacey saves Andie; Andie saves Pacey; and Mitch tries to live up to the hero worship Dawson has always had for him, but knows he has failed. Andie sums it up: 'Anyone can change their fate. Heroes are made, not born.'

The Last Word: A strong episode with a unifying theme that manages to encompass every ongoing storyline

perfectly. Subtle, but one of the best-thought-out install-
ments of Season Two.

209
The Election

1st US Transmission Date: 16 December 1998

Writers: Darin Goldberg and Shelley Meals
Director: Patrick Norris
Guest Cast: Jason Behr (Chris Wolfe),
Colin Fickes (Kenny Reiling), Richard K Olsen (Mr Milo)

It's election time for the Capeside High student government
and Andie wants to run for sophomore class president. She
recruits Joey as her running mate and Pacey as campaign
manager. Chris and Abby are running against them and
Abby uses some nasty smear tactics, revealing Andie's family
history and her mother's illness to the entire school. Andie
does not handle her humiliation well and backs out, so Pacey
tricks Abby into venting her nastiness over live school radio,
handing the election on a plate to the third candidate, Kenny.
   Jen thinks Dawson's script lacks any real edge and she
offers to sponsor him through regression therapy, teaching
him what it's like to be a teenager. He fails to cut class, or
shoplift, but he does paper a teacher's house and go
skinny-dipping.
   Mitch and Gale have sex, but this only pushes Mitch to
file for divorce.

The Ballad of Dawson and Joey: These two have drifted so
far apart that this is the first episode in the history of the
show where they don't share a scene or say one word to
each other. Joey talks about Dawson to Jack, telling him
how he used to hold her hand and comfort her when her
mother was dying.

The Ballad of Andie and Pacey: Pacey loves the way Andie
spouts perfect sound-bite politics: 'Your sincerity is so

appealingly sexy,' to which Andie replies 'Your sexiness is so appealingly sincere.' And why does she find him so sexy? Because he's so smart.

The Movie Brat: Dawson's finished his second movie script, the romance, and Jen thinks he's writing from too adult a perspective; no matter how much he protests that he is 'raw and dark' none of us are buying it, right? His second film is about 'the lives and loves of teens in a small town', 'the age of innocence ... sexual awakening, the magic of first love'. In other words, he's written all about himself and Joey. He admits to Jen that he does have 'perception disorder' and launches into a lengthy self-examination: 'I don't respond like a typical adolescent ... I am very much my age emotionally, maybe even younger, and my feelings are in constant conflict with my overachieving self-aware brain and it's a constant battle and that's what's driving me crazy.' He loves toilet-papering a teacher's house, but the skinny-dipping just messes with his head and when he tries to kiss Jen she tells him she just wants to be friends. Poor Dawson! He spends ages waking up to Joey's interest, kisses her and she dumps him. Then he spends ages resisting Jen's advances, finally kisses her and she tells him she wants to be friends. Is it any wonder he's confused? When he finally has to confront the reality of his parents' divorce he breaks down and cries, but not on Joey's shoulder as he once would: now it's Jen who's the comforter.

The Tomboy: Joey has a stellar grade point average (GPA), she's in the top 3 per cent of her class. She's so concerned about her family background that she doesn't want to be Andie's running mate until Abby calls her a 'born loser' in the Icehouse and Joey pours a pitcher of water over her. Jack thinks she has an 'amazing girl-next-door quality' and is 'a born leader'.

The Clown: Pacey takes his role as Andie's campaign manager seriously, researching the Clinton campaign for pointers and giving moral support. But his finest hour is his destruction of Abby on radio: never has he saved the day with so much style.

The Delinquent: Jen's philosophy: 'Life is composed of moments . . . and you have to take those moments as they come, impulsively.'

The Basket Case: Andie is astonishingly hyper about the campaign, so when the truth about her family is revealed she spirals into the lowest of lows. When Jack finds her staring out of the window in silence he confirms what's been hinted at before – Andie's hyperactivity is just that bit beyond normal and until recently she was on medication to control her mood swings. Jack wants her to resume the medication and by the end of the episode, crying and desolate, Andie starts taking her pills again. All she ever wanted was 'a normal family with a normal life, balance and order, order and balance', which explains her control-freak nature.

The Outsider: Jack's introverted, unsociable and aloof nature is explained when we discover Andie's problem. With his dad gone, his mother mad and his sister on the verge of instability, he's had to carry the whole weight of the family tragedy on his shoulders. Is it any wonder he's been withdrawn? He bites Joey's head off when she tries to comfort him after Abby's revelations, but later he apologises: 'When things get rough I tend to go on autopilot . . . protect the family, no one else matters . . . I can't allow myself the luxury of opening up . . . it's like my whole life is one big secret.'

The White-Bread, Country-Club Goody-Two-Shoes: Up to now Abby has been catty, selfish, gossipy and nasty but in a fun way. This week she finally becomes an all-out bitch, running the dirtiest of smear campaigns against Andie and Joey. She posts offensive flyers to start with, but when she publicises Andie's family problems, and the reasons for Tim's death, in front of the entire school she really goes to town. Her fake concern for Andie and the final look of triumph are chilling. When Pacey tricks her into revealing her true colours on radio we get a look at how unpleasant she really is and how much she loathes her running mate, Chris: 'I'm just using the walking penis for popularity and ultimately I'll destroy him just like I destroyed your little girlfriend . . . victory's so much sweeter when you have to walk on other people to get it . . . you and all those other halfwits are too stupid to stop me.' She gets her comeuppance and it's a miracle she dares show her face in school ever again.

Family Sucks!: Pacey on Andie's problems: 'Everyone comes from a dysfunctional family. It's the nineties: the only happy families are in TV syndication.'

That Three-Letter Word: Mitch and Gale swap the coffee table for the kitchen table, and, just like old times, Dawson catches them at it.

All Things Spielberg: Pacey calls Chris and Abby 'James Bond and Pussy Galore', from *Goldfinger* (Guy Hamilton, 1964).

All Things Freud: Jen deconstructs Dawson: 'Your hyperawareness is disarming. You've got to start responding like an adolescent and stop hiding behind that psychology degree you don't have . . . the reason you're not growing is that you never allowed the process.'

Grown-Up Stuff: Mitch is living in the warehouse space that should have been his restaurant and he has no job. So what's he doing? He's restoring antique furniture, of course. Is he independently wealthy or something? After having sex with Gale he's realised that 'it's insane to keep taking the same action expecting a different result – it's the action must change'. And so he decides to file for divorce.

Contempo Pop Music: 'Dead Yet' by Muddlehead, Switchfoot's 'Underwater', 'Sacred' by Kelly Brock, 'Kingdom' by the Slugs, Chumbawamba's 'Amnesia', 'Slingshots' by Morley, 'Troubled Mind' by Catie Curtis, 'You Look So Fine' by Garbage and 'Heart and Shoulder' by Heather Nova.

The Last Word: One of the most emotional episodes this year sees Meredith Monroe and James Van Der Beek surpassing themselves and turning in note-perfect perform- ances in some really heart-wrenching scenes. Also, the skinny-dipping sequence is particularly well shot by Pat- rick Norris in his first time directing the show.

210
High Risk Behavior

1st US Transmission Date: 13 January 1999

Writer: Jenny Bicks
Director: James Whitmore Jr
Guest Cast: Jason Behr (Chris Wolfe)

Dawson and his producer, Jen, begin casting for his new movie. Everyone tells Dawson that his script needs a new ending – his Dawson character needs to sleep with the Joey character. Dawson eventually gets so strung out by all the pressure that he climbs into Jen's room at night and they begin to kiss.

Jack's 'clumsy gene' rears its head again as he spills a drink all over Joey's art homework. In recompense he poses nude for her, which proves more than a little uncomfortable for both of them. One thing leads to another and they end up passionately making out.

Andie and Pacey begin to think about having sex and when she tells him her fantasy night, and how she wants to lose her virginity, he sets about making it happen. They have dinner and he takes her to a bed-and-breakfast. They talk about having sex, decide they will, then they won't, then they will. Eventually he drives her home and she thanks him for a wonderful night.

The Ballad of Dawson and Joey: With Dawson exploring his dark side and Joey courting danger with Jack in her front room, the writers are taking both characters on similar journeys, journeys that they needed to be apart to take. The one scene they have together, where he ribs her about her reaction to the nude model, reminds us how good their rapport is and how much the show is missing it at the moment. He doesn't tell her what his movie's about, though.

The Ballad of Andie and Pacey: Andie nagged Pacey to have an HIV test, and he did, even though he argued with her at first. This raises the sex question and they're so much more upfront and straightforward about it than any of the other couples in the show. They decide not to rush it, but when she asks him, if 'the time and the place were right, [would you] want to?' he gives a heartfelt 'hell, yes'. Pacey finds her at the pharmacy collecting her prescription – Xanax – and in a moment of utter tactlessness he seizes her bag and inspects the contents. Andie tells him they're for her mother. In the bed-and-breakfast Pacey gets all romantic: 'You have no idea what you've done for me, just being in my life ... you make me feel like maybe there's hope for my pathetic existence ... God, I am so lucky.'

The Movie Brat: Jen's regression programme seems to have worked, because Pacey calls Dawson's revised script 'dark ... obtuse ... very un-Dawson Leery', to which Dawson says he wants to 'ride the edge a little'. He wants Tom Hanks or Jimmy Stewart as the lead in his movie, begging the question: why doesn't he just cast himself and get the whole set: writer, director and star? The characters in Dawson's movie don't have sex at the end of the film but Jen, Pacey, Chris and Abby all think they should. Dawson thinks he's taking the riskier choice by having them not do it because cinema is full of teens having sex, but also because the film is 'about romance, not sex', which reveals that deep down he still has the Season One hang-up we thought he'd got over.

The Tomboy: Joey is proud of herself for going through with the nude sitting with Jack because it's 'something that most people would assume that Joey could not do'. She admits that her life is boring sometimes, but now her art feels risky, dangerous, and it allows her to take chances: 'I feel like I'm doing something special . . . just for me.' She's a virgin, and she's still terrified by sex.

The Delinquent: Jen seems to have pulled herself out of her destructive spiral recently. Maybe hanging around Dawson and being his producer is helping her sort herself out. She thinks the lead in the movie should be a Ray Liotta type, dangerous and brooding, because 'sexy will always win over nice'.

The Basket Case: Since Andie went back on the medication Meredith Monroe seems to be deliberately toning down her performance, reflecting Andie's more placid, drug-dulled state.

The Outsider: Jack is uncomfortable, but he's also brave for offering to pose nude and carrying it through, especially since he later admits that sex scares him. He's not a virgin, but he's done it only once (with Kate from **314**, 'The Valentine's Day Massacre'). He's not very good at expressing himself, which he thinks is his biggest flaw.

The White-Bread, Country-Club Goody-Two-Shoes: Abby crops up long enough to get French-kissed by Chris and run away in disgust. She gives a pretty good reading for Dawson's movie, though, and ends up cast as the Jen character, opposite Chris Wolfe's reading of Dawson.

That Three-Letter Word: This entire episode is all about sex.

Scrumping: in Britain it means to steal apples from an orchard; in Capeside it means to have sex. Had me confused for a while there. Why were Andie and Pacey getting so serious about apple stealing?

Joey and Jack: First there's the slip with the towel when Joey gets an eyeful of Jack *au naturel* and then, when he's been telling her about his first time, she gets an eyeful of him, erm, in all his glory, shall we say. What did she expect? She's a gorgeous girl asking a naked teenage boy to describe in detail how he lost his virginity. It would have been a superhuman act of restraint if he hadn't risen to the occasion. Once they're both dressed the awkwardness descends again but Jack says it should continue to be a night of new things. We leave them making out heavily on Joey's couch. Could they be about to . . .?

Dawson and Jen: These two go subtext crazy this week, with Jen upset that her role in Dawson's romantic life has been reduced to the first act of his movie. She tells him, 'If you hadn't gone for such an obvious choice of girl maybe the ending to your script would have been a little less obvious.' Then she tells him he should have chosen her to be his leading lady: 'True love is always fuelled by lust and people who care that much about each other will sooner or later end up having sex.' She says that if someone has sex because they're hurting, in pain, in lust, trying to forget someone, in denial or looking for a distraction, then 'sex has just become very interesting and not the obvious choice at all'. When she says he should think about a rewrite it's clear she doesn't just mean in the script. So, when he impulsively climbs in her bedroom window (does she have a ladder there too, now?) and they start making out, he tells her, 'Don't ask my motive.' Could they be about to . . .?

Andie and Pacey: Andie is very upfront about sex, and, although Pacey is joking about buying condoms in the pharmacy, she calls his bluff and buys a pack anyway. She doesn't think she's ready but she's all for the discovery of the physical side of Pacey Witter and so she's glad to have condoms available just in case. She has fantasised a lot about how she wants to lose her virginity and tells Pacey the whole scenario: dinner, walk, bed and breakfast. Pacey says he wants to be the one, but only when she's ready, and she replies, 'When you talk like that it makes me want to jump you.' Pacey gives her the fantasy evening and they end up in a bed-and-breakfast with a big four-poster bed and Andie quietly freaks. Pacey backs off, saying it was just about having a special night and there's no hurry, but once again his backing away makes Andie 'want to do it'. Then, amazingly, Pacey decides they're not ready, even though this just makes Andie 'want to do it even more'. In the end they check out and he drives her home. But did they or didn't they . . .?

Reality Bites: In one of the best teaser sequences in ages Pacey and Dawson appear to declare their love for each other, but they're just reading from Dawson's script. The introduction of Dawson's new movie reintroduces the playful reality bending that Season One did so well. Dawson is using his script to dissect his relationship with Joey 'on the page, just like every other narcissistic writer throughout history', as ever able really to analyse and understand his life only if it's a movie.

Metatextuality: One of *Dawson Creek*'s biggest strengths is the dialogue, the way that the teenage characters talk in the way the adult writers wish *they* had been able to talk when they were that age. Naturally, some critics miss the point and criticise the show for being unrealistic. So in the opening scene the show is gloriously sending itself up in Dawson's script, and Pacey's response to it is practically a big wink at the audience: 'You're writing too many syllables . . . what's with all the psychobabble insight? How many teenagers do you know who talk like that?' The gag goes even further in the audition sequence when we have ordinary teenagers trying to talk Dawson-speak and failing utterly.

All Things Spielberg: Joey and Jack basically re-enact the scene from *Titanic* (James Cameron, 1998), except with Jack as Rose. Jack says he likes the role reversal. Do you really, Jack? That's interesting . . .

All Things Freud: Pacey to Dawson: 'Only you could take your virginal insecurities and fear of deflowerment and turn them into "risky, edgy behaviour".'

Contempo Pop Music: Swirl 360's 'Hey Now Now', 'The World Is New' by Save Ferris, 'Please' by Chris Isaak, Sheryl Crow's 'Anything But Down', 'Driving You Crazy' by Tia Texada and 'Lover Lay Down' by Dave Matthews Band.

The Big Issue: Jen sums it up: 'Intent and motive are what make sex so interesting.'

The Last Word: With a 'to be continued' cliffhanger, nudity, condoms and lots and lots of sex talk, this is as close to the edge as the show's got so far. By the end of the evening Joey and Jack are on the verge of having sex, as are Dawson and Jen, while the couple we expected to be sleeping together, Andie and Pacey, chuck it in for a cup of cocoa and an early night. So the question is: come morning, who will still be a virgin?

211
Sex, She Wrote

1st US Transmission Date: 20 January 1999

Writers: Mike White and Greg Berlanti
Director: Nick Marck
Guest Cast: Jason Behr (Chris Wolfe),
Edmund Kearney (Mr Peterson)

Chris finds a note on the floor of English class that reads, 'I want to talk to you about last night. The whole thing was amazing but sex changes everything, and I think we should take some time before anything happens again.' He tells Abby and she decides to find out who wrote the letter as her mystery fiction assignment for class. She has three couples in the frame: Jen and Dawson, Pacey and Andie, Jack and Joey. Her attempts to solve the mystery consist of prodding, gossiping, lying, spreading distrust and suspicion and eventually, when everyone is at everybody else's throat, she calls them all together in a classroom for a denouement. By this time Andie isn't talking to Pacey because she thinks he blabbed about their night together; Dawson thinks Jen did the same, and he is also not talking to Joey because he's seen her picture of Jack and thinks she slept with him; Joey has read Dawson's revised script and assumes he's slept with Jen; and Jen and Jack just look embarrassed and bewildered. The truth is revealed – Dawson and Joey are both still virgins, but Andie and Pacey did sleep together after all, and it was he who wrote the note. In the end Abby doesn't hand in her assignment, Dawson and Joey start rebuilding their friendship, Jen and Jack bond, and Pacey and Andie declare their love for each other.

The Ballad of Dawson and Joey: Joey guesses that Dawson's movie is about them when he says his leading lady 'requires a certain mixture of spirit and passion, wide-eyed innocence and unparalleled external beauty . . . what I need is a you'. Although she's concerned it'll show her in a bad light, Dawson assures Joey he'd 'never write anything hurtful about you, ever'. She is jealous when she thinks Dawson has slept with Jen, and Dawson's the same about her and Jack, so when they snap and start shouting at each other they tell each other that they did have sex, when they didn't. After the dust settles they meet up and begin the slow process of moving back towards each other. He says, 'You and I cry sex till we're blue in the face but when it comes down to actually doing it all we're left with is a couple of harmless kisses,' to which Joey replies, 'It's not about the perfect setting, it's not about the perfect timing: it's about the perfect person.' They admit they're glad neither of them had sex, and say how much they miss each other.

The Ballad of Andie and Pacey: In spite of all their last-minute second-guessing (and the best efforts of the writers to convince us otherwise), Andie and Pacey ended up having sex at the B&B, and afterwards they are positively glowing. 'You were a perfect gentleman and I thoroughly enjoyed myself,' says Andie later. But Pacey pulls away from her, writing her the note and giving her the impression that he's the type of guy who runs a mile when things get serious. When the misunderstandings caused by Abby are cleared up, Pacey pours his heart out, explaining that the reason he's been so weird is that he got an A in his history test, and 'everything's always been so predictable for me but now my whole life's course has changed . . . it used to be the only comforting part about being Pacey Witter is that I always knew what to expect and now I don't have a clue and I'm terrified'. He says Andie is now 'the single most important being to ever grace my existence . . . I am falling hopelessly in love with you' and she replies that she shares the same fear. They kiss and make up.

The Movie Brat: Immediately after his make-out session with Jen, Dawson wants to analyse what just happened, but she wisely calls for a twelve-hour moratorium. In his script rewrite 'the so-called Dawson character does it with the beautiful neighbor from the big city he has a crush on'. He tells Jen 'you inspired me', so now she's his substitute Joey-muse. He's surprisingly cool about his fling with Jen, telling her, 'Last night was last night . . . we're still friends, and whatever word applies to what we are.' Joey thinks his script is mysterious.

The Tomboy: Joey has no regrets about her brief flare of passion with Jack, but it's so awkward afterwards that who knows where their relationship is going?

The Delinquent: Jen is discombobulated by Dawson's passion and finally she bonds with her natural ally in all this, Jack, opening up to him and getting him to open up to her. They're both getting used to being in the shadow of the Dawson/Joey drama.

The Outsider: Even though he really wants to, Jack doesn't have sex with Joey because he is so scared that he can't even take his clothes off and he isn't able to rise to the occasion. Which is ironic given that he was naked and priapic mere minutes beforehand. He thinks maybe he has a problem, but Jen reassures him that this sort of thing happens all the time.

The White-Bread, Country-Club Goody-Two-Shoes: 'Nancy Drew from hell' is the focal point this week (Nancy Drew was a teenager who solved mysteries in books and on TV), casting herself as a sleuth ('it's original, it's creative, it's *so*

Abby Morgan!') and ruthlessly exploiting any advantage she can get over her six prime suspects, all the time fighting off Chris's lecherous advances, yet bribing him to help her with a promise that she'll let him 'touch me in bad places'. If she fails to hand in her assignment she will fail the course and have to take summer school. After her little stage-managed denouement Abby gets it right in the neck from an outraged Jen: 'You are a lying, manipulative and cruel person and the fact that you're only sixteen makes me feel more sorry for you than for any of the people in this room whose lives you are so intent on destroying. You're pathetic.' Surprisingly, perhaps in the light of her old friend Jen's condemnation, Abby does the right thing and takes the F grade rather than hand in her assignment and reveal all.

Reality Bites: Not only would Dawson rather watch a movie than do whatever it is the movie's about, but instead of having sex with Jen he runs home and writes a movie script in which he *does* have sex with Jen in 'one of the kinkiest sex scenes since Mickey Rourke cracked open the refrigerator door in *9½ Weeks*'. When Jack tells Dawson he didn't sleep with Joey he says, 'This little movie life you're living, Dawson, is not in danger.'

Metatextuality: When asked to do a presentation on mystery literature for English class, Dawson turns in a presentation on movie mysteries, in which he establishes that 'the genre's constructed in three sections: the setup, the testimonies and the classic denouement where all the characters are gathered in one room', which is exactly how this episode is structured.

All Things Spielberg: *9½ Weeks* (Adrian Lyne, 1986) is an erotic thriller starring Mickey Rourke and Kim Basinger.

All Things Freud: Abby on Jack: 'Underneath Jack's sensitive, little-boy-lost façade I have a feeling that there's a real sex pig just waiting to jump out.' Oh, Abby, if only you knew! Jen on Dawson: 'As much as I love the guy he's just not there yet . . . I can take all the jerks in the world climbing in and out of my bedroom window, but, when Dawson Leery does it, it better be for me.'

Our Quips Are Wittier: Abby rejects Chris's unsubtle come-ons: 'Chris, your lines land like bricks.'

Contempo Pop Music: 'Human Beings' by Seal, 'Life's a Bitch' by Shooter and 'You Get What You Want' by New Radicals.

The Big Issue: The truth will out!

The Last Word: A playful episode, beautifully sending up the mystery movie genre. We are completely manipulated all the way through, first to believe Pacey and Andie haven't had sex when they have, then to believe Dawson and Joey have when they haven't. The moment when Dawson and Joey both shout 'Yes!' at each other, saying they did sleep with Jen and Jack respectively, jaws across the world hit the floor – except they were lying of course.

212
Uncharted Waters

1st US Transmission Date: 27 January 1999

Writers: Dana Baratta and Mike White
Director: Scott Paulin
Guest Cast: John Finn (John Witter)

Mitch and Dawson join Pacey, his dad and Jack, aboard the *Reel Action* for a weekend fishing trip. The tension between Pacey and his father is intense. They hit a bar after the first day and John Witter gets fall-down drunk and enjoys beating Pacey at darts. Pacey breaks down after his father has passed out, and reveals the depth of his despair at his father's harsh treatment. Eventually Pacey brings in a fish big enough to win the trophy they're competing for.

Gale hosts Jen, Andie, Joey and Abby for a night of bonding so she can interview them about what it's like to be a modern teenage girl. The girls raid Dawson's porn collection for fun. Later, when Abby gets too confrontational, Gale kicks her out. Next morning Andie finds that Abby has spent the whole night outside the house waiting for her mother to pick her up.

Dawson and Jack reach an uneasy truce after Jack admits to Dawson that his father ran away from the family not because of his business but because he just couldn't stand his wife's illness any more.

The Movie Brat: Dawson entirely fails, at first, to realise how difficult it must be having John Witter as a dad. He thinks his put-downs are jokes, unable to conceive of a dad so far below perfect, given his own superdad. Then, when he tries to empathise with Jack's being left by his dad, Jack takes him to task because Mitch has only moved up the road, whereas Mr McPhee is gone for good. By the time the weekend is over he's reached a new understanding of how lucky he is to have Mitch. Pacey's dad thinks Dawson is a cinematic genius and has a great 'brain and commitment to excellence'.

The Tomboy: Jack on Joey: 'She's got a strong will and is as intelligent as a Rhodes scholar.' Joey on herself: 'I'm just Joey Potter, the small-town girl who will live and die on the Creek . . . and as much as I disdain that identity it's all I've got.'

The Clown: John Witter's snide comments to and about Pacey begin in his first scene when he makes a crack about Dawson returning in the future to 'visit Pacey at whatever fast-food joint he's flipping burgers at' and they keep coming all weekend long. Finally we understand why Pacey has the low self-esteem and lack of self-confidence he does – it's because his dad is, as Pacey puts it, a bastard. His dad passes out on the beach and Pacey has a monologue that cuts right to the heart of things: 'Why can't you see me, huh? When did you give up on me, when I was five? . . . I'm here and . . . I'm trying *so* hard for you. It's your job to love me no matter who I am or what I become because you're my father . . . you're supposed to love me, you son of a bitch. I can't do this by myself.'

The Delinquent: Jen's assessment of herself for Gale's TV piece: 'I was on the fast lane to self-annihilation . . . but having all that experience came back to haunt me . . . in New York I was the precocious little ingénue and in Capeside all I'll ever be known as is the New York wild child, town slut, bad girl.'

The Basket Case: Andie reveals the cracks in her façade for Gale as well: 'I have this need to look and be perfect . . . my home life is in total chaos and I feel like if I don't get straight As . . . then people will know I'm this fraud and that I have no idea where I'm going or what I'm doing.'

The Outsider: Jack tries to make friends with Dawson but he's having none of it. Andie persuades Pacey to take Jack on the trip because he's got no friends in town and she wants Pacey to include him more.

The White-Bread, Country-Club Goody-Two-Shoes: Abby pushes it too far and gets thrown out of Gale's house after insulting Joey, Jen and Andie all in one sentence. But she stays outside because her mother was expecting her to be there all night. Andie finds her in the morning and accuses her of giving her a really hard time. Abby gives an interesting and revealing defence: 'I play a crucial role in this little circle . . . I'm the girl everyone loves to hate . . . I'm the one you can take all of your anger and aggression out on.' And why is she like this? Because 'sweet is boring. I don't have family lives like you guys: my parents' divorce is boring, my house is boring . . . there's no drama, so you know what? I create drama, and I think it's a valid extracurricular activity.' And suddenly, after a few weeks of being the villain, she's likable again.

Family Sucks!: We get to meet John Witter – and what a sad, lonely, obviously unhappy man he is, and poor old Pacey bears the brunt of it. John rides Pacey so hard because 'a lot of things in life suck, son, and it's my job to prepare you for that inevitability'. Later, after he's won the trophy, he says to him, 'Enjoy this moment, son – you probably won't have too many like it.' He gets so drunk

that Pacey has to carry him home, and he's hypercompeti-
tive to the point of enjoying beating his own son at darts
just a little too much. These are the actions of a man whose
ambitions have been thwarted and who's profoundly
dissatisfied with his life. The truth is, it's not Pacey who's
the loser but his dad, and, though Pacey's far too young to
realise that yet, he will one day.

All Things Spielberg: Dawson's renting movies to try to
inject some character layering into his script and one of his
rentals is *The Great Santini* (Lewis John Carlino, 1979),
about a bitter father–son conflict.

Grown-Up Stuff: Finally Dawson notices that his dad is
unemployed and rootless and gently nags him about
finding a job or getting a game plan. He even asks if
Mitch is all right for money, which he says he is. Mitch is
worried about disappointing Dawson but feels he has to
follow his dream, find 'something I can put my heart and
my passion behind'. Dawson tells Mitch how much he
respects him and thanks him for being all the things
Pacey's father isn't.

Girl Talk: Gale's interview technique is a total bust and so
she suggests a 'girls' night' and uses the dreaded word
'bonding'. How do the girls bond? By raiding poor
Dawson's porn collection and watching *Good Will Humping* (no, I'm not going to tell you who directed it!).

The Joey–Jen war reaches a climax, and maybe a peace
accord, at Gale's house. First Jen tries her compliment-
Joey strategy one final time: 'We need girls who are
thoughtful and articulate and no one speaks their mind
more eloquently and honestly than you do.' Then when
Joey is still not interested Jen tries confronting her instead:
'I just want to know why you're still treating me like I'm
this vixen that came into town and stole away your one
true love,' and Joey replies 'stop encroaching on what's
mine. I mean, you systematically cast yourself in my role.
Every time I turn around I'm being replaced by you in
some form and then ... you're shocked and surprised

when I resent you for it.' But then she lists the ways Jen is replacing her – with Dawson (but Joey, you dumped him), as movie producer (but Joey, you turned down the job), as best friend (but Joey, what do you expect?). Yes, Joey has finally lost all touch with reality, folks. Finally she opens up and admits in the interview that her defences go up because she feels inadequate in front of people with more experiences than she's had. Then she tells Jen, 'I respect you, I respect who you are . . . and I think there's room in Dawson's life for you without replacing me.'

Gale tells Joey she's her surrogate daughter and she's very proud of her.

Guy Talk: Pacey asks Dawson if he respects his father and Dawson replies, 'I'd hate to live in a world where I didn't.' When the question's fired back at him Pacey dodges it: 'John Witter, the most well-known, well-respected man in Capeside . . . how could you possibly not have respect for a man like that?' That makes it clear he doesn't respect him at all. Pacey gets increasingly frustrated with Dawson because, as Jack points out, Mr Witter has built Dawson up into such a paragon that Pacey can never live up to it. Pacey even loses it with Dawson at one point, which is fair enough because he's been wandering around making puppy eyes, entirely oblivious to all the relationship undercurrents on the boat. Just when it looks like Pacey's won some respect from his dad it gets undercut by John's snide comment and Pacey just about gives in: 'Do you have any idea how many times I've set myself up for that one? . . . over and over again I can't seem to stop myself trying to get an unqualified "Good job, son".' Dawson puts the opposing view, pointing out that 'there are people in your life who recognise and respect your talent and intelligence'.

Guest Cast: John Finn has been in practically everything. On TV he's appeared in 5 episodes of *The X-Files* as well as *NYPD Blue*, *Millennium*, *Brooklyn South* and many more. On the big screen he's been in *Carlito's Way*, *City Hall*, *Blown Away* and *Cliffhanger* among others.

Contempo Pop Music: 'Heaved Away' by Keel, 'Watch Your Step' by Matthew Ryan, Lyle Lovett's 'If I Had a Boat', 'I'm Cool' by Reel Big Fish, 'C'est La Vie' by B*witched, 'Slowly I Turned', 'Ode To Stevie' and 'Bottoms Up' by Black Toast, 'Suburbia' by Moxie, 'My Door Is Always Open' by Binge, Robynn Ragland's 'Pcacc In the Water', 'Best Of Me' by Far Too Jones and 'This Pain' by Adam Cohen.

Ker-THUNK!: OK, so Abby does add a much-needed tension and element of conflict to the proceedings, but, after all that's happened, how likely is it that Jen would invite her to an evening at Gale Leery's house when Andie and Joey are going to be there? It's a bit too much to swallow.

The Big Issue: Being a parent is a complicated gig, but being a daughter or a son is just as hard.

The Last Word: While the scenes with the guys on the fishing trip ring true and honest the scenes of the girls, occasioned by the contrived interview situation, feel mawkish and forced. They don't work – leave that trite bonding stuff to *90210*. However, Pacey's monologue on the beach is perhaps the most affecting, dramatic and brilliantly acted scene in the whole series to date. Hats off to Joshua Jackson for pulling out all the stops and turning in a superb performance. That's by far the biggest lump I've had in my throat while watching this show.

213
His Leading Lady

1st US Transmission Date: 3 February 1999

Writers: Shelley Meals and Darin Goldberg
Director: David Semel
Guest Cast: Jason Behr (Chris Wolfe),
Rachael Leigh Cook (Devon),
Eddie Mills (Tyson 'Ty' Hicks)

It's one week until the start of filming on Dawson's movie *Creek Daze* (set in the small town of Creekside) and he still hasn't found a leading lady. Delivering a new draft of the script to Joey in art class, he is stunned by a nude model, Devon. Later he bumps into Devon in the library and, when she reveals she is a drama major, he asks her to read for Sammy, the Joey role in his film. Devon turns out to be headstrong and opinionated but is a very good actress and Dawson casts her. Chris Wolfe is playing Wade, the Dawson role, and Abby is playing Jen's character. Joey is now helping with the film (as is Jack), and, as she sees her relationship with Dawson played out in front of the whole world, she becomes increasingly uncomfortable. Eventually, she confronts him and he reveals that he's not really over her at all and the movie is the only thing keeping him going.

Pacey finds Andie's pills and confronts her about them. She admits they are hers but she has finished her course and is now going to therapy on the advice of her doctor. But as she comes off the medication her behaviour on the set of *Creek Daze*, where she is working as prop girl, becomes increasingly erratic. Eventually she dumps Pacey. Pacey won't take this lying down and convinces her she's made a mistake.

Jen meets Ty, a young man who is helping out on set, and she asks him out. When they go out for a date, he takes her to a Bible study group.

The Ballad of Dawson and Joey: When the episode opens it's just like old times – Dawson and Joey in his bedroom – and Dawson is pleased they've managed their first movie night since breaking up. Joey seems less happy that Dawson is so all right with everything, nor is she entirely cosy with the idea that the Sammy character in Dawson's movie is supposed to be her. He says, 'Time to learn to let go . . . you let me go so, in turn, I let go of you.' Devon tells Joey that she thinks Sammy and Wade, and by extension Joey and Dawson, are 'soul mates who will be for ever connected by an overpowering transcendent love'. When Jack asks Joey if she's happy with being portrayed in the film she is adamant that Dawson is over her, something Jack doesn't believe at all. Devon also provokes Joey, asking her what it's like to 'date one guy when you're in love with another', and asking Jack what it's like 'being the transition guy'. You'd hate Devon if only she wasn't bang on the money.

Dawson describes to Chris how he felt when Joey kissed Jack, and, as he does so, he stares at Joey; it's clear Jack is right and Dawson's nowhere near over her: 'It's agony, complete excruciating agony, like your heart has been ripped out of your chest and stomped on.' Joey confronts Dawson, unable to accept that he's as comfortable with things as he appears to be: 'Why do you insist on reliving in excruciating detail one of the most painful experiences of our lives? . . . how can you be OK?, Didn't we mean anything to each other?' It's almost as if she dumped him just to get a reaction. Finally, he says what's needed saying for a while: 'You left me, you dumped me, I haven't moved on, OK? I haven't let go, and that's why I'm clinging for dear life to the one thing that's keeping me going.' Which is movies, fantasy and attempting to understand his life by putting it on film, which is all he's ever done.

In a calmer moment Joey apologises for shouting at him, and Dawson admits, 'I just thought if I made this autobiographical, cathartic movie then I could put the past behind me in one fell swoop.' But of course it doesn't work that way. Joey says it's been as difficult for her, but after all she dumped him. Why does *she* get to complain about how painful it all is? Anyway, she says, 'Our lives are destined to be intertwined.' But for now they have to move on.

The Ballad of Andie and Pacey: At first Andie tries to tell Pacey that the Xanax is her mother's, but he doesn't believe her. She tells him the truth and he makes her promise to tell him if she's ever not all right. His concern and almost panic when she begins to lose it is touching and he's conscious that whatever he does will be the wrong thing. Andie tells him that if he loves her he'll back off.

Pacey refuses to give in and goes so far as to climb a trellis to her bedroom window carrying a rose, even though she threatens to push him off: 'I'm actually a charter member of the Andie McPhee fan club and as a matter of policy our devotion never waivers through the good times or the bad . . . I'm not going to turn away from you, after all you've done for me, and certainly not when you need me most . . . because I love you.' Andie tells him she loves him too and they kiss.

The Movie Brat: The look on Dawson's face when he's confronted by a naked Devon is a picture, but when she's clothed and being prickly he handles her pretty well, very much the movie director, handing out scripts with his name and address on them, dropping it into conversation that he's directing a film. Very slick – he'll fit in perfectly in LA. Devon thinks his script is 'heavy-handed and overly verbose' and contains a lot of 'angst and overanalysing and the hesitancy to act on anything', which all sounds very familiar. In the end she thinks he's a good director, and, as we watch him handle the actors and extract a really good performance from Chris, it's clear she's right.

The Delinquent: Jen is confident and upfront with Ty, asking him out before he can ask her out. She's a great producer, focused and in control, and the dark days after her grandfather's death seem long gone.

The Basket Case: Andie comes off her medicine and starts losing it. Later she tells Pacey, 'I just want to feel better.'

The Wicked Witch: Grams is alive! She appears for only the third time this season after an absence of seven episodes. She's back on form, introducing Jen to Ty and encouraging her to go out with him because she knows he's a good, God-fearing Christian and she hopes he'll be a good influence on Jen. Still, she's not all sneaky, and lavishes praise on Jen's abilities as a producer. Maybe some of Jen's Angry Grrl music has been rubbing off on her, too, because she comes over all liberated: 'In my day women didn't have many options . . . but now, what a wonderful time to be a woman: you can do or be anything you want, and without a man by your side.'

Reality Bites: Dawson's reality disorder is finally getting way out of hand. When Devon reads a scene from his script we find she is repeating *word for word* things Joey said to Dawson in **111**, 'Beauty Contest'. Dawson is filming the bedroom scenes in his own bedroom, which makes Pacey remark that 'telling your life story in your own bedroom is a little perverse, even for you'. When Abby is late on set he has Jen read the part of Kim, which is of course based on Jen, who is then reading words she said mere months before. Devon notices that 'it's interesting that you put such effort into making this script almost precisely match reality and yet you change the ending.'

Guy Talk: Pacey asks Dawson for advice on Andie and tells him about her medication. When he asks if Dawson's noticed her being erratic, Dawson replies he's 'been too busy watching her bounce off the walls'. Pacey's worried about putting too much pressure on her but Dawson says he should just ask her about it. Later, after Andie's dumped him, Pacey confides in Dawson again, but this time Dawson's advice isn't so impartial or useful – he simply tells Pacey to move on. Pacey rejects his advice because 'I know what I want, I want Andie and ... whether she knows it or not she needs me'.

Guest Cast: Rachael Leigh Cook has a very successful movie career and has starred in *She's All That*, *Get Carter* and *Josie and the Pussycats*. She also stars alongside James Van Der Beek in *Texas Rangers*, which was directed by *Dawson's Creek*'s and *Halloween H20*'s director, Steve Miner. Eddie Mills has been in *Ally McBeal* and *Clueless* as well as being a regular in Kevin Williamson's other TV show, *Wasteland*.

Contempo Pop Music: 'It's All Been Done' by Barenaked Ladies and Bruce Springsteen's 'Sad Eyes'.

Backstage: During the Barenaked Ladies song there is a cut from filming outside to inside the school and during the cut there is a flash of Devon's face and, for one single frame, a clapperboard for episode #213 of *Dawson's Creek* filmed on 14 January 1999.

The Last Word: A superb episode, harking back to the themes of the first season and bringing Dawson's reality issues to the fore again. Rachael Leigh Cook is excellent, and kind of creepy, as Devon. Jen's blossoming capacity to handle other people is well handled in the background. It's nice to see Dawson finally shout at Joey a bit because her behaviour's been awful and she deserved it. But maybe that's just me.

214
To Be Or Not To Be . . .
1st US Transmission Date: 10 February 1999

Writer: Greg Berlanti
Director: Sandy Smolan
Guest Cast: Eddie Mills (Tyson 'Ty' Hicks),
Edmund Kearney (Mr Peterson),
Richard K Olsen (Mr Milo)

In English class Jack is forced to read out a poem he wrote that he thought would be for the teacher's eyes only. The poem is about a masculine image of perfection, and he breaks down while reading it and flees the class. Pacey tries to go after him but is told not to by the teacher, Mr Peterson. The rumours that Jack is gay begin immediately and culminate in someone spraying FAG on his locker, which spurs Joey into a very public kiss of support. Next English class, the teacher tells Jack to finish reading the poem or accept a fail grade and Pacey is so angered that he reads it instead. He refuses to stop and after a fierce confrontation Pacey spits in Mr Peterson's face and leaves.

Pacey is told to apologise or accept a week's suspension.
Though it will seriously damage his new-found academic
success, Pacey refuses to apologise, gives an impassioned
speech to the headmaster, and takes the suspension.
Meanwhile, Joey wrestles with whether to ask Jack the big
question and eventually she does ask if he is gay. He
promises he isn't.

The Ballad of Dawson and Joey: Dawson is concerned
about Joey's reaction to Jack's poem, but she takes it the
wrong way and accuses him of trying to split her and Jack
up. She later climbs through his bedroom window ('It's the
surest form of normalcy I know'), apologises and asks for
Dawson's advice. He tells her to confront Jack and says
that he thinks what she and Jack have is 'worth saving'.

The Ballad of Andie and Pacey: Andie's initial reaction to
Jack's poem upsets Pacey and he's shocked when she tells
him she'd be disappointed if Jack were gay. Her disapproval of Pacey's decision not to apologise also distances
the couple. When she finds him alone at the dock he is not
in the best of moods and says, 'Do you know how much I
needed your support? . . . I don't need you to agree with
everything I say . . . but what I do need to know is that
somehow, some way, you're there for me.' Andie's outraged until Pacey reveals that he has been acting out of
guilt because he feels Jack's humiliation was his fault but,
'You didn't want to hear it: you just wanted me to clean
up the mess. But there are some messes you just have to
live with.' She offers to walk him home but he declines, and
they're clearly on rocky ground.

The Clown: Pacey's academic rehabilitation seems almost
complete (as Dawson says, 'Pacey Witter leaving early to
do homework, slightly less believable than a *National
Enquirer* headline') when the school counsellor, Mr Milo,
tells him his mid-term results – three Bs and two As. The
provocation of Mr Peterson, though, leads Pacey to blow it
all. He knows his grade-point average can't take a suspension and that it will put him back to square one, but his is a

moral stand and he's determined to make it, regardless: 'Andie, everything I've worked for, everything that you've helped me to become, is somebody who believes in himself and his instincts, and every instinct I have tells me that what that man did in that classroom was wrong.' Jack tells Pacey, 'I didn't need a hero. I recognise it's an addiction of yours.' His poem was 'Ode To the Sports Car'.

The Delinquent: Ty won't leave Jen alone, even though his Bible studies class freaked her out. She wants him to go away because his religion is big a problem for her. He continues to call and badger her till she gives in. They go out on a date to a local blues bar. They dance and have a good time. Jen is surprised by his behaviour, 'student by day, ratpacker by night'. When he jokingly points out that Grams likes him Jen replies, 'She likes what she knows about you, which apparently isn't all that much.' He suggests they keep it that way.

The Basket Case: Andie's first reaction to Jack's poem is resentment at giving her something else to deal with. Andie is sure he's not gay because 'he's talked about girls his entire life, he's crazy about Joey, he hates Madonna', but after she's read the poem even she seems to think it's a possibility and tells him, 'I don't know if it means you're gay or not and I really don't care . . . I just want to let you know that I'm here for you, and I love you, and you're not alone.'

The Outsider: Jack's model of Creekside for Dawson's film is really good, and helps foster friendship between them at last. Jack is failing English. He is extremely reluctant to read out his poem, and he doesn't change the pronoun from 'he' to 'she' as he could have done, so some part of him perhaps wanted to confront what the poem meant. The poem describes a perfect male form, talks of 'shackles of guilt' and being afraid of 'what I could be', so it's no surprise that even Pacey and Dawson think it's possibly about Jack's sexuality. His explanation is, 'I wrote what I was feeling. One of the images that came into my head was masculine, nothing sexual about it ... it could have been me; it could have been the image of my brother ... but there was nothing gay about that poem. As for the crying ... it hit a weird nerve as I was reading it. It just unleashed some stuff that I've been dealing with in my family.' Later, when Joey asks him outright if he is gay, he says no, but the look on his face as he holds her is of confusion and fear.

School Sucks!: Mr Milo, the counsellor, seems genuinely pleased when Pacey gets good grades. He sticks up for him in front of the Principal, laying blame at Mr Peterson's door. The Principal also doesn't seem so bad, making it clear she has no choice but to suspend Pacey, giving him every chance to apologise, and barely stifling a smile after Pacey's brutal condemnation of Mr Peterson. So there *are* good teachers at Capeside High! Mr Peterson prides himself on being unfair, bears irrational grudges, writes people off even when they're trying their best, enjoys failing people and callously inflicts misery on Jack. Pacey's speech is a classic, and it seethes with a genuine and justified moral outrage: 'We students of Capeside come to a place where you guys are in charge ... we never ever question it because we're afraid to. To question it is to go against the belief that the entire system is built upon, the belief that you guys know what's right, and I'm not afraid to tell you that what happened in that classroom was not right ... while I do respect the system I do *not* respect men like you, Mr Peterson. I don't, I can't, and I never will.'

Guy Talk: Dawson admits to Pacey that he wouldn't have acted as Pacey did, but, when Pacey asks if he would be ashamed if Pacey couldn't apologise, Dawson replies, 'In my lifetime, Pacey, I will never be ashamed of you.'

Kiss and Tell: When Jack is getting stuff from his defaced locker, in front of lots of prying eyes, Joey runs up and kisses him long and hard, just to show the world, even though she believes that 'massive suck-face embraces are best left for bedrooms and private sunsets'.

Contempo Pop Music: 'Slide' by Goo Goo Dolls, 'Know What You Mean' by Sister 7, 'I Do' by Lisa Loeb, Jenifer Kruskamp's 'Come Rain or Come Shine', Chris Isaak's 'Walk Slow', 'In My Life' by Trina Hamilton, 'Smoke' by Natalie Imbruglia and 'Only Lonely' by Hootie and the Blowfish.

The Big Issue: All relationships, as Dawson realises, 'begin and end with honesty'.

Backstage: The writer, Greg Berlanti, said on the *Dawson's Creek* website that 'the most rewarding to me to write was the two-part "To Be or Not to Be . . . That is the Question." To be able to provide gay teens with the kind of character on television that I never had was very fulfilling.'

The Last Word: Jack's being gay is the biggest issue yet dealt with by the show and it's handled sensitively without being clichéd. Kerr Smith is finally given some real acting to do, and he does it very well, while the character of Jack moves from being a quiet cypher to suddenly acquiring layers of interest that the writers can work with. Pacey's speech is an all-time great moment too.

215
. . . That Is The Question

1st US Transmission Date: 17 February 1999

Writers: Kevin Williamson and Greg Berlanti
Director: Greg Prange

Guest Cast: David Dukes (Mr McPhee),
Eddie Mills (Tyson 'Ty' Hicks),
Edmund Kearney (Mr Peterson),
Richard K Olsen (Mr Milo)

Concerned by Jack's situation and Andie's erratic behaviour, Mr Milo calls Mr McPhee, who comes to town to sort things out. Over dinner he asks if Jack is gay, but he doesn't answer. Next day Mr McPhee is packing to leave when Jack tells him that he *is* gay, which is exactly what his dad doesn't want to hear. Andie and Jack ask their father, who is entirely unsympathetic, to leave. Later the next evening Jack tells Joey, and afterwards Joey returns to Dawson's bedroom to cry on his shoulder.

Pacey returns from his suspension determined to have his revenge on Mr Peterson. He studies local laws and prepares a document citing all the rules and codes of conduct that Mr Peterson has broken. He sends it, along with twenty testimonials from other students, to the board of governors. Mr Peterson resigns before he can be reprimanded.

Jen takes Dawson and Joey with her and Ty to the blues bar, where they dance.

The Ballad of Dawson and Joey: Dawson advises Joey to plan a romantic evening with Jack and neither of them can believe he's offering her advice on her relationship with his rival. At the blues club Dawson and Joey dance and he admits he has considered the possibility that Jack is gay. Joey says she 'can't read his eyes the way I can yours' and when Dawson asks her to tell him what his eyes are saying she says, 'How comfortable it is for us to be here together as friends.' And he replies, 'You're good' even though his eyes were clearly saying, 'I adore you unconditionally; will you bear my children?'

The Ballad of Andie and Pacey: Pacey and Andie aren't talking because she blames him for outing Jack, and he thinks she's being cold and insensitive. Eventually they trip over each other in their rush to apologise first – he says he was self-righteous, she counters that she had unrealistic expectations. Andie also addresses Pacey's need to be a hero, 'I don't need a white knight in shining armour: I need a partner . . . I'm proud to love and who's proud to love me back in spite of all my faults, and it's you – you're the one, Pacey.'

The Movie Brat: In the bar Dawson is left sitting with Joey and Jen and can't help but notice that he's sitting between two girls who've dumped him.

The Tomboy: Joey's face in the school corridor after Jack has left makes it clear the strain she's under and her doubts about him, so when Dawson suggests a romantic evening she decides to cook Jack dinner. Unfortunately, when he arrives it's to tell her that it's over.

The Clown: Pacey utterly destroys Mr Peterson and tries to apologise, but is told, 'That stunt was one of the most admirable moments of your life. Don't ruin it with an apology.' The one thing Pacey has learned from him is perhaps the most important lesson of all: 'that respect is not commanded through fear: it's earned through compassion'. You can tell, though, that Pacey feels bad, especially when Mr Peterson asks him, 'Should I respect you? You ended my career. Where's the compassion in that?'

The Delinquent: Jen has allowed Ty to talk her round and now she has 'this stupid junior-high crush'. She is surprised when he starts playing piano at the blues bar and even more shocked when his attitude to Jack and homosexuality in general turns out to be a little more Bible-belt than she had anticipated. Jen tells him it's over but he pleads his case, saying that he's 'open-minded; my narrow-minded ways are open for discussion . . . if you think my beliefs are wrong, teach me, show me another way.' Jen decides to give him another chance.

The Wicked Witch: Just when Jen expects Grams to side with Ty's homophobic views Grams surprises her by taking Ty to task. Grams and Jen stand united against prejudice and it's nice that they seem to be having more in common as the season progresses.

The Outsider: Jack has been keeping his head down but when taunted in school he's there with a comeback. He suggests that he and Joey should 'make love on the student green' or 'have a going-into-the-closet party'. Eventually, Jack tells his father that he is, after all, gay, and to Joey he says, 'When I wrote that poem something clicked inside of me that has been quiet for so long and it made me realise that whatever it is I'm going through isn't going to go away.'

Family Sucks!: Pacey stays with Dawson during his suspension because 'hiding out here and alienating you beats the hell out of torture and death at the hands of my father at home'. If Pacey's dad is a disaster, Jack and Andie's father is just as bad. He resents being called to Capeside because it's an inconvenience and sees Jack's sexuality as just one more problem for the family. He seems to think it's Jack's fault and insists that Jack is being selfish and has *chosen* to be gay. Andie adores her father and thinks that everything will be all right. Jack doesn't want him back and when Andie says she wants her father to be proud of her he replies, 'Did you ever stop to wonder if you're proud of him?' Next morning Mr McPhee packs to leave and when Jack tells him not to come back and shouts him down he loses his authority for the first time. Jack breaks down in tears and tells his father, 'I have tried harder than you know to be quiet and to forget it and to not bother my family with my problems but I can't any more because it hurts . . . I don't want to be going through this but I am.' Andie unites with Jack and they tell their father to get lost. So by returning to Capeside he's brought the remains of the McPhee family closer together, by uniting them against him.

That Three-Letter Word: Jack isn't the only one having a sexual crisis. Joey asks Dawson, 'Am I sexual? . . . I know Jack's not gay but he's obviously confused about something and it's always kept him at a distance and I was just wondering if he chose me because I'm safe . . . I'm Joey Potter, virgin at large.' Dawson assures her that she's extremely sexual but Joey is confused because Dawson initially chose Jen. Dawson says he was only being stupid and continues, 'Your sexuality is in everything you do, your wit, your intelligence, your anger, your feistiness . . . you're blossoming and it's amazingly sexy.'

All Things Spielberg: Pacey is watching and rewatching *Jerry Maguire* (Cameron Crow, 1997). Jerry's a role model for Pacey because 'he took a stand'. Dawson points out that in the movie Jerry lost everything and had to fight and beg to get it all back.

Guy Talk: The opening scene between Dawson and Pacey is so well played, understated and full of easy banter that it really emphasises how close and solid their friendship is. Jack says thank you to Pacey for standing up for him and the look of pleasure, gratitude and relief on Pacey's face speaks volumes.

Guest Cast: David Dukes had a long career in TV, appearing in miniseries such as *War and Remembrance* and *Kane and Abel* as well as numerous TV shows such as *Law and Order*, *Ally McBeal* and *Sliders*.

Contempo Pop Music: 'Tell Me' by Audra and Alayna, 'Waterfall' by the Din Pedals, 'Calling You', 'Queen Bee' and 'Sunday Kind of Love' by Jenifer Kruskamp, 'Where Are You Tonight?' and 'Reckless' by the Devlins, 'Intimacy' by the Corrs and Beth Nielsen Chapman's 'Wait For the Way'.

The Last Word: A powerful episode, which gives Kerr Smith a chance to show what he can do (see **214**, 'To Be Or Not To Be . . .' again); he delivers in spades with a powerful and moving performance. Meredith Monroe and Katie Holmes are also particularly good and if only the writer hadn't put in that final line, where Jack tells Joey, 'Thank you for being you', they would have avoided triteness altogether. The introduction of the McPhees' father also adds another layer to their characters and they cement themselves as proper regular cast members – so why aren't they in the titles yet?

216
Be Careful What You Wish For
1st US Transmission Date: 3 March 1999

Writer: Heidi Ferrer
Director: David Semel
Guest Cast: Eddie Mills (Tyson 'Ty' Hicks)

It's Dawson's sixteenth birthday and he decides to get Joey
back. When she refuses he sinks into depression. Andie's
begun her therapy and is told to cut loose for a night and
allow herself to be imperfect. When Dawson and Andie are
taken out by Pacey, who is supposed to deliver them to a
surprise party arranged by Joey, they end up at the blues
bar. Dawson and Andie get drunk and sing the blues on
stage. When Pacey does finally bring them to the party at
the Leery house Dawson makes quite a spectacle of
himself, telling some uncomfortable home truths before
retreating to the toilet with Andie, where they revisit their
dinners and swear never to drink again.

Abby sets her sights on Jack and manages to get him to
kiss her at Dawson's party. Joey walks in on them and
Jack has to explain himself.

Ty is so uncomfortable with Jen's sexuality that they
break up, unable to reconcile his religious views with her
liberal ones.

The Ballad of Dawson and Joey: Dawson decides that Joey
is the answer, although he doesn't seem sure what the
question is. He goes to talk to her and tells her outright, 'I
want more, I want you back . . . the only thing that makes
sense in my life is you . . . we're soul mates, Joey. You and
I were meant to be, period, the end, cue happy music.' Joey
reiterates that they broke up because of her, not him.
Dawson walks away upset, saying, 'If you and me weren't
meant to be together then I don't know anything.' When
he gets drunk Dawson kisses Joey and she pushes him
away, face first into his birthday cake. Afterwards she

forgives a tired Dawson and he asks the big question of the season: why did she dump him and then go out with Jack? She replies, 'Because he wasn't you ... it was about looking for someone who wasn't so close to me, where I could tell where he ended and I began ... our lives have always been so intertwined in so many ways that I feel like you partially invented me ... I need to find out if I can be a whole person without you.' Just before he falls asleep Dawson tells her to 'do it quickly, OK, because, God, I love you'. Joey tells him she loves him too, but he's already snoring. Given how annoying Joey's treatment of Dawson has been it's a surprise how convincing her reason is. That must have won her back a lot of viewer sympathy.

The Movie Brat: Dawson's birthday brings on a crisis of confidence: 'I'm still me, the whiny adolescent, big-talking, small-doing loser that I was a year ago', who thinks all he achieved in the last year was falling in love with Joey. But he has written and directed two films in twelve months. Not so shabby for a fifteen-year-old. He's never drunk before but when Andie suggests they do so he dives right in. The Dawson blues is one of the high points of the series:

My name is Dawson Leery
I'm feeling kind of weary
Today is my birthday
And you all look a little bleary
The girl I cared for left me and ran away
Straight into the arms of a guy that turned out to be gay

He ends his birthday by telling Joey, 'I'm sixteen years old and I'm so hopelessly lonely.'

The Clown: Pacey is very patient with his drunken friends but Dawson resents it and tells him, 'I wish that my best friend Pacey would just end this transformation into do-gooder, A-student and all-round sanctimonious angel and would go back to what he does best, which is make me feel good about my life because his is supposed to be worse.'

The Delinquent: Ty has issues with sex. He bails out of kisses because Jen tempts him and turns him on. He doesn't believe in sex before marriage and he knows of Jen's history, so he decides to end their relationship. Jen is furious and hurt because she wasn't going to sleep with him anyway: she was looking for 'something pure . . . and you ruined that'. Ty is history.

The Basket Case: Andie tells her therapist, 'It seemed like there needed to be someone to be the glue to hold the family together and I guess I was the most likely candidate . . . I felt like I was juggling all these balls in the air.' The therapist prescribes Andie a night of imperfection and she goes for it, wearing a showy red dress, acting on impulse, getting drunk and singing the blues. She's never been this much fun, and Meredith Monroe is clearly having a ball playing her; she quotes this as one of her two favourite episodes (the other is **207** 'The All-Nighter'). Dawson isn't the only one who can sing the blues:

> *My name is Andie*
> *And my brother's the one that's gay*
> *My other brother died*
> *And my daddy ran away*

The Outsider: Jack is apparently the only gay guy in Capeside, an accolade he seems to wish he could shrug off. When Abby tells him he's gorgeous he calls her 'Satan', which is fair. He turns up to Dawson's party with a new, gelled hairdo. He tells Joey he kissed Abby because she made him feel 'normal' and being gay seems so lonely to him. However, he 'realised from the minute I started that I was, that I am gay'.

The White-Bread, Country-Club Goody-Two-Shoes: Abby's at the height of her powers this week, playing wide-eyed innocent when Jack tells her he doesn't like her, telling him all the things he wants to hear, luring him into Dawson's bedroom, seducing him simply for the challenge of it and then crowing to her best friends.

Reality Bites: Pacey tells Dawson, 'You need to stop looking to movies for all the answers to life's questions.'

All Things Spielberg: When Ty and Jen are making out in Dawson's new car the hand hitting the steamed window is a total *Titanic* (James Cameron, 1997) riff.

All Things Freud: Andie is letting out 'what Freud calls your id: it's the part of you that holds your purest impulses and desires'.

Grown-Up Stuff: Mitch lets himself in and makes Dawson's breakfast without telling Gale. Then, when he tries to arrange a joint birthday present, Gale tells him he's too late – she's bought Dawson a Ford Explorer. Mitch doesn't approve and the bickering begins. Drunk, Dawson wishes that 'my mom had never slept with her co-anchor . . . that my father would stop talking about actually getting a job and go out there and get one . . . that the two of you would stop your petty bickering and at least pretend to be the adults around here'. Mitch tells Gale he's planning to be a substitute teacher at Capeside High. Does that mean he's a qualified teacher? Or docs Capeside High hire teachers on the basis of just being a nice guy? That's a credibility leap too far. After Dawson's party Mitch wonders if they've really messed up Dawson but Gale reassures him that Dawson's just a normal sixteen-year-old. She returns the Explorer and they agree to cover the down payment on an old car and let Dawson work to cover the rest.

Girl Talk: Joey thinks she turned Jack off from women completely and although she knows that's not really the case it still gets to her. Bessie replies that she thinks Joey's handling it all really well, and recommends that she focus on her art.

Kiss and Tell: Abby and Jack lock lips and I for one sure didn't see that coming! Jen's kisses put the fear of God into Ty, poor lad.

Contempo Pop Music: Amanda Marshall's 'Give Up Giving In', Kyf Brewer's 'Nothing To Do With Being In

Love', 'Freak of the Week' by Marvelous Three (as Jack arrives), 'Attic' by the Kickbacks, 'Truth Of Our Time' by Chickenpox, 'Maria' by Blondie and 'Frozen Charlotte' by Natalie Merchant.

The Big Issue: Joey sums it up this week: 'We're all going through the painful process of growing up.'

The Last Word: Hilarious performances from James Van Der Beek and Meredith Monroe wedded to the singing scenes, which clearly sacrifice believability for laughs, make this the funniest episode of the show ever. Dawson's drunken birthday wish is a great scene showing James Van Der Beek's unexpected talent for physical comedy. And still there's a real emotional core to the episode that rings true. Bravo.

217
Psychic Friends

1st US Transmission Date: 10 March 1999

Writer: Dana Baratta
Director: Patrick Norris
Guest Cast: Mädchen Amick (Nicole Kennedy),
Rachael Leigh Cook (Devon),
Nick Stabile (Colin Manchester),
Gareth Williams (Mike Potter)

It's carnival time in Capeside and while Dawson helps his new film studies teacher with her silent-film exhibition, Jack helps Joey set up a stall of her drawings and Pacey plays the part of Mr Skippy, the safety dog. A fortune teller tells the fortunes of Joey, Andie, Pacey and Dawson in turn, proving surprisingly insightful.

Joey flirts with a photography student, Colin, and gets to be a model for a day. She's hoping to be kissed, but he turns out to be more interested in Jack. Grams goes out on her first date since her husband died, but the guy's wife is ill so he has to cancel, to Jen's disappointment. Dawson shows *Creek Daze*, his new film (see **213**, 'His Leading Lady'), to his new film teacher and she tears into it, leaving poor old Dawson disconsolate.

The Ballad of Dawson and Joey: Joey misses Dawson and wishes they could get their friendship back. When Colin talks about dating a friend, then breaking up and losing both lover and friend, that clearly rings a bell with Joey, as it does when he says he can think of a million reasons why they broke up then, but almost none now. At the end Dawson rings her at home but she doesn't answer because she's standing outside looking longingly at his window.

The Movie Brat: Dawson's depression continues and now he isn't sleeping. We see one of his nightmares in which Jack steals both Joey and Dawson's movie. He tells Mitch, 'It's like I'm stuck alone in a dark theatre watching my life go by on the screen and all the coming attractions are box-office bombs.' He has a new edge of cynicism, too, and he doesn't intend to rely on people any more. Now that Joey is gone he's certain of only one thing and that's his ambition to be a filmmaker. He admits he is obsessed, which makes it all the more crushing when his new film studies teacher, for whom he has a bad case of hero worship because she is a major film writer, tells him that *Creek Daze* is uninspired and 'lacks emotion'. She is really tough on him and he's absolutely devastated. The fortune teller says to him, 'A soul mate walks your path, one you have known for many lifetimes before this one . . . that which is lost can be found again.' In frustration, Dawson trashes Jack's model of Creekside (see **214**, 'To Be Or Not To Be . . .').

The Tomboy: Joey is totally bored with her life and herself. She rates boys as Franks ('as in Stein') or Leos ('as in Di Caprio'); 'Dawson's definitely a Leo'. Although she 'decided to throw away relationships in pursuit of her true self', as Jack puts it, she still misses being kissed. She takes to modelling like a natural and really enjoys herself; she also sells her first picture. The fortune teller informs Joey that she has 'too much pain in your past, too much loss for one so young ... you must say yes to every new opportunity that comes your way ... you will be safe if you follow your heart.'

The Clown: Pacey looks set to slug a little brat who heckles him when he's playing Mr Skippy, but he doesn't. He won't have his fortune told partly because he doesn't believe it, and partly because he expects only bad news. But when the fortune teller does look at Pacey she sees 'a young man that wears a mask that is not his own. To the world he is strong and confident but beneath the mask is a little boy, afraid of the world, afraid of everything.'

The Basket Case: Andie was called 'Andie McGeek' in junior school. She believes in fortune tellers. The fortune teller says that 'the troubles of [her] past are only a preview of what's to come' and this upsets her because she doesn't think she can face any more hard times. Pacey reassures her and tells her, 'Your future is going to be so bright and magnificent it's going to be off the scale.'

The Wicked Witch: Grams gets a first name: Evelyn. An old school friend asks her out to dinner and after some persuading from Jen she agrees. Jen dolls her up until she looks a million dollars and off she trots, only to be stood up – because the guy's wife is ill. Still, she looks on the bright side and tells Jen that she's grateful to her for making her open up to new people and experiences.

The Outsider: Jack and Joey are really tight now and he insists on coming to her photo shoot to chaperone her. His 'gaydar' is sadly deficient, but he tripped Colin's, so he must be giving out some sort of signal. He's annoyed when Joey makes a date for him with Colin and tells her, 'I know I should be moving forward with this whole new sexual identity but the truth is I'm just not ready.'

Family Sucks!: Joey finds her dad standing on her porch, out of prison and home at last.

School Sucks!: Benji has left the school and is replaced by Miss Kennedy, 'every sixteen-year-old male's wet dream'. It seems Dawson did manage to get into film class after all, and so did Jen. When Mitch says hi to Dawson at school his son automatically calls him Mr Leery.

That Three-Letter Word: When Grams is confronted with the possibility of dating she obliquely says that she has said goodbye to 'certain things'.

Reality Bites: The final shot of Joey rowing up the creek exactly mirrors the shot of Sammy rowing from *Creek Daze*.

Metatextuality: *Creek Daze* is fundamentally an episode of *Dawson's Creek* made within the show itself, so, when Miss Kennedy critiques it, she's critiquing the show she's starring in: '. . . a preposterous soap opera about a bunch of teenagers who talk too much. I mean we've seen it all before, all that self-aware, self-referential hyperbole, filled with clichés that are disguised as send-ups. It actually borders on plagiarism.' She also says that the dialogue is unbelievable and there at least she's got a point.

All Things Spielberg: Film class discuss Frank Capra (again) and his film *Meet John Doe* (1941).

Grown-Up Stuff: Mitch takes the job vacated by Mr Peterson, but still no mention of qualifications of any sort. Well, at least he's off the streets. He doesn't waste any time settling in, either, bragging in the faculty lounge about Dawson's filmmaking while making moves on Miss Kennedy, to Dawson's dismay.

Girl Talk: Joey and Jack check out guys in the lunch queue and though you might think it'd be uncomfortable they both seem OK with it (well, what category would *you* put it in?)

Kiss and Tell: Joey can't get Colin to kiss her, but Jack obliges, on the forehead, just so she doesn't go home unkissed.

Guest Cast: Mädchen Amick got her big break in David Lynch's superbly unhinged TV thriller *Twin Peaks* and has gone on to star in *Fantasy Island*, *Central Park West* and many other films and TV shows. Nick Stabile has also appeared in an episode of *Charmed* as well as being a regular for a time on *Sunset Beach* and appearing in *Bride of Chucky*.

Contempo Pop Music: Semisonic's 'Completely Pleased', Blues Traveller's 'Run-Around', 'Angels in the Attic' by Debra Davis, 'I Could Be The One' by Donna Lewis, Natalie Merchant's 'Life Is Sweet' and 'How' by Lisa Loeb.

The Last Word: A weak episode that doesn't move the storyline forward much. It is raised mainly by the shock of Miss Kennedy's response to Dawson's movie and the brief story of Gram's date. A filler installment.

218
The Perfect Wedding
1st US Transmission Date: 24 April 1999

Writer: Mike White
Director: Greg Prange
Guest Cast: Mädchen Amick (Nicole Kennedy),
Rachael Leigh Cook (Devon),
Gareth Williams (Mike Potter),
Katy Selverstone (Pam, the Bride)

In spite of Joey's misgivings, her freshly paroled father and Bessie agree to cater a wedding at the last minute as a way of paying off some of the Icehouse's debts. Dawson, Jack, Pacey and Andie all agree to help out for the day. Andie nearly destroys the wedding cake and Pacey tries to fix it. Jack and Dawson talk the panic-stricken bride into going through with the wedding. Joey spends the whole day in a flap, afraid of the high-profile nature of the wedding and her father's re-entry into Capeside society. Gale arrives, dressed to kill and determined to get Mitch back, but he arrives with Nicole Kennedy, Dawson's film teacher. With the bride convinced, Joey and her dad reconciled, the cake saved and the food served, it all seems to have gone well.

Abby and Jen crash the wedding but Andie throws them out. They take a bottle of champagne to the docks. Abby slips and falls into the water. After seeing no sign of life, Jen jumps in to save her, but she's too late.

The Ballad of Dawson and Joey: Joey's dad is surprised to find that she and Dawson aren't an item, and he's the one who gets them to dance together. Dawson is very support-ive throughout the wedding stress and tells Joey he'll always be there for her. When they dance Joey says, 'Thank you . . . for being my friend, for understanding me better than anyone and for putting up with me for the last sixteen years. I love you.' Dawson says he loves her too and, hallelujah, they kiss. Jack looks on approvingly, as do Gale and Mr Potter.

The Ballad of Andie and Pacey: Andie says that when they get married it should be in Venice. Pacey replies that by the time that day comes it will have sunk into the sea.

The Movie Brat: Miss Kennedy's criticisms of *Creek Daze* still niggle at Dawson, and when he shows his mom the film he's unwilling to accept her praise as unbiased and decides to re-edit: 'I had such a distinct and clear vision for this movie . . . I just failed to translate that vision into film. And what about all the other visions that I have for my future? What if I fail to bring those to life either?'

The Tomboy: Joey is shocked by her father's return, and the gossip of the townsfolk makes her uncomfortable. The frightened girl comes out from inside her tough exterior and tells Dawson she's afraid of her father letting her down again.

The Clown: Pacey, perhaps surprisingly, loves weddings and thinks they are 'the most beautiful ritual that mankind has ever created'.

The Delinquent: With the movie wrapped and Ty gone, Jen is starting to get itchy feet again and tells Abby she's 'frustrated . . . bored . . . going berserk'.

The Basket Case: Andie tells Pacey she hates weddings because they're old-fashioned and an invitation to failure. Pacey doesn't believe her and later gets her to admit that she's a wedding fanatic and they make her weepy.

The Outsider: Jack's 'intuitive insight' calmed Joey down when she panicked about the wedding, and in seconds flat he was able to talk the bride into going through with her marriage. He's everybody's counsellor and his smile when Joey and Dawson kiss casts him as guardian angel.

The White-Bread, Country-Club Goody-Two-Shoes: Abby tells Jen that she'll never be happy: 'Wherever I am I'll always want to be somewhere else; whatever I have I'll always want something different . . . I just don't want to be a cliché.' And then she dies, so I suppose she got her wish.

Family Sucks!: The Icehouse has been in financial trouble but Mike Potter is determined to get it back on track. He plays the returned family man, telling his daughters not to worry, he'll take care of things. Joey thinks he's doing too much too soon, and tells Bessie, 'He tore our family apart and he thinks he can put it back together in a day. Well he can't.' Mike overhears her and apologises: 'You two have been so strong, you've done so well . . . I'm the one who's supposed to be the one protecting you from all the harsh realities of the world and here you are protecting me. Yet again I'm failing in my parental duties.' Joey lets her guard down at last and tells him she's proud of him, glad he's back and that she loves him.

School Sucks!: Dawson thinks it's weird seeing his dad around school, 'consorting with the enemy', and when he sees Mitch chatting to Nicole he asks Pacey, 'Should I really have to be subjected to this?'

All Things Spielberg: Gale to Dawson: 'Your movie may not be *Citizen Kane* but it's not *Bride of Chucky* either.'

Citizen Kane (Orson Welles, 1941) was a massively innovative and groundbreaking film, hailed by many critics as the best film ever made; *Bride of Chucky* (Ronny Yu, 1998) wasn't.

Grown-Up Stuff: Gale misses Mitch a lot and when she arrives at the wedding she tells Dawson she's there to win Mitch back. So, when Mitch enters with Nicole on his arm, and then has the gall to come over and introduce her to Gale, it's both cruel and antagonistic. Mitch says he doesn't want to put him in the middle, but Dawson replies that that's exactly what he's doing by dating teachers from his school.

Girl Talk: Jen needs to have some fun and tells Abby that she spent the best times of the year with her. Abby replies, 'I think that's the nicest thing anyone's ever said to me.' Later, on the dock, Jen and Abby discuss their nightmares of the future, 'married to some beer-swilling, football-watching bonehead . . . living in some cookie-cutter house with two snot-nosed brats, driving the car pool.'

Guy Talk: When Jack tells Dawson that Mr Potter's been paroled it's clear Dawson is hurt Joey didn't tell him first. Jack gives Dawson a pep talk, telling him Joey is his 'soul mate' and that she needs him because 'you're the only one that knows her history . . . what she's going through' and that he should 'force a connection'.

Kiss and Tell: Dawson and Joey kiss on the dance floor. Jack gets a thank you kiss from the bride.

Guest Cast: Katy Selverstone has appeared in *Seinfeld*, *Law and Order* and *The Drew Carey Show*.

Contempo Pop Music: 'Flush' by John Rouse, 'Reality Hurts' by Jenna Music, 'Kiss Me' by Sixpence None The Richer, 'All Mine' by Dance Hall Crashers, 'Little Differences' by Save Ferris, 'Shimmer' by Shawn Mullins, 'Not the One' by Vanessa Handrick, 'You' by Shelby Starner, 'Once Again' by Michael Brandmeier, 'You and Me' by the Spies, 'Any Lucky Penny' by Nikki Hassman and 'Feels Like Home' by Chantal Kreviazuk.

The Last Word: They killed Abby! Who's going to play the bad guy now? Who's going to stir things up, cause trouble, voice unpalatable truths and lead Jen astray? Plaudits to Monica Keena, who made the character so much fun and such an important element in the Capeside mix. I for one miss Abby a lot, and I think the show does, too. This is a good episode, better than **217**, 'Psychic Friends', and a real acting workout for Katie Holmes, who does some excellent work.

219
Rest In Peace
1st US Transmission Date: 5 May 1999

Writer: Mike White
Director: David Semel
Guest Cast: Michele Scarabelli (Mrs Morgan),
Gareth Williams (Mike Potter)

In the wake of Abby's death Jen spirals out of control again, drinking heavily, blaming herself but taking it out first on Andie and then on Grams, who unwisely tries to comfort Jen with religion. Jen is outraged at the hypocrisy that surfaces as everybody pretends to have liked Abby. She gives an angry speech at the funeral, telling the truth about Abby and attacking God. Grams is disgusted and throws Jen out, telling her to find somewhere else to live.

Abby's death makes Joey think about her mother and come to terms with her death three years ago. She attends Abby's funeral and then goes to her mother's grave for the first time and lays a flower there.

Mrs Morgan asks Andie to give a speech at the funeral. Her desire to say something nice leads her to Abby's bedroom and her diary, which is vicious and nasty, as you'd expect. When she gives her speech she avoids praising Abby but thanks her for being one of the people who pushed her. Later she returns to steal Abby's diary so that her mother won't read it and sees an apparition of Abby, smiling at her in the mirror.

The Ballad of Dawson and Joey: On the way home from the wedding Joey and Dawson are still kissing and they go upstairs to his room. Who knows how that would have ended if Jen hadn't been there, fresh from Abby's drowning? They decide not to analyse their actions because they've got so much else to deal with. After the funeral Joey kisses Dawson, tells him she's happy and then asks him to escort her to her mother's grave.

The Ballad of Andie and Pacey: Pacey is worried about Andie's stability under the pressure of giving a eulogy and, as ever, he tries to think of ways to rescue her. She tells him, 'Don't let our roles become etched in stone . . . me the helpless lunatic, you the hero on horseback. I need to take care of myself.' After her eulogy goes so well Pacey seems reassured and proud.

The Tomboy: Joey's never visited her mother's grave because 'that little girl inside of me is just waiting for her return . . . that her death was just some cosmic error and eventually God will realise he made a terrible mistake and he'll send her back to me like he did my dad'. She doesn't want to go to Abby's funeral because it will 'open a Pandora's box of emotions that, frankly, I'd rather keep sealed tight'. She admits, 'I never really liked Abby, I actively despised her'.

The Delinquent: When Grams starts trying to tell Jen that it's all 'God's plan' Jen's having none of it and drunkenly rants that 'there is no God and there is no heaven and there is no hope. The only truth I know is pain.' She pushes Grams away and tells her, 'If I can't just be myself and speak my mind maybe I should move out.' Her speech at Abby's funeral is a shocker: 'Abby had a toxic personality . . . bordering on radioactive. Abby could be cruel . . . spiteful . . . petty. She spent her days mischievously stirring up trouble and creating calamity and generally taking pleasure in other people's pain.' Then she moves on to God, and directs all her comments at a horrified Grams:

'Abby taught me the sadistic nature of God and, as much as that knowledge is disturbing, it's true and it's real ... for that little bit of honesty I will always be grateful to her.' Afterwards she admits to Andie that she's lashing out because she blames herself for Abby's death. She apologises to Grams but it's too late, so now she's homeless.

The Basket Case: Andie tried hard to befriend Abby and got only spite in return. However, she still feels upset and guilty about Abby's death, so when Mrs Morgan asks her to give a eulogy she agrees. In the end she says, 'In her own truth-telling way she gave me strength. I'm a much stronger woman because of her ... she gave me that gift. She was one of a kind.'

The Wicked Witch: Grams admits she didn't like Abby, so at least Jen won't be angry with her for being a hypocrite. Jen's drunkenness outrages Grams and she asks Jen, 'Does it give you so much pleasure to shock and offend me? I am trying to be understanding but you insist on disobeying my rules and polluting my house with your disrespectful blaspheming.' She comes to the funeral and tries to make peace with Jen: 'I do hope we can avoid ugly scenes like last night in the future. I wanted to let you know I forgive you.' But Jen doesn't want her forgiveness and replies, 'I'm looking for your understanding and that's something you've never been able to provide.' After Jen's blasphemous speech Grams walks out of church, goes home and packs all of Jen's stuff. When Jen comes home she tells her, 'The truth is that you deliberately tried to wound me in that chapel and take out all your pain and rage at the world on me ... How about a little compassion for me, your grandmother who loves you, who would do anything for you, who would die for you? You should be living with ... someone who you respect and clearly I am not that person.'

The White-Bread, Country-Club Goody-Two-Shoes: More obvious shows would have revealed that Abby's diary contained the lonely, broken-hearted thoughts of a misunderstood girl. Then all the characters would have agonised about how they never knew her and learned an Important Lesson. Happily *Dawson's Creek* is better than that, and we find Abby's diary is a spiteful, nasty collection of hateful rants, entirely consistent with the girl we knew (you can read it online at http://www.capeside.net/virtualeyes/abbysdiary/). When confronted by Andie's uncomfortable response to Abby's death, and the ludicrous yellow armbands that people wear in her memory, Jen says, 'Aside from me Abby didn't have a single friend in Capeside . . . Abby spent her entire life shattering our fragile egos and that's why people disliked her so intensely . . . even in her death she's still exposing hypocrisy.'

Family Sucks!: Joey tells her dad she feels as if her mother is fading from her memory. Mike tells her, 'You are so like your mother . . . she's not gone: she lives in you and that comforts me no end.'

Reality Bites: Dawson has to process a real emotion, so what does he do? True to type he looks at Abby on screen in his movie to try to work out his feelings. Interestingly, Abby appears to have been a very good actress. It must be deliberate that the clip Dawson watches is of Abby 'corpsing'.

Grown-Up Stuff: Gale's piece on Andie, Joey, Abby and Jen (212 'Uncharted Waters') has won an award for Excellence In News Broadcasting and this has led to a job offer in Philadelphia. Gale is going to take the job, leaving Mitch to move back into their home. She doesn't think Mitch is ever going to try to rebuild the marriage and so she's giving up. Dawson tells this to Mitch and is disgusted when Mitch seems to indicate that he'll let Gale go.

Our Quips Are Wittier: When Jack tells Joey that he was the last person Abby kissed, she says, 'At least she went out with a bang,' and then cannot believe what she's just said.

Blooper: Jen says she saw Abby in the water and she was so scared, and then Andie says the current was too strong and there was nothing Jen could have done. But, if that's so, why wasn't Jen swept away as well?

Guest Cast: Michele Scarabelli has appeared in many TV shows, from *Star Trek: the Next Generation* to *Dallas*, and was a series regular in both *Airwolf* and *Alien Nation*.

Contempo Pop Music: Appropriately enough 'Life's a Bitch' (and then you die) by Shooter plays throughout the episode. 'So Young' by the Corrs, 'Whatever Makes You Happy' by Paul Westerberg, 'It's Over Now' by Neve, 'Magic' by Ben Folds Five, 'To Be Loved' by Curtis Stigers and 'Lose Your Way' by Sophie B Hawkins.

Ker-THUNK!: It's very dramatic to have Jen appear in Dawson's room after Abby's death, but she was soaking wet and had just witnessed a death – would the police and medics *really* have let her just walk away from the scene?

The Big Issue: Normally it's best to tell the truth, but sometimes it's better to hold your tongue.

The Last Word: A powerful and mature episode that doesn't pull any punches and tackles hypocrisy head on. This is the sign of an increasingly confident show taking risks and pulling it off. Recently we've had a string of episodes in which the regulars have each taken their turn in the spotlight and acted their socks off. This time it's Michelle Williams's turn, and she is superb. The ghost at the end was a bit much, though, and smacked of a cop-out, with Abby benignly looking on as Andie tried to protect Abby's mom. However, **220**, 'Reunited' throws light on that incident and redeems it.

220
Reunited

1st US Transmission Date: 12 May 1999

Writer: Greg Berlanti
Director: Melanie Mayron
Guest Cast: Mädchen Amick (Nicole Kennedy),
Scott Denny (Tim McPhee)

Dawson takes Joey to a local restaurant to celebrate their one-month 'anniversary' (which is, kind of spookily, the 'anniversary' of Abby's death, though they never mention it). Unfortunately, his father is there with Nicole and they are seated together. To make matters worse Jen and Gale arrive too. Joey and Jen contrive to remove Nicole and have the band play Mitch and Gale's favourite song. Mitch takes the bait, asks Gale to dance and subtly lets her know he wants her to stay. She tells Jen afterwards that she won't take the Philadelphia job, but then she sees Mitch and Nicole kissing on the dock and runs home, in tears.

Andie's erratic behaviour takes a dramatic turn as she begins to hallucinate her dead brother. Pacey and Jack realise what is happening but Andie, in a panic, locks herself in the bathroom with her vision of Tim, who tells her she has to choose between him and Pacey. Pacey begs her to come out and she eventually chooses him and opens the door. Jack decides that their father needs to be called because Andie's deterioration is following the same path as their mother's illness.

The Ballad of Dawson and Joey: It's been a month since they got back together and they seem more together than ever. The banter in the boat as they head home is relaxed and friendly; things look good for them, for a change.

The Ballad of Andie and Pacey: Pacey confronts Andie about her change of hairstyle, realising that she's changed it back to how it was when Tim was alive. Then he hears her talking to Tim and thinks she's seeing someone else, so when he finds out the truth he's both relieved and horrified. Andie pushes him away when he tells her he thinks she's ill again: 'If you don't like having a wacko for a girlfriend then why don't you do us both a favour and just break up with me?' But you can't get rid of Pacey that easily. When he asks her to come out of the bathroom he's very, very scared of losing her and tells her, 'My life began when I met you, Andie, and you never gave up on me so I'm not going to give up on you.'

The Movie Brat: Dawson really goes for Nicole at dinner; it makes a change to see him so aggressive and unembarrassed. He accuses her of being a hypocrite by first trashing his movie (see **217** 'Psychic Friends') and then changing her tune because she's dating his father.

The Clown: When Andie's crisis comes and she locks herself in the bathroom Pacey deals with it brilliantly, talking her down, persuading her to come out and choose him. As ever, give him a situation to save and Pacey rises to the occasion.

The Delinquent: Jen is now living with Gale and Dawson and won't call Grams because it would only lead to 'a few weeks of mild reconciliation and then the inevitable ideology clash'.

The Basket Case: Andie is losing it big time and she's nervy, temperamental, difficult and terrified. Her vision of Abby (**219**, 'Rest In Peace') now seems less like a ghost and more like the beginning of her decline, and her psychiatrist thinks she needs to go back on medication because 'what's going on inside you, Andie, may not be healing itself properly'.

The Outsider: Jack's reduced to being an observer as Andie breaks down but he makes the difficult decision to call their dad because 'this is what happened with my mother . . . at first it was like this, a few minor episodes here and there, and by the time anybody wanted to deal with it she was too far gone . . . I wanted so badly to believe there was something I could do.'

That Three-Letter Word: After their dinner Joey playfully asks Dawson if he was anticipating 'closing the deal' and he calls her a 'vulgar little thing' and says he prefers the term 'consummating their ultimate desires'. She says they're too young, and Dawson's fine with that, but he gets her to admit she's seriously considered it.

Metatextuality: The opening sequence, where they discuss how *90210* they have become, all hanging out together as friends after everything that's happened, slyly acknowl-edges that it's a bit ridiculous. Nonetheless, it still thumbs its nose at those people who claimed that the show was possibly losing its edge and inevitably becoming more soapy and safe.

All Things Spielberg: Joey thinks the gang are like 'St Elmo's from hell', comparing them to the gang from *St Elmo's Fire* (Joel Schumacher, 1985), the last great eighties brat-pack movie.

All Things Freud: According to her therapist, Andie is experiencing 'complicated grief'. Abby's death 'seems to have upset you a great deal, which ultimately may have triggered unresolved issues with your brother's passing'.

Grown-Up Stuff: Gale admits that she thinks about getting Mitch back all the time but she's just about given up hope until she runs into Nicole at the restaurant and decides to take her on. Dawson impatiently tells his dad that Gale's decision on taking the Philadelphia job 'has everything to do with you'. Although Mitch replies that it's 'only a matter of paperwork and signatures now', he still asks Gale to dance. Gale said she was waiting for 'one of those small moments in life that provide some clarity' to indicate whether she should take the job, and after the dance she tells Jen she's staying because 'I realised I could move ten thousand miles away and never let Mitch go'.

Girl Talk: Gale and Jen settle down for a night of girl talk, but Gale burns dinner so that puts paid to that idea. At the restaurant Jen and Joey join forces to engineer a reunion between Gale and Mitch – perhaps the thaw in their relationship has really taken hold at last.

Kiss and Tell: Nicole takes the initiative and kisses Mitch, and later he manages to kiss her back, even after their disastrous dinner; he must be the world's most charming diplomat.

Blooper: Jack says, 'It's bizarre . . . the way we all started the school year and how we all managed to come out as friends.' But, since Seasons One and Two both cover the same year, and the McPhees arrived only at the start of Season Two, they must have moved school mid-year.

Guest Cast: Scott Denny has appeared in *Fantasy Island* and *Oz* and can be seen on the big screen in *Urbania*.

Contempo Pop Music: Appropriately enough, we hear 'Mania' by Babel Fish when Tim first appears to Andie in the school. 'Surrounded' by Binge, 'This Is Where It Ends' by Barenaked Ladies, 'Chasing You' by Seven Mary Three, 'Reunited' by Dennis McCarthy, one of the men who writes all the incidental music on the show, and 'Ready For a Fall' by PJ Olssen.

Ker-THUNK!: The constant absences of Mrs McPhee are really starting to strain credibility. Since she's gradually going nuts she's hardly likely to be out on the town, so where is she and why does she never hear the ruckus going on in her house?

The Last Word: As Dawson points out, the restaurant sequences veer close to farce at times, but they pull it off, just. The real business of the episode is Andie's breakdown and Meredith Monroe and Joshua Jackson do brilliant work portraying really difficult scenes that could easily have been melodramatic and overwrought. A minor triumph as the dramatic stakes continue to rise and the season nears its end.

221
Ch . . . ch . . . ch . . . Changes

1st US Transmission Date: 19 May 1999

Writer: Dana Baratta
Director: Lou Antonio
Guest Cast: David Dukes (Mr McPhee),
Gareth Williams (Jack Potter)

Dawson has to do a project on a person who has changed and so he decides to interview someone on film. Joey, Jen and Jack all refuse but Mr Potter agrees, and tells his life story on camera. This upsets Joey, who tells Dawson to stop and turn the camera on himself, but he's too afraid to do that. While helping out at the Icehouse he sees Mr Potter handling a bag of cocaine and realises that he's smuggling drugs again. Dawson builds Joey a white picket fence outside her house, to give her the one thing her now-perfect life was missing.

Mr McPhee responds to Jack's summons (**220**, 'Reunited'). He arrives and tells his children to pack because he is taking them back to Providence with him so they can get the help they need. Andie, Jack and Pacey are all horrified, and eventually Mr McPhee agrees to let them stay if they want. However, Andie acknowledges that she needs help and agrees to go. Jack stays behind with a distraught Pacey.

Jen phones her mother and asks to come home but is refused, so she packs her bags and buys a bus ticket out of Capeside, intending to head out on her own. Jack stops her and asks her to come and live with him, and she agrees.

The Ballad of Dawson and Joey: Joey likes Carpentry-Dawson and thinks that giving him a jeans-and-white-T-shirt makeover would be a 'definite turn-on', but the fact that he's a dreadful carpenter ruins the illusion. Dawson reveals his deep insecurity when he tells Joey, 'I'm afraid I'm not enough for you and I never will be and . . . you'll realise that you've grown way beyond me and I'm just going to lose you again.' Joey is astonished, gets positively gushy, which isn't like her at all, and demonstrates how much she's changing now that her dad is back and her life is finally perfect: 'I love you, and I believe in you and I am so proud of you and . . . proud to be with you.' This spurs Dawson on to his greatest hopeless-romantic moment ever, when he stays up all night to build the white picket fence.

The Ballad of Andie and Pacey: When Pacey is interviewed by Dawson he reveals both how insecure he still is and how dependent he is on Andie to maintain his composure: 'My only accomplishment this year was to find an inspiration like Andie. Everything else just stemmed from her.' Later, he admits to Mr McPhee that he's considering himself, too, when asking for Andie to stay because he doesn't know how he'll manage when she's gone. On their final night together he takes her out on a date to the place they first kissed, and they dance together, reflecting on how far they've come since they met, and how much they've changed. Even though they decide not to say goodbye, Pacey comes running to see her off and tells her to remember her promise: 'You and me together again, happy, healthy, more in love than ever.' Jack tells his dad, 'I've never seen two people have what they have together.'

The Movie Brat: Dawson is 'trying to figure out how people grow and change'. And about time, too, since he is exactly where he was when the series started while everyone else seems to have moved on and grown up a bit. His conclusion, that Rick in *Casablanca* doesn't change at all, and that many movie characters don't really have character arcs at all, seems to indicate that he'll remain pretty much the same old well-meaning but clueless, not-quite-there-yet teenager for some time yet.

The Tomboy: For the first time since the series started Joey is blissfully happy, all smiles and flirtiness, comfortable with Dawson in a way she never seemed before, and she seems to have learned to trust her dad again. So when Dawson's interview with her father stirs up memories she wants left buried she calls a halt to it because 'we've worked so hard to close those doors and move on'.

The Clown: Pacey's hero complex takes a battering when he finds that he can't save Andie from being taken away and he tells Dawson that 'ever since me and Andie ... collided, she mistook me for someone else and she gave me somebody to be and now that she needs my help there's not a damn thing I can do for her. I'm failing her, so you're going to have to find yourself another hero.'

The Delinquent: Jen has changed but her parents haven't, and they don't want her back. With Grams having thrown her out Jen feels abandoned and decides to leave for good. By the end she's moved out of the Leery house and in with Jack.

The Basket Case: Andie is now more hostile to her father than Jack was. She bluntly tells him he's not welcome and then, when he reveals he's been sent for by Jack, she accuses Jack of betraying her. In the end, though, she decides to leave because 'the more time I spend here with everybody, and with Pacey, the more I want to get better'.

The Outsider: Jack still confronts his father, but less angrily now. His dad thinks Jack's homosexuality is some sort of illness that can be cured or a choice that can be revoked. He blames himself for it, but Jack tells him, 'I'm gay for the same reasons Tim wasn't. It just happened that way.' Jack decides to stay in Capeside because he can't live with his father, although he does want to make him proud. Mr McPhee tries to tell Jack he's proud of him, but can't bring himself to do it. Later, he does manage some conciliation: 'I'm not the best father, I know that, but I do want you to be happy.'

Family Sucks!: Mr McPhee seems slowly to be realising how badly he's screwed up his family and starts a slow process of reconciliation, but he's not very good at it, and still seems to think that forcing decisions on his kids is acceptable. In the end he does relent, letting Andie and Jack make up their own minds and reaching out slightly to Jack. Maybe there's hope for him yet.

Reality Bites: Dawson fails to make the connection between his film assignment and reality, totally failing to realise that it will stir up real feelings in the real world. As ever, it's all through the lens for him.

All Things Spielberg: *Casablanca* (Michael Curtiz, 1942) is the greatest love story ever filmed and an acknowledged masterpiece. The 1983 TV series of the same name, starring David Soul from *Starsky and Hutch*, isn't.

Contempo Pop Music: 'Sell Your Soul' by Grammatrain, 'Everything Changes' by Bridget Benanate, 'Goin' Our Way' by Gus, 'Paper Cup' and 'London Rain' by Heather Nova, 'Cry Ophelia' by Adam Nova and 'Chrome' by Matthew Ryan.

Ker-THUNK!: Dawson somehow manages to build a white picket fence in total silence, because Joey sleeps right through its construction, even though it's on her front lawn. From total incompetent to genius of silent carpentry in one day?

The Big Issue: Dawson says it best: 'Love is change, or at least I hope so.'

The Last Word: Coming up on the season finale it's clear how all the characters have evolved. Joey's found her way back to Dawson and happiness, but her father looks set to destroy it all again; Pacey's become an A student, all because of Andie, but he's afraid that when she leaves he'll be back at square one; Jen has changed, but her parents haven't, so she feels trapped by the actions of the person she used to be; Dawson, always the still point in the middle of everyone else's crises, hasn't changed at all.

222
Parental Discretion Advised

1st US Transmission Date: 26 May 1999

Writer: Greg Berlanti
Director: Greg Prange
Guest Cast: Gareth Williams (Mike Potter),
John Finn (John Witter), Richard K Olsen (Mr Milo)

Dawson tells Mike Potter that he knows about the drug smuggling and it must stop, but Mike says he's trapped. Pacey's dad knows something is going on, and the Icehouse is being staked out. Later, when the gang are all studying at the Icehouse, a petrol bomb is thrown through a window just as Mike is flushing the cocaine down the toilet. As the Icehouse burns to the ground Jack saves Jen, Pacey saves Joey, and Dawson, heroically, saves Mike. After the fire Dawson tells his parents about Mike's drug smuggling and then, feeling that he has no choice, he tells Joey. Sherrif Witter, Gale, Mitch and Dawson talk with Joey and try to persuade her that she must act in order to protect her family and to prevent her dad going away for life. She confronts Mike and he confesses, then she tearfully reveals that she has been wearing a wire. The police take him away. Joey tells Dawson she never wants to see him again.

Pacey is failing all his finals because he isn't even writing them. His dad taunts him about Andie and then tells him to stop going to the Icehouse. When Pacey refuses he hits him. After the fire he's at it again, blaming Andie's departure for Pacey's bad mood and saying she's got a screw loose. Pacey decks his dad (yay!). Later, after speaking to Andie on the phone, Pacey's dad apologises and arranges for Pacey to take make-ups of his finals.

Jen starts dropping hints about committing suicide, which alarm Jack. Grams comes to school to try to make peace with Jen, but Jen doesn't want to know. When she doesn't run from the fire Jack confronts her and she admits she has lost the will to go on. She decides to return to Grams and patch things up, and she takes Jack with her.

The Ballad of Dawson and Joey: It's just like the old days: Dawson and Joey open the show in his bedroom on movie night and discuss the themes of the episode before it begins. This week it's love stories in movies and Joey's preference for doomed tales of endless but unrequited love. Joey thinks that it doesn't matter if circumstances tear a couple apart as long as they never stop loving, and she says it doesn't matter what the circumstances are for her and Dawson, because 'we get the happy ending'. Naturally, this being a season finale, they don't. When Dawson tells Joey about her dad she's panic-stricken because she realises she'll not only lose her dad, but will lose Dawson as well. She warns him, 'We won't survive this' and asks him to drop it, but he says it's 'a risk that I'm willing to take because I care more about you than I care about myself'.

Joey tries to keep it together but Dawson's movie morality is just not capable of dealing with a situation as complex as this one and she rounds on him: 'In that black-and-white world in which you live you didn't see any choices, but that's not my world. I see things in grey, and that's what makes us different, and that's what made me fall in love with you, and that's what's tearing us apart.' Finally, drained and betrayed, Joey coldly tells Dawson, 'I will never forgive you . . . there are certain circumstances that love cannot overcome and from now on I don't want to know you.'

The Movie Brat: For a change we see proactive Dawson, forcefully challenging Mr Potter, taking the initiative and telling Joey, running into a burning building to save someone. This is the first time he is ever really active in the crisis, and his actions cost him dearly. The final scene with Joey really shows up the inadequacy of Dawson's emotional armoury. Because movies are his only frame of reference he mouths endless bland film clichés – 'you did the right thing . . . we both did what we had to do' – at a moment when he should just have shut up and hugged her.

The Tomboy: Joey wants to believe her dad is innocent, but it gets harder and harder to do so. She makes him swear he knows nothing about the fire, but afterwards Dawson finds her sitting outside staring at the creek. When he tells her the truth she tries to deny it, but she's not fooling anyone, least of all herself. She's forced into selling her dad out, but in reality she'd probably have done it herself sooner or later.

The Clown: Mr Witter tells Pacey that he's gone off the rails since Andie left, and with Pacey not writing a word in his final papers and believing it doesn't really matter it's clear he's right. But Pacey's dad just doesn't know how to deal with his son, and resorts to hitting him to try to get him to obey instructions. After that it's just a matter of time before he loses Pacey altogether. In the ashes of the fire he taunts Pacey with the fact that Andie has 'a few screws loose' and Pacey snaps, flooring his dad with a mean left hook. Frankly, anyone who tells his boy, 'If God hadn't blessed you with my good looks I wouldn't know whose son you were' deserves to get punched. Pacey calls his dad a bastard and a 'rotten son of a bitch' and tells him, 'If you so much as make one more even slightly disparaging comment about the woman I love you'll be policing this town from a hospital bed.' Predictably, punching his dad is the best way to get his respect and attention ('I deserved it, good for you for doing it') and Mr Witter eventually even gives Pacey a hug. He apologises, says, 'I'm sorry I'm not the kind of father that you felt you could share your story with,' admits that Andie sounded sweet, and laments, 'As little as I know about her I know even less about you, my own son.' Pacey's relief at finally having a vaguely human father to turn to is amazing.

The Delinquent: Jen's suicide hints are a bit obvious and lack real conviction, but when Jack asks her about her reaction to the fire she admits, 'I'm not the kind of person that would take her own life . . . I just didn't care enough to run.' She agrees to try living with Grams again as long as 'we address the reality of why this didn't work out before', and Grams doesn't give her 'biblical judgment'.

The Wicked Witch: Surprisingly it's Grams who makes the first move to reconcile with Jen. She willingly accepts all Jen's conditions at the end, though, and even takes Jack's arrival in her stride.

Family Sucks!: Mitch tries, unsuccessfully, to put his family back together: 'The past twenty-four hours have reminded me how much I love to be a part of this family.'

Jen returns to the only family member who still wants her: 'I want a family, I want us to take care of each other.'

Joey tells Dawson he's a member of her family now and she defends her family through thick and thin. In the end though, she has to tear it apart to save it and both her dad and Dawson are cast out.

School Sucks!: Mr Milo, who was so pleased when Pacey turned himself around at school, calls Mr Witter and warns him about Pacey's exam performance. The school even lets Pacey do make-ups, so they're obviously feeling quite generous these days.

All Things Spielberg: Dawson and Joey resurrect movie night to watch *The Age of Innocence* (Martin Scorsese, 1993) a moody, mannered adaptation of Edith Wharton's novel of doomed love.

Grown-Up Stuff: Gale has decided to take the Philadelphia job because 'the someone I really care about has done nothing to even remotely suggest that he cares about me'. She asks Mitch to move back in with Dawson and, though he uses guilt to try to get her to stay, saying she's not considering Dawson, she stands firm. After the meeting with the police Mitch comes clean and admits that he wants her to stay and rebuild their family, but it's too late – she's determined to leave.

Guy Talk: With his dad gone, Dawson asks his mom for father/son advice and she gives him such a swift, straight-forward answer that he says, 'Wow, dad's got nothing on you.'

Contempo Pop Music: 'Hit So Hard' by Hole, Oleander's 'Why I'm Here', 'Letting Go' by Sozzi, 'Moon Beneath My Feet' by Kim Stockwood and 'That I Would Be Good' by Alanis Morissette.

The Big Issue: When push comes to shove you have to be able to depend on family.

The Last Word: All four main characters redefine their relationships with their parents this week. Pacey finally stands up to his dad and in doing so gains his respect; Joey gives her dad every chance to tell the truth but he lies to her until she is forced to betray him to save both of them;

Jen accepts Grams's offer of a reconciliation, but only on condition that they sort out what went wrong first time; Dawson finally shows his parents how grown up he can be and this gives them the strength and the reason to build some bridges. As with every season finale the tension is that much higher, the emotions that bit more raw, and the situations more extreme. No one could fail to have a lump in their throat when Jen and Grams reconcile, or when Pacey finally breaks down in front of his dad. Having Dawson and Joey split up may not be the best cliffhanger – after all, they've done that before but the vehemence of her rejection is chilling and the look on Dawson's face as we fade to credits reminds us that through everything this show is always about those two and their relationship. If that relationship is as dead as Joey indicates, how is the show ever going to continue?

Season Three

Co-Producers: Janice Cooke Leonard, Gina Fattore
(from episode 314), Tom Kapinos (from episode 314)
Producers: Jeffrey Stepakoff, David Blake Hartley
Co-Executive Producers: Greg Berlanti, Greg Prange
Executive Producers: Alex Gansa, Paul Stupin

Regular Cast

James Van Der Beek (Dawson Leery)
Katie Holmes (Joey Potter)
Joshua Jackson (Pacey Witter)
Michelle Williams (Jen Lindley)
Meredith Monroe (Andie McPhee)
Kerr Smith (Jack McPhee)
Mary-Margaret Humes (Gale Leery)
John Wesley Shipp (Mitch Leery)
Mary Beth Peil (Grams)
Nina Repeta (Bessie Potter)

Season Three's non-title-sequence regular guest stars were:
Michael Pitt (Henry Parker)
Obba Babatundé (Principal Green)

Kevin Williamson often said in the early days of *Dawson's Creek* that he would never leave the show. But at the end of Season Two he packed his bags and went off to start a new one, *Wasteland*, focusing on a group of six twenty-somethings trying to survive in New York. ABC commissioned thirteen episodes with an option to extend to 22, but in the end a mere three episodes were shown before the show was pulled. The production company tried to sell it to MTV, the WB and others, but it was dead in the water.

Two of the cast from *Wasteland* featured in *Dawson's Creek*: Sasha Alexander, later to appear as Gretchen Witter in Season Four, was one of the main leads; also featured was Eddie Mills, who played Ty Hicks in Season Two.

While Williamson was off sorting out his new show, *Dawson's Creek* carried on without him, but it was a bumpy ride . . .

301
Like a Virgin

1st US Transmission Date: 29 September 1999

Writer: Tammy Ader
Director: Greg Prange
Guest Cast: Brittany Daniel (Eve Whitman),
Niklaus Lange (Rob),
Vanessa Dorman (Belinda McGovern),
Kelly Cheston (Madison Blackner),
Aubrey Dollar (Marcy Bender)

Dawson has spent the summer with his mother in Philadelphia. On the bus home he meets a beautiful girl who vanishes before he hits Capeside. Dawson sees Joey at school and asks Pacey to keep him away from her, so Pacey takes him to a strip club where the waitress turns out to be the girl from the bus. She turns up again, the next day, in Dawson's living room and he takes his dad's boat out to impress her. On the waves she tells him her name is Eve and she goes down on a startled Dawson (in front of a *very* startled home audience), so startled in fact that he crashes his boat straight into a jetty at the marina where Joey has been working all summer. The damage comes to $3,000. Eve takes a collection of tips from the strip club, but it's not enough.

Pacey decides to turn the Leery house into a strip club for a night, charge $20 entry and pay for the damage that way. During the ensuing wild party Dawson retreats to his room and finds Joey there. She apologises for pushing him away after her father's arrest and takes off her top, trying to initiate sex (at this point the home audience's hair is turning white in shock). Dawson refuses and tells her they can't get back together because he can't go through it all again. Joey leaves in tears and Dawson asks Pacey to go and check on her, which he does. Mitch returns early from coaching camp, where he's been training to be the new coach of the Capeside High football team, so Dawson has to decline Eve's offer to sail away with her for the night and lose his virginity.

Jen is so outraged by the bitchiness of the head cheerleader, Belinda McGovern, that she signs up to try out for the squad. At the audition, instead of doing a cheer, she demolishes Belinda and causes a coup – the cheerleaders sack Belinda and elect Jen head cheerleader.

The Ballad of Dawson and Joey: Joey realised pretty quickly that she shouldn't have pushed Dawson away after her father's arrest, but she didn't contact him all summer because she was ashamed. She tells Bessie that she and Dawson made up and then talked themselves blue in the face, but later admits that was just how she wishes it had gone.

The Movie Brat: Welcome the New Dawson, all action and no angst. As ever, when he takes action it's a total disaster because it's just not him – 'a man's character is his fate', he says, but he's going against his character.

The Tomboy: Welcome the New Joey: no longer sweet, innocent, feisty or funny, she tries to excuse her mistakes by taking off her clothes and jumping Dawson while delivering the simply embarrassing line, 'I can be sexual.' The charming ingénue is gone; this Joey is a scattershot mix of brazen sexuality and bad psychology. She's spent the summer working at a local marina.

The Clown: Welcome the New Pacey: gone is the charming wide boy of old, and instead we have a crude, lewd imposter. The point of Pacey is that he confounds expectations; when you think he's going to be crude he's charming, when you think he's going to be stupid he's smart, and vice versa. The Pacey we get in this episode is an amalgam of every clichéd best-friend character from every third-rate teen movie ever made. All the subtlety and character is gone, replaced by a leering, over-the-top caricature.

The Delinquent: Welcome the New Jen: champion of the weak, scourge of the bully, popular girl and head cheerleader. Of all the characters this week she is closest to her old self – it's a stretch to accept her actions, but they are logical and she displays serious style in her devastating attack on Belinda. Her mortification when she finds out she's been elected head cheerleader is the only really funny moment in the episode.

School Sucks!: There's a new principal in town, Principal Green, and he seems pretty cool: 'You children are thinking like people twice your age . . . reclaim your youth, live, learn, screw up.' He still gives Pacey detention for talking in assembly, though.

That Three-Letter Word: Pacey has a vision and tells Dawson, 'Sometime during the course of this year you are going to get laid.' Dawson describes *Risky Business* as about 'a teenage boy who passes into manhood via a sexual encounter with a beautiful woman who's essentially a fantasy character of his own creation', so when Eve tells Dawson that she's 'a fantasy of your own creation' it's clear what she thinks her role is. She thinks 'the problem with teenage sex is that it's something you do, something you get done' and when he remarks that her name is biblical she says, 'I'll try and live up to it' before disappearing below the camera level and going for his zip. Then the boat crashes and at first we're not sure if Eve ever got any further than that, but Dawson later tells Pacey and his reply – 'at least her jaw didn't lock' – pretty much confirms that the deed was done. Also, when Dawson tells Pacey how much the damage to the boat will cost, Pacey remarks, 'Next to Bill Clinton you will have paid more for a certain service than anyone I know.' (These remarks appear to have been cut from all repeats of the episode, which leaves the deed ambiguous.) During his party Joey, thinking that 'sex is all [he's] about these days' tries to seduce Dawson. Mitch's return scotches a night with Eve.

Metatextuality: One girl sings her audition cheer to Paula Cole's theme music.

All Things Spielberg: Dawson is watching *Risky Business* (Paul Brickman, 1983) on the bus, and this whole episode is basically *Dawson's Creek*'s ill-advised version of it. It must have sounded like a good idea in the script meeting.

Grown-Up Stuff: Welcome the New Mitch: from substitute teacher to head coach of the school football team, the Minutemen, in a few short months. This is the great dream he's been waiting to pursue? And when did Mitch get a boat? In **212**, 'Uncharted Waters', he was hardly a seasoned sea dog.

Kiss and Tell: Eve kisses Dawson, who looks as if he'd been struck by lightning.

Our Quips Are Wittier: Pacey asks Dawson what happened to the girl on the bus and he replies, 'She morphed into an octogenarian Spanish woman with a hairy upper lip.'

Blooper: Sleepy ol' Capeside now has a strip club, but it's a club where the women *never take off their bras*! Nor do they disrobe at the Leery House Of Ill Repute. Obviously, this is merely an imposition of the timeslot, but it's just absurd.

Guest Cast: Beauteous Brittany Daniel was, with her sister Cynthia, one of the two leads in *Sweet Valley High*. She was also memorable as Blinkie opposite Leo DiCaprio in *The Basketball Diaries*. Kelly Cheston has had regular stints on the supersoaps *All My Children* and *One Life To Live* and can be glimpsed in Denzel Washington's vehicle, *Remember The Titans*. Vanessa Dorman was a regular on *Sunset Beach*. Niklaus Lange was the eponymous lead in *Kilroy* a TV movie co-written by George Clooney. Obba Babatundé has appeared in more television shows than I can name, but they include *The Fresh Prince of Bel-Air*, *Sliders* and *Chicago Hope*. He's equally ubiquitous on the big screen – you may have seen him in *The Silence of the Lambs*, *Philadelphia* or *Multiplicity*.

Contempo Pop Music: Bob Seger's 'Old Time Rock and Roll' opens the new season and serves notice that this is a raunchier, harder show. 'Who's Who' by the Pretenders, 'Push It' and 'Sleep Together' by Garbage, 'Let Us Sing' by Tricky Woo (surely the only band ever named after a fictional dog from a series about a Northern English vet), 'Dead Again' by Buckcherry and 'Hold On' by Mary Beth.

Mark Mothersbaugh makes his incidental-music debut and it just sounds all wrong. It's drums and organs and it's sassy and aggressive, and it's just not *Dawson's Creek*.

Ker-THUNK!: Dawson is throwing a party, his dad's away. It would be so much fun if his dad came back unexpectedly and found him at it! Actually, no, it wouldn't: it would be predictable and lame. No excuse is ever offered for Mitch's early return: it just happens because that's what's supposed to happen in TV when a young character thinks it's safe to throw a party. Lazy writing. And will someone please tell me where Pacey got a guy named Gino to be bouncer for the evening?

The Big Issue: Pacey: 'Teenage boys will come. They will most definitely come.'

The Last Word: Dawson says it best: 'There's something *so* not right about this.' Kevin Williamson leaves and it all goes horribly wrong. Just consider this for a moment: Dawson gets picked up by a strange girl on a bus; he then meets her again in a strip bar; she gives him a blow job in a speedboat which he then crashes before filling his house with strippers and charging admission! What were the writers and producers *thinking*? Had they never seen the show before? This is a disastrously ill-advised mess of an episode that sets entirely the wrong tone from the start and just gets worse with every passing frame. In an interview on Channel 4 later in the year James Van Der Beek explained that the season started terribly because they hired someone 'who didn't like the show', but it didn't need him to say that for it to be crystal clear (for more see **Backstage** in **305**, 'Indian Summer'). At one point Dawson says, 'This past year has been a hellish nightmare. I spent it verbalising and angsting instead of living.' And it's hard not to take that as an explicit condemnation by the writer of the show they're writing for. Every scene feels wrong to a greater or lesser degree and only at the very end, with Pacey and Joey at the dock, does this resemble the Capeside of old. All the characters are wrong; Dawson tells Eve 'this isn't me' and then tells Joey 'this isn't you'. And this isn't *Dawson's Creek*.

302
Homecoming

1st US Transmission Date: 6 October 1999

Writer: Greg Berlanti
Director: Melanie Mayron
Guest Cast: Brittany Daniel (Eve Whitman),
David Dukes (Mr McPhee), Chris Demetral (Marc)

It's time for Andie to return to Capeside and Pacey goes to fetch her a day early. Joey tags along and helps him get into the hospital without permission. He finds Andie with a guy, Marc. Pacey and Andie leave and, although Andie is trying not to show it, she is crying as they drive away. She then avoids being alone with Pacey until he confronts her at the football team's pep rally and she admits she slept with Marc. Pacey is disgusted and walks away. Later he tells her he can't face being with her any more and they break up.

Eve is now a senior at Capeside High and she offers Dawson sex, which sounds fine to him. She tells him to be prepared. She will choose the time and place and surprise him. Dawson edits a film for the pep rally that will feature the debut of Jen's newly sardonic cheerleading squad. At the rally Eve arrives, tells Dawson it's time, and starts taking his clothes off behind the screen showing this film. It looks like Dawson's going to lose his virginity but he sits on a button that raises the screen and there they are – semi-clothed and making out in front of the entire school. Joey is appalled, but comes to visit Dawson later and they agree they will just be friends for now.

Jack is recruited to the football team as wide receiver to the new quarterback, freshman Henry Parker. Jack's dad has moved to Capeside but Jack remains with Grams.

The Ballad of Dawson and Joey: Dawson is glad that Pacey is looking out for Joey. Eve asks if Dawson is over 'the brunette it took you all of five minutes to bring up on the bus' and, when he tells her he is, she knows he's lying. After the incident at the pep rally Joey comes to see Dawson and says, 'In some weird way it helped me . . . we really do need to move on and to meet new people and have new relationships.' She now agrees it would be wrong to get back together and they decide to just be 'Dawson and Joey'. Dawson gives her the necklace he has worn since the first episode as a symbol of their new beginning.

The Ballad of Andie and Pacey: Pacey is nervous about seeing Andie again but his early arrival catches her unawares and it's clear from the very first moment that there is something going on between her and Marc. Pacey tries to shrug it off and Andie tries to pretend nothing's wrong, but it's too obvious that Andie's keeping a secret. When she avoids being alone with him time after time Pacey has to force the issue. He's worried she wants to end things and she says, 'That's the last thing I want.' But, when she admits that she slept with Marc and asks Pacey to forgive her, he just can't get over it. Joey persuades him to talk to Andie, and he does, reluctantly, and with this speech their relationship ends: 'Our relationship was like this beautiful thing . . . you inspired me to be a man I'd only ever dreamed of being . . . it dawned on me I might not be that person for you. I can never go back to loving you the way I did knowing that my love wasn't strong enough first time around. I could always forgive you, Andie, but I will never forget.' It's surprising that there's no long drawn-out storyline to end such a major saga, just a quick admission, a shocked response and that's all. It's brutal but it rings true, and Monroe plays it superbly.

The Movie Brat: Dawson has never been closer to losing his virginity but he seems to be cursed. Eve tells him to be prepared, so he has to go to the pharmacy and buy condoms. Trying to build up the courage, he buys power bars, films and lifesavers before making the mistake of asking for them at the counter when they're on an aisle like everything else. It's a classic humiliation/rite-of-passage scene and Dawson's face is a mask of embarrassment as other shoppers hand on advice till he wants the ground to open up and swallow him. Maybe because he's had his fill of humiliation for the day he actually handles their impromptu appearance before the school with great aplomb, taking a bow and seeing the funny side.

The Tomboy: Pacey got Joey in to see her father in jail at the end of Season One (**112**, 'Decisions'). Now she repays the debt by distracting the receptionist at the sanatorium so he can get in to see Andie. Joey seems to be almost back to her old self. The resolution of her feelings for Dawson also gives the character room to breathe again.

The Clown: The shock and hurt of Andie's betrayal could be enough to destroy Pacey's tenuous grip on his school results and send him off the rails again. He's angry, hurt and disappointed, and he doesn't leave any chance for reconciliation. Like Joey, he has been freed from previous storylines in preparation for a new beginning.

The Delinquent: Jen's cheerleading debut is a riot. In cowboy boots and ripped fishnets, she leads a lacklustre chant, which goes: 'We've got style, we've got class, so what if those other guys kick our ass.'

The Basket Case: Andie's the bad girl of the piece, betraying Pacey and destroying their love, but her story is so believable and she was so vulnerable and alone that she doesn't really lose our sympathy: 'I was scared they were never going to let me out of there or that whatever was broken inside of me wouldn't be fixable.' Her character existed last year only as a foil for Pacey, but within one episode of the new season that relationship is ended and so she too is released for new storylines.

The Outsider: Mitch's first act as coach is to appoint Jack as wide receiver of the team, and Jack's not happy because 'a gay kid on the football team – now if that isn't a written invitation to ridicule, what is?' He allows himself to be persuaded, against his better judgment, and when he makes his entrance at the pep rally he looks as if he wants to vanish, but he gets a stirring round of applause and visibly bucks up. Grams on Jack: 'After a year with Jennifer, having Jack was like boarding St Francis.'

The Puppy Dog: Welcome Henry Parker, freshman student, star quarterback of the Minutemen and as persistent and annoying as a hyperactive terrier. When he first sees Jen the world goes slo-mo and he looks as if a truck had hit him.

Family Sucks!: Mr McPhee has moved his business to Capeside and returned home to live with Andie and his wife, but he tells Jack, 'The changes that you are going to make in your life right now, the changes you have every right to make, would be too difficult with me around.' He thinks it would be best for Jack to stay with Grams, a decision Jack resents. It seems, however, that his dad may actually be trying to do the best thing for Jack, because he approaches him after the pep rally, and asks him to come home because 'when I saw you in that jersey, for the first time in a while, I saw myself in you'. Jack refuses but says his father should ask him again sometime.

That Three-Letter Word: Eve, whom Pacey describes as 'a femme fatale whose entire genetic coding screams "objectify me"', offers Dawson 'a night of scorching hot, unbridled, mind-altering sex' and he accepts. After the screening incident, Dawson decides not to spend the night hanging out with her because 'all you are to me is sex . . . the first time I sleep with somebody I don't want it to be for just any reason: I want it to be for every reason'. Never has Dawson been so close and yet so far. Jen's advice to Dawson on sexual technique is a masterpiece of unsubtle innuendo that pushes it about as far as possible without getting the show yanked off air: 'First you have to watch the sundae, admire the sundae, then, just before it's about to drip, you let your lips lick round the exterior, savouring every inch . . . if you remember one thing let it be this: if you don't get the whipped cream all over your face, you're not doing it right.'

All Things Spielberg: Principal Green is a film buff. When asking Dawson to edit the Pep rally footage he cites Capra's use of film to recruit during the war and the influence *Annie Hall* (Woody Allen, 1977) had on women's fashions. Dawson, on the other hand, thinks that using film for propaganda purposes is too much like Leni Riefenstahl, a brilliant female director whose famous documentary *Triumph of the Will* (1934) contains some of the most powerful images ever captured on film, but uses them to glorify Nazi Germany.

Grown-Up Stuff: Mitch got the coach's job because 'nobody wanted to coach a team that had been so bad for so long . . . it couldn't actually be any tougher than the last year of my life'. He seems to have them pretty well drilled already. Maybe he's found his calling.

Kiss and Tell: Eve locks lips with Dawson in a closet at school and then on stage in front of the whole world.

Our Quips Are Wittier: Try saying this three times fast: 'nervous anticipation doesn't cause spontaneous combustion'.

Blooper: James Van Der Beek fluffs a line at the start when he says to Josh, 'It's nervous that you're . . . It's natural that you're nervous'.

Guest Cast: This was Michael Pitt's big break, but he has since chosen his movie projects with care, appearing in *Finding Forrester* with Sean Connery and in the critically acclaimed *Hedwig and the Angry Inch*. At the time of writing he has roles in two forthcoming films, *Bully* and alongside Sandra Bullock in *Fool Proof*. Chris Demetral has an impressive list of TV appearances in shows from *Star Trek – The Next Generation* through *Blossom* and *Beverly Hills 90210*; he plays Jules Verne in *The Secret Adventures of Jules Verne*.

Contempo Pop Music: 'Bodyrock' by Moby, 'Days And Days' by the Nines and Tuck and Patti's cover of Cyndi Lauper's classic 'Time After Time'.

The Big Issue: Joey tells Pacey, 'We talk like we know what's going on but we don't: we don't have any idea. Look, we're really young and we're going to screw up a lot . . . we're going to keep changing our minds and sometimes even our hearts, and through all of that the only real thing we can offer each other is forgiveness.'

The Last Word: That's a relief! After the previous episode it seemed that the show was dead, but although there are still elements that feel out of place, most notably Eve, this almost feels like *Dawson's Creek* again. Andie remarks, 'Jen's a cheerleader, Jack's on the football team, I got sane and everyone else went crazy?' which somewhat deflates the wrongness of things. The characters seem largely back to normal, although Dawson still seems a bit off, and there's some real emotion and fun. With the resolution of the two major relationships of Season Two, Dawson/Joey and Andie/Pacey, the characters all feel fresh and the opportunity to tell new stories with them makes this feel like a season opener, so let's just pretend **301**, 'Like A Virgin', never happened.

303
None of the Above

1st US Transmission Date: 13 October 1999

Writer: Bonnie Schneider and Hadley Davis
Director: Patrick Norris
Guest Cast: Brittany Daniel (Eve Whitman),
Niklaus Lange (Rob)

Eve gives Dawson a copy of the upcoming Preliminary Standard Aptitude Test (PSAT) and he takes it to the gang for advice. The fire alarm goes off and Dawson has to leave the envelope with the test in it, behind. When he returns it's been taken. He gives the culprit till 5.30 to return it to his locker, but it isn't returned. Eve leads him to think of Pacey as the thief and he confronts him. They end up punching each other. When the test comes Dawson gets up and leaves, as does Pacey. They walk off, friends again, while in the classroom Andie begins filling in the answers – without having opened her test!

Andie collects all the things that remind her of Pacey and gives them back to him to symbolise the end of their relationship. Pacey gets drunk and turns up at the marina to cry on Joey's shoulder. He slips and drops the box into the creek.

Jack runs the gauntlet in football practice. Henry tells Jack he's in love with Jen.

The Ballad of Andie and Pacey: Their banter is now a bitter version of its previous self. Andie decides that 'this isn't going to be one of those long, drawn-out break-ups', dumps their history in a box and gives it back to him without a word of regret. When the photo of Andie and

Pacey sinks beneath the waves it takes all hope of reconciliation with it. And only Pacey seems to care.

The Movie Brat: Dawson wants to get to know Eve so they have a movie night, but her preference for TV kills it dead. Later she tempts him with a metaphorical apple, then with the real thing – the test paper. He doesn't throw it away, but takes it to the group and Joey remarks, 'Once again Dawson Leery proves that the groin is mightier than the brain.' And indeed he breaks into school, considers cheating on an exam, and starts a fight with his best friend. As Joey says, 'Throwing parties, crashing boats, upstaging marching bands – Dawson, if your rope was any more yanked you'd be a church bell.' Finally, after all the trouble she's led him into, he decides that he doesn't actually like Eve, says goodbye and walks away.

The Tomboy: Joey's losing sleep because of nerves but according to the principal she has a 'shot at a National Merit Scholarship'. She's pretty blunt about Eve, calling her a 'bleached blonde ho-bag' to Dawson's face. Her employer at the marina, Rob, asks her out and she politely declines, but later, when she makes a mistake, he docks her pay and revokes a night off in punishment for her refusal.

The Clown: When Andie cuts him loose, Pacey runs straight to Joey and the friendship between them continues to grow. He feels low because 'I thought if I'd earned anyone's respect it was Dawson's' and he starts into his old 'I'm a loser and nobody loves me' tune, which Joey soon dissipates by joking, 'I thought you were a loser for years but you've never believed me.'

The Basket Case: Last season Andie was a sympathetic character, but this year she's emerging as a hypocritical, heartless and unpleasant person. Her break-up with Pacey is merely a hiccup and she is now driven and single-minded: 'I have my life in order and I intend on doing everything I can to keep it that way. I have a plan.' Her treatment of him is harsh and she doesn't seem to care. To top it all, she steals the test from Dawson and then has the face to complain about how dishonest the thief is.

The Outsider: Jack thinks he's being singled out for rough treatment in football practice because he's gay, but Mitch assures him it's because he's a new boy. He wants to quit, but Jen points out that maybe he's meant to be 'a well known gay athlete who inspires others to come to terms with who they are'. He eventually slo-mos his way through the chute of players in triumph chanting his mantra, 'fug'.

The Puppy Dog: Henry is a spiritual quarterback, telling Jack he needs to chant a mantra before going into battle. He wants Jack's help to get close to Jen, and launches into the most impressive rhapsody: 'Every night, heavy dreams about her lips, her breasts, her legs. If she would just allow me near her, just smell her sweet smell, maybe even kiss me, take me in her arms, deliver me from suffering and falsity, it would prove there wasn't anything bad or anything empty-hearted in this world that couldn't be corrected.' Jack tells him he's got no chance at all, but later on, transfixed, Henry chants Jack's mantra as he runs towards Jen, veering off at the last minute and heading into space, leaving a very bewildered Jen behind.

That Three-Letter Word: Eve bluntly asks Dawson if they can have sex after watching TV and he doesn't rule it out. Given that the titles to the episode begin when they do it's possible to construe that they did. But they couldn't have – there's no angst!

Metatextuality: The teaser sequence is the best the show has ever produced. Dawson hates TV and says, 'If you've seen one hour of whiny, overanalytical teen angst, you've seen them all,' and goes on to describe Felicity, in the show of that name that comes on the WB after *Dawson's Creek* as 'indecisive . . . paralysed by some romantic notion of the way things are supposed to be . . . kind of chatty'. So they're criticising their stable mate on the grounds that it's too much like, um, *Dawson's Creek*. Eve instantly points out that she's Dawson, and, although Dawson protests that he's not a fictional character on a television show we all know he is. Eve thinks he's 'straight out of central casting, perfect hair, perfect skin, you're a hero', to which Dawson, wonderfully, replies, 'You obviously weren't watching last season: it was far from perfect.' It just gets better as Eve tells him, 'That's where I come in, second season, shake things up, screw with the status quo'. She's the 'temptress who will test our hero's moral fibre', according to Dawson. 'Will he survive unscathed?' she asks. Stay tuned at the start of the episode when she tempts him most explicitly. Finally, as she moves in to kiss him, Dawson moans, 'You know what else I hate about television? . . . they always cut to commercials at the best part' – and cut to credits. Genius.

All Things Spielberg: Jen's 'half-assed . . . reverse psychology' is so obvious that Jack protests, 'I'm not Beaver Cleaver and we're not in black and white here.' The homey old TV show *Leave It To Beaver* ran from 1957 to 1963.

Guy Talk: Pacey calls Dawson a 'self-righteous son of a bitch who cares more about his rose-coloured, defunct 1950s' belief system than the people who fail to live up to it', while Dawson calls Pacey 'weak . . . self-motivated, a smug cold-hearted son of a bitch who just dumped his girlfriend after she begged and pleaded for an ounce of sympathy'. When Pacey accuses Dawson of sending Joey's dad to prison, and Dawson accuses Pacey of sending Andie crazy, it's inevitable that they're going to swing for each other. At the end Dawson decides that 'if we're gonna beat the crap out of each other it should at least be over a chick'.

Our Quips Are Wittier: While practising for the PSAT, Jack basically tells the audience: 'What, you thought that Dawson was the only one with such a prolific vocabulary?'

Contempo Pop Music: 'Absolutely (Story of a Girl)' by Nine Days, 'Swaying' by Train, 'Speak of the Devil' by Chris Isaak, 'You Won't See Me Cry' by Sue Medley and 'From My Head To My Heart' by Evan and Jaron.

Ker-THUNK!: The episode is predicated upon Dawson's getting the PSAT in advance, but we never get a hint of how Eve got it for him. Also, the security guard would not only have to be blind to not see Eve and Dawson under the school desk, but deaf not to hear them talking as he walks past.

The Big Issue: 'The most obvious choice is usually the wrong one.'

The Last Word: A nice little mystery, with Eve filling a recognisable and interesting narrative role – made explicit when she brings Dawson an apple. The MacGuffin of the stolen test is unexplained and a bit too convenient, but the tensions it reveals in the group play well, as do the shock ending and the revelation that Andie was the thief. Apart from the teaser sequence, this season still doesn't feel like *Dawson's Creek*, though.

304
Home Movies

1st US Transmission Date: 20 October 1999

Writer: Jeffrey Stepakoff
Director: Nick Marck

Dawson is commissioned to do a piece on Jack ('gay kid on the football team') for his mother's TV show. Mitch tries to persuade Dawson not to shoot the piece because he doesn't want the whole world to know about Jack's sexuality and footballing ability before the game. Dawson defies Mitch and the piece is broadcast. Mitch blames Dawson for ruining his plans, and when the game is played Capeside is losing massively at half-time because the opposing side is destroying Jack. Dawson and Jen come to the rescue. They smear mud on the jerseys so the opposition can't identify Jack. They also put make-up on every member of the Capeside team. The opposition are put off their game and Jack scores the winning goal. Mitch apologises to Dawson and they patch things up.

Jen discovers that the cheerleaders are running an auction, the prize being a kiss from Jen. She resigns rather than go through with it, but when someone pays $500, and she finds out the money goes to orphans, she agrees. Henry has paid the money and Jen kisses him in front of the whole school. Then she is crowned Homecoming Queen.

Pacey persuades Joey to skip school to go on a secret mission with him. They walk out of town to the post office to collect a package and on their way back are picked up by Principal Green. As punishment they have to dress up as the football mascot – the Minutemen Mule – and let the auction winner ride them on his way to kiss Jen. They get two freshmen to do it instead. Pacey takes Joey to see a wrecked boat he has bought and intends to renovate. The package they collected is the nameplate for the boat – *True Love*.

Andie meets a man from the Educational Testing Service in school and is worried that her cheating on the PSATs (**303**, 'None of the Above') has been discovered. Later, Principal Green approaches Andie and makes an appointment with her to discuss a discipline problem. Andie prepares a speech of apology for her cheating, but it turns out he wants her to head a new student discipline committee.

The Ballad of Dawson and Joey: Dawson finds an old tape of his first meeting with Joey. The first thing Joey did when she met Dawson was push him over and run away!

The Ballad of Pacey and Joey: In this episode it becomes clear that the writers are pushing Joey and Pacey together. Their banter is starting to resemble Andie and Pacey at the same point last season, and even Principal Green recognises that they've got an 'affinity with one another'.

The Clown: Pacey's boat, *True Love*, makes its first appearance; it will be a regular feature for the rest of the season.

The Delinquent: Jen never wanted to be head cheerleader, so it was only a matter of time before she resigned. Her soft heart leads her to agree to the kiss auction, and she seems touched by Henry's mad gesture. Her utter horror at being crowned Homecoming Queen is hilarious.

The Basket Case: Andie is a mess of panic when she thinks her cheating has been discovered, and she nearly gives the game away to Principal Green before he stops her. The apology speech she rehearses is touching and details how she's been destroyed by losing Pacey, who she says is her soul mate.

The Wicked Witch: Grams used to be a cheerleader in school.

The Outsider: Jack seems pretty relaxed about coming out now, and doesn't seem concerned about going on national television to talk about being a gay football star. He gets pummelled by the opposing team but manages to stay the distance and win the game.

The Puppy Dog: The first word Henry manages to say to Jen is the hopelessly romantic 'mouthpiece'. When he gets to kiss the girl whose 'very name is fire in my loins', he looks stunned.

Family Sucks!: For the first time real chinks appear in Dawson's relationship with Mitch and they come into conflict over Dawson's TV piece. Mitch is at first patronising and then angry that Dawson went through with it, believing it lost him the game before it even started. Dawson responds by saying that he's the one who has to parent Mitch and resents not being able to be the child every now and then. Mitch realises that his role as a father is not to provide all the answers, but to 'try to help'. He reaches out to Dawson and offers to go home and watch *Close Encounters* . . . with him, but in the end settles for leaving the football on the pitch and not letting it interfere with his relationship with Dawson again.

School Sucks!: Principal Green is crazy about football. Mitch isn't doing well as a substitute teacher so the coach's job is crucial to keeping his place at the school. The mascot of the Capeside football team, the Minutemen, is a mule.

Reality Bites: Dawson's decision to film a TV news item surprises Pacey but Dawson sticks to his credo: 'Real life is interesting but it'll never be as dramatic as a well-conceived narrative ... as soon as I get my foot in that proverbial door I'll be right back in the magical land of make-believe.'

Metatextuality: Pacey says that no narrative could be 'more thrilling, more sexy and more far-fetched' than Dawson's recent adventures. Normally this self-aware commentary would be amusing, but the episodes with Eve were way too far-fetched for comfort.

All Things Spielberg: Pacey lectures Joey on the art of hitching a lift and cites the classic teen flick *The Sure Thing* (Rob Reiner, 1985) as demonstrating that a girl will always get picked up more quickly than a guy.

All Things Freud: When Dawson asks Joey for advice on how to handle his problem with his father, afraid that challenging Mitch will 'kill him', she tells him that 'according to Freud, that's exactly what sons are supposed to do'.

Kiss And Tell: Henry sells his lucky charm – the famous quarterback Doug Flutie's mouthpiece – to raise $500 to kiss Jen, who doesn't know whether to be disgusted or flattered. When he offers to let her back out she gives him a smackerooni and the world goes slo-mo again.

Contempo Pop Music: 'Static' by Bleach, Sue Medley's 'Break the Chain', 'I'm Sorry Now' by Jude, Mad Lion's 'Go To War', 'Man With a Hex' by Atomic Fireballs and 'I Do', also by Jude.

The Last Word: This isn't up to much. In Season One the show ridiculed bad football movies with *Helmets of Glory* but now they're reduced to making their own version, and it's lame. Having conflict between Mitch and Dawson is an interesting move, but the sappy speech that resolves it is mawkish and leaden. Andie's proving difficult to write for – her storyline is not only contrived but it's unconnected to everything else in the episode. Having the team wear make-up stretches believability beyond breaking point: we're expected to believe that a group of rough-and-ready high school footballers doesn't contain one muscle-brained homophobic oaf who would refuse? The Pacey and Joey scenes work beautifully, and Jen's role fits nicely into the main story, but otherwise this is another disappointment.

305
Indian Summer

1st US Transmission Date: 27 October 1999

Writers: Gina Fattore and Tom Kapinos
Director: Lou Antonio
Guest Cast: Brittany Daniel (Eve Whitman),
Niklaus Lange (Rob Logan), Dylan Neal (Doug Witter)

Dawson sees a flashlight in Grams's house and calls the police to report a break-in. He goes to investigate and finds Eve climbing out of Grams's window. He demands an explanation but she threatens to report him for taking the PSAT test and so he tells Deputy Doug that he made a mistake. Eve vanishes. Dawson checks at school and finds out she was never enrolled there and the strip joint won't give him any help because he's underage. Doug suggests that Dawson stake out the Laundromat, but he eventually sees her buying an ice cream and follows her back to a large yacht in the harbour. After she has left, Dawson breaks in and finds a faded old photograph of a young woman, which he steals. Doug finds him, thinking he is a thief, and tells Dawson that the boat belongs to an eighty-year-old couple who are not here, so Eve must be squatting. Doug also says that they're looking for someone who stole a speedboat a few weeks back (the implication is that this was the boat Eve was driving in **301,** 'Like a Virgin'). Eve turns up in Dawson's room demanding her photo back. He refuses until she tells him the truth. She says that she found out last year that she was adopted and she knows her mother came from the coast, so she's looking for her. The picture is of her mother. She was in Grams's house looking to steal something to pay for her next bus fare. Dawson returns the picture. Eve leaves, saying she's going to try a new town. Later that day Dawson sees a picture of Grams's daughter, Jen's mother, and recognises her as the woman in Eve's picture.

Henry cannot bring himself to ask Jen out on a date, so Jack arranges a meeting with Jen and sends Henry in his place. Jen is very angry at being set up, tells Henry to ask her next time, and storms off home to give Jack a piece of her mind.

Rob, Joey's boss from the marina, takes Andie out on a date to the newly reopened Rialto. Joey is horrified, because Rob has been making endless unsubtle passes at her all summer. She leaves work early and crashes the date, trying to prevent Rob doing anything nasty to Andie. Andie resents Joey's intrusion, but she refuses to leave. Next day Rob fires Joey for leaving work early.

The Movie Brat: Dawson doesn't understand film noir: it's too murky, dangerous and sexually driven for him ever to comprehend. The hapless hero who falls for the femme fatale because he's blinded by lust is a character Dawson could never identify with, as he's proved by his ability to reject repeatedly the lovely Eve's advances. But he does lie to the police for her, play detective to try to track her down, follow her across town, break into her home and steal from her, so maybe he's got more in common with the doomed heroes of noir than he thinks.

The Delinquent: Jen just wants a male friend who's not going to walk away when she says she won't sleep with him, and that's what Jack's for. She now considers him her best friend.

The Basket Case: Andie meets Rob at the country club and agrees to go out with him because he went to prep school with her dead brother, Tim. She's flirtatious and confident and resents Joey's interference. She attacks Joey's judgment, citing Dawson and Jack as examples of Joey's lack of sophistication with guys, and tells Joey that she's 'moving on with [her] life'.

The Outsider: Jack tries to help Henry and Jen by bringing them together but it backfires. He feels alone in Capeside because there isn't really any gay community. Jen reassures him that he'll have a love life one day, and it'll be great, but he's not convinced.

The Puppy Dog: Henry clams up when he sees Jen in school: 'My hard drive crashes, I go pre-verbal.' When he waits to meet her at Jack's rendezvous he is preparing phrases he's written on his hand to help him get through the evening. He tells her how he feels, although the eloquence he's displayed when describing her to Jack in previous episodes is all gone: 'You're awesome, you look awesome, you smell awesome, everything about you is awesome.' Jen is so annoyed that he tried to arrange a date by stealth it seems he's damaged his chances. Jen is disturbed by the way he 'looks at me like I'm a pornographic fantasy come to life'. He is fifteen.

Family Sucks!: Deputy Doug makes a welcome return but Pacey's fascination with Doug's sexuality reaches ever greater heights (see **104**, 'Hurricane') and is becoming, as Doug says, 'plain weird'. In the face of an onslaught of innuendo from Pacey, Doug screams that he is not gay and walks off.

That Three-Letter Word: Pacey on Dawson: 'Not all of us are as immune to the allure of sex as you are . . . most of us are just big dumb guys happy to sell our souls for the *slimmest* chance of getting some.' Eve tries to distract Dawson from telling the police with 'the suggestion of teen lesbianism' – she fantasises that she and Jen are having an affair. Jen is glad that sex will never be an issue between her and Jack because he's the only guy she's ever been friends with who hasn't wanted to go to bed with her.

Metatextuality: Eve describes Dawson's friends as '*Sweet Valley High* extras', the show in which Brittany Daniel was the lead.

All Things Spielberg: The Rialto reopens with *Blue Streak* (Les Mayfield,1999). The noir film that Dawson is watching at the start stars Orson Welles. It's hard to identify from the brief glimpse but it looks like *Trent's Last Case* (Herbert Wilcox, 1952). Pacey tempts Dawson with *Wild Things* (John McNaughton, 1998).

Guy Talk: Pacey dispenses classic Capeside wisdom to Dawson: 'There are some women who come on to the movie set that is your life and function solely as day players. They'll show up, they know their dialogue, they'll hit their marks, they'll occasionally steal a scene or two from you, but they will remain always and for ever an impenetrable mystery.'

Our Quips Are Wittier: Pacey, tiring of movie night: 'All this rapid-fire deconstruction is making me weary, Leery.'

Contempo Pop Music: In keeping with the film-noir theme of the episode, Mark Mothersbaugh provides a lot of moody saxophone music, so there are only two songs in this episode: 'Before You' by Chantal Kreviazuk and 'Swim' by Madonna.

Ker-THUNK!: Eve is Jen's half-sister. And Eve is breaking into Jen's house at night. Eve has never had a scene with Jen, and prior to this episode we have no reason to believe she even knows Jen exists, yet she throws her name around Dawson's bedroom as if they were old buddies. We're supposed to believe that Eve's breaking into that house, the only house in Capeside that holds the evidence she was searching for, was just a coincidence?

Backstage: In a chat on the *Dawson's Creek* website, the writer and producer Tom Kapinos had this to say about Eve: 'Eve was an absolute mistake from the word GO. She was the product of a show runner who, on the first day of work, boasted that he had never seen the show, didn't like the show, and was being paid $2 million a year to run the show! The show runner is the person who is in charge of the day-to-day creative voice of the show. He's in charge of putting out every script, making sure it's up to his standards, and he's the person the network and the studio will come down on in the event that they don't like something.'

The Last Word: The film-noir pastiche is well done – the music, camera angles, the hot summer setting all help conjure an authentically noirish air. By the end Eve has left for good and although a new storyline emerges for her they never bring her back to the show. In **306,** 'Secrets and Lies', Rob is also written out and the show effectively reboots and begins the season again. It's clear that the characters of Eve and Rob don't really fit well in the world of *Dawson's Creek* and have skewed the balance of the show away from its core merits – character, dialogue, real emotional development. This isn't a bad episode, and it continues the trend of episodes that play with movie genres, but, as Pacey says to Dawson, 'No self-respecting son of Spielberg would feel comfortable in a morally ambiguous world populated with hard-boiled antiheroes and duplicitous femme fatales.' And that world sits uneasily in Capeside.

306
Secrets And Lies

1st US Transmission Date: 10 November 1999

Writers: Greg Berlanti and Alex Gansa
Director: Greg Prange
Guest Cast: Niklaus Lange (Rob Logan),
K Callan (Constance Freckling)

Jen meets Constance Freckling, Capeside's oldest living Homecoming Queen (or HQ as they're called), who plans a gala every year with that year's HQ. Constance's insistence on decorum and presentation irritates Jen, but Henry, who lives next door to Constance and considers himself her best friend, persuades Jen that she's all right and vice versa. Jen agrees to arrange the entertainment and invites Henry to be her date. On the night Jen arrives with a quartet of drag queens. The night goes very well and Constance has a good time in spite of her initial reservations. Henry asks Jen out and tells her he loves her. She tries to let him down gently, but he's devastated.

Andie goes to a party at Rob's house and later calls Joey in tears. Pacey and Joey arrive and Andie says that Rob tried to force himself on her. Pacey storms into the house and punches Rob. Andie refuses to call the police since nothing really happened. Pacey takes her to his boat and Andie tells Pacey she wants him back. Pacey spends the night with her.

Next day, Rob visits Joey and protests his innocence. When Joey mentions this, Andie becomes very defensive. So, when Pacey tells Andie that they made a mistake and their relationship is over, Andie thinks Joey has told him that she made up the incident as a way of forcing Pacey and her back together. Joey denies it and it becomes clear that Andie *did* make up the incident for those reasons.

Gale returns from Philadelphia for the HQ gala. Dawson finds out that she's been fired from her job for being too old. She doesn't want to run back to Capeside but, on Dawson's urging, she goes and talks about it to Mitch.

Joey and Bess are using their insurance money from the Icehouse fire to turn their house into a bed-and-breakfast.

The Ballad of Andie and Pacey: Andie tells Pacey how devastated she's been since breaking up with him. She's not over him, says that he's the one, seduces him and tries to get everything back to the way it was. The day after they sleep together is the first time she's felt happy since leaving hospital. Pacey, however, takes her to his boat to demonstrate that he's OK since they split, and that he's channelling his frustrations into something positive. He resists her overtures at first, but finally goes with the flow, although it's clear that he regrets it instantly. She thinks their night together was perfect; he thinks it was a terrible mistake, and tells her, 'There used to be a time when you and I were so in sync with everything we did, just connected, and look at us now – we have the opposite reaction to the exact same event.' She thinks he's punishing her and is still angry but Pacey just tells her she's not the one and that he feels as if he went against what he knew was right.

The Ballad of Henry and Jen: Jen sees the softer side of Henry and tells him, 'You keep wearing your heart on your sleeve like that and you're going to bleed to death.' She flirts with him, wraps his arm around her, strokes his leg, holds his hand – the poor lad doesn't know what's hit him. Constance tells Jen Henry adores her and warns Jen not to break his heart, so when he tries to kiss her Jen stops him. He tells her he's in love with her but she dismisses it gently and tells him that she won't be ready for a relationship until she can 'look at [herself] without judgment or condemnation'.

The Tomboy: Joey suspects Andie's duplicity after Rob's visit but she dismisses it because she believes in her friends. Eventually, though, she finds out what Andie has done and comforts her as Andie confesses how lost she feels without Pacey.

The Clown: Pacey makes turning the Potter house into a B&B a lot easier by drafting in the local Police Auxiliary to help. The banter between him and Joey is still there. He's gutted when he finds out Andie is dating Rob and when confronted by a crisis he acts as he always does: he charges in to be Andie's hero, just as she knew he would.

The Delinquent: Jen's mother was Miss Cape Cod and tried to mould Jen into a debutante. Jen is horrified at being HQ and worries that she's sold out and is turning into her mother. She rejects Constance at first, unwilling to play a role that isn't her, but she finds a way to get through it – hiring four drag queens to make a point about dressing up to pretend to be someone you're not.

The Basket Case: If the Andie of this season is the sane, cured Andie, then give us back the mad one. First she sleeps with someone else (**302**, 'Homecoming'), then she gives Pacey back all his stuff and steals the PSAT paper (**303**, 'None of the Above'), she dates sleazeball Rob (**305**, 'Indian Summer') and now she's so far gone that she fakes a sexual assault to try to get Pacey back. Andie may be driven, determined and stubborn, but this season she's also dangerous, selfish and out of control.

The Puppy Dog: Henry's quite the little softie: he's Constance's best friend, builds bridges and helps out and is altogether a mother's dream. He becomes a de facto regular when he is shown walking alone, broken-hearted, in the final broody-music montages.

Grown-Up Stuff: Gale surprises Dawson and Mitch by returning for the HQ gala – she was HQ herself sometime in the seventies. Mitch seems nonplussed when she asks Dawson, not him, to be her escort for the gala. She's reluctant to talk to Mitch about being fired because they may end up becoming friends again. Dawson persuades her and we see Mitch and Gale at the end talking like old friends.

Kiss and Tell: Andie kisses Pacey and, after trying not to, he kisses her back. Henry tries to kiss Jen but she's having none of it.

Bloopers: Henry falls off Constance's roof and lands at Jen's feet after disturbing a bee's nest. But the house we saw Jen walk into was *huge*. Such a fall would have killed him outright.

Guest Cast: K Callan has had a long career on television and film. Her most high-profile role was as Mrs Kent in *Lois & Clark: The New Adventures of Superman*.

Contempo Pop Music: Meredith Brooks's 'Shout' is the song playing at Rob's party when Pacey confronts him, 'Get Me Through December' by Natalie MacMaster, the drag queens sing 'It's Raining Men', which was originally recorded by the Weather Girls, 'Super Good Feeling' by Bleach, and the final collection of brooding moments is accompanied by Chantal Kreviazuk's 'Eve'.

The Last Word: The show seems to be finding its way back to its old self, although the drag queens, amusing though they are, seem out of place. Also, it's hard to know where the writers are taking Andie, but her character this year feels very out of place and lost and her actions in this episode really deserve to be examined more closely because it was a major thing she did and should have had more serious repercussions. Constance is a terrific character, and it's great to have Gale back in town.

307
Escape From Witch Island

1st US Transmission Date: 17 November 1999

Writer: Tom Kapinos
Director: James Whitmore Jr
Guest Cast: Vanessa Dorman (Belinda McGovern),
Wayne Peré (Boatman), Liz Vassey (Wendy Dalrymple)

'In November of 1999 four hyper-verbal teenagers wandered off in the woods on Witch Island to film some ridiculous documentary for history class, and eight hours later two of them started making out . . .'

The class has to do a paper on *The Crucible* but Dawson gets permission to make a movie instead, with the help of Jen, Pacey and Joey. Off the coast is Witch Island, where thirteen young girls, accused of witchcraft, were banished in the 1700s. Local men used the island as a brothel until, one night, an outraged mob arrived, locked all the girls in a church, and burned it to the ground. Dawson and the gang go there to make a movie on witchcraft, which is a thinly veiled rip-off of *The Blair Witch Project*. On the island Dawson and Joey spend the time analysing their relationship and arguing over the island's mystery: there is one gravestone too few and one of the girls was due to be rescued by her lover the night of the fire. Dawson thinks they escaped; Joey thinks he betrayed her and she burned in the fire.

Jen and Pacey talk about why they've never hooked up and decide that there's nothing between them except friendship, so Jen playfully finds a love potion in a souvenir shop book and tries it out on Pacey.

The guide, Wendy, warns the gang not to go into the woods, but they take a map and go to find the church. Afterwards Pacey nips off to pee and Jen goes to find him while Joey and Dawson go to hold the boat. But the boat won't wait for them, and all four are stranded on the island for the night. Drawn by the ringing of the church bell, they all gather there and find the church *has* no bell. Pacey and Jen make a deal to try a sexual relationship without love, to save complications and hassle. They start to make out in the church. They are interrupted by flames and the sound of an angry mob, as the church doors lock, the missing bell tolls and fire bursts out at them from the walls. Almost as soon as the manifestation has started it stops again and they flee to the dock, where they find the boat and escape. When Dawson shows his documentary to the class a student spots two figures in seventeenth-century dress standing on the dock watching them leave. Dawson thinks it's the two lovers; Joey thinks it's the guide and the boatman, dressed up, playing tricks on them.

Andie takes her new job as discipline officer (**304**, 'Home Movies') too seriously and hands out hundreds of punishment slips. Principal Green is furious because she's been sticking strictly to guidelines written in 1956.

The Ballad of Dawson and Joey: When Joey and Dawson talk in the video shop he doesn't know about her being fired from the marina (**305**, 'Indian Summer') or starting a B&B (**306**, 'Secrets and Lies'), and she doesn't know that Eve left town. Joey feels that she and Dawson have drifted too far apart and she wants that old feeling back, but he still wants to be just friends. Dawson believes that they will find a way back to each other if they're truly meant to be. Joey is much less optimistic, thinks Dawson has a 'cloying and annoying world view' and is worried that their connection is broken for ever: 'Is this just the first act or is our story ended and we're just to stupid to realise it?' She admits that his rejection of her (**301**, 'Like a Virgin') really hurt. Back in Dawson's bedroom, she sums up their new beginning: 'We've spent years intellectualising every little feeling and it doesn't count for anything. All that matters is what we do, how we take care of each other. So let's not talk this to death: let's take it slow and check in with each other every once in a while.'

The Movie Brat: Dawson has missed movie making and regrets that things got so angsty that he lost sight of his cinematic ambitions.

The Clown: Pacey thinks he's 'brooding and comely' and admits that Jen is gorgeous, but she's not his type.

The Delinquent: Jen feels bad about breaking Henry's heart but admits she did it 'accidentally on purpose'.

That Three-Letter Word: Jen thinks a witch was simply 'a girl who happened to follow her completely healthy, totally natural urges and explore her sexuality' and admits that, were she living in 1690, 'I would *so* have been burned at the stake by now.'

Pacey decides that love is too much hard work and comes to the conclusion that 'casual sex is the way to go . . . the concept of two horny teenagers coming together for some gleefully nasty coitus and parting as friends is positively revolutionary.' In the end they agree that if they ever have any urges to vent or itches to scratch they can call each other up for guilt-free sex.

Reality Bites: The boatman allows Dawson to film him for his documentary as long as he can film Dawson for his – a film about people who are making films about Witch Island!

Metatextuality: When Pacey says he doesn't want to have sex because he's tired, Jen replies, 'Fine, *Roswell*'s on in five minutes, anyway.' She was right – at the time *Roswell* was on the WB right after *Dawson's Creek*.

All Things Spielberg: *The Blair Witch Project* (Daniel Myrick, Eduardo Sanchez, 1999) was a groundbreaking film made on a tiny budget and shot as a long improvisation. It was either the scariest movie ever made or a tedious student film of no merit, depending upon your viewpoint. Pacey and Jen hated it; Dawson and Joey loved it.

All Things Freud: Pacey out-deconstructs Dawson, and lays out all the writers' guidelines on character, with a stunning analysis of why he and Jen never got together: 'you needed the affection of the unblemished small-town pure-heart to validate you in your oh-so-vulnerable time; me, as the perennial black sheep of the Witter brood, I needed the love and affection of a woman whose drive and commitment would . . . force me to get in touch with . . . my inner achiever.'

Grown-Up Stuff: Mitch and Gale first made love on Witch Island – information Dawson wishes he didn't possess!

Guy Talk: Dawson asks Pacey if he was right to keep his distance from Joey, and Pacey says that if it felt right to do it then it probably was.

Kiss and Tell: Pacey and Jen kiss in the church and it's weird.

Bloopers: Examined too closely, this episode falls apart. Where did all the candles come from in the church? How did they light them (unless one of the gang is a secret smoker)? What *was* going on in the church? But all of that can be happily dismissed because it's clear the production team is just having fun. The only serious blooper, though, is the church itself: it was supposed to have been the site of a terrible fire, but it's still standing in perfect condition.

Guest Cast: Liz Vassey was the female lead in the criminally short-lived TV series *Maximum Bob*. She also appeared in four early episodes of *ER*, was a regular on *All My Children* for three years and is now playing Captain Liberty in the live-action TV series of the animated show *The Tick*. Wayne Peré has been in such films as *Out Of Sight*, *The Limey* and *Galaxy Quest*. He was a semi-regular in *The Flash*, which also starred John Wesley Shipp (Mitch).

Contempo Pop Music: 'Puzzle Girl' by Kim Stockwood, 'Gone' by the Tea Party and 'If' by Dragmatic.

The Big Issue: Jen and Pacey: 'Love has this horrible habit of messing things up', but 'sex is nice'.

The Last Word: The third film pastiche this season after *Risky Business* (**301**, 'Like a Virgin') and film noir (**305**, 'Indian Summer'), this is the first one that really works. After a very dodgy start to the season we get a whole episode in which Dawson and Joey talk about their relationship and Pacey and Jen talk about sex. What could be more Capeside than that? That's not to say there aren't problems – integrating Andie continues to be a headache and her slight storyline is irritating and serves only to make her even more unsympathetic. But the music is right, the pacing is good, the dialogue sparkles and it feels as if the show is back from the brink.

308
Guess Who's Coming To Dinner
1st US Transmission Date: 24 November 1999

Writer: Heidi Ferrer
Director: James Charleston
Guest Cast: Mel Harris (Helen Lindley)

It is Thanksgiving and Grams invites everyone to her house for dinner. Andie and Pacey each arrive thinking the other will not be there and after some awkwardness when they both try to leave, Jack tells them to get over themselves and stay. Jen's mother Helen arrives unexpectedly. Jen doesn't really want to talk to her, but Joey persuades Jen to give her mother a chance. Dawson tells Helen about Eve and says he thinks it best she tell Jen, which she eventually does. Jen is outraged that her mother could be so like her and yet punish her so severely. Angry, she grabs Pacey and drags him to the potting shed to take advantage of their guilt-free sex arrangement. Pacey backs off because she's so angry. Jen comes to realise that her mother is trapped in a loveless marriage and is deeply unhappy – she doesn't hate Jen: she hates herself.

Gale is living at home again in the guest room, although she is looking for a flat. They tell Dawson that the divorce is final, which, though he's stunned, he seems to take with a sort of relief.

The Ballad of Andie and Pacey: Pacey tries to make small talk with Andie but she rails at him for trying to be nice. Pacey meekly agrees and tries to leave until Jack stops him. Pacey grills Jack about Andie; Andie grills Joey about Pacey. Neither finds out much except that the other is broken-hearted and mending slowly.

The Movie Brat: When he finds out about his parents' divorce he wants to 'act out our teenage ennui in wanton destructive ways' but settles for a long talk with Joey.

The Tomboy: Joey is astonishingly mature and calm this week, counselling Jen, Dawson and Andie through their problems. She persuades Jen to give Helen a chance and tells her, 'We're all strangers to our parents . . . they love us but they don't really know us.' She adds that she should talk to her while she still can.

The Clown: Pacey once again does the right thing – Jen throws herself at him and actually begins undressing him but he stops her, talks to her about her problems and gives her a hug when she starts crying. When she's calmed down, and got over the embarrassment, Jen is very appreciative of his superhuman restraint.

The Delinquent: Jen now considers Capeside home, not New York. She feels as if she is at a crossroads and she 'could just go either way', but Grams has faith she'll follow the right path: 'for the past fourteen months I've been watching you . . . change. You're more serious now, you're at peace with yourself.' Jen describes her mother as 'the most intensely selfish person that I have ever known', but tries to give her a second chance. By the time Helen leaves, Jen has realised that her parents' relationship is cold and empty, but Helen relies too much on the social status it provides and can't face being alone, as she would be if she divorced. Jen ends up pitying her mother and that brings them closer together.

The Basket Case: Andie misses Pacey desperately but is slowly accepting that it's over.

The Wicked Witch: The judgmental, unpleasant Grams of old would never have thrown open her doors to all the town as she does here. She's become a sort of vaguely grouchy matriarch to everybody, and the role suits her.

Family Sucks!: Pacey goes to lengths to avoid having dinner at his house, where his dad will get drunk and watch football all day before complaining about the food. Mr McPhee stays in Chicago for work and Jack resents it.

That Three-Letter Word: Poor old Pacey every time he and Jen kiss she gets the giggles. He protests: 'Foreplay is no laughing matter. How do you expect a guy to do his best work in the face of scorn and derision?' The deal between the two of them has yet to be consummated, but it's still on the table.

Grown-Up Stuff: Gale and Mitch are trying to become friends again and seem to be succeeding, although it's making Dawson very uncomfortable.

Guest Cast: Mel Harris is best known for her role as Hope Steadman in the zeitgeisty eighties soap *thirtysomething*.

Contempo Pop Music: 'Beginner's Luck' by Ariel's Worm, 'America' by Bree Sharp, 'Better Than Anyone' by Mary Beth, '17 Again' by the Eurythmics, 'Getting Over You' by Janis Ian and 'That I Would Be Good' by Alanis Morrissette.

Backstage: In the original version of this episode Jen and Pacey were going to have sex. Unfortunately the network weren't happy and vetoed it at the last minute.

The Big Issue: 'The only homes we have are the ones we make ourselves.'

The Last Word: While the actual Thanksgiving scene is mawkish at best, and the episode is saddled with ending the Eve storyline, there are a lot of really good scenes here, mostly two-handers between various combinations of the cast. It's well written and performed and the episode, mostly shot outside, looks beautiful. The dialogue between Jen and Pacey, not characters who often get a lot of scenes with each other, is light and funny and works wonderfully.

309
Four To Tango

1st US Transmission Date: 1 December 1999

Writer: Gina Fattore
Director: James Whitmore Jr

Pacey discovers he's failing maths and asks Joey to help him. She agrees, as long as he comes with her to a ballroom dancing school and helps her compete for some scholarship money. They agree to keep the dancing a secret. He tells her about his arrangement with Jen, but doesn't name her. Joey thinks it's sordid.

Pacey and Jen are still trying to have sex, but they're finding it difficult because there's no sexual tension. They sneak into Dawson's room to make out while he's at school. Dawson returns early and Jen escapes through the window, but he finds Pacey, who pretends he was playing video games. Unfortunately, Pacey drops a condom, which Dawson later finds. When he hears Joey and Pacey talking about the dancing, and they obviously lie about it, he comes to the conclusion that they are sleeping together.

Dawson tells Jen his suspicions and they follow Pacey and Joey to the dance hall and are press-ganged into dancing. During a game where they switch dance partners, Dawson confronts Pacey and Joey. In the end Pacey gets annoyed at Dawson for even caring about whether he and Joey are together, and tells him that he should get used to the idea that Joey will have other men sooner or later. Pacey storms off to the cloakroom, where Jen comes to calm him down. They start making out and Joey and Dawson find them. Dawson is amused, but Joey blows her top as she realises it's Jen that Pacey had the sex pact with.

Jen interprets Pacey's anger at Dawson, and Joey's anger at Pacey, as clear signs that they're developing a relationship, but Pacey denies it, perhaps too strenuously. Jen and Pacey agree it'll never work between them. Dawson persuades Joey not to be so judgmental of Pacey and Jen, so Joey goes back to the dance hall and talks to Pacey. They make up and leave, but not before finding out that there's no scholarship this year anyway.

Dawson put his news item on Jack (**304**, 'Home Movies') online and Jack's received loads of emails, many of them homophobic. One guy writes that he has had a similar experience, and when he instant-messages Jack they start chatting online, after a lot of persuading from Andie. They swap pictures and Andie agrees, on Jack's behalf, to a date that night. Jack chickens out.

The Ballad of Pacey and Joey: Penny, the dance instructor, susses immediately that Pacey and Joey are 'clearly in the early stages of some screwball mating ritual . . . there's enough sexual tension here to power a KISS reunion tour'. They deny it, but Joey's reaction to Pacey and Jen's arrangement is way too extreme to be anything other than sublimated jealousy. Pacey gives Dawson a lecture on Joey, says that 'she's a freakin' goddess' and that sooner or later some other guy is going to be interested in her and 'he's not going to be your best friend and he's not going to ask your permission'. When Joey forgives Pacey she's all embarrassed smiles and takes him by the hand. As they walk out of the episode, hand in hand and smiling, it's inevitable that something is going to happen – their rapport is just so good.

The Movie Brat: Dawson goes silent, hard-faced and accusatory when he thinks Pacey and Joey are having an affair. There's a dark, bitter edge to his reaction that doesn't flower because he realises he's wrong, but it strongly indicates that his reaction would be extreme and unpleasant if they were. When he finds out that it's Jen, not Joey, he changes instantly to being understanding and nonjudgmental.

The Tomboy: Joey's attempts to gain money are becoming increasingly desperate. Does she *really* think she has a chance of being voted 'High School Student Who Best Exemplifies the Spirit and Grace of Ballroom Dancing'?

The Clown: Pacey's in big trouble at school – he's got four D pluses and one C minus. He associates studying with sex because both Tamara and Andie would reward him when he had worked hard, so now he finds it hard to study because there's no reward.

The Basket Case: After a number of poor episodes for her character, Andie's role in this one – supportive and slightly annoying sister – feels right and works well. She pushes Jack to get a boyfriend, but accepts it when he tells her he needs to slow down.

The Outsider: Jack talks to another gay high school student online and although he really enjoys the conversation, and fancies him when he sees a picture, he's unsure about taking the next step: 'When I walk through that door . . . my entire life is going to be different. I'm not just going to be telling the world that I'm gay: I'm actually going to *be* gay.'

School Sucks!: The Capeside Minutemen didn't make it to the regionals, so Mitch's coaching career hasn't been *that* successful after all.

That Three-Letter Word: Jen and Pacey just can't find that spark, no matter how hard they try. Joey says she could never sleep with someone she didn't love, and so does Dawson.

Reality Bites: Pacey says that 'the storyline is starting to stretch the limits of believability' when he and Jen haven't managed to have sex even though they're both horny teenagers who decided to do it weeks ago. Dawson looks at the Pacey–Jen dalliance 'from a storytelling perspective' and concludes that, in script terms 'Pacey's brooding, disillusioned, tough-guy persona was destined to collide with Jen's fake sexual bravado'.

All Things Spielberg: Andie tells Jack to 'say anything – it worked for John Cusack'. *Say Anything* was the second film from the *Dawson's Creek* favourite Cameron Crowe. Jen says Pacey and Joey are preparing for 'Capeside Dinner Theater's version of *Strictly Ballroom*'. *Strictly Ballroom* (Baz Lurhmann, 1992) is an Australian comedy about, unsurprisingly, ballroom dancing.

Guy Talk: Pacey gets frustrated at Dawson: 'This is the way it always is with you: you talk and talk but you don't listen to yourself; you say you're over her but you're not; they're just words, they don't mean anything to you.'

Kiss and Tell: Jen and Pacey kiss and kiss but just can't get past how weird it is.

Our Quips Are Wittier: Pacey on dancing: 'On the sliding scale of embarrassment and decidedly non-butch activities for a teenage male to be involved in, waltzing is right up there with painting your own pottery.'

Contempo Pop Music: 'World You Want' by Violin Road, 'Hateful' by Peter Searcy, 'Me, Myself and I' by Vitamin C and 'Knock It On the Head' and 'Stay You' by Wood.

The Big Issue: You can't force sexual chemistry where it doesn't exist, but neither can you prevent it where it does.

The Last Word: This is a lovely episode. The badinage between Jen and Pacey, and Joey and Pacey, really has a light romantic-comedy touch. The scene where they're dancing and swapping partners is particularly well done. The characters all feel right; there's some good foreshadowing of things to come; and the difficulty of integrating Andie is overcome by focusing on her relationship with Jack. It's as though the dodgy start to this season had never happened.

310
First Encounters of the Close Kind

1st US Transmission Date: 15 December 1999

Writer: Leslie Ray
Director: Greg Prange
Guest Cast: Bianca Lawson (Nikki Green),
Adam Kaufman (Ethan), Robin Dunne (AJ Moller),
Marla Gibbs (Mrs Fran Boyd)

Harvard University is having an open day for prospective students. Dawson goes to show his Witch Island documentary (**307**, 'Escape From Witch Island') in a film competition; Joey goes to have a tour and spend the weekend with a student who will teach her about college life; Andie goes to try to have an interview with the dean; Jack goes, too, saying he's there to take the tour, but he's actually there to check out the gay scene in town.

Dawson meets Nikki Green, who enrolls him in the competition and then watches as his film is a total failure – the audience barely applauds and leaves as soon as it's ended. Nikki comes to talk to him after the Q&A and, although she tries to be supportive, she admits she thought the film was poor. Later it turns out that Nikki has a film entered as well – it's a huge success and gets a standing ovation. Dawson congratulates her, but only grudgingly. At the prize giving Nikki's film doesn't even rank and she's very upset. Dawson comforts her and tells her that he really thought her film was wonderful and should have won. He meets her on the train home and discovers that she's the daughter of Principal Green. Her parents have divorced, and her mother's just moved to a new town, so she's coming to live in Capeside.

Joey has been listed as Joseph and finds herself sharing a room with a guy, AJ Moller, who tells her to get lost while he finishes a paper. She attends an English seminar that he turns out to be chairing and she's asked what her favourite great book is. She says *Little Women* and the class tear her choice to pieces. Afterwards Joey berates AJ for being so mean. He apologises and they agree to start over again. He takes her to the library and shows her Louisa May Alcott's own copy of *Little Women* and they read together from it. They stay up all night talking about James Joyce.

Jack buys a copy of the *Pink Pages* and hits town to check out a gay bar. A guy hits on him and he flees in terror, totally freaked out. On the train home he meets Ethan, who's going to Capeside and who is also gay.

Andie tries to jump the queue and secure an interview with the dean but the secretary, Fran, tells her she's got no chance. They end up having lunch together and Fran gives Andie some useful advice about ambition and life.

The Ballad of Dawson and Joey: Pacey's prophecy from **309**, 'Four To Tango', comes true and AJ takes an interest in Joey. Dawson's face when he sees them say goodbye is as jealous as it was when he thought Pacey was with Joey.

The Movie Brat: Poor old Dawson! An early success with his first movie has now led to two flops, both of which have received critical maulings that have crushed his ambitions. He begins to doubt if he really can cut it as a filmmaker, but Joey's support and Nikki's film remind him why he wanted to do it in the first place: 'To reach people . . . no matter what happens to me I'm not gonna give up until I reach that goal.' But when he gets back to his bedroom he looks as if he wants to hide there for a while. He was born on 14 March 1983.

The Tomboy: AJ tries to put Joey off by being rude and unpleasant, but feisty ol' Jo just rises to it and takes him on until he realises what a jerk he's been. She's so unintimidated that she even spends the night in his room. When he asks her if he can call she says yes and gets all bashful. She has always seen college as her way of getting herself out of Capeside, but now she sees it as an exciting opportunity in its own right and she can't wait. She's named after Jo in *Little Women* and her mother used to read it to her at night.

The Basket Case: Andie has dreamed about going to Harvard since she was tiny – her father is an alumnus. She did the tour a year early and already has an appointment to see the dean in a few months' time but her impatience leads her to try early. When she talks to Fran it's about her mother and her illness. Fran tells her to stop blaming herself for things that aren't her fault.

The Outsider: Jack takes the opportunity to check out a gay club but it's far too intimidating for him. His relief when Ethan turns out to be both gay and nonthreatening is palpable. Ethan can tell Jack's gay and that he's new to it and a little afraid. Ethan's just ended a two-year relationship.

All Things Spielberg: Dawson proclaims his love of Spielberg to Nikki and she's sceptical and asks, 'Where's the edge?' Dawson replies, 'Edge is fleeting, art lasts for ever.'

Our Quips Are Wittier: Joey thinks the weekend could be 'when all of our hopes and dreams just come crashing down around us . . . forcing us to withdraw from mainstream society and spend the rest of our days as these cynical, embittered shadows of our former selves.' Ever the optimist!

Guest Cast: Bianca Lawson was originally cast as Cordelia in *Buffy* but had other obligations and couldn't accept the role. (As originally cast, *Buffy* would have featured her as Cordy and Katie Holmes as Buffy – I wonder how different the show would have been . . .) She was eventually cast as Kendra, another slayer, and appeared a few times in *Buffy*'s second season. Adam Kaufman also had a recurring role on *Buffy*, as the dastardly Parker Abrams, in the first few episodes of the third season. He now stars as Mathew in *Metropolis*. Robin Dunne had a regular role as Franz in a TV series based upon Louisa May Alcott's other little book, *Little Men*, the sequel to *Little Women*. He also played Sebastien Valmont in the short-lived TV series based upon the movie *Cruel Intentions*, which starred Sarah Michelle Gellar, of *Buffy*, and Joshua Jackson.

Contempo Pop Music: Ben Folds Five's 'Kate', 'Mrs Potter's Lullaby' by Counting Crows, 'Run Into You' by Last December and 'Never Ending' by Wood.

The Big Issue: As Andie somewhat pretentiously puts it, 'You get this picture in your head of the way things should be and you end up closing yourself off to some of the wonder and serendipity of the actual experience.'

The Last Word: As a potential blueprint for how the show could work in its fifth season, when all the characters leave Capeside for college, this works on every level. Joey and Dawson open and close the episode in his bedroom discussing the plot and it feels like old times, but in between we have our characters' first real adventure in the wider world. Dawson's and Joey's storylines take precedence over Jack's and Andie's, and we have the first ever episode of *Dawson's Creek* not to feature Pacey or Jen at all. A great coming-of-age story and a good introduction to two new characters – Ethan and Nikki.

311
Barefoot At Capefest

1st US Transmission Date: 12 January 2000

Writers: Bonnie Schnieder and Hadley Davis
Director: Jan Eliasbcrg
Guest Cast: Bianca Lawson (Nikki Green),
Adam Kaufman (Ethan Brodie)

Dawson has picked himself up from his humiliation in **310**, 'First Encounters of the Close Kind', and is ready to make another film using the school's 16 mm camera. Unfortunately, Nikki Green has signed it out for four weeks. He goes to her house in a bad mood and accuses her of being rude and selfish, but before a fight can start Principal Green appears and invites Dawson to dinner. Afterwards, Dawson is surprised that Nikki's bedroom shows no sign of her movie madness and they each talk about the divorce of their parents. Dawson gets upset and leaves. At home Joey finds him taking down all his Spielberg posters – she thinks he's following another girl's lead and selling out; hc says he's moving on. Joey leaves in a bad mood. Later she returns, with a peace offering – a poster of John Lennon, which they put up above his bed.

Out shopping, Jack meets Ethan, who's returned to Capeside to attend the Capefest alternative-music festival (Capeside gets less sleepy and small every episode!) and says Jack should come along. Jen and Jack get to the campsite at the festival and Jack immediately leaves Jen and goes to find Ethan. When he finds him they go for a walk and talk. When they return, all Ethan's stuff has been stolen, so Jack tells Jen to get lost and offers Ethan a place in their tent. Ethan just wants to go to sleep, to Jack's disappointment. Next morning Ethan admits he might be interested in Jack, but he doesn't think Jack's ready yet. He gives Jack his number.

At the festival Jen meets Henry, who's selling veggie burgers. He's been giving her the silent treatment for a month and she hasn't noticed, so he's angry with her and doesn't want to be friends. Later that night she sees him playing guitar and singing, and realises there's even more to him than meets the eye. She finds him next morning, apologises, and makes the first tentative moves towards being more than friends.

Andie signs on as assistant director for the school play, but the teacher who is directing is incompetent and rude. Pacey is cast in the lead and she asks him to quit because it's too awkward to work with him. He refuses and they learn to work together.

The Ballad of Dawson and Joey: Joey is furious with Dawson for tearing down his posters and accuses him of 'tossing [his] identity out the window' because a new girl has come to town. She's offended that he talked about his parents' divorce with Nikki instead of her, but Dawson retorts that she's just jealous. He points out that he's not mentioned AJ once but Joey thinks that's just as bad. When Joey returns to make up she tells him that 'no matter how much we yell, or no matter how quiet we are, I hear you' and he agrees that he hears her, too. She admits her jealousy can get a bit out of control sometimes.

The Ballad of Andie and Pacey: Andie's first reaction to Pacey's casting is to insist he quit, because she got into the drama class to help her get over him. She's fuming when he stays put. As the teacher's direction gets worse, and Andie's gets better, Pacey backs her up, they start to thaw to each other and he refuses to let her give up.

The Ballad of Henry and Jen: Jen is really pleased to bump into Henry but he's even angrier with her than he was when she broke his heart in **306**, 'Secrets and Lies'. When she sees him sing he finally gets an 'awesome' from her in return for all the ones he's thrown at her, and she admits that she misses him and the way he used to look at her. He replies that it's too hard to be friends with her because he loves her and she doesn't love him. Jen's apology, when it comes, is lovely and wins him over completely – she apologises 'for being callous with your heart, for thinking that just because I'm older I know better . . . if one of us is younger than the other here I don't think it's you.'

The Movie Brat: Dawson's picked himself up from his Witch Island flop but he's not happy at having a competitor in town and gets stroppy with Nikki. On one hand he's relieved his parents' divorce is over, but he tells Nikki he feels 'a disappointment of being the product of something that didn't work out'. He takes down his posters because he doesn't see the world in the same way as he did when he put them up. It's a major coming-of-age moment for Dawson and marks the beginning of a new stage for the character. Nikki's statement that she loves movies only because they allow her to explore her other interests, and that if she *only* loved movies she'd only be able to make movies *about* movies, hits Dawson hard because he recognises that it describes his problem entirely.

The Clown: Pacey takes the part in the play mainly because it will get him a C grade in English, but he turns out to be quite good as an actor, and his teacher thinks he's 'a natural with comedy'. Maybe that's his calling! According to his teacher, though, he's also 'a deplorable student and he has the ethics of a billy goat'.

The Delinquent: Jen eggs Jack on in his pursuit of Ethan and doesn't seem to mind being cast out of the tent into the night for the sake of Jack's love life.

The Basket Case: Andie is a pretty good theatre director. It seems the perfect arena for her overenergetic control-freakery.

The Outsider: After bailing on his first date (**309**, 'Four To Tango') and fleeing in terror from his first gay club (**310**, 'First Encounters of the Close Kind'), Jack finally finds a gay guy who's willing to talk about it and be his friend. However, he was so nervous that he didn't ask for his number after the train ride (**310**). His relief at finding Ethan is enormous and he admits that he's 'the first guy I was ready to take that next step with'. Jack sees Ethan as a potential partner, but Ethan sees himself more as a mentor and guide for Jack. He's a breakfast-cereal addict and although he tries to pretend he knows something about alternative music he's not convincing.

The Puppy Dog: Henry continues to stretch the limits of believability. Not only is he a jock – star quarterback no less – who helps out old ladies and has a passion for flowers, he is also a good cook, a vegetarian and a sensitive singer!

Family Sucks!: Principal Green embarrasses Nikki at dinner, telling Dawson that her first film was *A Day In the Life of Daddy*. Pity her when she brings boyfriends home to visit!

School Sucks!: Mr Broderick is the worst teacher Capeside High's produced yet and it's a miracle Andie and Pacey don't stage a mutiny and get rid of him.

All Things Spielberg: The school play is *Barefoot In the Park* by Neil Simon, which was filmed by Gene Saks in 1967.

Grown-Up Stuff: Gale has found a flat of her own and moved out of the Leery house, taking all the furniture from the family and guest rooms as part of the divorce settlement.

Guy Talk: Ethan tells Jack about being gay: 'It's about moments, it's about being too nervous to ask for my number, it's about conversations like this ... it's about who and what you love and that's why you can't erase it because it's not just part of your life: it's everywhere.'

Contempo Pop Music: 'No Chance' by Little Jinn, 'The Frug' and '85' by Rilo Kiley, 'Finally Found You' by

Weekend Excursion. Henry sings 'No Surrender' by Bruce Springsteen, but it's not Michael Pitt's voice. Pete Stewart's 'Better Off', 'Scared Of Me' by Channeling Owen, 'DeCapo' by Declan Nine, 'Angels In the Attic' by Debra Davis and 'Imagine' by John Lennon.

The Last Word: A watershed episode for Jack and Dawson as they begin to cope with redefining themselves and growing older. The Andie storyline, because she's got Pacey to bounce off, manages to be funny and involving, pretty much rehabilitating a character who was cruelly served by the first few episodes of the season. Jen and Henry's relationship is touching and well played and Nikki makes a good foil for Dawson.

312
A Weekend In the Country

1st US Transmission Date: 19 January 2000

Writer: Jeffrey Stepakoff
Director: Michael Katleman
Guest Cast: Obi Ndefo (Bodie Wells),
Carl McIntyre (Fred Fricke)

It's time for the grand opening of the Potter B&B but they've got no bookings and no money left. Bess considers taking out a mortgage on the house, which Joey opposes. Pacey invites an influential writer for *B&B Quarterly* to come and stay and arranges for Grams, Jack, Jen, Andie and Mitch to come along as fake guests. Mitch brings Gale. Joey is outraged – the B&B isn't ready and there's too much at stake, but before they can cancel Fred Fricke, the reviewer, arrives to find a broken boiler and a flooded bathroom. As the gang talk around a log fire and share memories, Fricke comes in and overhears Joey saying that they're all fake guests. Joey hits the hay convinced their chances of staying in business are gone. Next morning she finds Bodie making pancakes, a big group breakfast, and a happy Fricke, overwhelmed by the friendliness and good atmosphere.

Andie keeps working on Jack to move home and he assumes it's at his dad's behest. He eventually realises that it's Andie who misses him, so he decides to return home.

Henry unilaterally arranges a date with Jen. She decides to tell him all about her New York days, and he's not bothered by it at all.

The Ballad of Pacey and Joey: You can tell Pacey's falling in love with Joey, because he's started doing his knight-in-shining-armour bit. When Dawson thanks Pacey for looking after Joey as he asked (**301**, 'Like a Virgin'), Pacey goes a little overboard with his downplaying: 'She ain't easy, all right? She's physically incapable of keeping her mouth shut for more than two seconds at a time. She's got an opinion about everything ... I am eager to return to our regularly scheduled programming.' Grams remarks that you know you love someone when you can just sit and watch them sleep; we play out with Pacey, watching Joey sleep in her living room, rapt.

The Ballad of Henry and Jen: Henry has fixed the roof at a local restaurant but has accepted a meal for two as payment. He *tells* Jen she's eating there with him because he knows she'd say no and he's not going to give her the chance to. By telling him all about her past Jen's cleared the decks for a relationship and proved that she's still capable of trusting. Henry's response is perfect, and floors Jen: 'Whatever you did before is part of what makes you who you are, and I'm thankful for that.'

The Movie Brat: 'Everything's in question.' Dawson is confused and lost. He can no longer imagine what his future's going to be like, and everything around him is changing so fast that he's lost his bearings.

The Tomboy: Joey is desperate about the state of the B&B and tries to forbid Bess from taking out a mortgage on the house because it's their only link to their mother. Bess reminds her that she's only sixteen and can't forbid it, which leads Joey to deliver a virtual précis of the series premise: 'Do you even remember what it's like to be sixteen? It's like you have all the responsibilities of an adult but none of the authority: you can't vote, you can't drink, you can't make any definitive decisions about your life.'

The Clown: Pacey feels guilty because he encouraged the B&B idea and so he goes all out to make it work. When he gets Fricke to turn up, which took a lot of doing, only to find the boiler blown and the toilet flooded and Joey fuming mad, he gets the inevitable attack of self-doubt, and tells Mitch that everything he touches goes wrong.

Family Sucks!: Bodie, the missing cast member, returns from who knows where at last and we find out that he's been working elsewhere and hasn't been able to afford to come home often.

Reality Bites: Jen and Dawson watch the moon turn many colours and, while she thinks it's beautiful and magical, he has 'a bitter sense of the reality behind the magic'. That's post-Spielberg-poster Dawson, more cynical and resigned than before.

Metatextuality: The guy who comes to the door of Joey's house at the start and tries to convert her to Christianity is the writer, Jeffrey Stepakoff.

All Things Spielberg: Dawson hires *The Big Chill* (Lawrence Kasdan, 1983) for movie night because it's 'the definitive movie of the entire baby-boom generation'. Everyone else hates it.

Grown-Up Stuff: Pacey asked Mitch to come to the B&B, and Mitch asked Gale. Dawson has to watch his newly divorced parents play happy families, which 'pisses [him] off'. Gale is being passed over by every network she's approaching, so Mitch is trying to be supportive, but Dawson finds their relationship confusing and hates the fact that they don't seem to know what they want. Mitch reminds Gale that they used to dream of running a fish restaurant and gives her the number of a property downtown that he's had his eye on. Gale dismisses the idea, but then goes to see it anyway.

Guy Talk: Dawson tells Pacey how impressed he is with how Pacey's changed, and how he's not glib or predictable any more.

Mitch also gives Pacey a pep talk and tells him Joey and Bess are lucky to have someone who will go to such lengths for his friends: 'That goes to the heart of who Pacey Witter is.' At last, someone on the show really gets Pacey!

Contempo Pop Music: Julie Plug's 'Starmaker', 'Fear' by Bryan Kelley, 'Getting By' by Weekend Excursion, 'Will You Ever Know' by Kind Of Blue, 'Ain't Too Proud To Beg' by the Temptations, 'Absence of an Angel' and 'Promise Me This' by Pancho's Lament and 'Both Sides Now' by Joni Mitchell.

The Last Word: A good episode but it's kind of high on the schmaltz factor: Fricke's final comment, 'The heat didn't work last night but this is one of the warmest places I've ever stayed,' is gagworthy. The love-in around the fire recalls the mawkishness of the Thanksgiving scene (**308**, 'Guess Who's Coming To Dinner'), and yet it's not badly done and the cast are great. This episode develops the storylines well and it's a feel-good piece. Just a bit too sweet, really.

313
Northern Lights

1st US Transmission Date: 26 January 2000

Writer: Gina Fattore
Director: Jay Tobias
Guest Cast: Bianca Lawson (Nikki Green),
Robin Dunne (AJ Moller)

It's the opening night of the school play, see **311**, 'Barefoot At Capefest'. Joey can't come because AJ is coming to town and has asked her out on a date. The director, Mr Broderick, drops out due to kidney stones and Andie is left in charge. Jen postpones her dinner with Henry because of the play and he says he'll come with her instead.

AJ takes Joey to a party thrown by some college professors because tonight is a rare chance to see the aurora borealis from Capeside. He's nervous but when cloud obscures the view Joey agrees to go for a walk with him. On the beach he kisses her and she asks him to take her to the after-play party so she can congratulate Pacey. AJ waits in the car park and then follows her in to ask Joey if he did something wrong. She tells him that she panicked because he's so much smarter than she is and she feels intimidated.

Jen keeps a seat for Henry but she's brought Grams as well. Grams says she'd gladly have stayed home to let Jen and Henry be alone. Jen sits on the other side of Grams to Henry. At the party she goes to talk to Pacey and Henry gets left with Grams. Eventually Henry snaps and, inspired by a scene from the play, stands in the rafters and makes Jen admit that she's embarrassed to be with him. Afterwards, walking home, she and he finally kiss.

Pacey has chronic stage fright but a pep talk from Dawson and a shove from Andie get him on stage in time, where he shines. He's worried about Joey being on a date and upset that she's not there to see the play. At the party he sits alone and broods, but when Joey turns up he lights up. Afterwards, when Joey's gone off with AJ again, he broods some more. He finally makes peace with Andie.

Dawson quits film class, to Joey's amazement. Nikki tries to talk him out of it but he stands firm and comes to wait for Joey at her house. Joey returns from her date with AJ and she and Dawson talk about his current confusions. The northern lights burst out above them, right on cue.

The Ballad of Dawson and Joey: Dawson shoots hoops with Pacey before the play and he's doing well, but as soon as Pacey reveals that Joey's on a date Dawson misses the basket by a mile. When he tells Nikki he's lost his sense of joy she asks him where he was when he had it last – and the next thing we know he's turned up at Joey's door in the middle of the night. He still runs to her when he feels confused and lost. But, when Pacey and Joey talk at the party, she talks about her feelings for Dawson in the past tense, to her own surprise.

The Ballad of Pacey and Joey: If there were any doubts left they're gone by the end of this episode – Pacey is head over heels in love with Joey and just can't help himself. His frantic, hyperactive pleas for her not to go on the date with AJ look like stage fright to Joey, but he's panicking for very different reasons. It's the same when he's late for the show – he's fretting about Joey when Dawson comes to find him. Pacey actually gets annoyed that Dawson's not more worried about the date and projects all his own anxiety on Dawson. After the show he's not depressed because his family didn't turn up, but because Joey didn't, and Jen realises it instantly. Immediately after AJ kisses her, Joey thinks of Pacey, so maybe Pacey's love is not unrequited after all. When Joey arrives he guesses that AJ kissed her because 'he'd have to be a moron not to'. He almost admits his feelings and tells her, 'You fall in love, it doesn't work out and you think that it'll never happen again, but it does, believe me it does, in the strangest of places.'

The Ballad of Andie and Pacey: Andie says she isn't disappointed with the slump in Pacey's grades because girls often try to change their boyfriends and it never works. Pacey replies, 'In your defence I wasn't exactly a luxury model: I did have fixer-upper written all over me.' But she says he didn't need fixing or changing because he's perfect as he is, and he says the same about her. It seems like the final appraisal of their relationship, and they walk off to a new one, as friends.

The Ballad of Henry and Jen: At the end of 312, 'A Weekend In the Country', Jen and Henry seemed to be connecting at last, but when this episode opens she's been avoiding him for a week, so he's taken to avoiding her so she can't cancel their dinner date. Her attempt to postpone for the play backfires when he invites himself along. But Jen's still having second thoughts and her decision to invite Grams is a real slap in poor Henry's face. Henry's grand gesture is dangerous and funny and he tells her he won't come down until she says, 'I, Jen Lindley am embarrassed to be here on a date with Henry Parker. I've ignored him, I've taken him for granted and spent the last five months of my life making him miserable, all to disguise the horrifying fact that I like him.' Walking home, she tells him he's unique and bizarre and she's amazed by his ability to be totally honest, something she's never been able to be. He promises to teach her and at last, after twelve episodes, she kisses him.

The Movie Brat: The crisis that began in **312**, 'A Weekend In the Country', continues as Dawson tries to get a handle on who he is and what he wants. Dropping film class is an even more dramatic gesture than removing his posters, but he's still not sure where that leaves him. Pacey's right when he calls him 'Zen': there's a detached, calm side to Dawson that's beginning to emerge, and, despite a bumpy ride at the end of this season, it will grow until his Season Four self is positively Buddhist at times. This is the start of a major character change. It was long overdue.

The Tomboy: Joey's determined to try for an Ivy League college because she wants to do big things with her life. Her passion for art has faded and she's not clear why, but says that she's not sure where she begins and the persona she puts on to please other people ends (which mirrors, to an extent, Dawson's plight at the moment).

The Clown: Pacey's all over the place this week, as his feelings for Joey send him into a tailspin. **111**, 'Beauty Contest', demonstrated that he could charm an audience on stage, and he proves it again in this episode with his performance as Paul in *Barefoot In the Park*.

The Delinquent: The only unsatisfying thing in this episode is the lack of explanation for Jen's treatment of Henry. She goes to absurd lengths to keep Henry at arm's length. Still, she gets there in the end.

The Basket Case: Andie's mantra in hospital was 'structure and purpose' and that's what directing the play has given her.

School Sucks!: Mr Broderick finally realises that the play has been Andie's show all along and hands her his director's folder. So he can do some things right.

All Things Spielberg: Joey says that AJ comes across as a '*Good Will Hunting* impersonator'. *Good Will Hunting* (Gus Van Sant, 1997) starred Matt Damon and Ben Affleck, who also wrote the script, for which they won an oscar. Damon plays a young boy who realises he's a mathematical genius.

Kiss and Tell: AJ kisses Joey on the beach, and it seems likely he kissed her again after the second stage of their date, too. Jen kisses Henry (yay!).

Our Quips Are Wittier: Joey asks Pacey if he's ever heard of the aurora borealis and he replies, 'I may not be Ivy League material but if you give me a road map and a remote control I can probably find my way to the Discovery Channel.'

Contempo Pop Music: 'Affirmation' by Savage Garden, 'No Regrets' by Sue Medley, 'Get On the Bus' by Pancho's Lament, 'Even Now' by Trina Hamlin and 'What Can Never Be' by Sinead Lohan.

The Last Word: A cracking episode. Having all the action revolve in different ways around the opening of the play gives it a focus and unity that doesn't feel contrived at all. Each love story is addressed and moves forward, and we get more of Nikki, who's a great character. Pacey gets to shine, Joey looks stunning and Andie gets a good role, too. The only off note is Jen's treatment of Henry, and Robin Dunne's performance as AJ seems to lack the spark it had in **310**, 'First Encounters of the Close Kind', but these are minor gripes.

314
The Valentine's Day Massacre

1st US Transmission Date: 2 February 2000

Writer: Tom Kapinos
Director: Sandy Smolan
Guest Cast: Dylan Neal (Doug Witter),
Alex Breckenridge (Kate Douglas),
Michael Hagerty (Matt Caulfield)

Dawson is trying, and failing, to teach Joey to drive. Pacey suggests they go to a party being thrown by Matt Caulfield, a notorious hellraiser and Capeside High student. Dawson agrees; Joey refuses. Andie invites her friend Kate to come along, because she's just been dumped by her boyfriend and wants to have a good time. She was Jack's first girlfriend and doesn't know he's gay. On the way to the party Jack is about to tell her when she reveals her boyfriend just dumped her because he discovered he was gay!

Joey does turn up after all, to keep Dawson on the straight and narrow, and they hit the party – an illicit get-together at the golf club. To get in they have to drink a shot of vodka jelly but Andie and Joey refuse and go driving in a golf cart. Deputy Doug arrests them. Dawson goes for a walk with Kate and they are just about to kiss when she throws up, and then Deputy Doug arrests them. When Doug drives into the main party everyone runs except Pacey, who's tied upside down to a tree chugging beer through a hose.

In the cell Jack tells Kate he's gay, Joey finds out about Kate and Dawson and is outraged, and Pacey delivers a drunken dissertation on the dynamics of the Dawson-and-Joey relationship. Mitch arrives to bust them out, but

Doug says Sheriff Witter thinks Pacey should spend the night in the cells, so he's left alone. He admits to Doug that he's screwed up over a girl and Doug advises him to tell her how he feels. Next day Pacey goes to Joey's, apologises for his behaviour and is just about to tell her he loves her when he chickens out. He ends up teaching her to drive, with far more success than Dawson had.

It's time for Jen and Henry's dinner and Jen is nervous. Henry persuades a nurse at the hospital to let him donate blood twice, so he can raise money for a gift. By the time of the date he's pale as a vampire and slightly dazed. He passes out in the restaurant. When he's being wheeled to the ambulance he gives her his gift – a ring that turns out to be too small. Jen's first instinct is to call it a day, but she thinks twice after talking to Grams, and visits Henry in hospital. She admits that she's never had a date on Valentine's Day before and that's why she was so nervous. They eat hospital jelly and decide to stop trying so hard.

'Here we go again kiddies, for the 476th time this hour, our Number One billboard chart topper "**The Ballad of Dawson and Joey**". Will those two crazy kids ever get back together again? Boy, I hope so!' And thus begins Pacey's rant, when he tells it like it is and pulls no punches. He says Joey treats Dawson 'like some weird, neutered, virginal creature' and '[pleads] sheer frustration. Do you have any idea how exhausting it is to exist on your periphery? To witness this perpetual dance that you two have? One week you're soul mates, the next week you're giving each other up for the greater good . . . could you make up your mind? Please? And the reverence that you two treat this little saga of yours with is enough to make a guy wanna puke.'

The Ballad of Pacey and Joey: Joey and Pacey literally banter across Dawson in the car as if he weren't there. And in the prison cell Dawson again fades into the background as Joey and Pacey again go at each other hammer and tongs. Pacey repeats what he said about Joey to Dawson in **312**, 'A Weekend In the Country', and tells Doug that she's annoying and opinionated, but he also waxes rhapsodic about her beauty, sweetness and intelligence. Joey surprises Pacey by saying that her banter is just a cover for her concern and she's worried no one's looking out for him right now. Nothing better illustrates the changes in the group than the opening and closing scenes: Dawson can't teach Joey to drive, they're not in sync any more and they just argue; Pacey and Joey are much more on each other's wavelength, and he does manage to teach her, and they laugh about it.

The Ballad of Henry and Jen: Their meal becomes the date from hell, all because of Henry's flair for the grand gesture. Their real date is in the hospital, when Jen suggests that they start acting their age and stop trying to be like some older, mature couple. Jelly suits them far better than fine cuisine.

The Movie Brat: Pacey and Joey agree that 'Dawson is lost right now', but they spend the whole episode as good and bad angels on his shoulder fighting over his actions, and Dawson resents it. He goes to the party, drinks the alcohol, tries to kiss the pretty new girl in town and attempts to act without thinking and have a good time. The fates conspire against him, but he's still trying to find a new way of going about things. He tells Mitch that he's trying to get back to the heart of being a sixteen-year-old, and Mitch says that's fine, but in that case he's going to *treat* him like a sixteen-year-old, and instructs him to work all the free time he has at Gale's new restaurant until he grows up a bit.

The Tomboy: Joey comes down hard on Dawson for going to the party, and expresses outrage that he would try to kiss Kate the way he did. It's the same as her reaction to Pacey and Jen's kiss in **309**, 'Four To Tango', and it demonstrates how closely her feelings for Pacey and Dawson mirror each other – she reacts the same way to both their peccadilloes.

The Delinquent: Valentine's was the night the boys at Jen's old school had dates with the girls they really liked, hence she never got asked out on Valentine's.

The Outsider: Jack's old nickname was Jackers, and Kate was his first girlfriend. He always felt something was slightly wrong when he was dating her but couldn't quite identify what it was.

Family Sucks!: Doug redeems himself for not attending Pacey's play in 313, 'Northern Lights', by giving some good big-brotherly advice, so at least one other Witter isn't a total jerk.

That Three-Letter Word: Jack slept with Kate when they were going out, and she gives his performance rave reviews.

All Things Spielberg: In *Say Anything* (Cameron Crowe, 1989) John Cusack's character, Lloyd Dobler, teaches Ione Skye's character, Diane Cort, to drive, but Dawson and Joey just don't have that dynamic and she tells him he's no Lloyd Dobler. At the end, when Pacey's teaching her to drive, they're driving in circles while she practises gear changes, and that's exactly what happens in *Say Anything*.

Grown-Up Stuff: Gale has bought that property that Mitch told her about in 312, 'A Weekend In the Country', and is opening a restaurant in Capeside.

Girl Talk: Andie and Joey discuss Pacey. They agree that he's like an overeager, destructive but ultimately lovable puppy. Andie remarks that Joey sounds just like she did before she got together with Pacey.

Kiss and Tell: Poor Dawson! Mere seconds away from kissing Kate when her dinner makes a return visit.

Our Quips Are Wittier: Pacey's lurid description of what would happen if he told Joey how he felt is a classic: 'There is a strong possibility that the sun would cease to shine, that the tides would cease to rise . . . that the very earth would crack open and Capeside would become home to a huge Hellmouth that would spew forth endless hordes of monsters and demons that would choke the denizens of this city, making them fall to their knees and pray for a return to the days before I took action.'

Bloopers: The greenscreen work as the gang drive their golf carts is lame – the long shots show them cruising over humps and hillocks, but when we cut to them they're on smooth ground. And their hair stays perfect – there's no breeze even though they're driving in open vehicles. Couldn't someone have rigged up a fan?

Contempo Pop Music: 'Passion' by Patria, 'Real World' by Universal Honey, 'Charming the Gods' by Bryan Kelley, 'Bad Girl' by DJ Rap, 'Taste Test' by Beanbag, 'What Can I Say' by Julie Plug, 'Point #1' by Chevelle. Jack and Kate discuss their younger days to 'The Way Things Used To Be' by Debra Davis and we play out with 'Never Be The Same' by Susan Aglukark.

Ker-THUNK!: We see two cells of the Capeside police lock-up. One is crammed full of teenagers while, the other is spacious and roomy because it contains only our characters.

The Last Word: The Pacey–Joey–Dawson triangle is re-vitalising the season and this episode crackles with subtext, tension and secrets. Joshua Jackson and Katie Holmes are at the top of their games; Dawson's identity crisis continues to work well for the show as his character redefines itself; Jack's subplot with Kate is amusing and shows his increased confidence in his own identity. All this and Deputy Doug too, who's always fun.

315
Crime and Punishment

1st US Transmission Date: 9 February 2000

Writers: Gina Fattore and Alex Gansa
Director: Joe Napolitano
Guest Cast: Dylan Neal (Doug Witter),
Michael Hagerty (Matt Caulfield),
Obi Ndefo (Bodie Wells)

Joey has been commissioned to paint a mural on the wall of Capeside High, to express school unity. At the grand unveiling however, we find that it's been daubed with black paint. Pacey and Dawson both try to comfort her, and Dawson gives her Mitch's keys to the school and urges her to repaint it overnight, but she doesn't. Pacey finds out that it was Matt Caulfield and tells him to apologise. A fight ensues and Pacey and Matt are hauled in by the principal and told to explain. They won't, so one of Matt's friends and Dawson are called in to explain. When it becomes clear that Pacey could be suspended, ending his hopes of going to college, Dawson speaks up and Caulfield is forced to admit he defaced the mural. Principal Green expels him, although Caulfield makes it plain that his rich, influential father will not be pleased. Pacey is put on the mentor programme and will have to be a big brother to some small Capeside kid.

After the fight, when Joey comes to tell Pacey off for being the hero, he says he's been spending time with her only because Dawson asked him to look out for her (**301**, 'Like a Virgin'). Joey's fuming but Dawson reminds her how clear it is that Pacey really does care about her. She eventually decides to repaint the mural and finds Pacey already cleaning off the vandalism. They paint together.

Andie's PSAT score has put her in the top 50,000 students in the country and she's on the way to a National Merit Scholarship. She's racked with guilt and admits to Jack that she stole the paper (**303**, 'None of the Above'). She resigns from the Disciplinary Committee and tells Principal Green that she cheated. He doesn't punish her, even though she thinks she should be expelled.

The Ballad of Pacey and Joey: When Joey has a go at Pacey for getting into trouble it's obvious that she's just worried about him; as she said in **314**, 'The Valentine's Day Massacre', 'you have to read between the banter'. But Pacey becomes defensive, and says he's around her only because Dawson told him to be. Joey's so hurt that she asks if that's what 'you and me is all about', and says she thought . . . But she doesn't say what she thought, only that she thought 'something else'. That's the closest she's come to acknowledging her feelings for Pacey and he knows he's blown it. His next gesture, repainting the wall so she can begin with a clean slate, is better judged. Joey thanks him for 'being yourself . . . not caring what anybody else thinks . . . knowing in your heart what's right and wrong, and for being there this year when I needed you the most'.

The Movie Brat: Dawson's happy that Pacey and Joey are getting on so well, and pats himself on the back for pushing them together.

The Tomboy: Despite implying (in **313**, 'Northern Lights') that she's no longer interested in art, Joey has spent a month conceiving, planning and executing a huge mural for the school, and it means a lot to her. She feels like she's making a statement, baring her soul to the world for the first time. In her unveiling speech she says the only thing that unites the students is a sense of possibility and her mural is to remind them that no matter the odds you can realise your dreams. She's humiliated and depressed when it's defaced. Dawson confronts her about why she won't repaint it and she tells him that her life isn't as full of possibilities and options as his and she can't afford the time to explore her art because the grind of daily life takes too much effort. Dawson thinks she's just scared of showing her work to the public.

The Clown: The object of Pacey's affections is in trouble and so, Joey says, he goes 'tilting at windmills while in the throes of a misguided hero complex'. He refuses to back down in the face of Caulfield's resistance. And even when they're in front of the principal his misguided sense of schoolboy honour won't let him spill the beans and he needs Dawson to save the day for him.

The Basket Case: Andie's strictness on the Disciplinary Committee has been a way of punishing herself because she's felt so bad about stealing the test. She did it because she wanted to show the world that she was better, but now she is better she feels awful. By doing the right thing and telling the principal she puts that guilt to bed for good.

Family Sucks!: Pacey's oldest sister is named Kerry. She's married to a tattoo-covered sergeant major, Jerry, and has come running home with her kids because the marriage has failed. She's moved into Pacey's bedroom *so* Pacey's been thrown out and sent to live with Doug; Mr Witter even gives Doug a cheque to pay for any damage Pacey may cause to his obsessively neat, musical-poster-covered flat.

School Sucks!: Principal Green takes a drastic step when he expels Matt Caulfield. Race and social issues have never really featured heavily or explicitly in the show, despite the references to Bodie's colour throughout Season One. But when Caulfield says 'I'm white, I'm rich' and stares down Principal Green, we finally get a hint of the real dark side of high-class Capeside (see **316**, 'To Green, With Love'). Bodie also remarks on this when he laments that there are only ten black kids at Capeside High. Joey corrects him: there are eleven. We also get to see the soft side of the principal. He's angry and disappointed in Andie, but refuses to punish her because she's hurt only herself and knows how badly she's behaved.

Bess hated school because the Potter family finances meant she never had the right clothes and was always teased.

All Things Spielberg: Pacey remarks that Joey's mural looks like something you'd find tattooed on 'Kwai Chang Caine's forehead'. Caine was the hero of *Kung Fu*, a TV series that ran for three years between 1972 and 1975.

When Pacey moves in Doug says, 'This is not *Party of Five*.' This was a TV show about five siblings who lived together in one house after their parents died. It ran for six years and launched Neve Campbell and Scott Wolf on an unsuspecting world.

Our Quips Are Wittier: Pacey on American art: 'This is the US of A. We're a prosaic nation and when we have art in public places we want it to be about as subtle as Godzilla.'

Contempo Pop Music: 'Believe Again' and 'One Turn Deserves Another' by Susan Aglukark, Julie Plug's 'Devoted' and 'Flower Days' by Trina Hamlin.

The Last Word: Another excellent episode, with Pacey doing what he does best – trying to save the day and getting it all slightly wrong. Dawson's fading into the background a bit; it's as if, since he doesn't know how to define himself right now, neither do the writers. The focus is shifting firmly to Joey and Pacey, which is no bad thing because their burgeoning love affair is dramatic, touching and funny.

316
To Green, With Love

1st US Transmission Date: 16 February 2000

Writers: Gina Fattore and Greg Berlanti
Director: Ken Fink
Guest Cast: Bianca Lawson (Nikki Green),
Robin Dunne (AJ Moller), Obi Ndefo (Bodie Wells),
Jessica Collins (Sherry Eisler),
Lawrence Pressman (Dr Fielding),
Michael Hagerty (Matt Caulfield)

The parents of Capeside are outraged at Matt Caulfield's expulsion (**315**, 'Crime and Punishment') and Dr Fielding, Capeside's Superintendent of Schools, decides that if Principal Green does not rescind Caulfield's expulsion by Friday he will demand his resignation. The students are outraged, and Pacey encourages Joey to take action. Joey talks to AJ on the phone and he also encourages her, so when she begins to organise rallies and meetings she credits AJ with inspiring her to do it. AJ comes to town to help, leaving Pacey feeling left out. Joey meets Dr Fielding and tells him she's got a petition with 300 signatures and has organised a big rally. She was bluffing, so all the gang, especially Pacey, rally round to help and the Potter B&B becomes their base of operations. Bessie receives a threatening phone call telling her not to let them use the B&B and she asks Joey to stop, but Joey, backed up by Bodie, refuses. At the meeting the students take turns to talk about how Principal Green has helped them, and then the man himself arrives to thank them. Bessie arrives and tells Joey how proud she is of her. Principal Green refuses to back down and so he packs and leaves, to a standing ovation from the students.

The reporter covering the story for the local TV station, Sherry, used to be an intern, and Gale trained her. Her coverage is biased and deliberately uses quotes from Joey in the wrong context. Gale is angry, so Dawson persuades her to let him film a piece, fronted by her, which she could then try to sell to the station. Principal Green refuses to be interviewed because he feels that if he shows his anger to the community they will use it against him. They interview Dr Fielding, who keeps going on about his responsibility to the community coming before the feelings of the students. Gale shows him his contract and demonstrates that he is in no way beholden to the community, and Dr Fielding, realising he's been caught out, terminates the interview. The station runs the piece and asks Gale to be a special reporter for it. She turns it down to concentrate on the restaurant.

The Ballad of Pacey and Joey: 'I have it on pretty good authority that my rough charms don't really register on her rarified romantic palate.' Pacey knows how impossible the situation is. He can't fall for Joey because the implications would be huge. He admits to Jen that it really hurts and she tells him, 'That just means it isn't pretend any more.' He stays in the background, organises everything for Joey, supports her and does all he can to make her notice him, but she doesn't. In the end he goes for another grand gesture and rents her a wall on Capeside main street that she can paint a mural on. This floors Joey, who tells him, 'As soon as I think I've got you all figured out you go and do something so outrageous that completely challenges me in a way that no one else would even think of . . . in case I don't say it enough, thank you.'

The Movie Brat: Dawson brings his camera to the rescue, so filmmaking is still instinctual to him even when he tries to put it aside. Gale tells him, 'As much as you think you've changed . . . you're still the quiet hero, stepping in at the right time.' He's enormously proud of Joey.

The Tomboy: Joey blossoms in this episode. She's forthright, driven, organised, inspirational and right. All the defensive feistiness has developed into genuine bravery and a willingness to stand up and fight for what she believes in. She still takes Pacey a bit for granted, and AJ and she are tight even though he still seems awkward and hesitant around her.

The Clown: First he got Mr Peterson fired (**215**, '. . . That Is The Question'), then he persuaded Fred Fricke to come to Capeside (**312**, 'A Weekend In the Country'), now he's organising rallies and flyers. Pacey's turning into quite the fixer.

The Delinquent: Jen and Pacey have become good friends in the wake of their deal (see **307**, 'Escape from Witch Island') and she can read him like a book now. She sees his increased discomfort around Joey and calls him on it, giving him a talking to and helping him out.

Family Sucks!: Bessie *did* take out the mortgage (**312**, 'A Weekend In the Country') and she's very worried about annoying the people who run the bank because they could foreclose on her. So her request to Joey to stop using the B&B as a base is understandable, although she comes around in the end.

School Sucks!: So farewell Principal Green, by far the best faculty member Capeside High's produced so far. Will the next incumbent be so willing to cut Pacey so much slack?

All Things Spielberg: Jen tells Pacey he's like Duckie, Molly Ringwald's best friend from John Hughes's teen flick *Pretty In Pink* (1986), and actually goes through the whole plot of the film with him to buck him up.

Grown-Up Stuff: Gale's restaurant is coming on nicely, but she admits she misses reporting and Dawson's idea of the news report gives her a chance to get back to what she loves. When she's given the opportunity to do more work for the station she turns it down because she just needed a chance to leave the job on her own terms.

Our Quips Are Wittier: When Sherry tries to interview Joey she replies, 'In your frosted blonde dreams, Barbie.'

Guest Cast: Jessica Collins has appeared in *Beverly Hills 90210*, *Lois & Clark: The New Adventures of Superman* and many other TV shows. Lawrence Pressman has appeared in too many TV shows and movies to name them all, but they include *NYPD Blue*, *Star Trek: Deep Space Nine* and *Ally McBeal*; on the big screen you may recall him in *American Pie* or the original *Shaft*.

Contempo Pop Music: 'Better Off' by Pete Stewart, 'Two Beds and a Coffee Machine' by Savage Garden, Mary Beth covers 'Tracks Of My Tears', and James Taylor's 'That Lonesome Road'.

The Big Issue/The Last Word: It takes half an hour before Bodie finally says what everyone's been thinking – this confrontation would never have been so divisive, and the parents and board so strict, if Principal Green had been white. Mr Caulfield's initial statements at the PTA meeting are thinly veiled racism. As he bangs on about Community Values it's clear that what he means by that is white, rich community values. He states that Principal Green should feel more at home in an 'urban war zone than our civilised community', and his attack on Joey is based on her family's rejection of their values, an obvious reference to Bess's relationship with Bodie. Playing the race card in *Dawson's Creek* is a brave move for a show in which such issues are referred to but never really addressed. They handle it very well and without sensationalism. It's a subtext and a factor, but it never really emerges fully fledged and polemic, which makes it feel far more pernicious and real than a crass, blunt, issue-driven, bang-you-over-the-head script could. It manages to be moving, too, and gets away with its schmaltzy ending in much the same way that *Dead Poets Society* did. Principal and Nikki Green were good characters, though, and they'll be missed.

317
Cinderella Story
1st US Transmission Date: 1 March 2000

Writer: Jeffrey Stepakoff
Director: Janice Cooke-Leonard
Guest Cast: Jonathan Lipnicki (Buzz Thompson),
Robin Dunne (AJ Moller), Deborah Kellner (Morgan)

AJ has won an award for creative writing and Joey goes to visit him at college for the presentation ceremony, where he is due to give a reading. Pacey drives her to the station and warns her that she's chasing a fairy tale and will only get hurt. Morgan, a stunning blonde student who is AJ's oldest friend, meets Joey at the train station. As the day progresses and Joey, Morgan and AJ hang out together it becomes clear that Morgan is Joey to AJ's Dawson, and she has returned from her studies in France because she's realised she's in love with him. Morgan recommends the piece that AJ should read, and when he reads it he looks at her – it's about unspoken love and he obviously wrote it for her.

Afterwards Joey tells him to go to Morgan, and she goes to the station to catch a train home. There are no trains till the morning so she calls Pacey to come and collect her. She won't tell Pacey what happened until they're just outside Capeside. She tells him he knows her best in the world apart from Dawson and he was the first person she thought to call. Pacey pulls the car over, gets out and asks her what she means. They talk back and forth until he seizes the day and kisses her.

It's a week till the opening of Gale's restaurant. It doesn't have a name, a chef or any staff, so Gale leaves Dawson in charge of tasting food from possible chefs and hiring staff. He hires Jen as a waitress, but she breaks everything. Andie and Jack help with the tastings, but all the chefs are dreadful. Dawson calls Mitch and asks him to come and help. Gale is furious because she wants this to be her enterprise, not Mitch's. Dawson goes off to sulk but Jen finds him. When he returns to apologise he finds that Gale has hired Mitch as her general manager, that the restaurant is called Leery's Fresh Fish, and Bodie has been given a 20 per cent stake in the business and will cook in the evenings.

Pacey begins his mentoring duties with a nine-year-old boy called Buzz, who is precocious and talkative. He takes Buzz to an arcade but he starts a fight with some other boys so Pacey drags him away to work on *True Love*, his boat. Buzz tells him that his father is dead, but when Pacey goes to see the supervisor he finds out that his dad ran off with another woman and his mother works long hours. Buzz tests people to see if they will come back to him. Pacey goes to Buzz's house and cooks him dinner while Buzz pumps him for information about his True Love, Joey.

The Ballad of Pacey and Joey: Pacey tells Joey that her relationship with AJ isn't real. It's long-distance and she's just travelling up there to put on a dress and go to a dance like Cinderella. Later she tells AJ the same thing, that their relationship is 'exciting, romantic and unbelievable' but it's not real, and what he has with Morgan is. She doesn't seem to realise, though, that her real thing is Pacey. Morgan is AJ's muse, Joey says, and cites Morgan's story of buying paper for AJ and forcing him to write, but she doesn't equate that to her life and Pacey buying her the wall.

The Tomboy: Joey knows that she's in the middle of an unspoken love because she recognises the symptoms from her own experiences with Dawson during Season One. She takes control, pushes AJ towards Morgan and exits stage left. It's a mature and selfless thing to do.

The Clown: Buzz is the perfect foil for Pacey, a smartass who thinks he knows it all, gets defensive when feelings are raised and isn't reluctant to throw a few punches. Everything Buzz says is a gem, although the precocious nine-year-old strays a bit too close to the stereotypical cutesy little kid that crops up in so many TV shows. Pacey goes to the supervisor, obviously to try to get a different kid, but when he finds out the truth he decides to stick with it and even goes to Buzz's house to cook. Looks like he's found someone else to rescue.

The Delinquent: Jen has been out of circulation for a while because she's been spending lots of time with Henry. She wants to be a waitress to meet people and raise money to take Henry out on dates. She's the world's worst waitress, but they keep her on as a hostess instead.

Family Sucks!: Since Bodie will now be working for the Leerys he will spend the days at the B&B and evenings at the restaurant. So Joey has a family again.

Reality Bites: Jen to Dawson: 'On the outside you're not that naïve little boy any more – you've been through too much recently – but deep down at your core there's always gonna be a part of you that rejects reality, and that's eternally hopeful.'

Grown-Up Stuff: Dawson has a perfect excuse to invite Mitch to help Gale. She really does need the help, but he admits to Jen that he is trying to get his family together again. Gale apologises for losing her temper with Dawson and admits she really needed the help and so now she's Mitch's boss.

Girl Talk: Morgan and Joey are forced together by circumstances and get on well. Morgan likes Joey's wit and tells her all sorts of things about AJ, such as his name – Arthur Jr. Morgan is an artist and she's studied in Paris, which was always one of Joey's dreams. If they weren't in competition for AJ they'd be good friends.

Kiss and Tell: Both times AJ and Joey try to kiss, at the café and in his room, Morgan interrupts. Pacey and Joey kiss – at last!

Bloopers: When Pacey pulls the car over to the side of the road you can see the tyre tracks on the grass from previous takes.

Guest Cast: Jonathan Lipnicki began acting at the age of five, when he had a regular role on *The Jeff Foxworthy Show*, but it was his award-winning role as Ray in *Jerry Maguire* that made him a star at the age of six. He has since appeared in *The Little Vampire* and both *Stuart Little* films. Deborah Kellner has appeared in *Blast From The Past* and *Mighty Joe Young*.

Contempo Pop Music: 'Gone' by Sue Medley, 'I Can't Try Hard Enough' by Dag Juhlin, Brooke Ramel's 'The Answer', 'Dry Land' and 'Settling' by Tara McLean and 'I Know' by Kind Of Blue.

The Big Issue: 'The loudest sound of all is love unspoken.'

The Last Word: Buzz is the cute kid that only *Dawson's Creek* would produce – hyper-articulate, self-aware and dripping irony. If he's like this at nine, by the time he's Dawson's age he'll be able to out-verbal the entire cast.

Pacey and Joey continue to be at the forefront of the show. The mirroring of the Dawson–Joey–Pacey situations – in which one is always in love with the other but never able to say it – with the AJ–Morgan situation is nicely done and allows all the issues to be aired obliquely. Chances are you were either groaning or punching the air when Pacey kissed Joey. Some fans hate the Pacey–Joey relationship and want her to get back with Dawson; some think it was just a desperate move by the writers to stretch out the show; some think it works really well and is the best relationship the show has yet given us. I'll pin my colours to the mast and admit that I'm in the last camp. I was cheering for the guy.

318
Neverland

1st US Transmission Date: 5 April 2000

Writer: Maggie Friedman
Director: Patrick Norris
Guest Cast: Jonathan Lipnicki (Buzz Thompson),
Dylan Neal (Doug Witter),
Adam Kaufman (Ethan Brodie),
David Dukes (Mr McPhee)

Joey freaks out at Pacey for kissing her and refuses to talk to him during the rest of the drive home. She tells Bess and admits that she let Pacey kiss her. He tells Doug, who advises him to tell Dawson about his feelings for Joey in a place that reminds them of their strong friendship. When they find out that some local woods, where they built a fort as kids, are being turned into housing, Pacey suggests they go camping and Dawson agrees. They find their old wooden fort and just as Pacey is about to tell Dawson Buzz turns up with two friends. Dawson tells the kids scary stories and Pacey digs up a time capsule he and Dawson buried years ago. After the kids are asleep Pacey again tries to tell Dawson, but Dawson starts going on about how loyal Pacey is. Pacey can't do it. When Pacey and Buzz bump into Joey in town, Joey and Pacey apologise to each other, agree to forget the kiss and swear that they are just friends.

Jen finds out that Henry is having a birthday party and has not invited her. Andie suggests a girls' night out and Jen and Joey agree. They meet at Andie's for popcorn, toenail painting and face packs. Joey wants to go roller-skating, and Jen's activity is to try on underwear – so they go rollerskating in their underwear and bathrobes (Jen also

has a big pink feather boa). Jen stumbles on Henry's party
at the rink – he didn't invite her because he thought she'd
think it was too juvenile. She reassures him, they make up,
he gets to see her rollerskating in her underwear –
everybody's happy. Joey tells Jen about the kiss.

Jack invites Ethan to come and visit on a weekend when
he knows his dad will be away. Unfortunately, Mr McPhee
cancels his business trip and, upon finding an unexpected
house guest, tells Jack to send Ethan home. Jack refuses.
Mr McPhee tries to hang out with the guys but Jack keeps
telling him to get lost until Ethan invites him to join them
for dinner. Ethan and Mr McPhee talk about cars and they
end up visiting a vintage-car museum. Jack finally snaps
and rails at Ethan for inviting his dad. Mr McPhee leaves,
but not before saying that he cancelled his business trip to
spend time with Jack. Back at the house Ethan persuades
Jack to give his dad a chance and Jack asks his dad why
he's started making an effort – Mr McPhee's realised
Jack's a good kid and he thought he'd better make the first
move.

The Ballad of Pacey and Joey: 'Do you have any idea the
monumental implications of that meaningless little impulse? The ripple effect that it could create on our small
but fragile universe?' Joey shoves Pacey into the middle of
next week in her shock at being kissed, and at herself
allowing him to. She instantly raises the spectre of Dawson
and goes into a huge sulk. They both make it clear, to Bess
and Doug respectively, that the only reason they don't feel
they can be together is Dawson. As Doug and Jen point
out, Joey's reaction wouldn't have been so extreme if she
didn't feel something too – just compare this reaction with
the first time he kissed her (**109**, 'Double Date'), when she
definitely didn't reciprocate. Joey tells Jen that she's
'freaked out and angry . . . it came out of nowhere' and Jen
correctly points out that it can't have done because she's
not at all surprised by the news. When Pacey and Joey
meet in the shop it's awkward and stilted but friendly, and
he apologises, admits it would be a disaster to get together

and says the kiss was just an impulse and it meant nothing. Joey looks disappointed but agrees that she overreacted. When Pacey walks away she gives him the long lingering look of love.

The Ballad of Henry and Jen: The roller-rink birthday party is a Parker tradition but Henry agreed only because his mother promised it was the last time. He thought that Jen would have seen him as a little kid if she'd come and he would have been humiliated. Jen protests that his innocence is the best thing about him and he should have told her. She bought him a mint-condition vinyl copy of Bruce Springsteen's 'Born To Run' LP (it was a Springsteen song Henry sang in **311**, 'Barefoot At Capefest'), but when she found out she'd not been invited she traded it back to the dealer and bought 'angry chick music'.

The Movie Brat: When Dawson sees the fort he's disappointed because he remembers it as being larger than life, but it's pretty ordinary. 'Maybe my whole life has been ordinary.' He says he's 'been trying to reconnect with who I was in the past . . . I knew who I was'. He decides that the two things that haven't become jaded in his life are his friendships with Joey and Pacey: she's his 'conscience . . . soul mate . . . inspiration', he's 'pure loyalty'. When he tells the boys stories he tries to retell them old Spielberg plots. It's only when he's forced to that he creates something of his own. Even though he's taken the Spielberg posters down his instinct to homage rather than creativity is still there and that's what's holding him back.

The Delinquent: Jen is everybody's best friend these days. She counsels Pacey in **316**, 'To Green, With Love', Dawson in **317**, 'Cinderella Story', and now Joey. It's an interesting thing to do with the character who was everybody's big worry last year, to make her the stable one in the midst of everybody else's crises.

The Outsider: Jack tries to avoid a fight by not telling his dad about Ethan's visit and he's mortified when he finds out his dad will be at home. He tells Ethan that his dad hates him, isn't interested in knowing him, and 'can't muster a shred of emotion for his own son'. Jack is so angry that he can't see that his father's reaching out to him until Ethan points it out.

Family Sucks!: Deputy Doug is wise and cool when Pacey asks his advice, and Pacey's grateful and surprised. It's good to see these two bonding a bit now that they're cohabiting. But let's not go too far: Pacey still tells his brother that Dawson was 'the brother I never had', which has got to hurt.

Mr McPhee only needs to tell Jack that he's upset about Ethan's visit because he cancelled the weekend to be with his son, but instead he tries to lay down the law and sabotages his own best efforts. He tries to bond over cars and hang out with them when all he really needs to do is come clean. By the end he's told Jack how he feels and there's a feeling that maybe they could start to connect again.

All Things Spielberg: Joey is the bus, Dawson is the bomb underneath, Pacey is the heroic cop who's trying to stop the explosion and to do that he has to diffuse the bomb by telling Dawson. Doug riffs on *Speed* (Jan de Bont, 1994) and proves he's as much a Capeside film victim as everyone else in town.

Girl Talk: Andie's girls' night out is a far more satisfying way of hothousing the characters than Gale's news report (**212**, 'Uncharted Waters'). They need an 'oestrogen boost' and Andie thinks that they need to build some bonds of sisterhood. Joey the tomboy misses the days when she could hang out with boys and get dirty, climb trees and never worry about sex getting in the way – now she just wants to eat ice cream. Jen's mom was the exact opposite and insisted that Jen be clean and proper, eat properly and never mess with her mother's expensive clothes. Andie talks about her mother and how she used to feel protected and safe. And, by the way, where *is* her mother? She's vanished from the show without a trace!

Guy Talk: Pacey's uncomfortable with being the loyal one in Dawson's world, especially since he's fallen for Joey. When he describes Dawson he's almost describing the premise of the series: 'If I'm loyal to you it's only 'cause you cast me in the role. You're the storyteller . . . you're the guy who builds this fantastic world, you just let the rest of us live in it.' The time capsule contains Deputy Doug's pocketknife, ticket stubs from the first three times Dawson saw *Jurassic Park*, a photo of Dawson and Joey and a code he and Pacey devised the day they became blood brothers and wrote an oath of loyalty.

Kiss and Tell: We open with the Pacey–Joey kiss and she's kissing him right back.

Our Quips Are Wittier: Andie on Joey's and Jen's social lives: 'Don't you guys think it's a little abnormal that the two of you never hang out with anybody that doesn't have a penis?'

Contempo Pop Music: 'In My Life' and 'Even Now' by Trina Hamlin, 'Give Me A Reason' by Mission Delores, Brooke Ramel's 'Anything', 'If You Leave' by Last December, 'I'll Stay Right Here (Moments)' by Eli, 'Chosen Family' by Leona Naess and 'Go Be Young' by Edwin McCain.

The Last Word: All in all a slower episode. Not much happens in the Dawson–Pacey storyline, but then that's the whole point. Joey and Pacey have only two short scenes together, leaving us gagging for more, and there's a sense of stalling for time, or, more charitably, extending the suspense. Jack's story stands out as the best thing in the episode by some distance. David Dukes is very good as Mr McPhee and the relationship developing between him and Jack looks to be an interesting one.

319
Stolen Kisses

1st US Transmission Date: 26 April 2000

Writer: Tom Kapinos
Director: Greg Prange
Guest Cast: Rodney Scott (Will Krudski),
Julie Bowen (Aunt Gwen), Sarah Lancaster (Shelley)

Dawson and Joey are going to visit Dawson's Aunt Gwen and Pacey, his friend Will, and Andie are all coming along too. The sleeping arrangements for the first night mean that Pacey and Joey end up sharing a bed, which makes them both very awkward. While Joey and Dawson go shopping with Gwen and try to explain their relationship to her, Andie, Will and Pacey hit a pool hall and Will hustles some guys out of a lot of money. Later that night they sing karaoke and, when Gwen gets Dawson and Joey up to sing their old song, Pacey goes outside. Joey comes to find him, admits she has feelings for him too and Pacey kisses her. Gwen interrupts them and Pacey scarpers. Gwen tells Joey that she has to tell Dawson. Joey tries, but Gwen comes in at the wrong moment and Joey can't go through with it. Dawson starts making noises that indicate he thinks maybe he and Joey should get back together. That night Joey and Pacey talk outside and he gives her an ultimatum – she has to let him know how she feels, he can't keep initiating things. So she kisses him.

Henry is working at Leery's Fresh Fish as a bus boy. A new waitress, Shelley, fancies Henry, and Jen gets increasingly jealous as Shelley moves in on him. Eventually she causes a scene in the restaurant and calls Shelley a 'slutty wench' in front of all the customers before running off to cry in the storeroom. Henry finds her and they make up – she says being jealous freaked her out.

Mitch's friend Tom, who gave the toast at his and Gale's wedding, has died. His wife visits and gives them a copy of the toast, which moves Mitch to dig out the video of the wedding. After watching that, and reading the toast, they feel their problems are insignificant and, perhaps, over. They end up dancing together in the restaurant.

The Ballad of Dawson and Joey: Gwen wants to know why Joey and Dawson are not together any more and gets a potted history of the last two years' plot. Even after that she still can't understand why, since they're now past their issues and friends again, they aren't together. This sets Dawson thinking, and he tells Joey that *he's* forgotten why they're not together as well because 'we make sense of each other's lives'.

The Ballad of Pacey and Joey: Pacey agreed not to come to Gwen's, and later refers to his and Joey's 'arrangement', which implies that at some point between episodes they've talked about their situation and come to some sort of explicit understanding. He later admits he came because he wanted to be with Joey. They fight when they get into bed and if anyone on the floor had been awake at that point it would have been obvious something was going on. He tells her he can't compete with her history with Dawson and she replies, 'You're not supposed to compete: we're supposed to have our own his–', which pretty much gives the game away. Pacey thinks the situation is 'uncomfortable ... weird and I hate every single second of it'. She feels awful and they're both terrified lest Dawson or Andie find out. He's tried to get over it but he can't; she's tried to tell Dawson but she can't. In the end she has to admit she feels the same way he does.

The Ballad of Henry and Jen: When she finds out that Shelley fancies Henry, why doesn't Jen just say 'he's my boyfriend'? She gives Shelley extra work, gets jealous, rails at Henry and finally throws a tantrum, and all of it was entirely avoidable. She admits she has issues, and I should think so given that she refers to Henry as 'a funny little creature'. Mostly she feels vulnerable because he's broken through all her defences and she can't stand the thought of losing him.

The Movie Brat: Dawson's not sure where his efforts at reinvention have got him. He still feels the same as he always did. Joey nails it, though: 'You had to be the centre of attention; life revolved around you and your dreams; and recently I've watched you fade into the background and let others shine. You're different.' That's what the character's been doing in the show too, as the focus has moved away from Dawson. He tells Gwen he 'just can't find the inspiration any more'.

The Basket Case: Andie takes the lead integrating Will into the group, quizzing him in the diner. She plays right into Will's hands at the pool hall, though, shouting about how badly he sucks and setting him up to hustle without even realising it. She thinks it's seedy and wrong, but pockets her share of the winnings and seeks him out to talk to later. She wants to move on and lets Pacey know she's finally OK with his doing the same.

The Outsider: Jack's nickname 'Jackers' (**314**, 'The Valentine's Day Massacre') has stuck and Pacey calls him that twice. He passes on the trip to spend time with his dad, so it looks like that relationship's doing well.

The Puppy Dog: He's got a job as a bus boy at the restaurant throughout spring break, just so he can spend more time with Jen.

Family Sucks!: It isn't explicitly stated whose sibling Gwen is, but she remembers meeting Pacey when he was little at her sister's house, so I take it to mean she's Gale's sister. She was married to a boring suburbanite lawyer but later fell in love with a much older painter and ran away with him. He died of a heart attack after only a few years.

That Three-Letter Word: An attractive girl offers Henry sex whenever he wants and he totally freaks out, starts shaking, and runs to tell his girlfriend. Bless.

All Things Spielberg: Andie refers to Will as Tom Cruise in *The Color Of Money* (Martin Scorsese, 1986), a film about pool hustling that was a sequel to the classic *The Hustler*

(Robert Rossen, 1961). Will's favourite movie is *Planet of the Apes* (Franklin J Schaffner, 1968).

Grown-Up Stuff: Mitch and Gale seem to be on the point of getting back together. It was inevitable, really, but it's been handled really well.

Kiss and Tell: Joey tells Pacey she feels the attraction too and no man could walk away from a statement like that, so he gives her ten seconds to prevent him from kissing her and she doesn't. At the end he says he can't keep kissing her, that she has to kiss him sometime or it's never going anywhere – so Joey plants one on him good and proper, and the crowd goes wild.

Guest Cast: Julie Bowen was a semiregular, as Roxanne Please, throughout Season Five of *ER* and was a regular on *Extreme* and *Ed*. She's also appeared in *Happy Gilmore*, *Multiplicity* and *An American Werewolf In Paris*. Sarah Lancaster was a regular on *Saved By The Bell – The New Class*. Rodney Scott's character Will was spun off into the short-lived WB series *Young Americans*.

Contempo Pop Music: 'Walking In My Sleep' and 'One And Only' by Better Days, 'Goodnight Moon' and 'Idiot Waltz' by Shivaree, 'Wild Thing' covered both by Generation X and by Pacey in the karaoke later. The other karaoke tunes are 'Louie, Louie', originally recorded by the Kingsmen, 'Ooh Child' by the Five Stairsteps and 'Daydream Believer', recorded by the Monkees. Mary Beth plays us out with her cover of 'Daydream Believer', one of the very few songs on the show specially recorded at the request of the production team.

Ker-THUNK!: The sleeping arrangements just don't make sense. There's a double bed, and Joey and Pacey are last in the room, but Andie, Dawson and Will have all camped out on the floor. The assumption seems to be that Pacey has the bed no matter what, but why would that be? Surely it would be Dawson – after all Gwen's his aunt.

The Big Issue: Will: 'It's better to have a short time with somebody that you really love than a lifetime with somebody who's basically your roommate.'

The Last Word: The Jen-and-Henry storyline is a bit irritating. Both this episode and **319**, 'Stolen Kisses', have featured storylines based upon a character (this episode Jen, last one Mr McPhee) who fails to say a simple thing at the right time and then compounds that error time and again. I just want to shake them both and tell them to wise up. Mitch and Gale's thread is engaging, in spite of a touch of implausibility. (After all, how many kids really *do* manage to get their parents back together?) It again goes to prove that this show is a cut above the rest, giving the adults real problems and allowing them to be more than just adversaries and spoilsports. The two big scenes with Pacey and Joey sparkle. Their relationship is shaping up really well, and the promise of conflict with Dawson leaves us on quite a cliffhanger. A good installment – it stretches credibility with the sleeping arrangements and the Mitch–Gale developments, but mostly gets away with it.

320
The Longest Day

1st US Transmission Date: 3 May 2000

Writer: Gina Fattore
Director: Perry Lang
Guest Cast: Rodney Scott (Will Krudski),
Jonathan Lipnicki (Buzz Thompson),
Dylan Neal (Doug Witter)

True Love is finished and it's time to name her. Everyone gathers at the dock. Pacey and Joey are making out in the boat house and he asks her to give him one day to tell Dawson. Pacey goes out first and Joey follows a minute later through a different door. Dawson gives Pacey a bottle of champagne to name the boat. The rest of the episode is told following three different points of view.

Pacey: Pacey has Buzz for the day but dumps him with Doug so he can go to Dawson's. He stands outside the house unable to go in. Jen notices Pacey and tells him Joey told her she wants to be with him. Mitch comes out and tells them Dawson's at the library. Pacey misses him there but bumps into Andie and Will, who are going out on a date that evening. Back at Doug's, Buzz has destroyed the answering machine and driven Doug nuts. Pacey tells his brother about himself and Joey and Doug prophesies that when it's all over Joey will go back to Dawson and Pacey will be left alone. That night he's walking up to Dawson's front door when Joey runs up and tells him to stop. Dawson comes out to see what they're talking about and Pacey tells him that he and Joey are together.

Joey: After the naming of *True Love* Joey tells Jen that she's fallen for Pacey but doesn't know what to do about Dawson. Jen says she must tell him, and Joey replies that Pacey's doing it right now. Joey then goes to the library to finish an assignment and bumps into Andie, who tells her about her date with Will. Andie admits that she's not over Pacey at all, which mortifies Joey. Outside she sees Dawson, who asks her if she fancies movie night, but she says no and runs away. She phones Pacey at Doug's and leaves a message on the answering machine telling him not to tell Dawson. She runs to Dawson's bedroom, where she finds him watching *The Last Picture Show*, a film about a girl who comes between two best friends. She can't bring herself to tell him and leaves, but just then she sees Pacey going in and runs to stop him. Dawson comes out to see and this time we discover that he already knew about them.

Dawson: In the library Dawson meets Will and gives him advice on what to do on his date with Andie – take a boat out on the creek. He tells Will he's thinking of looking up an old friend – which obviously means Joey. Jen and Henry are hanging out on Grams's porch when Dawson arrives and Jen ushers Henry inside so she can talk to Dawson alone. Jen, thinking Pacey has already told him, offers her sympathies, which leads to Dawson figuring out what's going on. Henry comes out and tries to kiss Jen to make it better. Jen gets very angry and throws him out. In his room Dawson's watching the film when Joey arrives and then leaves. He waits a minute, then goes outside to see her and Pacey arguing. He totally loses it, disowns his friendship with Pacey and, like Doug, prophesies that Pacey will be alone when all this is finished. Andie and Will arrive. Dawson tells them what's gone on and runs inside with Joey running after him. Andie shouts at Pacey for being such an idiot and she too tells him he'll lose Joey to Dawson and be left alone.

In the house Dawson tells Joey they are no longer friends and she must choose between him and Pacey. Then he tells her to leave. Jen comes to see him later and he tells her he's going to fight for Joey. Joey finds Pacey at the dock and, as they both cry, tells him it has to be over. She walks away and when she looks back Pacey is gone.

The Ballad of Dawson and Joey: Dawson indicated in **319**, 'Stolen Kisses', that maybe he thought he and Joey should think about trying again, and when he asks her over for movie night it's clear he's got an ulterior motive. That makes the timing of the revelation all the more difficult for him. Andie tells Pacey that Joey will never love him as she did Dawson because he was her first love. Dawson tells Joey, 'If things are complicated between us it's because you made them that way'. And he's got a point.

The Ballad of Pacey and Joey: It's a week since the visit to Aunt Gwen's and Pacey and Joey have been making out at every opportunity since then in an 'embarrassing grope-fest'. Joey describes her feelings as 'a bizarre gravitational pull' towards Pacey and she can't stop thinking about him or wanting to kiss him.

The Ballad of Andie and Pacey: Andie meets Pacey at the library and all her feelings for him come flooding back and she realises she's not over him at all. Her speech to him about Dawson being Joey's first love and how you never love anyone like that is clearly meant to reflect on her and Pacey. She runs off in tears at Pacey's behaviour.

The Ballad of Henry and Jen: Henry's inappropriate response to Jen's little crisis gets Jen so angry she threatens to hit him. His exact words – and, boy, doesn't he wish he'd kept his mouth shut! – are 'I want to put us before whatever little mini-drama you and your friends have whipped up this week.'

The Movie Brat: Dawson's reaction to the news is about as extreme as it can be. He says that he is no longer friends with either Pacey or Joey, calls them malicious liars, asks Joey if she's punishing him and finally tells her that this has ruined everything and that there is no going back. His resolution to fight is the worst thing he could do in the circumstances.

The Clown: Everyone tells Pacey how alone he will be at the end of the day, but he forges ahead anyway. He's not sure if *True Love* is seaworthy yet, but he finished her, which is quite an achievement.

The Delinquent: Again Jen is the confidante, advising Pacey and Joey and trying to help Dawson. In fact it's her newly developed role as everyone's sounding board that gets her in such trouble as she lets the secret slip.

That Three-Letter Word: Sex instantly raises its head when Dawson tells Joey that Pacey will expect her to do it with him.

All Things Spielberg: Jen borrowed *All The President's Men* (Alan J Pakula, 1976) from Dawson. Michelle Williams had already filmed *Dick* (Andrew Fleming, 1999), a comedy version of the same story. Dawson rents *The Last Picture Show* (Peter Bogdanovitch, 1971) and uses it to make his point to Joey, narrating the plot and letting her figure out what she should do. It's the movie they went to see on their first date (**201**, 'The Kiss').

Girl Talk: Joey wishes she could be like Jen, able to act on her feelings without fear. Jen replies that the fearless get broken hearts just like everybody else. Andie tells Joey it's good that Will doesn't know how cute he is "cause God save us from the ones who do'.

Contempo Pop Music: 'Matter Of Time' by Jennifer Parsignault, 'Thank You' by Dido (probably best known from its sampling in Eminem's 'Stan'), 'Miss Fortune' by Eagle-Eye Cherry, 'Mend' and 'In Your Keeping' by Jann Arden.

The Big Issue: You rarely, if ever, get a second chance.

The Last Word: The best episode of the season and one of the top ten *Dawson's Creek* episodes ever. Nothing falls short, everything fits beautifully. The tension builds and each time we get a longer glimpse of the final confrontation until it all makes sense. Gina Fattore deserves enormous credit for crafting such a fine script. The direction is excellent as well. We see some scenes three times but each time the emphasis is different, the angle or the viewpoint revealing nuances that were hidden last time. After asking the audience to invest so much in Pacey and Joey throughout the season, and fading Dawson into the background, to have him behave this way brings him dangerously close to being the bad guy on the show and losing audience sympathy altogether.

321
Show Me Love

1st US Transmission Date: 10 May 2000

Writers: Liz Tigelaar and Holly Henderson
Director: Morgan J Freeman
Guest Cast: Rodney Scott (Will Krudski)

It's the Capeside regatta and Pacey has entered *True Love*, with Will as his mate. Weeks ago Leery's Fresh Fish agreed to sponsor him and, though Mitch wants them to rescind the offer, Gale sticks to it. Dawson decides to enter as well, persuades Andie to let him use Mr McPhee's boat, and gets Bess to sponsor the boat for the Potter B&B. Joey asks Pacey to sort it out with Dawson and he tries, but Dawson thinks that by winning the race he can prove how much he loves Joey. Mitch and Jack help Dawson crew the boat and he charges *True Love* on the finishing line and forces Pacey to swerve and lose the race. Dawson is disqualified and Pacey is *really* mad. Dawson argues with Pacey about Joey right in front of her and admits he still loves her. She tells him she just needs him to be a friend and he agrees, if that's what it takes. Pacey renews the lease on Joey's wall and tells her he's not giving her any ultimatums but he wants to know where he stands. Pacey tears the name off his boat and throws it away, but Andie picks it up, gives it back and makes her peace with him. Joey comes to Dawson's for movie night.

Henry has taken to standing outside Jen's house bearing a sign that reads JEN LINDLEY PLEASE FORGIVE ME. Grams suggests it's time to do just that, and when he appears in front of Leery's Fresh Fish Gale tells Jen to get rid of him, so Jen forgives him. He takes her to the roof, where he's prepared a picnic so they can watch the regatta fireworks. They sleep there and next morning Grams assumes they've had sex. She tries to give Jen the Birth Control Talk, but is relieved when Jen tells her she didn't have sex with Henry, that they really did just sleep together.

Gale isn't happy that Mitch backs Dawson in the regatta but he retorts that sometimes it's better to act than let everything go unspoken, as he and Gale have been doing. She takes the hint, closes the restaurant and prepares a special dinner for them. They end up in a passionate clinch.

The Ballad of Dawson and Joey: Pacey's assessment of the Dawson-and-Joey saga: 'Fifteen years of watching PG movies in your bedroom followed by another year and a half of pretending to be grown up only to drop each other at the first sign of crisis.' Dawson tells Joey his relationship with her is the one he needs most. He says he's glad Pacey kissed her because it forced him to confront the possibility that he might lose her and realise that he couldn't let it happen. His entering the race is about his trying to show her he loves her rather than just saying it, but talking is all he's good at, so he should have really stuck to that.

The Ballad of Pacey and Joey: They haven't spoken for two weeks and the first thing she talks to him about is Dawson, which upsets him. She asks him to sort things out and he tries his best. He finds her contemplating the wall he hired for her to paint and admits that he thought Dawson's outrageous behaviour would have made her resent him, but it hasn't and he's amazed. He asks if she could ever love him as a soul mate, like Dawson, and she begs him not to make it harder or make her choose. He takes the hint and walks away.

The Ballad of Henry and Jen: His stunt with the sign is endearing at first but Gale's right: it does become creepy after a while. He wants to show Jen that he's not like other guys, and that's why he stage-manages the rooftop picnic, to be 'the most original person in [her] life'.

The Movie Brat: Dawson said he was going to fight for Joey, and fight he does. He's childish, rude, dangerous, petty and quite clearly the bad guy here. Pacey tries to sort it out, Joey tries to sort it out, but Dawson just goes ahead and storms around like a spoiled brat. He tries to win Joey back by being more like Pacey – impulsive and confrontational – but when Pacey does it it's heroic and for the right reasons, and when Dawson does it he comes off as petulant and stupid. Has any other series ever made its titular character so completely the bad guy? (See **Backstage**.)

The Tomboy: Joey hates being in the middle of this war and wants everything just to go back to the way it was because she can't believe she's worth so much trouble.

The Clown: Pacey tells Dawson just to punch him and get it over with. He apologises but Dawson just turns it into a contest: Pacey versus the history of Dawson and Joey.

Dawson accuses Pacey of being interested only in 'girls you can save or screw' and he's got a point.

The Delinquent: Grams gives Jen back the dress she wore in the first episode and Jen says it's not her style any more. Grams agrees and tells her, 'You've become a beautiful, poised, confident, mature young woman'. She thinks that she's crossed the most important barrier – that she's worthy of being loved at last.

The Wicked Witch: Grams has made the winner's wreaths for the regatta on her own since 1953. She jumps to conclusions when Jen is out all night and hugely disappoints Jen, who thought it was obvious that she had changed. Even when she still thinks Jen's had sex with Henry she manages to accept it with grace, although her proposed talk about birth control would have been interesting!

The Outsider: Jack's the only one who stands up to Dawson and tells him he doesn't think he's right to enter the race, but Andie overrules him.

Family Sucks!: Joey's furious with Bess for sponsoring Dawson's boat but Bess just tells her to get over it.

That Three-Letter Word: Henry tells Jen that he'd 'be lying if I didn't think about it pretty much every time I breathe in or out'.

All Things Spielberg: Joey rents *E.T.* (Steven Spielberg, 1982), the same film they were watching in the first scene of the first episode, and she says that the words 'I'll be right here' – the *E.T.* quote that was first line ever spoken in *Dawson's Creek* – are 'some of the most comforting words in the world'.

Grown-Up Stuff: Gale and Mitch are back together and she tells him, 'You're more important, you always were, you always will be.'

Our Quips Are Wittier: Pacey's advice to Will: 'Avoid public nudity, stay off drugs, try not to murder anybody, and . . . don't sleep with any of your teachers – believe me it never works out as well as you think.'

Bloopers: Jen says that her reason for being angry with Henry is that he tried to have sex with her, and later he says he was glad they didn't have sex, as if it had been clear at the time that he was trying to bed her. But that's not really what happened in **320**, 'The Longest Day', at all – he kissed her because he didn't know what else to do, and because he was misjudging the situation, or at least that's how it looked.

Contempo Pop Music: Nik Kershaw's 'Fiction', 'Sunday Morning' by Better Days, 'Somewhere In New Mexico' by Jill Sobule, Megadeath's 'Crush 'Em', Dawson makes his peace with Joey to 'Let That Be Enough' by Switchfoot. 'Hazel' by Troy Young Campbell and 'Music To My Ears' by Jenny Bruce.

Backstage: When asked about the character of Dawson in Season Three, Greg Berlanti said, 'I think that the effort is always to make our characters as real and as truthful to who they are as possible. That does mean that sometimes they behave in ways that aren't as likable. I think that in the earlier half of [Season Three] we probably presented too many stories concerning Dawson that weren't as positive as they should have been. And hopefully we won't run into that problem again, but I don't want to make him boring either. You know? Likable doesn't always mean good. What you want to strive for is a character that is "understandable".'

The Big Issue: Actions speak louder than words – just make sure they're the right actions. Henry gets it right with the picnic, Pacey got it right with the wall, Gale gets it right with dinner, and Dawson gets it *spectacularly* wrong with the boat.

The Last Word: Somehow this feels reminiscent of the dark days of early Season Three, more dramatic and over-wrought than it needs to be. But it can't be denied that the love triangle is providing loads of drama, a real dilemma and no easy answers for any of the characters. The Henry-and-Jen story feels like it's treading water a bit: he keeps getting things wrong then saves the day with a Grand Gesture, but where's it going? Grams is great and Gale and Mitch finally get it sorted, which is grand. Also, Will is totally extraneous, as he was in the last two episodes. He just tells Andie he got his scholarship to Rawley, says goodbye to Pacey and leaves to start *Young Americans*. Did anyone think such a minor role would inspire people to follow his character in a new show? He should have been given much more to do if that was the intention. The two references to **100**, Pilot, are nice – the dress showing how far Jen's come since then; the scene of Dawson and Joey uneasily watching *E.T.* mirrors the very first scene and demonstrates how things have changed so much since then and can never really go back to the way they were. Not a favourite episode, but there are some nice touches, and the triangle keeps it afloat, dramatically.

322
The Anti-Prom

1st US Transmission Date: 17 May 2000

Writer: Maggie Friedman
Director: Greg Prange
Guest Cast: Adam Kaufman (Ethan Brodie)

The school year is ending and it's time for the prom, which has the theme of couples this year. Dawson asks Joey, who says yes but then regrets it because it'll cause conflict with Pacey. Andie tries to get Pacey to ask her and he takes the hint and does so. Jack wants to bring Ethan as his date, but the girl selling tickets unleashes a barrage of prejudice and refuses to sell him one. Dawson suggests they throw their own prom at the restaurant and Mitch and Gale agree. Dawson gives Joey some diamond earrings to wear and asks her to dance, but she keeps looking at Pacey, who keeps looking back. Joey accuses Dawson of arranging the prom, and parading her around all night, just to get at Pacey. Dawson denies this, but is angry that Pacey turned up at all.

Joey excuses herself and asks Pacey to dance. This upsets both Andie and Dawson, who walks out, with Joey chasing after him. He tells her he did arrange the whole evening to try to win her back, then kisses her and leaves. Pacey apologises to Andie but she says she's all right and tells him he has to fight for Joey. Next day Joey visits Dawson, returns the earrings and tells him she refuses to choose and he has to back off.

Ethan admits to Jack that he never did anything as brave as bring a guy to the prom. Jack's angry because he thought Ethan was more experienced than he was. Jack feels cheated. He tells Joey he feels totally out of place and thinks he made a big mistake coming to the prom at all. Ethan leaves to catch a train and Jack runs after him and tells him that he's confused about the nature of Ethan's feelings. Ethan dares Jack to kiss him. Ethan leaves, unkissed.

Jen tells Henry that they definitely won't have sex after the prom. He tells her he's going away to football camp for eight weeks, upon which revelation she flips and tells him they probably would have had sex after the prom, but now they certainly won't. Henry's baffled and when Jen closes her front door on him she makes it clear their relationship is over.

Dawson and Joey find Gale kissing Mitch goodbye at the Leery house in the morning. Mitch forces Gale to define the nature of their new relationship, and she does – by asking him to marry her again. He accepts.

The Ballad of Dawson and Joey: Joey and Dawson made a pact as children to go with each other to the prom if they didn't have dates and Dawson holds her to it. He sells it to her as just a friend thing, but later he tells her that he wanted to show her what she'd be missing by choosing

Pacey. Dawson misjudges it badly – he gets huge credit from Joey for suggesting the prom when she thinks it's in support of Jack, but then he loses all that credit by trying to use the event to influence Joey. She's not impressed: 'You might as well get on the PA and scream, "She's mine, Pacey. Ha, I win!"' Finally he accepts that he's got to stop trying to force a choice out of her.

The Ballad of Pacey and Joey: Joey takes the lead by asking Pacey to dance, which is pretty courageous given the circumstances. The attraction between them kicks in instantly when he whispers about how right it feels, compliments her on her mother's bracelet, disses the earrings even before he knows they were from Dawson, and reveals that he remembers everything about their times together in remarkable detail. He calls her elegant and beautiful and she closes her eyes. It's clear just how much she wants to be with him.

The Ballad of Andie and Pacey: Andie comes to study at Pacey's house, and he comes to visit her at home. Andie's the only one of the gang still spending time with Pacey, perhaps out of sympathy, but more likely because she's not over him, no matter how much she tells Jack she is. She wants him to ask her to the prom, but not out of pity, so she tells him she's got other offers, although she hasn't. The look on her face when Pacey and Joey dance is resigned and reflects that she really does just want Pacey to be happy and if that means his being with Joey then she's willing to encourage it.

The Ballad of Henry and Jen: Poor old Henry! He just can't win. Jen's sophisticated sex plans leave him totally clueless and he manages to misread the situation entirely. His decision to go to football camp for eight weeks in the summer without telling Jen is very stupid indeed, and then to drop that information into conversation at the prom without realising that she'd be upset is more stupid still. Most stupid of all is his protest that his decision had nothing to do with her, when of course it should have done. When she says goodnight he delivers an ultimatum – if she goes inside it will be the end, no more grand gestures or banner. And she closes the door in his face.

The Tomboy: Joey just wants things back the way they were but by trying not to choose she's only making things worse. She feels trapped and powerless. Dawson is still trying to force her to choose and Pacey is still refusing to put pressure on her, but it's clear whom she'd rather be with – she just can't think of a way to follow her heart without devastating Dawson.

The Clown: Pacey's spending most of his time moping. With final exams coming up, we've had no mention of how this is affecting his schoolwork, but it can't be good. He has decided to sail *True Love* down the coast to Key West during the summer and intends to leave straight after the last exam.

The Delinquent: Jen feels betrayed by Henry and feels stupid for opening up to him. It's just his inexperience that causes all the misunderstandings rather than malice or lack of care, but she's too sensitive and defensive to see that.

The Basket Case: From the selfish, untrustworthy, slightly unpleasant character that started the season Andie has grown back into a sympathetic and likable person; her support of Pacey, even though she wants him back, is touching and mature. She looks a million dollars at the prom, too.

The Outsider: Jack makes a brave decision when he tries to take Ethan to the prom, but when he's refused a ticket he wants to back down because he doesn't want it to be a political choice: he just wants to be left alone to have fun without having to fight for it.

School Sucks!: Barbara Johns's refusal to sell Jack a prom ticket, and the withering attack she makes on him for being gay, is the first time we've really seen any evidence of homophobia in Capeside High. It's overdue and should have been dealt with earlier.

That Three-Letter Word: Jen's opinion of prom-night sex is not high: 'You end up doing it fifteen minutes before curfew and it's completely unromantic and it's way too fast and it generally sucks.' Henry's all right with not doing it on prom night as long as they get to do it eventually. But at the dance they can't talk about anything else, silence falls and then Jen says that she said they wouldn't do it only to take the pressure off so they could do it spontaneously.

Metatextuality: Ethan has been spending time in Capeside and demonstrates that he has learned the rules of life there when he starts talking in TV-world analogy and tells Jack to kiss him: 'No lights, no cameras, no network television to cut to commercial – it's just you and me.'

Grown-Up Stuff: Dawson's reaction to finding Gale and Mitch kissing in the morning is just to feel numb. There have been so many changes in their relationship that he's given up trying to predict or understand it. Now he just goes with the flow. But he's happy when they agree to remarry.

Kiss and Tell: Dawson kisses Joey at the end of the evening and she later confesses that she did feel something, even though she didn't expect to. Poor old Jack can't kiss Ethan, even though he has the golden opportunity. Gale and Mitch are back to their old ways and Dawson, as ever, has to watch them snog to within an inch of their lives, not once but twice in an episode.

Contempo Pop Music: 'In Every Corner' by Julie Plug, 'This Misery' by Wild Colonials, when Dawson collects Joey we hear 'London Rain' by Heather Nova, which also played when he collected her in **201**, 'The Kiss', for their first ever date. 'It's Not Unusual' covered by Wild Colonials, 'Foresight' by Granian, 'I Believe' by Kind Of Blue, 'Once In a Life' by Twila Paris, 'My Invitation' by Sarah Slean and 'Little Things' by Chantal Kreviazuk.

The Last Word: The idea of an alternative prom is a good way of taking the staple of US teen flicks and TV and turning it on its head so that it's dealt with in an unexpected way. The love triangle continues to dominate and Dawson, while less out of order and slightly more sympathetic than in 321, is still getting on my nerves. Pacey continues to be quiet and unconfrontational but the fun is in trying to work out how long that can last. The highlight of this episode is in fact Gale's proposal to Mitch. It may be the minor storyline but it packs quite a punch and it's played very well.

323
True Love

1st US Transmission Date: 24 May 2000

Story: Greg Berlanti and Jeffrey Stepakoff
Teleplay: Tom Kapinos and Gina Fattore
Director: James Whitmore Jr
Guest Cast: Adam Kaufman (Ethan Brodie),
David Dukes (Mr McPhee), Obi Ndefo (Bodie Wells),
Dylan Neal (Doug Witter)

Gale and Mitch are getting married and Joey is maid of honour (see 212, 'Uncharted Waters') to Dawson's best man. Andie tries to persuade Dawson to make the first move towards making peace with Pacey. Doug tries to persuade Pacey to make his feeling for Joey clear, and later he pulls over Joey in her car and tells her that Pacey is leaving and she should do something about it. Joey confronts Pacey and accuses him of running away without even saying goodbye, but he responds that unless it ended with her asking him to stay the goodbye scene would be pointless. There is a farewell party for Pacey and during the wedding rehearsal it's obvious Joey wishes she were there instead. Dawson tells her to go because she's making him feel like she's stuck with him, but she stays. Later she tells him that if she thought he could forgive her she might be with Pacey. Joey finds that Pacey has written ASK ME TO

STAY across the wall he rented for her. He says he's not ready to give up and tells her it's time to choose. Pacey attends the wedding and Joey tells him she can't choose because of her feelings for Dawson. And that's it: she's chosen and she tells him goodbye. Pacey congratulates Dawson, they agree that things are never going to be the same between them, and he leaves. Dawson and Joey dance and she tries to convince herself that they'll have a great summer, but as she talks she can't hide that she's crying. After the guests have left Dawson tells her he has to let her go, and she must go to Pacey. She runs, leaving Dawson sobbing on the jetty outside his house. She just catches Pacey, tells him she loves him, they kiss and she says she wants to join him on his boat trip.

Henry apologises to Jen but she refuses to accept his apology and says she wishes they'd never met. He gets on the bus and leaves for football camp. At Pacey's leaving party Grams tells a story about a lost love and Jen ends up feeling awful for letting Henry leave the way he did. So on the way home Grams swerves the car around, with Jen, Jack and Andie in it, and takes off through the night after the bus. Next day they find it parked at a roadside stop and Jen runs out and finds Henry, declares her love and kisses him in front of a cheering crowd. Jen then decides they must do the same for Jack, so off they drive to Boston to find Ethan. They arrive at the school and find him outside with a friend. Jack walks up and kisses Ethan, only to find that the friend is Brad, Ethan's ex, with whom he's just got back together. Jack is devastated and returns home where his dad surprises Jack by comforting him. Then, hearing of Joey's decision and Dawson's misery, Andie, Jack and Jen gather in his bedroom with some movies to cheer him up.

The Ballad of Dawson and Joey: Joey tries to make her friendship with Dawson work because she's terrified of losing the one person with whom she's shared every event of her life: 'You're so much of my life, Dawson . . . your house is my house and your family is my family and there's not a significant event I've experienced that you haven't

experienced with me and I was so afraid of losing that.' She
tells him that he's the reason she broke up with Pacey. She
says they can spend the summer catching up, taking trips,
waterskiing and having fun, but she can't convince herself
or Dawson. Dawson finally stops fighting and accepts that
he has to let Joey go. He blames himself for preventing her
taking the scholarship to Paris (**201**, 'The Kiss') and
decides that 'Pacey is this year's Paris'. He accepts that
Pacey loves her and she loves Pacey, and although he still
loves Joey she can't love him back. He does say, though,
that it'll all end in tears and that all roads will eventually
lead Joey back to him.

The Ballad of Pacey and Joey: Pacey to Joey: 'Let's be
honest here: the decision to be together or not to be
together has always been yours.' He takes a leaf out of
Henry's book with his Grand Gesture, inspired by Grams's
tale at his party. Joey thinks that by leaving he'd be giving
up on her, and he agrees, so he finally decides to fight for
her. When she tells him at the wedding that she can't
choose because of Dawson, he tells her that she's finally
made a choice and he wishes she could have made it
months before and saved a lot of trouble. Joey's final
declaration to Pacey is great and she thanks him for being
there for her and challenging her and being the only one
of the gang who's not been trying to stop growing up.
When she tells him she loves him I cheered. And so they
sail off into the sunset for three months alone together on
the seas.

The Ballad of Henry and Jen: When Jen finds Henry and
tells him how she feels it rounds off a terrific storyline in
which she's grown hugely as a character. Jen tells him her
anger was all defensive and she was more nervous than
Henry about sex because she's never slept with anybody
she loved before. They kiss and make up in spectacular
fashion and he disappears for eight weeks.

The Movie Brat: Having sworn to stop fighting for her in
322, 'The Anti-Prom', Dawson has no choice but to accept

that he's lost Joey. When he tells her to leave and breaks down at the end he's finally a sympathetic character again.

The Basket Case: Andie's still not got over the pain of losing Pacey but she's still trying to mend fences between him and Dawson.

The Wicked Witch: It's Grams's finest hour as she whisks Jen and Jack off on a '*carpe diem* roadtrip' so they can have a chance of the perfect kiss and never regret things left undone. When she was young she worked in a naval hospital and met a young soldier, Thomas Culpepper, and spent a perfect day with him. He asked her to wait for him but she didn't reply and he flew off to fight in the Korean War. The next day she realised her mistake, hitched a seven-hour ride in a cargo plane, caught him at San Diego and kissed him in front of his entire ship, USS *Missouri*. He was killed soon after. (The USS *Missouri* served two tours in Korea so the date of Grams's perfect kiss was either August 1950 or September 1952.)

The Outsider: Poor Jack! He finally gets to the point when he can kiss Ethan and it's the worst possible timing. He tells his father that his life is like 'having all the problems of a typical teenager and there's this whole other level of constant fear and pain'. When his dad tells him he's glad Jack's gay, and holds him as he cries, there's a real sense that their relationship is mending.

Family Sucks!: Doug comes up trumps with good advice for Pacey and goes out of his way to impress the need for action on Joey. His character has come a long way since the endless (hilarious) closet-homosexual taunts that Pacey used to throw his way.

Metatextuality: The last scene in Dawson's bedroom is absolutely definitive and sums up the show in all its glory:

> *JEN*: . . . the words 'I want to be alone' are used far too often around here.
> *ANDIE*: Kinda ranks up there with, 'uh, can we talk?'

JACK: Yeah, and all those countless references to all things Freud and Spielberg.

JEN: I'm pretty sure of it. We're not in Capeside any more, Toto. This is some alternate reality where our intellects are sharper, our quips are wittier and our hearts are repeatedly broken while faintly in the background some soon-to-be-out-of-date contempo pop music plays.

When Jen delivers that last line she stares off as if she were straining to hear, and, yes, there it is, there's a song playing in the background! For sheer self-referentiality it's challenged thus far only by the opening scene of **303**, 'None of the Above', but they're both actually topped by the opening scene of Season Four (**401**, 'Coming Home').

All Things Spielberg: Pacey accuses Doug of being warped by watching too many Katherine Hepburn movies. 'We're not in Capeside any more, Toto' is a misquote from *The Wizard Of Oz* (Victor Fleming and King Vidor, 1939).

Grown-Up Stuff: So Gale and Mitch are married again. During Season One they drifted apart, in Season Two they split up, this Season they've got back together. It's been quite a ride.

Kiss and Tell: Jack feels able to cross the line and kiss a guy for the first time. Yay for Jack.

Contempo Pop Music: 'Jealous' by Sinead O'Connor, 'Sleepless' by Jann Arden, 'The Riverside' and 'I Will Be There For You', by Jessica Andrews, 'Promise Me This' by Pancho's Lament, Janis Ian's 'Days Like These' and 'Walking In My Sleep' by Better Days.

Backstage: The final cut of this episode ran fifteen minutes too long and so some elements were taken out. The most important cut featured the engagement of Bess and Bodie, an element that has yet to make it into a broadcast episode.

Greg Prange, one of the co-executive Producers, on Jack and Ethan's kiss: 'To be perfectly honest, we shot one version of the episode with the kiss and one version without. But, after we looked at both versions, we felt that the kiss was absolutely necessary for the storyline. I have to say, we were kind of nervous about it. But the studio and the network both supported us in our decision, and we feel very grateful for that.'

The Big Issue: Andie sums up not only this episode but delivers a manifesto for the entire series: 'Our pain makes us real . . . but we can't do it alone, none of us can.'

The Last Word: Now *that* is how to end a season. A wedding, a dramatic journey, a break-up, a make-up, a disappointment and two lovers riding off into the sunset – it's all in here. It's been a mixed season but it ends on a real high note.

Season Four

Regular Cast

James Van Der Beek (Dawson Leery)
Katie Holmes (Joey Potter)
Joshua Jackson (Pacey Witter)
Michelle Williams (Jen Lindley)
Meredith Monroe (Andie McPhee, up to **407**)
Kerr Smith (Jack McPhee)
Mary-Margaret Humes (Gale Leery)
John Wesley Shipp (Mitch Leery)
Mary Beth Peil (Grams)
Nina Repeta (Bessie Potter)
(although credited as Special Guest stars, the following were effectively
series regulars)
Sasha Alexander (Gretchen Witter)
Mark Matkevitch (Drue Valentine)

Adam Fields, who provided all the incidental music for Season One, returned to the show for Season Four and again provided all the incidental music.

401
Coming Home

1st US Transmission Date: 4 October 2000

Writer: Greg Berlanti
Director: Greg Prange

Guest Cast: Dylan Neal (Doug Witter),
Garikayi Mutambirwa (Jean),
Jason Daniel Roberts (John-John)

Three months have passed, school starts in a few days, and
Joey and Pacey sail back into town. Everyone wants to
know if they slept together during the summer, but they're
telling no one. Pacey's sister, Gretchen, is now staying at
Doug's, and Bess has rented out Joey's room, so both
Pacey and Joey are homeless for a few days. Jen persuades
Joey to come to the Dive-In – a film show at the waterfront
– and Dawson also agrees to go. Joey brings Pacey to the
Dive-In and much awkwardness ensues. Dawson and Joey
say hi, Pacey stalks off and later loses his temper with Joey.
Dawson drives Joey home and she gives him a present to
inaugurate a new friendship, about which Dawson is
doubtful. She then drives to the dock and finds Pacey on
True Love. They make up and we fade out on them reading
to each other in their hammocks.

Andie meets two French students on the beach and
shows them around town. They don't speak much English
and she speaks about them while they're present, assuming
they don't understand. Andie fancies Jean, who speaks a
little English but has a girlfriend. Then the other one,
John-John, reveals he's American and has understood
everything she's said, to her embarrassment. He asks if he
can kiss her and she agrees.

The Ballad of Dawson and Joey: Dawson doesn't want to
talk to Joey but he does, and it goes exactly as he expects:
'Joey and I are going to engage in some semi-casual
conversation until the awkwardness overwhelms us both
and then we're just gonna part.' But when they do part
Dawson has to stop and catch his breath, he's so shaken
by it. He looks both surprised and relieved when he
discovers Joey's still a virgin.

**The Ballad of Pacey and Joey – they Argue and Make Up,
Take 1:** This episode's bone of contention: Joey's relationship with Dawson.

Gretchen on the Pacey–Joey romance: 'It didn't take Nostradamus to call it . . . look at your similarities: you're both classic scrappy underdogs. She's sassy, you're a legendary annoyance; she's beautiful and you're lucky.'

Pacey and Joey have spent a magical summer, sailing up the coast and living on odd jobs. Pacey's reluctant to go to the Dive-In and avoids Dawson entirely. When he and Joey argue he accuses her of getting off the boat emotionally long before she did physically. She later agrees that she had been worrying about Dawson.

Dawson is still a presence in Joey and Pacey's relationship. They've discussed him on the boat and he's the cause of their first real fight. Joey buys Dawson a brick from Hemingway's house but tells Pacey it's a present for someone else – the first thing she does this season, after the teaser sequence, is lie to Pacey about Dawson. Pacey is the one who brings Dawson up, though, setting the pattern for the season – every time he gets insecure he raises the spectre of Dawson.

On the boat at the end Joey tells Pacey: 'My heart? That's a fixed point. Three months riding the open waters couldn't shake it, I'll be damned if I'll let your insecurities shake it . . . my heart never left this boat, it's never left you.'

Pacey reads Joey to sleep with 'The Little Mermaid'.

The Movie Brat: Dawson has developed a passion for photography during the summer, and his parents have built him a darkroom under the stairs. His bedroom is now covered in his own black-and-white photos of Andie, Jack and Jen. He says it's been the best summer of his life.

The Delinquent: Jen has spent the summer sunning herself on the beach. She nags Joey about coming to the Dive-In, and nags Dawson about talking to Joey when they're both there, because she feels guilty about letting Dawson find out about Joey and Pacey the way he did (**320**, 'The Longest Day').

The Basket Case: Andie loves Paris and has always wanted to visit. When she describes it she rattles off the names of famous painters: Degas, Cézanne, Monet, Van Gogh. She's almost right: they were all French except Van Gogh, who was Dutch. She avoids Pacey at the Dive-In, so she must still have some feelings for him.

The Wicked Witch: Grams doesn't approve of Jen and Henry's phone and email relationship – she thinks life is for living in the now. Which is, as Jen points out, a surprising stance for her to take.

The Puppy Dog: Henry is gone and will never return to the show. However, when we left him last season, he and Jen were tight, so the writers have to deal with him off screen. That begins when Jen tells Joey that Henry did so well at football camp that he won a scholarship to a boarding school and, since that will greatly improve his college chances, his parents have sent him there.

The Big Sis: Welcome to the stage Gretchen Witter, Pacey's older sister and Dawson's first crush. She has come home from college and is taking some time off, but it's not clear why she left or how long she's staying in Capeside, and she won't tell Pacey.

Family Sucks!: One of Pacey and Doug's three sisters, Kerry, and her kids are still at his parents' house. Doug is putting up Gretchen on the couch that used to be Pacey's, and driving her nuts because he's so clean. Pacey and Gretchen have an easy rapport and get on well – it's nice to see he has an ally in the family whom he can really talk to at last.

Bess surprises Joey by telling her that the Potter B&B is one of the most successful in the state. They've doubled their rates and they're booked up well into autumn.

That Three-Letter Word: Three months alone on a boat, deeply in love, hormonally poisoned teenagers, one of whom is Pacey, whose track record speaks for itself. So did they or didn't they? Joey thinks no one would dare ask; Pacey assures her they will. They agree to say nothing. Jack, Bess and Jen all ask Joey; Doug and Gretchen ask

Pacey; none of them get a crumb. But when Joey raises it with Dawson, and he says her answer could kill him, she says it wouldn't – she and Pacey didn't have sex.

Metatextuality: The opening scene brilliantly sets up the season. Pacey suggests that he and Joey don't go home and she asks if he's serious. He replies, 'Just what would we be missing from the land of poorly scripted melodramas, huh? Recycled plot lines, tiresome self-realisations, you throw in the occasional downward spiral of a dear friend and maybe a baby here and a death there, and all you've really got is a recipe for some soul-sucking, mind-numbing ennui, and I, for one, could skip it.' And indeed, throughout the season we do get a downward spiral, a death, a birth and lots and lots of self-realisations.

All Things Spielberg: The Dive-In movie is *Jaws* (Steven Spielberg, 1975). When Joey and Pacey see Dawson, and he sees them, the ominous shark music from the film underscores the scene. Gretchen calls Doug 'Felix Unger on crack' – Felix was the obsessive tidy-freak from Neil Simon's hit play and film *The Odd Couple* (Gene Saks, 1968). The sequel, *The Odd Couple II* (Howard Deutch, 1998), again by Neil Simon, features Mary Beth Peil, who plays Grams.

Grown-Up Stuff: Mitch and Gale are back to their old tricks – making out on the sofa, where Jen and Dawson find them. Have any of Dawson's friends *not* seen his parents getting it on?

Kiss and Tell: Andie gets to kiss the American/French exchange student.

Our Quips Are Wittier: Dawson on finding his parents making out: 'Welcome to the Leery household, where it's déjà-screw all over again.'

Bloopers: When Dawson is developing pictures with Jen he's developing shots that have already been seen on his bedroom wall.

Guest Cast: Garikayi Mutambirwa was the lead in the TV series *Van-Pires* and is also in the film *Clockstoppers*. Jason Daniel Roberts appeared in MTV's *The Real World*, something that garnered a lot of publicity for the start of the new *Dawson's Creek* Season.

Ker-THUNK!: Gretchen was Dawson's first big crush. It was a huge family joke. He loved her beyond all things when he was little. And she's never, ever, *ever* even been referred to in passing during the last three years of his life?

Buzz, the little kid whom Pacey mentored towards the end of the previous season, has gone, never to return. Didn't they establish that his emotional problems were largely caused by his male role models disappearing out of his life? And what has Pacey done? Gone off for three months. Does he go to see Buzz on his return, or do we even get a throwaway line to end the relationship off screen? Nope.

In terms of dramatic mileage, it's better to have the Pacey–Joey sex dilemma, and any actual consummation and its consequences, on screen. So it has been saved for future episodes. But can anyone really believe that during those three months alone on that boat, if they were real teenagers in anything other than a TV show, they *wouldn't* have had sex?

Contempo Pop Music: 'AM Radio' by Everclear, 'Souvenirs' by Mary Beth, 'This Year's Love'. Adam Fields is back doing incidental music and the show sounds right in a way it didn't in the previous two seasons. He set the musical style from the very beginning and having his music, and the themes from Season One, running throughout the episode makes this a Coming Home in more than one sense.

The Big Issue: Dawson says, 'You don't choose what you love: it chooses you' – which directly contradicts what Mitch said in **104**, 'Hurricane', when he told Gale, 'Love is a choice you make.' The push and pull between these two viewpoints has always been central to *Dawson's Creek*.

The Last Word: The introduction of Gretchen is clunky –
giving Dawson this never-mentioned crush is both stretching credibility and telegraphing too obviously a potential
relationship. The French-boy subplot for Andie again
brings it home how hard the writers find it to integrate her
into the storylines of the other characters. She kisses a boy,
but he never appears again, so what's the fuss? The episode
does have a lot to achieve and it's bound to creak under
the weight of it a bit. On the whole this is a good intro to
a new season, especially the teaser sequence. Future plot
lines are set up efficiently and it's clear that the writers are
well in control of things and have a plan for the year – the
difference between **401** and **301**, 'Like a Virgin', couldn't
be more marked.

402
Failing Down

1st US Transmission Date: 11 October 2000

Writer: Tom Kapinos
Director: Sandy Smolan
Guest Cast: Carolyn Hennesy (Mrs Valentine)

Pacey discovers that he flunked three classes last year and
is in danger of not graduating at all. He is determined not
to tell Joey, but he's worried about it, so he gets defensive
and tries to pick a fight with her. Mitch, the school's new
guidance counsellor, tells Dawson that Pacey's in trouble.
Dawson refuses to help Pacey, but he does go and tell Joey,
who confronts him with the truth. She's hurt that he didn't
share his problems with her.

Joey needs a job to raise money for college. She gets a
position as waitress at the Capeside Yacht Club. The boss,
Mrs Valentine, is a nasty piece of work but Joey drops the
name of a local rich couple and their son, Owen Ross, and
she gets the job. One obnoxious customer gives Joey a hard
time, but when he signs his cheque 'Owen Ross' she has to

start being nice to him in case her deception is discovered. Mrs Valentine finds that the Rosses are out of town, however, and she is all set to fire Joey until the obnoxious customer (who turns out to be her son Drue) tells her he saw Owen Ross the other day, and saves Joey's job.

Henry is avoiding Jen's online attempts at contact. He emails Jack and asks him to tell Jen that he's breaking up with her. Jen guesses before Jack can tell her and she's very angry with Jack, and hurt by Henry's cowardice. Jack and Dawson both manage to cheer her up.

The Ballad of Pacey and Joey – they Argue and Make Up, Take 2: This episode's bone of contention: Pacey's insecurity about Joey's far rosier prospects for the future. And her relationship with Dawson, of course.

Pacey clams up, Joey gets annoyed, she finds out about his problems at school, she tells Pacey off, and Pacey comes to apologise. When he does, it's a great scene (only diluted by the fact that we get it a number of times throughout the coming season). He tells her that she's 'wrecked' him. He expected her to choose Dawson, and ever since she chose him he's been waiting for her to realise what a mistake she's made. Dawson would never have screwed up school as Pacey has. Joey says that Dawson could also never have persuaded her to run away with him for the summer: 'We shared something that I'm gonna remember for the rest of my life. Don't you see? We're creating our own history here, a history that has nothing to do with Dawson . . . it's going to be the details that define us.' His insecurity is a constant problem in this relationship.

The Ballad of Henry and Jen: Henry, who was totally thrown by a girl coming on to him (**319**, 'Stolen Kisses'), is finding it really difficult being away from Jen and surrounded by girls who are interested in him. Andie sums up her disbelief when she says: 'After all that? After doggedly pursuing her for an entire school year? After scores of grand romantic gestures? After behaviour that clearly licensed professionals would call stalking . . . he wants to take a break?'

The Movie Brat: This is the episode in which Zen Dawson appears for the first time. He's laid back, mellow, reserved and just very, very Zen. The character evolution that began when he tore down his posters (**311**, 'Barefoot At Capefest') seems to have finally ended and brought us a wholly different person. He's a million miles away from the Dawson of Seasons One and Two, and I prefer him this way.

The Tomboy: Her feistiness with Drue is the Joey of old, and he likes it a lot. Her response to Mrs Valentine's interview is classic Joey: 'Before I submit to another second of your thinly veiled bitchery, do you need a waitress or not?'

The Clown: Pacey's worried that making up the classes and graduating may be beyond his abilities and he's terrified that he's really screwed up this time.

The Delinquent: Jen works out what's going on with Henry long before she has it confirmed. He was her only real boyfriend and she's really angry that he's dumped her this way.

The Outsider: Poor Jack, stuck in the middle of Henry and Jen's long-distance breakup. He tries to break it to Jen gently, and even seems about to back out, but in the end he has to seize the day, knowing full well he'll cop it for being the messenger.

The Big Sis: Gretchen tries to persuade Dawson to make up with Pacey, but the look Dawson gives her makes her back off right away. She is appalled at Dawson's musical taste and was a huge grunge fan when she was ten. She's also very good at giving Pacey motivational speeches: she tells him to sort things out with Joey and he actually takes her advice.

The Dark Horse: Welcome to the stage Mr Drue Valentine, whose parents divorced when his father ran away with a younger woman. His mother, who runs the Yacht Club, is obsessed by money and privilege, and Drue hates her. He's playful and confident, and he toys with Joey for fun but stops short of getting her fired.

Family Sucks!: Gretchen and Pacey have moved in together, into a ramshackle place on the beach. It's cheap but needs a lot of work. Gretchen comments on Doug's sexuality, implying he's gay – so it's not only Pacey who's convinced of that.

School Sucks!: Pacey flunked science, history and English last year and should have been in summer school, but he didn't check his report card before taking off on the *True Love* and so he didn't know. He has to take those classes again to stand any chance of graduating and going to college. Otherwise, he will have to retake his senior year.

Grown-Up Stuff: OK, so first Mitch was a substitute teacher, without qualifications. Then he was sports coach, again without qualifications. Now he's stand-in school guidance counsellor, responsible for psychological counselling of distressed teens? People spend years training to do this job to ensure they don't irreversibly screw up some poor kid. But Mitch is obviously such a nice guy that he gets handed it on a plate.

Kiss and Tell: Joey and Pacey have a policy on kissing in public: often and heavily. They're just getting used to the novelty of snogging in school corridors when poor old Dawson has to push past them to get into class. Oops.

Guest Cast: Carolyn Hennesy was a regular on Jenny McCarthy's short-lived sitcom, *Jenny*, and is a regular on *Strip-Mall*.

Contempo Pop Music: 'How Could We Know' by Say-So, 'Packing Blankets' by Eels, 'Cavity' by Stew, 'Homecoming' by Five Way Friday, 'Alone' by the Lads and 'Superman' by Five For Fighting.

The Big Issue: Dawson: 'If you do it right, loving someone is gonna hurt . . . . love sucks . . . feelings change, passion fades, partners come and go, but through it all one thing remains sacred – and that's friendship.'

The Last Word: It's their senior year at school and all the problems that brings with it are laid out. Joey hasn't got the money to go to college although she will probably get the grades, hence her job at the Yacht Club. Pacey's grades are terrible and there's a danger he won't even graduate at all. Both these elements will loom large in later episodes. Gretchen is fitting in very well and having her live with Pacey, yet be good friends with Dawson, helps bridge the gap between storylines that might not otherwise meet. The final scene between Pacey and Joey is superbly written and played, but there's a danger that their relationship will become all angst and no fun. Following the more over-wrought season opener, this is a definitive episode, containing all the strengths and weaknesses of Season Four.

403
Two Gentlemen of Capeside

1st US Transmission Date: 18 October 2000

Writer: Jeffrey Stepakoff
Director: Sandy Smolan
Guest Cast: Harve Presnell (Mr Brooks),
Carolyn Hennesy (Mrs Valentine)

Dawson and Joey are paired with Drue to present a talk on *The Two Gentlemen of Verona*, Shakespeare's play about a woman who comes between two best friends. Pacey and Jen take *True Love* out for the day but get caught in a hurricane. They make for a cove to shelter and Pacey says Dawson will come and rescue them because he and Pacey sat out a storm in that cove when they were little. At the Yacht Club, where he and Joey are studying, Dawson hears about the *True Love*'s plight and steals a boat from Mr Brooks, a cantankerous Yacht Club regular, and sails off, with Joey in tow, to rescue Pacey and Jen. Pacey doesn't want to leave the *True Love*, but Dawson forces him to, and they make it safely back to land.

Mrs Valentine is an alumnus of a college Andie is applying to, so Andie has an interview with her to have her suitability assessed. Mrs Valentine harps on about Andie's mental illness and makes it clear, in her sneeringly bitchy way, that she won't recommend Andie. When the storm hits Andie takes control at the Yacht Club, orders everyone around and deals brilliantly with the situation, whereas Mrs Valentine just flaps about uselessly. After the drama Mrs Valentine congratulates Andie and promises to write her a glowing recommendation. Andie and Jack tell her they couldn't care less and rip her to shreds.

The Ballad of Dawson and Joey: Drue is perceptive enough to pick up on the vibe between Dawson and Joey. After the rescue, Dawson looks mournfully at Pacey and Joey kissing and you can tell he's thinking, as Mitch points out, that it's not fair that he got to be the hero but didn't get the girl.

The Ballad of Pacey and Joey: Pacey wants to stay on the boat because all his best memories – of his summer with Joey – are tied up with it. When Dawson drags him off the boat it's a highly symbolic moment, signifying Pacey's final acceptance that he has to let the summer go and deal with Capeside and the day-to-day struggles of keeping a relationship together in the real world. Joey was incredibly scared for him: 'In the future when you're dealing with life-and-death matters, remember that you're thinking for two.'

The Movie Brat: Dawson tells Joey, 'Pacey and I are not going to be friends again. End of story ... after the greatest betrayal of my life, what's done is done.' He's unforgiving and resents that Pacey hasn't even tried to apologise. But when things get rough he knows exactly where Pacey is and risks his life to save him. He even jumps on to *True Love* and drags Pacey to safety. When Pacey thanks him, Dawson simply replies that it's exactly what Pacey would have done.

The Tomboy: Joey insists on coming with Dawson to rescue Pacey because she can't face the idea of losing both of them. It's her cry that finally persuades Pacey to jump ship. She tells Pacey that he must make peace with Dawson because 'how can you really be whole if you continue to pretend like he doesn't exist?'

The Clown: He has run down the batteries on the boat's engine and sails straight into the biggest storm in thirty years to hit Cape Cod. With sailing skills like that it's a miracle he and Joey stayed alive through the summer. He tells Jen he has no regrets but admits he hates how things are between him and Dawson. In **402**, 'Failing Down', Gretchen had to persuade him to tell his problems to Joey; this week Jen tells him to apologise to Dawson and try to square things there because, again, he's keeping it all in. Will he never learn? His speech to Dawson at the end is the first real contact the characters have had this season and it's a powerful moment: 'I'm really sorry that I ruined our friendship because I miss it badly, and, however far off it may be, I do look forward to the day when you and I might be friends again.'

The Delinquent: Jen's no longer depressed about her breakup with Henry: she's now officially pissed off. She tells Pacey that her one regret is never having been in love, and dismisses her feeling for Henry, saying that she couldn't have been in love if it disappeared so quickly.

The Basket Case: Andie is on new medication – Nardol – and it is making her a little light-headed.

The Wicked Witch: Grams is worried about Jen following her breakup with Henry and tries to put a cap on Jen's melancholy. Her faith deserted her when she thought Jen was going to die at sea, but she still tries to get Jen to come to church with her. When Mr Brooks has a go at Dawson for damaging his boat, and seems about to get some money out of Dawson for the damage, Grams wades in and lets him have it with both barrels: 'If I find out that you let him dip into his college fund, I will personally kick your shrivelled old butt.'

The Dark Horse: Drue is now attending Capeside High and shares English class with Joey and Dawson. He provokes them, gets them assigned to a project together, deconstructs their relationship and generally makes a nuisance of himself. But when things get rough he gives them the keys to the boats and directs them to the best one. He knew Jen back in New York, but didn't know she was living in Capeside. When Jen sees him she says, 'God help us all!'

The Grouch: Welcome to the stage Mr Brooks. He always comes to the Yacht Club on Thursdays for prime rib special and he's a grouchy, bad-tempered pain in the ass. His boat, *The Artful Dodger* (after the character from Charles Dickens's novel *Oliver Twist*), is gashed during the rescue, and even though he knows the circumstances he is not amused. He's silenced by Grams's outburst, though, so perhaps he's more bark than bite.

Family Sucks!: Andie gives Mrs Valentine the phone numbers of Grams and the Leerys, and tells her to call and reassure them. But she doesn't give her contact details for Bess or any of the Witters.

School Sucks!: Pacey manages the seemingly impossible – he gets his first A grade.

All Things Spielberg: This episode is basically a rip-off or, if you prefer, homage to *The Perfect Storm* (Wolfgang Petersen, 2000) – Joshua Jackson admitted as much in an interview with Channel Four recorded during filming. They even reference the film directly: when Pacey tells Jen he's seen weather like this before, she replies 'Where? In *The Perfect Storm*?'

Drue proves that he fits perfectly into the Capeside scene by deconstructing the Pacey–Joey–Dawson love triangle in terms of *Star Wars*: 'You [Dawson] are obviously Luke to this Pacey guy's Han Solo . . . you're the stuff of pre-teen daydreams: cute, smart, nonthreatening. Which is great and all, but not for princess Joey here, who's clearly smack dab in the middle of her bad-boy phase.'

Grown-Up Stuff: Gale is suffering from nausea, but she thinks it's a cold.

Guest Cast: Harve Presnell has a long and illustrious career behind him, featuring in musicals, television and film. On TV he's been Dr Sam Lane in *Lois & Clark* and Mr Parker in *The Pretender*; on the big screen he's appeared in *Face/Off*, *Fargo*, *Saving Private Ryan* and *Paint Your Wagon*.

Contempo Pop Music: 'I'm Gonna Make You Love Me' by the Jayhawks and 'Never Saw Blue Like That' by Shawn Colvin.

The Last Word: Given the scope of their ambition in this episode it's amazing they pull it off as well as they do. There are some moments where the storm seems really tame and the live-action shots don't quite match the CGI effects, but this is dramatic stuff and on the whole they get away with it. The final scene between Pacey and Dawson, with its pull-back long shot of them walking away in different directions, is really well done.

404
Future Tense

1st US Transmission Date: 25 October 2000

Writer: Gina Fattore
Director: Michael Lange

Drue wants to reacquaint himself with the bad old Jen he knew in New York, the girl he took lots of drugs with. She tells him she's changed but he doesn't buy it. He organises a party for her and invites the whole school to celebrate her birthday – only it isn't actually her birthday! At the party she guesses that it isn't Drue's house, but a deserted summer house, and if they get caught she'll get busted for it because everyone thinks it's Jen's party. Jen finds out, however, that Drue lives with his mother in an apartment above the Yacht Club and couldn't have thrown the party there. She apologises and seems ready to accept that he has changed and really threw the party for her benefit. Then he gives her a birthday present – two tablets of ecstasy. She is angry with him; he walks away leaving the two tablets on the table for her.

Joey is fourth in her class and has good prospects of being accepted to an Ivy League college. This really bothers her, because it will cost a lot of money and she's worried about getting so close but not getting in. She's reluctant to talk to Pacey about it because he's got a good chance of not even graduating, but she does tell him and he's not very sympathetic, so she drags him to Drue's party. She gets drunk and talks with Jen and Dawson before eventually joining Pacey and Drue for strip poker. Pacey decides she's had enough and takes her home. Dawson is upset by seeing how close she and Pacey are and talks about it with Leery's Fresh Fish's newest bartender – Gretchen.

Jack breaks his shoulder in football practice and will have to sit out the rest of the season. Andie is concerned about his late applications for college and nags him until he loses his temper and tells her to back off. Since football was the only thing that made him feel like he fitted in at school, he's now more concerned about simply surviving senior year than which college he's going to attend. Andie apologises and tells him that when she's nervous about her future she looks for things to fix and she's been trying to fix him.

The Ballad of Dawson and Joey: Dawson tells Gretchen that seeing Pacey and Joey have a lovers' spat was worse than seeing them kiss because he can't escape noticing how much Joey loves Pacey.

The Ballad of Pacey and Joey: Pacey is unsympathetic to Joey's problems with college but she doesn't get angry with him about it. He tries to lay down the law at the party and prevent her from drinking but realises that she'd kill him if he stuck to that, so he backs away slowly. Throwing her over his shoulder and taking her home is hilarious and the fact that she doesn't scratch his eyes out indicates how much she's willing to let him get away with. No episode has even shown Joey this obviously happy and in love. She may be drunk when they get back to her place but she's all over Pacey. She offers to stay in Capeside to be with him, but he tells her he's going to follow her wherever she goes to college. He also tells her he's in love with her, which puts her on cloud nine.

The Ballad of Dawson and Gretchen: The final scene, with Gretchen prising confessions out of Dawson and giving him a pep talk to get him sorted, sets the tone for their relationship – she's the older, wiser, experienced one who's very good at giving advice and listening to Dawson's moaning. He tries to turn the tables and get her to tell him her problems, but she's not ready yet.

The Movie Brat: During the opening montage of the gang talking to the guidance counsellor they all seem hyper or animated, and then in the middle of all this angst is laid-back Zen Dawson – no scene better demonstrates the changes in the character and the bizarre detachment he exhibits these days. He isn't convinced about college and tells his mother, 'College is basically just a holding pen for eighteen- to twenty-two-year-olds . . . kind of like prison with a better meal plan.' He's applying only for colleges on the west coast, which he says is because he's movie-obsessed and wants to study in California; Gale thinks it's because he's running away from Joey.

The Tomboy: Drunk Joey is a sight to see, loving everyone, waving her arms about to stay upright, giving Pacey puppy-dog eyes to get him to carry her home. She will definitely need a good financial-aid package to get into college, and the counsellor tells her to be prepared for possible disappointment if she applies only to Ivy League colleges. She still wants to leave Capeside and do great things, but she's willing to postpone it, or even give it up entirely, to be with Pacey.

The Clown: Pacey is very worried he won't get into college at all, but will follow Joey wherever she goes. His aptitude test suggests he should pursue a career in law enforcement. Ha!

The Delinquent: Jen is shocked at Drue's gift, but did she leave the tablets there or take them with her?

The Basket Case: Andie is way ahead on her college applications and Harvard say she has a good chance of acceptance.

The Outsider: Jack's out of football for the season and he hates that. He feels very insecure without it giving him the kudos in school and the social position that goes with it.

The Big Sis: Gretchen assures Mrs Leery, when she's applying as a bartender, that she's on leave from college indefinitely, but won't give her reasons for leaving.

The Dark Horse: Drue was not one of Jen's ex-boyfriends, but he was an 'indiscretion'. He and Jen were on drugs at the time so she's not sure how much of it he remembers (this becomes important in 417, 'Admissions'). He used to buy lots of drugs in New York and Jen would try whatever he threw at her. His stunt with the party is a classic and helps him get to know people who were not even talking to him beforehand. Jen comes to believe he's changed and seems ready to become friends with him before he gives her the ecstasy. After that she cuts him dead.

Metatextuality: At the end of Season Four the characters in the show are all going to leave school and go to college. How can the show survive that and remain believable? In *Beverly Hills 90210* and *Buffy*, all the characters went to college in the same town. Will *Dawson's Creek* go down the same route? Not according to Joey: 'Maybe I'll just go to one of those fictional colleges. You know, like on those lame high school TV shows that go on for way too long. And then, just in time to save the franchise, all of a sudden it turns out that there's this amazing world-class college that's right around the corner where all the principal characters are accepted.'

All Things Spielberg: Jen says that Drue can convince you that he's 'the sausage king of Chicago', which alludes to a scene in *Ferris Bueller's Day Off* (John Hughes, 1986). Drue calls Capeside 'Pleasantville', after a town in the film of the same name (Gary Ross, 1998), in which everyone lived in a cutesy, black-and-white, fictional 50s sitcom. Gretchen admits she's not '*Coyote Ugly* material'; this bizarrely named film (David McNally, 2000) featured the adventures of glamorous bartenders.

Girl Talk: Joey drunkenly toasts Jen's un-birthday and tells her she loves her, even though she can't remember when they actually became friends. Andie asks Jen and Joey if she's 'too controlling' and in unison they answer, 'Yes!' Joey's Dadaist explanation of Andie's nature is that 'some people like salad dressing on the salad, and some people like it on the side', whatever that means. Joey asks where they all see themselves in five years. Jen says she'll be starting her master's thesis, 'Are Men Necessary?' Andie says she'll be in PR. Jen thinks Joey will have graduated from an Ivy League college and accepted a job in a trendy art gallery in Soho, New York. They agree to meet again in five years and see if their predictions came true.

Contempo Pop Music: 'Sorry' by Moxie, 'Something To Say' by the Mike Plume Band, 'Backstreets' by Filibuster, 'Never the Same' by Supreme Beings of Leisure, 'Sugar Star' by Crushing Velvet, 'Five Alive' by Medium, 'Please, Please (Stacy's Song)' by Plug, 'You Won't Fall' by Lori Carson, 'Respect' by Train, 'Day Ditty' by Wild Colonials and 'What You Don't Know' by Kate Reider.

Backstage: So Andie and Jack are both in the same year at school. Does this mean they're twins? This question has never been addressed and it became a running joke among the writers, so much so that a whole conversation in this episode deliberately muddies the waters:

ANDIE: Do you realise that next year is gonna be the first year ever that we're not gonna be in the same school together?

JACK: Hey, I tried to start kindergarten without you.

ANDIE: What? That is such a story that Mom and Dad told you. And besides, how could your version of the story possibly be true when everybody knows it's a fact that I, the more responsible one, am definitely the older sibling in this relationship.

On the website, however, staff writer Liz Tigelaar gives the answer: 'Jack and Andie are not twins. Jack is older than Andie. They are a little less than a year apart in age but he didn't want to start school without her so he was held back so they could begin together. That is why they are in the same grade.'

The Big Issue: Gretchen: 'All the things you want to be, you already are.'

The Last Word: Following the drama of **403**, 'Two Gentlemen of Capeside', this is a mellower, more contemplative piece when the spectre of college really begins to make itself felt, and the possible gulf between Joey's and Pacey's futures starts to shadow their relationship. Katie Holmes as drunk Joey is hilarious.

405
A Family Way

1st US Transmission Date: 1 November 2000

Writer: Maggie Friedman
Director: Nancy Malone
Guest Cast: Obi Ndefo (Bodie),
Harve Presnell (Mr Brooks), Carly Schroeder (Molly),
Bridgett Newton (Caroline)

Gale is pregnant but decides she and Mitch are both too old and too in debt to have the child. Dawson, at first shocked when he finds out she's pregnant, then manages to talk himself into being happy for them just before he's told they're not keeping it.

Jack takes on a coaching position for a little-league soccer team. Caroline, the older sister of one of the players, Molly, makes a very obvious pass at him and when she won't take no for an answer he tells her he's gay. When the next game rolls around two boys have been taken out of the team because their fathers think Jack, as a gay man, is dangerous around kids. Jack considers quitting but decides to stick it out.

Joey can't decide if she's ready to sleep with Pacey but, on Jen's advice, she goes to the free clinic for a consultation. Bess finds the pack of booklets and contraceptives that Joey is given at the clinic and provokes an argument. Eventually Joey tells Pacey she's not sure she's ready.

The Ballad of Pacey and Joey – they Argue and Make Up, Take 3: Sex has become an issue for Pacey and by stopping their make-out sessions he tries to kick-start a conversation about sex. Joey thinks it's 'one of those times when you say that you're kidding around but we're really having a fight'. She takes his point and addresses the issue but tells him, 'If you do turn into some typical silly-ass teenage boy and try to manipulate me again I'm out the door.'

The Ballad of Dawson and Gretchen: With Pacey no longer his best friend, and Joey making him feel awkward, Dawson has chosen Gretchen as his first port of call when he needs to talk about the things that are bothering him. His photograph of her is the only one Mr Brooks thinks shows a real connection with the subject. She trusts him with her secret (see **The Big Sis**) and knows he won't tell anyone.

The Movie Brat: Dawson's initial reaction to Gale's pregnancy is disappointment – they're in debt, in their forties, he's about to leave for college and they've only just remarried – and he thinks having a baby is 'completely irresponsible'. He tries to feel happy for them, and

Gretchen, by pointing out how hard it must be for Gale, helps him accept it. The next stage is supportive Dawson, when he tells his parents how happy he is only to be told that Gale doesn't want to have the baby. He's unable to understand her decision, but again Gretchen helps him to see things in a different light. He tells Gale, who is in part unsure about the baby because she's unsure of her own ability as a mother, 'You are the best mother I know . . . all you've done is make me proud. You're not afraid to make mistakes and then pick up and to keep going and keep trying new things, and I owe so much of who I am to you.'

The Tomboy: When Bessie tells Joey that she can't understand the consequences of having sex, Joey retorts, 'I am the oldest seventeen-year-old in Capeside . . . my whole life is consequences and responsibility.' She moans to Bodie that Bessie really should be grateful for her since she's most mothers' dream child.

The Outsider: Jack was mediocre at soccer in junior school, but Andie's persuaded him to take up coaching to help his college applications. He shows an instant ability with kids and handles the initially sullen Molly very well indeed. Her older sister, Caroline, though, leaves him tongue-tied. He doesn't want to tell her he's gay because he fears a homophobic backlash and 'I want to put "soccer coach" on my apps, not "gay civil-rights campaigner" '. When the backlash does come he's understandably gutted, but Molly supports him. He wants to quit because he's sure it'll get worse, but Andie talks him out of it. Jack: 'I'm a good person, Andie. When people look at me they see something awful. Do you know how that feels?'

The Big Sis: Gretchen is the one who guesses that Gale is pregnant rather than ill, and so Dawson guesses that she has been pregnant herself. She got pregnant by her boyfriend in the back seat of his car with Lynnard Skynnard on the radio (and she hates Lynnard Skynnard). She had a 2.9 Grade Point Average and lots of student loans, so she had a hard time deciding whether to keep the child, but she made a decision. We never find out whether she would have kept it or not, but either way she had a miscarriage.

The Grouch: Dawson is painting Mr Brooks's house to pay off the money he owes for gashing *The Artful Dodger* in **403**, 'Two Gentlemen of Capeside'. Mr Brooks tears into Dawson's photography, saying it lacks talent or emotion. But when he does see a picture he likes, of Gretchen, he grudgingly offers praise and encouragement.

That Three-Letter Word: After Joey's summer cruise with Pacey, Bessie was eager for salacious sex news, but now she tells Joey she's too young to be having sex at all. The doctor at the health clinic is alarmist, batters Joey with scary stories and brutal questions, and comes close to freaking her out before backing off and showing the good side. Do sex clinic doctors really employ such shock tactics with nervous teenage girls? Joey tells Jen, 'Pacey's not the problem, it's me ... the waiting just goes on and on and at this point even I'm getting impatient, but for some reason I just keep waiting ... of course I want to have sex, the question is, am I ready?'

Reality Bites: Dawson's reality issues have faded throughout the run of the series, as he's grown up and become more relaxed, and that's demonstrated when he tells his parents, 'I used to idealise this perfect childhood with this perfect house ... you guys gave me something so much better, you gave me something real.'

Grown-Up Stuff: Gale and Mitch tried for three years to have Dawson, and then five more years for more children before giving up hope. Mitch obviously wants to have the child but respects Gale's decision.

Contempo Pop Music: 'Everyone' by Five Way Friday, 'Just Another' by Pete Yorn, 'Feel the Movement' by Bright Blue Gorilla and 'Crest of Mary' by Verbow.

The Last Word: Jack gets a storyline at last and it's promising. Mitch and Gale also need to have a storyline this season and, since we've had the affair, the divorce and the remarriage, they've pretty much exhausted the marital-strife options. The pregnancy was an inspired idea and gives the characters, and the marriage, a new lease of narrative life. Gretchen gets a new layer of depth with the revelation about her pregnancy, and Mr Brooks reappears, promising a new character in the mix. There is a sense of beginnings in this episode; it was necessary if the show was to avoid becoming solely about the Pacey–Joey–Dawson triangle.

406
Great Xpectations

1st US Transmission Date: 8 November 2000

Writer: Nan Hagen
Director: Bruce Seth Green
Guest Cast: David Dukes (Mr McPhee)

There's a rave outside Capeside. Gretchen persuades Joey and Pacey to come but fails to persuade Dawson. However, when Gale and Mitch tell him they've decided to have the baby he is in such a good mood that he turns up anyway, and he drives Gretchen, Joey and Pacey there. Drue tries to get Jen to go and relive her party days but she refuses. However, she bows to pressure from Andie, who is going with Jack.

Andie cannot feel happy about her Harvard acceptance. When she sees Jen with the ecstasy tablets Drue gave her in **404**, 'Future Tense', she pumps Jen for information on how it makes you feel. Jen tells her it's great, at first, and makes you feel really happy but leads to a great downer. Andie, desperate to feel happy, takes one without Jen's permission. Despite Jen's attempts to look after Andie at the rave she goes off with Drue, tells some unpleasant truths to Joey and Pacey, and passes out as the drug interacts with her medication. She's rushed to hospital and is stabilised, but it's close. The gang follow, except Jen, whom Jack tells to get lost. Pacey stays with Jack and Andie, while Dawson drives Gretchen home and then stays up till sunrise talking to Joey.

The Ballad of Dawson and Joey: Jocy looks uncomfortable when she sees Dawson and Gretchen listening to a CD together in the record shop, but tells Pacey that it doesn't bother her. When Joey asks Gretchen if something's happening with Dawson, Gretchen replies, 'If Dawson is waiting for some childhood crush to come around again he's not waiting on me.' Joey's thrilled by Gale's pregnancy and she and Dawson conjure the image of the new Leery and Alexander Potter rowing across the creek to each other in the years to come, and it makes them feel old. She tells him she finds it hard to imagine life without him. His reply – that she managed pretty well throughout the summer – betrays his lingering bitterness.

The Ballad of Dawson and Gretchen: It's Joey who first suggests to Gretchen that Dawson might be interested in her as more than a friend. Gretchen confronts Dawson and he says they're just friends and that's that, but when they say goodnight on her porch there's an awkward should-I-kiss-her? moment, as there is when they fall on each other on the bouncy castle at the rave.

The Movie Brat: Following his confusion in **405**, 'A Family Way', Dawson's overjoyed when he finds out he's going to have a sibling. He turns down the rave invitation from Gretchen because it's totally alien to him, although he says he may accept 'if and when I'm ready for you to see how insufferably uncool I am'. He feels awkward driving Pacey and Joey to the rave but he's getting used to them. It's significant of the change in his allegiances that he tells Gretchen about the baby before Joey.

The Clown: Pacey misses the *True Love* and what it represented for him and Joey. Raving is not even his idea of music, let alone a good time. He's uncomfortable with the idea of Dawson dating his sister. When Andie's taken to the hospital he blames himself for not realising she was high, and stays to help look after her.

The Delinquent: Jen used to rave all night long, on ecstasy, at a New York club called the Haunt; Drue calls her 'the über-raver'. Jen denies she still feels the urge to party, but she's looking mighty thoughtfully at those tabs when Andie finds her, and she does take them with her to the rave, presumably intending to take one there. She gives Andie a summary of the effects and unwittingly makes it sound exactly what Andie's looking for, but she's horrified when Andie takes one. Jack blames her for Andie's collapse and says it should be her in the ambulance. Drue gives it to her straight, and plays on all her worst fears: 'You came here as the banished bad seed, Jen, that's all you'll ever be to them . . . they want you to play that role so they can feel better about the pathetic, plastic, Mayberry existence they're living.' She's started looking for colleges to apply to.

The Basket Case: Andie's got what she always wanted – an acceptance to Harvard – but her medication evens out her highs and lows so much that she can't even feel happy about it. The ecstasy seems like a good solution. Under its influence she admits she's not over Pacey, and she thinks Joey's dumping Dawson and going out with Pacey was cold.

The Outsider: Jack's condemnation of Jen is instant and brutal, and he doesn't even spare Andie, berating her in her hospital bed and telling her how angry he is with her. He's very proud of her Harvard acceptance, though.

The Big Sis: Gretchen loves raves and was the queen of all her high school dances. Her friendship with Dawson is very important to her and has helped her make the transition to being back in Capeside.

The Dark Horse: Drue relentlessly teases and hassles Jen and dances with Andie even when he knows she's high. He admits to Jen that he's 'damaged'.

Family Sucks!: Mr McPhee is hugely proud of Andie and he and Jack seem to get on well, too – the relationship appears to have mended nicely over the summer.

That Three-Letter Word: Jen on size: 'I think size only matters when you have a full view of the entire package.'

Metatextuality: Drue fulfils the same narrative function as the dear, departed Abby, so when Gretchen asks Dawson who Drue is he replies, 'Did you ever meet Abby Morgan?' Joey says, 'Any one of us could go at any moment for the silliest of reasons'; has she seen **407**, 'You Had Me At Goodbye' perhaps?

All Things Freud: Joey on Dawson's inability to grow up (which seems out of date now, a reflection on his Season Three self rather than his more mature, Zen, Season Four persona): 'Dawson has this way of hanging on to things since he was, like, twelve . . . sure, he outgrows them, puts them in their proper perspective, but that doesn't always mean they're gone.'

Grown-Up Stuff: Gale and Mitch have the balloons out; they're slow-dancing in the kitchen; and they're happy when Dawson goes out for the night. It's just like old times.

Contempo Pop Music: 'Hey Pretty' by Poe, 'Far From Saved' by Granian, 'Block Rockin' Beats', 'Setting Sun' and 'Leave Home' by Chemical Brothers, 'Protocol' by Symbiosis and Eva Cassidy's cover of Sting's 'Fields of Gold'.

The Big Issue: Drugs bad, raves not much better.

The Last Word: As Joey says to Dawson, 'It's scary how real everything's been this year', and mortality is close at their heels – the storm nearly took Jen and Pacey, and now the drugs nearly take Andie. Sleepy Capeside now has a rave culture, again stretching their one-horse-town schtick beyond plausibility, but this is a good episode and reflects the more adult tone of the show. Meredith is particularly good, as is Mark Matkevitch as Drue.

407
You Had Me At Goodbye
1st US Transmission Date: 15 November 2000

Writers: Chris Levinson and Zack Estrin
Director: John Behring
Guest Cast: Carolyn Hennesy (Mrs Valentine),
David Dukes (Mr McPhee), Harve Presnell (Mr Brooks)

Following Andie's near death from drugs (**406**, 'Great Xpectations'), Jack and Jen are not talking to each other, although Andie keeps telling everyone it wasn't Jen's fault. Mr McPhee suggests that Andie might like to take the rest of senior year off and stay with her aunt in Florence, since she already has enough credit to graduate. Jack wants her to stay, but when Andie asks Pacey for his advice he tells her she has to choose for herself. She decides to leave but before she does she invites everyone to dinner at Leery's Fresh Fish. She tells them all to sort themselves out – Jen and Jack have to patch it up, and so do Pacey, Joey and Dawson. She gives an impassioned speech telling them all how lucky they are to have each other. They get the message and bridges are built.

Joey has to get the person who knows her best to write a peer recommendation for one of her college applications. She wants Dawson to do it but is afraid of upsetting Pacey. Dawson decides not to do it because it's no longer his place, but when Pacey finds out that she did ask Dawson he's angry and hurt. In the end Pacey realises he overreacted, while Dawson agrees to write it after all.

Drue tells the school about his and Jen's part in Andie's drug experience and they are both given a hundred hours of community service.

The Ballad of Dawson and Joey: Joey thinks that Dawson will be hurt if she doesn't ask him to do her peer recommendation and she admits he knows her best, but his initial astonishment at being asked and reluctance to do it reflect the remaining distance between them. Eventually, when he agrees to do it, he reveals that he was afraid of putting his knowledge of, and feelings for, her down on paper.

The Ballad of Pacey and Joey – Argue and Make Up, Take 4: Pacey doesn't know that Joey is asking Dawson to do her recommendation until he sees Dawson refusing to do it. His problem is that he knows he's not the person who knows her best, but he wants to be. After Andie's speech at the restaurant he apologises to Joey and she tells him that in ten years' time he will be the person who knows her best and that 'Dawson knows my past, my future lies with you'.

The Tomboy: Joey broke her left arm after jumping off a swing in third grade, and she came home from Lake Emandal (presumably some kind of summer camp) because she was homesick. After her mother's death Dawson was the first person she saw and he sat with her all day and didn't say a word because he knew there were no words to say.

The Clown: Pacey is surprisingly ruthless when he tells Andie, 'Maybe not all friendships need to be saved. Maybe we're meant to just spend a certain part of our lives with certain people and then move on.' He's all for letting Jen slip out of the picture, it seems. Andie relies on him when she has a difficult choice to make, and we see the deep bond of affection that remains between them; in fact Pacey has spent more time with Andie since her accident than he has with Joey.

The Delinquent: Jen has been emailing Jack, asking him to talk to her. Eventually, Andie emails Jen, pretending to be Jack, so Jen comes to the McPhee house and begs Jack to forgive her: 'When you're close to somebody and they do something unexplained or out of character . . . you don't just abandon them . . . it's killing me what you're doing.' Drue's attentions start to get to her as well and she has to keep telling him to go away. When Grams finds out about her role in the drug incident Jen's distraught at losing her good opinion.

The Basket Case: The last time Mr McPhee can remember seeing Andie happy and relaxed was in Italy when she was very young. Her decision to leave is surprising but before she can go she decides she has to try to fix the gang, who are, as Pacey puts it, 'not the most huggy of groups right now'. Her speech to them all is wonderful, putting their current squabbles in perspective and actually achieving what she set out to do – fixing some rifts and moving the gang closer together again. They are the only real reason she can think of to stay in Capeside, because they have supported her through so much and she will miss them when she's gone. She takes full responsibility for taking the tablets and tells Jack that Jen is like a sister to him and he has to make it up with her because his actions have been inexcusable. She finally feels she has the strength to take control of her life and make her own decisions.

The Wicked Witch: Grams tells Jen, 'I have never in all my life been so deeply disappointed in anything or anyone.' She can't bring herself to talk to Jen about her actions or even hear her side of the story.

The Dark Horse: Drue is, in some twisted, perverse way, trying to win Jen's affections, or at least her friendship, by causing conflict and tension and trying to resurrect the Jenny of old New York. He tells Jen, 'That which does not kill me makes me more diabolical.' And, by admitting his role in the drug incident, he sacrifices a hundred hours of his time just to put himself on an even playing field with her. He's really screwed up, this boy.

The Grouch: Mr Brooks, not content with having his house painted, gets Dawson to paint his fence as well. His house is lined with photographs of friends and family who never visit him any more, partly because of an incident when he lost a lot of money that he invested in a business his brothers set up. He's a good cook.

Family Sucks!: Mr McPhee tells Andie that things between him and Jack are really OK now, and he's trying to fix all the mistakes he made with the family in the past. He has a sister called Georgia who lives in Florence.

Metatextuality: Pacey tells Andie, 'Isn't this what this year is supposed to be about, moving on?' And indeed that is the theme of the whole season as we build inevitably to the end of senior year and the departure of the gang from Capeside.

All Things Spielberg: Jen refers to Drue's 'inner Iago'. Iago is a character in Shakespeare's play *Othello* who engineers the destruction of Othello and his wife, seemingly from pure spite.

Girl Talk: Gretchen and Joey do a bit of bonding when Gretchen hassles Joey to tell her about the peer recommendation and why it's bothering her.

Guest Cast: Sadly, this is David Dukes's last appearance as Mr McPhee. He died of a sudden heart attack on the set of a movie in October. This episode was dedicated to his memory.

Contempo Pop Music: 'Wonderful' by Everclear, 'Two Wrongs and a Right' by the Normals, 'Freedom From Shame' by Michele Cummings and 'I Will Remember You' by Sarah McLachlan.

The Big Issue: As Mr Brooks says, 'You don't always lose people from your life by choice. Sometimes it just happens, when you make the wrong ones.'

The Last Word: So farewell, Andie McPhee. After a great first year in Season Two she was really underused in Season Three and badly used when she did get a storyline, so it's perhaps not surprising that Monroe decided to leave. Truth be told, she was the most expendable character, but that was not the fault of the actress. This episode is very angst-ridden, but the angst is not the witty, self-aware angst of seasons past: it's more melancholy, adult and mournful. While the show is taking the characters in interesting directions it would be nice for them to have a little fun, to inject a little joy into the show again lest it become too depressing. Happily, the next episode delivers in spades.

408
The Unusual Suspects

1st US Transmission Date: 22 November 2000

Writer: Jonathan Kasdan
Director: James Whitmore, Jr
Guest Cast: Dylan Neal (Doug Witter),
Carolyn Hennesy (Mrs Valentine),
Harve Presnell (Mr Brooks), Carly Schroeder (Molly),
Bridgett Newton (Caroline),
Harry Shearer (Principal Peskin)

The Charge: That one or all of Dawson, Pacey and Jack did steal Principal Peskin's yacht and his dog, Chester. That they did paint CLASS OF 2000 on the sail and then deposit the boat in the school's indoor swimming pool.

The Evidence: Dawson had Mitch's keys, which could have given him access to the school; Pacey had the code to the lockup where the yacht was stored because *True Love* used to be kept there; Pacey and Dawson made a pact in ninth grade to stage the best senior prank of all time; the dog, when released from the yacht, went straight to Jack.

Dawson's Alibi: Dawson, having lost his father's car keys the night before, is driven by Gale to Mr Brooks's house, where he is employed to sort out the Brooks archive and study. He stays there all morning but takes a three-hour lunch break during which he returns home and finds Drue waiting with Mitch's keys. Dawson bumped into Drue the previous night at the cinema and they hung out. Dawson dropped his keys in Drue's car. He returns to Mr Brooks, they fight and he leaves, although he eventually returns and continues the job.

Pacey's Alibi: Pacey spent the entire day with Deputy Doug seeing what it's like to be a police officer. He and Doug actually investigated the disappearance of Chester the dog. That night, alerted by an anonymous phone call, they go to the Yacht Club to investigate a possible break-in. There they find Drue, also claiming to be investigating a phone call on his mother's behalf. Pacey gets a lift home from Drue.

Jack's Alibi: Jack helped Drue collect some stuff from the hardware store for his community-service project before heading to the soccer pitch for a day of coaching and the first game of their play-offs.

Conclusion: Principal Peskin concludes that Drue copied Dawson's keys, had the code to the lockup because his mother runs the Yacht Club, and got the paint for the sail from the hardware store. He is suspended for two weeks, although he protests his innocence.

Reality: It was a setup. Jack, Pacey and Dawson pulled the prank and manipulated events to implicate Drue (Dawson left the keys in his car on purpose; Jack volunteered to help him on community service; either Dawson or Jack made the anonymous phone call that led Drue to the lockup). In fact Jack took Chester during a break in soccer training and left him at a rendezvous point; Dawson got the lockup code from Pacey, took the boat during his three-hour lunch and also left it at the rendezvous point; Pacey collected boat and dog after Drue dropped him off on the way home, and used copies of Mitch's keys that Dawson gave him to put the yacht in place.

The Outsider: Jack gets the authorities to allow Jen to assist him at soccer practice as part of her community service. He puts Molly in goal even though her parents threaten to fire him if he does. Although the team win the game, the parents use the three goals scored against them as an excuse to fire Jack – although it seems clear he's fired mainly because they disapprove of his being gay. It's a shame because Jack's demonstrated that he's really good with children and a career as a teacher or coach of some sort looks to be his vocation. Molly apologises because she blames herself for letting in the goals, but Jack assures her she's not to blame.

The Dark Horse: Drue thinks for a while that he's making friends – he's especially grateful to Dawson for spending time with him at the cinema and going for a burger with him afterwards. When he realises what's really happened, he accepts it and actually seems kind of amused by the elegance of his punishment. Mrs Valentine tells Drue she should have known he'd get in trouble in Capeside 'after last year's ferret incident'. The mind boggles.

The Grouch: Dawson insists that his debt to Mr Brooks is paid now that he has finished the house and fence, but agrees to clean out the study if he's paid. He finds Mr Brooks's high school yearbook and discovers that he wanted to become a great Hollywood filmmaker. Dawson spends too long at lunch and is fired, but refuses to accept that and returns to confront Mr Brooks. He's horrified by how Mr Brooks's dreams and his are the same: 'It scared the hell out of me, 'cause I don't ever want to be like you. I don't ever want to be the kind of person who pushes everything and everyone away from him. I don't want to be alone.' He decides not to let himself be pushed away and returns to work in the study. Mr Brooks gets a name – Arthur Isaac – so Dawson looks him up on the Internet and discovers that as Al Brooks he was a succesful director in the fifties. His first film was made in 1953 when he was 23, which makes him 70 years old. His films were: *A Kiss Before Midnight* (1953), *Her Dying Kiss* (1953), *Cradle to the Grave* (1954), *Murder On Front Street* (1954), *Hollywood and Vice* (1955), *White of Their Eyes* (1955), *Dead Man's Stare* (1955), *One Fine Dame* (1956) and *Turn Away My Sweet* (1956).

Family Sucks!: This is the best episode to ever address the Doug–Pacey relationship and a lot of home truths are spoken and respect earned. Pacey is unbelievably harsh to Doug, calling him a nothing and a waste of life, and generally being rude and insensitive. Doug is deeply hurt and delivers the character's definitive speech to Pacey: 'If you ever in your life care about anything as much as I care about being an officer in this town, I will be shocked. If you ever in your life are as good at anything as I am at being an officer in this town, I will be shocked. If you ever in your life presume to judge me again, so help me, God, I will beat the ugly right out of you.' When Pacey sees Doug helping a blind man take his shopping home he starts to realise the importance of Doug's role in the community. He later apologises to him for his diatribe and tells him that his job really does matter and he understands that now. Doug in turn tells Pacey, 'I think that you're a daring original. I think you have a talent for flying in the face of conventionality, and I think that you were born to break the rules, not enforce them' – and he actually admires that.

School Sucks!: Principal Peskin seems to be pompous, and easily fooled.

All Things Spielberg: Lots of cop show references in this episode: Dawson accuses the principal of playing the *NYPD Blue* angle a bit too hard; Principal Peskin watches *Poirot*; Joey accuses Pacey of taking his career aptitude test (**404**, 'Future Tense') too seriously and watching episodes of *Cop Rock*, an astonishingly ill-advised TV series from the 80s in which cops burst randomly into song whenever anything interesting happened (no, really, I'm serious); Doug says a day with him will teach Pacey more about police work than any episode of *Cops*, the reality TV show about, well, cops; Pacey says Doug aspired to be Elliot Ness (from *The Untouchables*) or Harry Callahan (from the Dirty Harry movies), but ended up as Barney Fife (the deputy from *The Andy Griffiths Show*).

Grown-Up Stuff: Mitch knows Dawson organised the stunt with the boat and congratulates him on it.

Guy Talk: Dawson's telling him he couldn't trust him any more was, says Pacey, one of the top five worst moments of his life. Dawson counters that seeing him and Joey on the porch was the worst of his. Pacey asks him, 'Do you think it's possible that someday I could convince you that maybe I'm the type of person that you could trust again?' He also says, 'Something's been right tonight that hasn't been right for a long, long time. I just keep on forgetting why we're not still friends.' Unfortunately, Dawson isn't ready to declare peace yet, although he hopes it'll happen one day.

Guest Cast: Harry Shearer has a long career as a comic actor behind him, the highpoint of which was his performance as the bass player Derek Smalls in *This Is Spinal Tap* (Rob Reiner, 1984). He also provides a plethora of voices for *The Simpsons*.

Contempo Pop Music: 'Crazy for This Girl' by Evan and Jaron (the video for which featured clips of the Joey–Pacey love story from Season Three) and 'After All' by Dar Williams.

The Big Issue: What goes around comes around – it's a karma thing.

The Last Word: Absolutely superb. Funny, clever, intricate, and it moves the continuing stories along well while also being a good self-contained episode. The music and editing, the lighting and flashbacks all construct a genuinely noirish feel far more effectively than **305**, 'Indian Summer', and we get to see flashes of the Dawson–Pacey friendship that this season has so far lacked. Jack's storyline is harsh and effective, Mr Brooks continues to get more and more interesting, and Drue gets his comeuppance. Straight tie with **415**, 'Four Stories', for best episode of the season.

409
Kiss Kiss Bang Bang
1st US Transmission Date: 29 November 2000

Writer: Tom Kapinos
Director: Perry Lang
Guest Cast: Carolyn Hennesy (Mrs Valentine),
Harve Presnell (Mr Brooks), Peter Jurasik (Mr Kubelik)

Dawson is applying to the University of Southern California (USC) film school and has written an essay about why he wants to be a filmmaker, but the counsellor returns it to him and tells him he's avoided the question and must do better. He watches one of Mr Brooks's films and loves it, so he asks Mr Brooks for advice on his essay. He also asks him why he stopped making films, hoping that it might help him understand his own creative drought. Mr Brooks's answer inspires Dawson to take up filmmaking again, and complete his essay.

Joey is invited to a party for applicants to Worthington College and asks Pacey to go with her. She feels awkward and is mostly silent, but Pacey is a huge hit, which leads Joey to lose her temper with him. He tells her he was just trying to make everyone see her through his eyes. She apologises to him for misunderstanding his actions.

Jen is not making any college applications because she won't ask her parents for money for fees. Grams and Jack make a lot of applications for her and Grams promises to help Jen get to college.

Gretchen organises a big Christmas party at the Leery house and winds up kissing Dawson under the mistletoe.

The Ballad of Pacey and Joey – they Argue and Make Up, Take 5: Pacey really doesn't want to go to the party but Joey talks him into it. At dinner with the alumni representative, Mr Kubelik, he tells jokes and, when he's asked why he won't come to Worthington, he lies about applying to Yale rather than admit his poor academic situation. Joey takes him outside and shouts at him for putting on an act and trying to impress everybody; before he can defend himself he's taken back in to meet the dean and Joey's left crying. Later, Mr Kubelik tells Joey that Pacey's been singing her praises, and tells her how lucky she is to have someone like him. She and Pacey have a little mutual-appreciation moment where he tells her that she has 'more class and intelligence and beauty and grace than anyone else who's walking the face of the planet'; she in turn calls him 'the perfect boy'.

The Ballad of Dawson and Gretchen: Movie nights are now Dawson-and-Gretchen affairs, and she likes him when he raves about films, 'passionate, opinionated, irritating even'. She seeks him out at the Christmas party and tells him he's cute, and then there's that kiss ...

The Movie Brat: Gretchen asks Dawson why he stopped making films and he can't answer her, although he later says he had 'a crisis of faith'. He turns to Mr Brooks for advice and when he tells Dawson why he stopped directing, and it so closely parallels Dawson's experiences, something clicks in him and he decides to start directing again. His next project is going to be a film about Mr Brooks's life and career.

The Tomboy: Joey's lack of self-belief comes into play at the party and she clams up, stares into her food and is convinced she's blown it. Mr Kubelik sets her straight: 'Your academic record stands on its own. You're a stunningly bright young lady. No one is grading you on your social skills.'

The Clown: Pacey finally gets to be the knight in shining armour, a role Joey almost never needs him to play, and he takes to it instantly, as he always does.

The Delinquent: Jen doesn't want her parents' Christmas presents or financial aid, and if that means she can't go to college then so be it. It takes Jack and Grams's intervention to get her sorted out and headed for higher education – otherwise she'd have blown it completely. Jack read her journal while he was doing her applications and discovered that Jen still dreams about him!

The Wicked Witch: Since turning her back on Jen after the drugs incident in **407**, 'You Had Me At Goodbye', Grams has not said a word to her. So when she tries to talk to Jen about her college applications Jen tells her she no longer has the right to try to motivate her. It's Grams's idea to fake Jen's college applications and she later tells her, 'You must understand that, no matter how angry or upset or disappointed I may be in you, I will always be there for you ... you are the most important thing in my life, Jennifer, and I love you.' She also says she will 'beg, borrow or steal' to get Jen into college.

The Grouch: Mr Brooks is by far the most interesting new character on the show. In this episode we get a glimpse of the heart underneath his grouchy exterior. He even flirts with Grams at the Leery party – he can smile! He stopped making films because his best friend and his girlfriend, the two leads in his last film, *Turn Away My Sweet*, fell in love with each other on set. After wrapping the film he left Hollywood and started a new life, unable to face directing again. As a young man he must have been almost exactly like Dawson, and Dawson's started to realise that. Mr Brooks is uncomfortable with Dawson's new respect for him, but admits he's 'not an idiot, merely a nuisance'. He gives Dawson a copy of *Kiss Kiss Bang Bang* by the film critic Pauline Kael.

Family Sucks!: Joey has been going for Sunday dinner with Pacey and his parents every week.

Metatextuality: Gretchen tells Dawson that, if he goes to Hollywood, he may be lucky enough to date a girl from the WB. Then his character, a boy on the WB, kisses her character, a girl on the WB. Jen wants to go and see the new film with Dean Cain that everyone's calling '*St Homo's Fire*'. This is *The Broken Hearts Club*, which was written and directed by Greg Berlanti, *Dawson's Creek*'s co-executive producer. It also features a brief cameo by

Kerr Smith as a gay baseball player! So Jen tells Jack, a gay sportsman played by Kerr Smith, that she wants to go see a film featuring Kerr Smith playing a gay sportsman. My head's spinning!

All Things Spielberg: Mr Brooks says he's never heard of Cameron Crowe, who is the director perhaps most often referenced in *Dawson's Creek*, but he is a fan of Sam Fuller, director of such classics as *Shock Corridor* (1963) and *The Big Red One* (1980). Mr Brooks also didn't appreciate *Star Wars*.

Kiss and Tell: On Mr Brooks's urging, Dawson and Gretchen kiss under the mistletoe. It's a far from platonic kiss and it ends with a long eye-locked stare – but Pacey and Joey enter the room just in time to get a grandstand view.

Our Quips Are Wittier: We never hear the joke Pacey tells Mr Kubelik, but the punchline is 'Rectum? I damn near killed 'em!'

Guest Cast: You may not recognise Peter Jurasik without the huge hairdo, but he was brilliant as Londo Mollari in the sci-fi series *Babylon 5*.

Contempo Pop Music: 'Sorry Charlie' by Hathaway, 'Teenage Dirtbag' by Wheatus, 'Piece of Soul' by Katie Reider, 'Souvenirs' by Say-So, 'Jingle Bells' by Mark Shane, 'The Christmas Song' by Vikki Carr, 'Love Came Down At Christmas' by Shawn Colvin, 'Christmastime' by Smashing Pumpkins and 'Have Yourself a Merry Little Christmas' by Mary Beth.

The Last Word: It's been so long since Dawson was the focus of an episode's main storyline that it's good to have him back. Harve Presnell steals the show as Mr Brooks, and Dawson's resumption of filming gives the show, and the character, its heart back to an extent; it's an element that's been missing for too long. A little gem of an episode, mostly for the Dawson–Mr Brooks relationship.

410
Self Reliance

1st US Transmission Date: 20 December 2000

Writer: Gina Fattore
Director: David Petrarca
Guest Cast: David Monahan (Tobey Barrett),
Harve Presnell (Mr Brooks), David Downes (Mr Kasdan)

Bessie is away for three days and has left Pacey and Joey at the B&B. Joey has a test to study for and throws Pacey out for distracting her, but when guests arrive she has no one to help and consequently she flunks the test. Pacey thinks she's distracted because of witnessing the Dawson–Gretchen kiss (**409**, 'Kiss Kiss Bang Bang'), and he's right. She goes to talk to Dawson about it and tells him to follow his heart, while Pacey talks to Joey's teacher, Mr Kasdan, and asks him to let her retake the test, which he does.

Jen takes Jack to a local 'gay–straight team coalition' where Jack feels incredibly uncomfortable and locks horns with rude, militant Tobey. Jen tries to persuade Jack to come for a gay bowling night and he declines, but she goes on her own and so Jack inevitably turns up. Again he and Tobey argue and Jack leaves.

Mr Brooks agrees to co-operate with Dawson's plan to make a documentary about him. He is on medication but stops taking it because it affects his memory and is interfering with his ability to talk properly on camera.

Gretchen tells Dawson that their mistletoe kiss was just a friendly thing, and he reluctantly accepts that. Later, however, inspired by Mr Brooks's tales of youthful risk taking, he tells Gretchen he likes her and is interested in her, although she maintains they're going to remain just good friends.

The Ballad of Dawson and Joey: Dawson gives Joey a Christmas present – a beautiful framed photo of her and Pacey which he took at the party. As a gesture of acceptance and friendship it's hard to beat and it really touches Joey. She kisses him on his forehead and tells him, 'Gretchen would be really lucky to have someone like you.'

The Ballad of Pacey and Joey – they Argue and Make Up, Take 6: This episode's argument is about, yes, you guessed it, Dawson. Pacey confronts Joey about her distractedness; she denies she's freaked by Dawson and Gretchen and stomps off in a huff. Pacey's worried that they never talk about the future, but Joey tells him that when she looks at the future she sees her and Pacey. Joey then manages to encapsulate the difference between her relationships with him and Dawson, and gives a speech that is germane to the whole love-triangle dynamic: 'Me and you, Pace, we grew up together . . . Dawson and I, we didn't grow up. We are in that house, in Dawson's bedroom, eternally having the same argument over and over again in this endless cycle that goes on and on. And I can't stop it, because whenever I'm around him I become fifteen again.' This is one of the best resolutions they have as a couple – conflict arises, they talk about it, she takes Pacey's advice, he doesn't crowd her, they end up lovey-dovey again; if only it were always this easy with them.

The Ballad of Dawson and Gretchen: The Dawson of earlier seasons would have agonised and analysed and managed to alienate Gretchen completely. Instead Zen Dawson understands she just wants to be friends and accepts the friendship. Then, when he does decide to seize the day, he does it simply, straightforwardly and with no little aplomb: 'That kiss meant more to me than just happy holidays . . . and I'm really glad that I said it because you're worth risking everything for.' She almost seems to melt at that point but sticks resolutely to her line that it was just a friendly kiss, no more.

The Ballad of Jack and Tobey: Although Jack has previously stated that he was the only gay guy in Capeside (**216**, 'Be Careful What You Wish For'), he finally comes face to face with the wider gay community and he hates it. Jack's essentially a nonpolitical guy – he doesn't want to fight for gay rights, or make a point or protest: he just wants to get on with his life. So, when he meets the highly politicised Tobey, he reacts against it. Tobey, in turn, reacts against Jack's all-American, football-playing, clean-cut, popular-guy image. Tobey is used to people who look and act like Jack being his oppressors, not his friends, but, as Jack rightly points out, 'There's something about me that obviously intimidates you . . . it's not my fault, and I'm not going to let you push me around any more than I should have let those damn soccer parents.' (See **408**, 'The Unusual Suspects'.) Jen thinks Tobey likes Jack, but Jack's not convinced.

The Clown: After his stellar performance at the Worth-ington party (**409**, 'Kiss Kiss Bang Bang'), Pacey is again trying to save Joey – help her with studying and running the B&B, fixing it for her to retake the test. He's back to his knight-in-shining-armour complex and, because it works this time, and he feels he is useful and helpful, he is happy and content. Still, he's heading for a fall because the more comfortable he gets in his role as saviour, the role he adopted for Andie and to which he always defaults, and the more he resorts to defining his relationship with Joey in those terms, the harder he's going to fall to earth when he's not required to save her any more.

The Delinquent: Jen drags Jack to the gay group against his better judgment, and then manipulates him into coming bowling as well, but she feels way more comfortable there than he does. She likes Tobey and is trying to engineer something between him and Jack, to Jack's obvious horror.

The Grouch: Brooks met his great lost love, Ellie Andrews, working in a diner on his way to LA. She jumped across the counter and came with him. Presumably she is the girlfriend he was referring to in **409**, 'Kiss Kiss Bang Bang', who fell in love with his best friend on the set of his final movie, *Turn Away My Sweet*. He misses her to this day.

School Sucks!: Mr Kasdan distinguishes himself as that rarest of creatures – the good teacher at Capeside High. He lets Joey retake the test, even gives her hints on what to study, gives her a life lesson about friendship, and compliments Pacey on his plea for Joey's sake.

Metatextuality: Mr Kasdan tells Joey that the test is being retaken and is, therefore, available for her to retake because 'Ian Prange was at the orthodontists again'; Greg Prange is one of the executive producers.

All Things Spielberg: Mr Brooks lied when he said he didn't know Cameron Crowe (**409**, 'Kiss Kiss Bang Bang') and he admits he's talented. He prefers Curtis Hanson, though, and thinks *L.A. Confidential* (1997) is the best film, or, as he would say, best picture, since *The Man Who Shot Liberty Valance* (John Ford, 1962). He says he's waiting for Clarence, a reference to Frank Capra's classic *It's a Wonderful Life* (1946), which features Clarence the angel. It would take up too many lines to reference all the classic movies he and Dawson discuss this episode!

Guy Talk: Dawson tells Jack that his fantasy is to be locked in an elevator with Kate Hudson. Jack has become Dawson's main male confidant this season, filling the gap left by Pacey's estrangement.

Kiss and Tell: Pacey on Gretchen's kiss with Dawson: 'There's no such thing as *just* a kiss, *especially* not in Capeside.'

Our Quips Are Wittier: At the bowling alley Jen asks Jack if he's embarrassed to be there: 'On gay bowling night? Yeah, I'm embarrassed. Not the gay thing, though. The bowling.'

Guest Cast: This will be the first time you've seen David Monahan, because his role on *Dawson's Creek* was his first big break.

Contempo Pop Music: 'Don't Need a Reason' by Beth Orton.

Backstage: Jen's hair has grown alarmingly between episodes. It's also become blonder and is now wrapped in headscarves all the time. This is because Williams went off to do some film work and when she came back her blonde hair was dyed brown, hence the wig she sports from now on.

The Big Issue: Mr Brooks dissects the love triangle beautifully, and it reflects on the Dawson–Gretchen kiss and its ramifications: 'For every piece of happiness, there's also a piece of unhappiness. If you haven't told both sides, you haven't told the whole story.'

The Last Word: Harve Presnell continues to steal the show from everyone as Mr Brooks. His performance prevents the character becoming the stereotypical curmudgeon with a heart of gold, and keeps Mr Brooks believable, layered and just irritating enough to not be *entirely* likable. He says the thing that makes a picture great is 'complex human emotions'; the same goes for TV, and this season is proving to be the most emotionally complex to date.

411
The Tao of Dawson

1st US Transmission Date: 10 January 2001

Writer: Jeffrey Stepakoff
Director: Keith Samples
Guest Cast: Carolyn Hennesy (Mrs Valentine),
Harve Presnell (Mr Brooks), Christian Kane (Nick Taylor)

Gretchen takes Pacey with her when she goes back to her old college to collect her truck from her ex-boyfriend, Nick. But the truck has no wheels, so Gretchen and Pacey stay for a party that night. Pacey tries to force Gretchen and Nick back together, largely because he doesn't want her going out with Dawson. However, when Nick encourages him to cheat on Joey, Pacey finds out what a jerk

Nick really is and changes his tune. Gretchen nearly sleeps with Nick but realises that she came here to say goodbye to him, not to spend time with him.

Drue's father asks him to come and stay with him in New York for the weekend, but before Drue can catch the bus he accidentally on purpose locks himself in the Yacht Club storeroom with an enraged Joey. They spend the night in there, although, as Joey finds out next day, Drue had a mobile phone all along.

Grams and Mr Brooks are now dating, but Dawson disapproves because he knows Mr Brooks is dying. He tries to tell Grams but fails, only to discover that she knows but is determined to pursue the relationship anyway.

Dawson, after being inspired by Grams and Mr Brooks, leaves a love letter, which he wrote many years earlier, for Gretchen.

The Ballad of Pacey and Joey: Drue can't understand Joey and Pacey, because they are such opposites. Joey sets him straight: 'Part of his recklessness is that he's constantly surprising me, and part of his rashness is that he's intensely passionate. Those differences are important; they make for a richer relationship.' But Drue is right when he says that things will get tough when college comes around, because she and Pacey will certainly not be at the same institution.

The Ballad of Dawson and Gretchen: Gretchen is still telling anyone who will listen that she and Dawson are just good friends, but the lady doth protest too much. After all, Dawson is making her mix-CDs and she's listening to them a lot. Dawson's corny old letter to Gretchen reads, 'If I tried to tell anyone else, they would say that you and I are impossible, that our lives are too different, that we could never be right for each other. But we understand each other and we care about each other.'

The Movie Brat: I've been calling him Zen Dawson all season and now the writers make it explicit, as Pacey refers to the 'Tao of Dawson' and Jack accuses him of starting a new movement: 'Zen and the art of dating'. His strategy of doing nothing and waiting for Gretchen and himself to end up together is very Zen indeed, and it's a surprise that he doesn't just adopt a full lotus position and levitate through the episode.

The Tomboy: Joey is a 34C. Which is nice to know.

The Wicked Witch: Grams hasn't felt this way since her husband died, so she must like Mr Brooks a lot. She knows he's dying but 'a moment, a single moment of true joy is more powerful than a lifetime of sorrow'.

The Big Sis: This episode is largely about Gretchen dealing with her past and confronting how she has changed since college: 'I left school to work on who I want to be . . . I can't try fitting that into everybody else's idea of what that is.' She tells Pacey about her pregnancy scare (see **405**, 'A Family Way') but is resolute that she was not a victim and liked Nick even though she knew all about his faults.

The Dark Horse: Drue found his dad having sex with another woman on the kitchen floor and would rather lock himself in a storeroom with a girl who hates him than ever spend time with his father again. Although he manipulates the situation, and is out-and-out evil about it, it's hard not to feel sorry for him when it becomes obvious it was all just a trick to avoid his father: 'Having to spend time with my dad is like being in prison.' Joey lets him off the hook when she realises.

The Grouch: The soft heart is even more in evidence now he's dating Grams, and he buys her some earrings as a token of affection. His rationale for their doomed relationship is similar to Grams's: 'You fall in love with the wrong woman, you tell fate to piss off, you don't like its plans for you.'

Family Sucks!: Gretchen and Pacey bond after he has fixed her car. She tells Pacey she got her strength to leave Nick from him, that he treats her really well, and she's always taken her cues from him about how she should be treated.

Metatextuality: Drue says that in the TV movie of their storeroom experience Joey should be played by 'some former teen-series idol who's trying to break into features'. Like Katie Holmes, perhaps?

All Things Spielberg: Lots of Cameron Crowe references again in this episode. Grams and Mr Brooks go to see his latest film, *Almost Famous* (2000); Pacey asks Dawson if he's going to find him outside his house with a boombox over his head – a reference to the famous scene where John Cusack does just that in Crowe's 1989 masterpiece *Say Anything*; Dawson's final line to Gretchen – 'What took you so long?' – is a crib from Crowe's 1992 film *Singles*.

Guy Talk: The pre-titles sequence is a joy – Pacey and Dawson, hanging out together again at last, fishing off the dock and talking about girls. Dawson tells Pacey that he's interested in Gretchen, and not in a platonic way. He thinks it's best to be upfront about these things, especially in the light of what happened when Pacey waited too long to tell Dawson about Joey last season. Pacey is not happy and tells Dawson that 'sisters are off limits: they're like mothers, only pretty', but Dawson isn't asking permission. Dawson later tells Jack that he's past trying to prove his feelings because the last time he did that was the boat race (**321**, 'Show Me Love'), and he realises it was a terrible mistake, but Jack works on Dawson to give Gretchen the letter and tell her how he feels.

Kiss And Tell: Drue catches Joey when she falls off some storeroom shelving while looking for food. But when he's got her in his arms he can't resist planting one on her for good measure. Bad move – she has a mean right cross. Gretchen and Nick get kissy, too, before she realises she's not interested any more. Dawson and Gretchen kiss again, this time a full-on romantic snog with rising background music and pull-away aerial camera shot to end the episode.

Our Quips Are Wittier: Drue to Joey, locked in the storeroom without food: 'If something happens to me, you have my permission to pursue whatever indelicate though life-sustaining tastes-just-like-chicken measures you see fit.'

Bloopers: So Joey is locked all night in a storeroom and no one comes to look for her? Where are Bessie and Bodie? Jack and Dawson are painting the room for the new Leery baby, but do they wear crappy old T-shirts like normal people? Nope: Jack's in a designer sweater; Dawson's in a nice clean shirt.

Guest Cast: Christian Kane got his big break in the short-lived *Fame LA*. He has a semiregular role as Lindsey the villainous lawyer on another WB show, *Angel*.

Contempo Pop Music: 'Broken Boy' by Michal, 'If I Am' by Nine Days, 'Understand' by the Lads, 'Want Me', 'Nocturne' and 'Siren' by Red Delicious, 'Love Is the Movement' by Switchfoot and 'I Think God Can Explain' by Splender.

Ker-THUNK!: Gretchen is twenty-one and has been at college for three years; Dawson is seventeen. He wrote her his love letter when she was just starting high school, which would be when she was fourteen, which makes Dawson ten when he wrote it. No ten-year-old on Earth, not even a precocious Capeside wunderkind, is capable of writing a letter like that. And finding the letter, discarded seven years earlier and left in a chest of drawers, was just the wrong side corny.

The Big Issue: Mr Brooks: 'One thing worse than the pain of loss is the aching void of inaction.'

The Last Word: The letter is contrived, there are no two ways about it, and the Grams–Mr Brooks relationship seems to come out of nowhere; but the stuff with Dawson works nicely, demonstrating how much he's changed and grown. Gretchen gets the lion's share of the episode, though, and Sasha Alexander carries it well, adding a lot of depth to the character. Drue also gets another layer, moving him further away from being the cartoonish villain he could so easily have become. Perhaps not the greatest episode, but continuing the run of quiet, nicely crafted character pieces.

412
The Te of Pacey
1st US Transmission Date: 17 January 2001

Writer: Maggie Friedman
Director: Harry Winer
Guest Cast: Dylan Neal (Deputy Doug Witter),
John Finn (Sheriff John Witter), Jane Lynch (Mrs Witter),
David Monahan (Tobey Barrett)

It's Pacey's eighteenth birthday and, even though he makes her promise not to, Joey organises a surprise party for him at the Witter house. Pacey is depressed and keeps trying to tell Joey something throughout the day, but the party keeps getting in the way. His parents keep telling Pacey he's a disappointment and isn't college material, and, although Joey defends him and says he is, Pacey reveals that his fall-back college turned him down.

Dawson and Gretchen were supposed to have their first date but they go to the party instead. Gretchen wants to keep their relationship secret and Dawson doesn't. She tells him she's worried about getting involved with him because she is going to leave town soon, but he says he is, too – for college – and they should live in the moment. Pacey and Joey find them kissing passionately in the basement at the party.

Jen is driving drinkers home from local bars as the final part of her community service and Tobey is riding with her as a volunteer. She drags him to Pacey's birthday bash in the hope that he and Jack will hit it off. They don't.

The Ballad Of Dawson and Joey: Joey tells Dawson that she doesn't care whether he and Gretchen are together or not: 'You guys can run off to Vegas and elope for all I care. I have much bigger things on my mind right now.'

The Ballad of Pacey and Joey: When Pacey is rejected from college it's a major blow and a huge problem for him and

Joey, who have so far glossed over the different routes their lives are taking: 'You and I are just on opposite paths, Jo. On different roads. And we are heading farther and farther away from each other.' Joey tells him that they will just have to work harder to stay together. Pacey is reassured, but he is right when he says it's getting more and more difficult to believe they have a long-term future.

The Ballad of Dawson and Gretchen: Gretchen's eagerness to keep her relationship with Dawson a secret annoys him and he says that, if she doesn't feel she can tell anyone about it, perhaps it's something she feels she shouldn't be doing. He avoids her at the party until she confronts him about it and he tells her, 'I think this is about you, and I think you need to figure out what you want.' Her explanation – that she's not going to stay in Capeside for ever and is afraid to break his heart – rings true. His response, that they should live in the moment, reflects Grams's and Mr Brooks's decisions in **411**, 'The Tao of Dawson'.

The Ballad of Jack and Tobey: Jen's still trying to set them up, but Tobey invents a fictional boyfriend – Greg – to put her off. When he and Jack meet at Pacey's party, Tobey is incredibly rude and defensive. Jack politely asks about the gay group and Tobey responds with, 'And what about that club of yours? What's it called? Self-hatred and denial. How's that going, Jack?' From this display Jen somehow manages to conclude that Tobey must really like Jack.

The Clown: The many birthdays of Pacey. Twelfth – he's sick all over a girl he has a crush on; fourteenth – he is mauled by a dog; sixteenth – he fails his driving test, Dawson forgets his birthday and no one comes to his party. The low self-esteem that has plagued Pacey throughout the series is explained and put into context – with the treatment he receives at the hands of his family it's no wonder he's so insecure and keeps trying to prove himself to others with grand gestures and last-minute rescues. He wanted to be a vet when he was younger, but his parents kept telling him to set his sights lower, on a job as a dog groomer. He got up early one morning and tried to cook pancakes for the family, but accidentally started a fire that killed the family dog.

The Delinquent: Jen's finished her community service.

Family Sucks!: Pacey's family almost defies description. His mom forgets his favourite meal and cooks Doug's favourite instead; she calls Joey 'Josie' and 'Joanne'; she tells Pacey she has faith that one day he'll stop being a disappointment and will succeed at something, apparently thinking that this is motivational; she says it was such a relief that Pacey was a 'late bloomer', by which she really means a stupid child; and she thinks that Pacey is the kind of kid who might join the army, which shows how much she knows. His dad gets drunk in front of hockey on the TV at his son's birthday party; forgets who Jack is even though they went sailing together (**212**, 'Uncharted Waters'); tells Joey stories about how he had sex in Vietnam on his eighteenth birthday; openly abuses his daughter Kerry in front of the whole family, and calls her a 'cow'; tells everyone that he expects Pacey to flunk out or drop out of college, and calls Gretchen a waste of money and effort for leaving college herself. Kerry spends all her time eating and buys Pacey an ashtray for his birthday even though he doesn't smoke. When Doug tells a tale about how the whole family once left baby Pacey at a diner and would have driven home without him had a woman not run after the car, it perfectly sums up their attitude to him. Gretchen sticks up for him, telling a story of how he defended her when she was picked on at school – Pacey with his hero complex again. Pacey tries to tolerate all the put-downs, jibes and insults, but finally he snaps, 'No one gives Pacey a break. Everybody expects the absolute worst out of Pacey. Pacey gets the short end of the stick. Pacey gets ... endlessly harassed because how dare he want to go to college so he can possibly get out of this place?' After his outburst Pacey storms off but his father finds him and they have a proper conversation, only the second time that's ever happened (**222**, 'Parental Discretion Advised'). His dad didn't get into the police academy first time. He comes the closest he ever has to complimenting his son: 'I know that I've been hard on you about school, and it's not because I don't think you're good enough to go or to get in, Pacey. I just don't know if it's the right thing for you ... But ask me if I think that you're meant to do great things ...'

School Sucks!: Pacey desperately wants to go to college, even though he admits he's probably not college material. He's applied for a number of places but the first to reject him was his fall-back, the one place he felt sure he could get into if no one else wanted him.

That Three-Letter Word: Jen notices that Grams is all smiley and cheerful, and correctly divines that she's thinking about sex. Grams admits she likes Mr Brooks but denies they're sleeping together and then skilfully directs the conversation elsewhere, but she does admit that 'when it comes to safe sexuality, I've got my bases covered'.

Kiss and Tell: Gretchen and Dawson, on a sofa, making out at a party. Whoever thought we'd see the day Dawson would do something so normal for a teenage boy!

Guest Cast: Jane Lynch has appeared in many TV shows, including *The West Wing*, *Married ... With Children* and *Frasier*; on the big screen she can be seen in *The Fugitive* and *Best In Show* among others.

Contempo Pop Music: 'Night and Day' by Ella Fitzgerald, 'Jello' by Arlibido, 'Rock Out' by 6X, 'Camelot' by Sweetsalt, 'Loving You' by Tammy Raybould and 'Lean On Me' by Beth Orton.

The Big Issue: You can choose your friends, but not your family.

The Last Word: Painful, awful, gruesome ... watching poor old Pacey get systematically eviscerated by his family's careless, thoughtless put-downs left me squirming in my seat. It takes a very well-written episode to get me feeling as uncomfortable as this one did – all the insults are so well phrased that you can see how they're not deliberate, just utterly stupid and thoughtless. A very good episode indeed, but not easy to watch.

413
Hopeless

1st US Transmission Date: 31 January 2001

Writer: Nan Hagan
Director: Krishna Rao
Guest Cast: Carolyn Hennesy (Mrs Valentine),
Harve Presnell (Mr Brooks),
David Monahan (Tobey Barrett),
Sabine Singh (Anna Evans), Rachel True (Kira),
Deron Barnett (Will)

Gretchen invites Dawson out on a date with her two best friends from college. Throughout the evening Dawson is conscious of his age – the girls talk about sex, reminisce about songs he's never heard, go into a club where he has to have his hand stamped UNDER 21, and after the club the girls head to a bar. Dawson, knowing he won't get in, drives home as Gretchen goes off with her friends. She feels guilty, however, and gets a cab home immediately afterwards and catches him at his house. She reassures him that the age difference is no problem and he was a hit with her friends.

Joey wants to get time off work to go on a school trip. Mrs Valentine says she can have the time if she and Pacey accompany Drue on a date that evening and ensure that the girl, Anna, whose father is very important, has a good time. The quartet of Pacey, Joey, Drue and Anna go to play miniature golf. Drue spends his whole time putting Anna down until Pacey is so annoyed he wants to punch him. Anna blames herself for sleeping with Drue too early and walks off; Pacey comforts her, Joey talks to Drue. At the end of the evening Drue admits he likes Anna and they kiss. Joey's theory is that Drue was freaked out only because Anna liked him back.

Tobey invites Jack to help out at a literacy project he volunteers at, helping kids to read. Jack agrees and afterwards goes out for a coffee with Tobey. But Tobey's friends are at the coffee shop and Jack realises it's a date by stealth. Tobey admits he's interested in Jack, but Jack doesn't reciprocate.

Dawson's film about Mr Brooks is finished. Grams discovers he has not been taking his medicine, and Dawson finds him unconscious on his living room floor.

The Ballad of Pacey and Joey: Even Mrs Valentine knows that Pacey and Joey are 'the perfect couple'. Pacey says it's 'the most amazing relationship I've ever had'.

The Ballad of Dawson and Gretchen: Gale tells Dawson that Gretchen is crazy about him, but her concerns that she's both too old for him and in the wrong place in her life to be with him seem fair. Gretchen's very eager to show him off to her friends. He wants to be sure he won't just be some nice, bland, risk-free guy she dates to recover from all the losers. He wants to 'make an impression'. She tells him he already has.

The Ballad of Jack and Tobey: Tobey joins the literacy programme because Jen has told him Jack likes working with kids and he thinks it's a good way to spend time with him. Jack is wary and Tobey is, at first, as rude as ever. But as the evening wears on Tobey starts flashing longing looks Jack's way. Tobey comes flat out and says he wants their coffee to be a proper date, and, while Jack admits maybe he'd like to feel something for Tobey, he just doesn't: 'We don't click, and even if you wanted to change that, you couldn't.'

The Clown: Pacey feels comfortable with Anna and tells her that she and he are alike in that they're both not good with books: 'People like you and I, we just have to figure out what our thing is and then become good at it.' Pacey comes over all prudish and tries to persuade Gretchen to wear something less revealing to her date with Dawson.

The Outsider: Jack is really good with Will, the boy he tutors at the literacy programme, accentuating the natural teaching skills that we saw when he was football coach earlier this season. He's totally wired afterwards, as well. Jack plays golf.

The Big Sis: Gretchen has slept with six boyfriends that she now considers losers. She even had a leprechaun, 'Lucky', tattooed on her hip to impress Loser No. 5, who was a musician. Dawson asks when he's going to get to see Lucky, and Gretchen just says they'll have to wait and see.

The Dark Horse: Drue has spent most of his childhood at boys-only schools so he doesn't know how to relate to girls – he knows only how to 'pick on women or sleep with them'. As soon as he's shared a genuine moment with Joey he reverts to cruelty and nastiness. He admits he's 'damaged' again.

The Grouch: Mr Brooks is now confined to a wheelchair and we discover that he is suffering from pancreatic cancer. He gets Dawson to sign a form, which he says is to give him permission to collect medicine for him. He tells Dawson that the movie, which lasts 93 minutes, is finished, and when he gets Dawson to help him out of his wheelchair into a normal chair he hugs him fiercely, as if he knows it will be the last time they meet. He tells Grams he's not been taking his medication because 'living without dignity is not living'. It seems Grams respects his decision.

Family Sucks!: Gale is worried about Dawson and Gretchen's relationship and she gets massively overprotective. She picks on Gretchen at the bar, glares at her whenever she can, and utterly humiliates Dawson in front of Gretchen and her friends by insisting on a curfew and treating him like a little boy. She later apologises – but, boy, she's harsh on the poor kid when he just wants to go out on a date.

That Three-Letter Word: Pacey hints to Gretchen that he's sick of waiting to sleep with Joey. After the double date Joey and he admit they have a problem with sex and that they've avoided talking about it for so long that it's becoming a *big* problem, especially for Pacey: 'I am happy that you and I took the time to really fall in love with each other, but we're here now ... I need for you to know that if our relationship is not gonna be progressing on to that next level it's not because of me.' Joey admits that she wants him, and he's glad to hear it, but she doesn't know why she's so scared and keeps holding back. Pacey tells her he's scared too, which comes as a huge relief to Joey. They agree to be scared together.

All Things Freud: Joey turns her psychoanalytical skills on Drue: 'You have this whole witty Drue routine you do. But it's just a front for some really scared kid who's desperate for people to love him and desperately trying to keep any sort of intimacy away.'

Kiss and Tell: Drue manages to be nice to Anna long enough at the end of the date to get her to kiss him again.

Our Quips Are Wittier: Drue asks Joey and Anna what they were talking about and Joey says they were 'discussing the beauty industry and how it manipulates and contorts the perception of ourselves in service of a capitalistic economy'.

Guest Cast: Sabine Singh had a regular role in *Student Affairs*, a TV show produced, and occasionally written and directed, by Adam Fields, who composed all the music for Seasons One and Four of *Dawson's Creek*. Rachel True is best known for her role as one of the four witches in *The Craft*.

Contempo Pop Music: 'What a Wonderful World' by Louis Armstrong, 'Hopeless' by Dionne Farris, 'Firecracker' by John Lardieri, 'Give You the World' by the Flying Cordovas, 'Waiting For a Sign' by Mary Beth (who appears on stage at the club Dawson and Gretchen go to).

The Last Word: OK in itself, but a bit too laid back and mellow, even for Season Four. Characters are consolidated but don't really progress. The Jack–Tobey interplay and the scenes with Mr Brooks are the best things here. Nonetheless, the scene where Grams and Mr Brooks discuss his decision to die without medication is very powerful stuff, and his final scene with Dawson is one of the most affecting the show's ever produced.

414
Winter's Tale

1st US Transmission Date: 7 February 2001

Writers: Zack Estrin and Chris Levinson
Director: Greg Prange
Guest Cast: Harve Presnell (Mr Brooks),
Sabine Singh (Anna Evans),
Andy Griffith (Mr Brooks's friend),
David Downes (Mr Kasdan)

It's the senior ski trip and Jack, Jen, Pacey, Joey and Drue are along for the ride, as well as Anna, whom Drue smuggles along. Pacey and Joey spend the whole weekend arguing about sex, continuing the discussion they began in **413**, 'Hopeless'. Anna offers herself to Pacey after he and Joey have had a fight but Pacey is not interested. Come the last night of the trip Joey decides it's time, and she and Pacey sleep together.

Jen sprains her ankle immediately upon arrival, and then sprains the other one that night. She and Jack are sharing a room. He finds her raiding the minibar one evening; they get drunk, leading to a very unexpected outcome . . .

Mr Brooks is on a life-support machine and the document that Dawson signed in **413**, 'Hopeless' means he has to decide whether to switch it off or not. After a visit from Mr Brooks's friend, the one who ran away with his girlfriend (**409**, 'Kiss Kiss Bang Bang'). Dawson decides to switch off the machine.

The Ballad of Pacey and Joey – they Argue and Make Up, Take 7: This episode's bone of contention: sex and Dawson.

Joey phones Dawson from the ski lodge to talk about Mr Brooks, and Dawson tells her that he thinks Mr Brooks was waiting to say goodbye to his friend. When she then says goodbye to Dawson it's in a way that indicates she's letting go of the last vestige of her attachment to him, ready to give herself wholly to Pacey at last.

As she seduces Pacey she lists all the little things that have made her fall in love with him: the way he looks after her, the fact that he never pressured her about sex during the three-month boat trip, the fact that he knew it was her mother's bracelet she was wearing at the anti-prom (**322**, 'The Anti-Prom').

The Ballad of Jack and Tobey: Jen is still trying to persuade Jack to go out with Tobey but Jack refuses because Tobey's too gay, and he finds that a turn off.

The Movie Brat: What a tough choice Dawson has to make. He puts it off, and waits for a sign, and when Mr Brooks's friend arrives he feels he's got one. He decides to commemorate Mr Brooks with a special movie night and he gets his folks, Gretchen and Grams together, makes popcorn and shows one of Mr Brooks's pictures.

The Delinquent: Jen can't ski and can't even stay upright on ice, taking two tumbles and messing up her whole weekend. She's a good lock picker, though, and the minibar stood no chance against her assaults. But Mr Kasdan sees her disposing of the bottles, so she's in trouble for drinking again.

The Outsider: Jack admits that his biggest fear is always being the friend or brother, never the boyfriend. This loneliness, coupled with the fact that he's a maudlin drunk, leads him to want to sleep with Jen, and he would have, too, had she not stopped him.

The Grouch: Mr Brooks took all the pills he had been hoarding and tried to kill himself but only put himself into a coma. He wrote to his best friend a month ago and asked to be forgiven for not talking to him or Ellie, his long-lost love, for fifty years.

Family Sucks!: One of Dawson's grandfathers died when he was two and he's never lost any other close family members. So why have we never seen any of his three remaining grandparents? In fact we've not seen any of Pacey's, Jack and Andie's or Joey's grandparents either. One of Gretchen's grandfathers died when she was eight.

That Three-Letter Word: Sex is everywhere on the ski trip. From the moment a student yells out of the bus that everyone who wants to get laid should get on board, through Drue telling Pacey how awful it would be to be the only guy to not get laid on the trip, to the porn that comes on as soon as Pacey switches on the TV, it's inescapable. Anna demands to see all the guys' wallets to find out if they carry a condom, and Pacey declines, lying that he left it back in the hotel so that Joey wouldn't know that he also keeps a condom in there. Of course she knows he's lying and gets angry when she sees the offending item – although she was the one who went to the sex clinic and got all that safe-sex stuff herself back in **405**, 'A Family Way', so it seems a bit rich. There's been tension between them ever since they talked about sex in **413**, 'Hopeless', and Pacey pleads for it to end: 'Tell me that we can laugh about sex now, 'cause it seems to me that's the only rational thing to do. You can't enshrine it. You can't run from it 'cause it's everywhere. It's like food and water and air.' Joey admits to Jack that sex is a big problem for her: she keeps waiting but she doesn't know what for, and she just gets more and more afraid the longer she waits. When Anna invites Pacey to come and join her in the hot tub Joey just throws snide defensive remarks at Pacey until he says the one thing they've both been avoiding: 'What I am scared of is that little piece of your heart that will always belong to Dawson Leery, OK? I'm scared of that piece of your heart that always envisioned your first time being with him. I'm scared of that part of you that just doesn't want it to be me.' When Anna subsequently offers Pacey sex he responds with exactly what Joey would want to hear, although he doesn't know she is behind him and can hear every word: 'It's not about wanting to have sex. It's about wanting to share the most intimate thing that you can possibly share with someone, no matter how long you have to wait.' After saying goodbye to Dawson on the phone, Joey seduces Pacey, who, frustrated though he was, was still willing to wait.

Reality Bites: As a young man Mr Brooks shared Dawson's reality issues and believed that the answers to all of life's questions could be found in the movies.

All Things Spielberg: Jack says the ski trip has a real 'John Hughes eighties vibe', referring to the king of teen movies. Mr Brooks's friend quotes *Miracle on 34th Street* (George Seaton, 1947) to Dawson.

Kiss and Tell: Jen and Jack – who saw that one coming? Jack's the one who tells her he loves her, but it's Jen who calls a halt to the proceedings, though not before they've migrated from kissing by the bed to full on-the-floor making out. She tells him that it's all a big mistake and when the moment fades they'll feel really awkward, which Jack is at first reluctant to accept.

Our Quips Are Wittier: Jack on Drue's repartee: 'Since when did obnoxiousness become an adequate substitute for wit?'

Bloopers: When Dawson is standing on the steps of the hospital there's a hair in the camera. The doctor tells Dawson that Mr Brooks has no immediate family, but in **407**, 'You Had Me At Goodbye', he told Dawson that he has two brothers.

Guest Cast: Andy Griffith is a huge American TV star, best known for *The Andy Griffith Show*, which ran between 1960 and 1968, and *Matlock*, which ran between 1986 and

1995 and which was filmed, like *Dawson's Creek*, in Wilmington.

Contempo Pop Music: 'Impossible' by Brian Charles, 'Hideaway' by Epstein's Mother, 'Do It Again' by Splytz, 'Sucker For the Count' by Revelation Darling, 'Summer of '69' by Bryan Adams, 'Dumb Love' by Brian Charles, 'Sugar Star' by Crushing Velvet, 'How Does It Feel?' by Radford and 'Takes My Breath Away' by Tuck & Patti.

Ker-THUNK!: I know it's good drama and it hits on big issues, but can anyone really believe that a simple form ostensibly for medication collection would give a seventeen-year-old kid the power of life and death over someone?

The Big Issue: As Jack says, 'The only really exciting things in life require . . . courage.'

The Last Word: Pacey and Joey having sex was long overdue, and the arguments they have throughout the episode – should we, shouldn't we? – just get kind of annoying. I was relieved when Joey finally seized the day because, although sex is a big thing, they were starting to make it way too big a deal. It's a surprise just how sensual the seduction scene is, as Joey takes the lead and real heat is generated on screen. Jen and Jack making out was a big mistake and felt really out of place. Andy Griffith's guest spot was a lovely touch but the dilemma that faced Dawson, while gripping, stretched credibility a bit too much.

415
Four Stories

1st US Transmission Date: 14 February 2001

Writer: Tom Kapinos
Director: David Petrarca
Guest Cast: Rob Nagle (Tom Frost),
David Downes (Mr Kasdan)

About Last Night: Drue manages to convince Mr Kasdan that Pacey and Joey are on the bus when they're still in bed; hence they are left behind after the ski trip. Their morning-after conversation is very awkward indeed.

The Big Picture: Following Mr Brooks's funeral, Gretchen and Dawson meet Grams in his garage, which is filled with props and memorabilia from his film career. Dawson tries to come to terms with his friend's death, and gets a visit from a solicitor regarding the will.

Excess Baggage: As punishment for her drinking on the ski trip (**414**, 'Winter's Tale') Jen is sent to see a therapist. She's nervous, uncomfortable, and eventually decides to leave. Her therapist manages to get her to stay by analysing her pretty accurately based upon only a brief acquaintance.

Seems Like Old Times: Joey and Dawson bump into each other in Capeside and she suggests they go for a drink and a talk. He tells her that Mr Brooks has left him a lot of money in his will, and he remarks that Joey seems different somehow. He guesses that she and Pacey have slept together but, when he asks her flat out, she lies.

The Ballad of Dawson and Joey: Dawson can instantly tell that Joey's changed. They sit on the swings they sat on back in **201**, 'The Kiss', and reflect on how far they've come. He tells her she's still his best friend and she always will be. He implies that she and he had a pact to sleep together first, that a promise was made, and he releases her from it. He's relieved when she tells him she's not slept with Pacey, even though he tries to tell her it would be OK if she had. So why does she lie to him? Perhaps because he tells her he hasn't slept with Gretchen yet.

The Ballad of Pacey and Joey – they Argue and Make Up, Take 8: Once again when things get difficult Pacey brings up Dawson. Joey doesn't want to hurt him but promises Pacey that if Dawson asks her she'll be honest and tell him she and Pacey have had sex. When they trade quips in the morning Pacey tells Joey, 'I could do this for the rest of my life . . . with you as my partner in irreverence.'

The Ballad of Dawson and Gretchen: Dawson gives Gretchen a long list of things he likes about her: 'You're smart and you're funny and you always know what to say to make me feel better . . . You're beautiful in a way that makes me remember those old-time movie stars . . . all style and grace. Plus, you smell good . . . not like in a perfumey way, but in a really pretty-girl kind of way.' She gives thanks he has no idea how charming he is. Gretchen tells Dawson that the moment she realised she was falling for him was when he got enthused about *Turn Away My Sweet* (**409**, Kiss Kiss Bang Bang).

The Movie Brat: Dawson is afraid of ending up as bitter as Mr Brooks was, of giving up and dropping his ambitions. He's confronted with the reality of death for the first time and is shocked that a whole life can come down to a pile of stuff in a garage.

The Grouch: Mr Brooks's will leaves money to Dawson and tells him, 'Mr Leery, this is the money with which one achieves greatness, so don't go blowing it on women and booze. But should that be your choice, make sure it's great women and great booze.' There were only five people at Mr Brooks's funeral: three Leerys, Grams and Gretchen. There is a play in his garage – *Delia and George* – which he wrote in 1949, when he was Dawson's age. Dawson's eulogy for Mr Brooks: 'He was a grumpy, misanthropic, smarter-than-thou pain in the ass . . . but he was a friend of mine, and I'm gonna miss him.'

School Sucks!: Capeside High sends its alcoholic children to a psychiatrist? In my day they just used to suspend them.

That Three-Letter Word: Jack is fine with what happened between him and Jen on the ski trip, but in order to sleep with her he'd need to be fantasising about Ryan Phillippe. Pacey is desperate to find out how he performed and badgers Joey for a review of his prowess. Joey is embarrassed talking about it and wants to keep it private and secret. Her choice of word to describe the encounter is unfortunate – she says it was 'nice', and every guy knows 'nice' is the kiss of death. Pacey is upset that she is keeping her distance and not touching him. He's insecure whether or not she was satisfied; she's insecure that she might not measure up to Tamara or Andie. Eventually she tells him that the things she'll remember best will be how sweet he was and the way he brushed her hair out of her eyes, which made her feel safe and protected. She's glad they had sex and wants to go home so they can do it again!

All Things Spielberg: The Rialto is showing *His Girl Friday* (Howard Hawks, 1940).

All Things Freud: Jen is in therapy. After a lot of banter and nervousness the therapist tells her that he thinks her 'smart, sarcastic exterior masks a scared, lonely young woman whose relationship with her parents has scarred her in ways she hasn't even begun to process'.

Our Quips Are Wittier: When Pacey asks Joey about his sexual prowess she responds, 'Just when I think you're the antithesis of the typical male, there you are, dragging your knuckles with the rest of the primates.'

Contempo Pop Music: 'Spectre Chase' by King Lear Jet, 'In the Sun' by Joseph Arthur, 'Color Blind' by Counting Crows, 'The White Trash Period of My Life' by Josh Rouse, 'But Not For Me' by Elvis Costello and 'They Can't Take That Away From Me' by Lisa Stansfield.

The Last Word: This is a beautifully written episode. Focusing on a series of two-hander dramas, almost like a stage play, it allows the characters room to breathe and speak for themselves in a way that the fast-cutting TV of today rarely does. It almost feels like a small independent art-house film. This is the point at which the show conclusively proves that it is a drama rather than a soap opera. The performances, the dialogue, the wonderfully appropriate music and the direction are all top notch. One of the best *Dawson's Creek* episodes ever, and a blueprint for how supposedly routine network TV can challenge and surprise.

416
Mind Games

1st US Transmission Date: 28 February 2001

Writer: Gina Fattore
Director: David Straiton
Guest Cast: Rob Nagle (Tom Frost),
Melissa Ponzio (Robin)

Pacey persuades Gretchen to spend the night at Doug's. Gretchen, unsurprisingly, concludes that he and Joey are sleeping together but Pacey swears her to secrecy. Joey is upset that Gretchen knows and makes her swear not to tell Dawson. Gretchen spends the evening watching videos with Dawson, and he notices that her bag is packed for a sleepover. This leads to some embarrassment and she provokes the sex conversation to clear the air. Dawson mentions Joey once too often and Gretchen discovers that Joey lied to him about sleeping with Pacey (**415**, 'Four Stories'). She is so angry and upset that she leaves, without explaining why. He calls by next day to see if she's OK. Joey hides when she hears Dawson and Pacey come in. Later, after Joey has left, Gretchen tells Pacey about Joey's lie, although he doesn't confront Joey about it when he sees her. Gretchen tells Dawson to keep being honest with her about his feelings.

Jen drags Jack along with her as she stalks her therapist, Tom, trying to find out about his personal life. He bumps into them in a bookshop and mentions a poetry reading he's attending the next day. Jen, who seems to have a bit of a crush on him, thinks it's an invitation and she and Jack go and meet him there. The poet turns out to be his girlfriend. He knew she was stalking him and he let her, to demonstrate that she can trust him.

Drue fixes the yearbook election and has Joey and Dawson elected class couple. Dawson infiltrates the yearbook staff and changes it to Joey and Pacey.

The Ballad of Dawson and Joey: Drue's assessment of Dawson and Joey is right on the money, and he thinks they've 'fatally wounded each other's psyches and doomed all [their] future relationships'. Dawson says he wishes Pacey and Joey had slept together on *True Love*, and 'put the final nail in the coffin of Dawson and Joey'. He admits (to Gretchen, of all people) that he was relieved when Joey told him she wasn't sleeping with Pacey because there's a part of him still clinging to the notion that they'll lose their virginity together.

The Ballad of Pacey and Joey: They seem so together and relaxed but every time they feel free the shadow of Dawson appears and the awkwardness comes crashing down. Joey's lie is ruining her relationship with Pacey because she's preoccupied with being found out. And when Pacey does find out, and decides not to tell Joey he knows, a sense of doom settles over the pair and we get the sense that Pacey knows the relationship can't last much longer. He never was good at bottling things up but he's decided to keep this to himself and it's bound to explode sometime.

The Ballad of Dawson and Gretchen: After Gretchen leaves his house in a bad mood Dawson thinks that she has 'seen the light' and realised she shouldn't be with him. So he buys her a toothbrush as a parting gift – she left hers at his house and it was worn out. Since she was just mad at Joey and the whole triangle thing, she and Dawson are back together by the episode's end.

The Movie Brat: Dawson's reaction to Drue's practical joke is to laugh it off as absurd (as he levitates past him in the school corridor chanting his mantra of peace and light). Never has Zen Dawson been more laid back and unconcerned.

The Big Sis: How nice it is in talkative, sort-it-out Capeside to see a character we like actually get angry and a bit destructive, and act like a normal human being. By telling Pacey about Joey's lie, Gretchen could be causing huge problems, but it's easy to understand why she did it.

The Dark Horse: Dawson says Drue is like one of the lamer Batman TV villains – 'evil with a short attention span'. He fixes the class-couple vote but then leaves the yearbook staff before it's printed, allowing Dawson to step in and rejig the result.

That Three-Letter Word: It's been two weeks since the ski trip and Joey and Pacey have trouble finding ways of spending the night together. Joey seems on the verge of accepting Pacey's invitation to skip class and have sex in the boiler room before Drue's practical joke interrupts the mood. When she turns up at Pacey's house she jumps on him without even a hello – a far cry from the reticent, frightened Joey of old, she's now very sexually confident. She sometimes wishes they'd had sex on *True Love*, to get it over with sooner. Pacey asks her if she thinks they're doing something wrong by sleeping together, and seems about to ask her, if not then why did she lie to Dawson? But he backs off.

Gretchen lost her virginity to her high school boyfriend, a 'moronic basketball player' whom Dawson hated. When he asks her if staying the night is a possibility she asks him if he wants it to be. Instead of saying 'hell, yes', he ums and ahs, talks about Jen and Joey, and manages to sabotage the moment completely. Never has a boy worked so hard to preserve his virginity.

Metatextuality: Throughout Seasons Three and Four a huge fan debate raged about which couple should be the focus of the show – Dawson and Joey or Pacey and Joey. The writer panders to this by having Drue express an opinion on the subject and call Dawson and Joey 'by far the most compelling couple'.

All Things Spielberg: Gretchen and Dawson watch a movie with Nicolas Cage and Jim Carrey, which has to be *Peggy Sue Got Married* (Francis Ford Coppola, 1986). Jack gets all his information about the gay community from the hit HBO show *Sex and the City*.

All Things Freud: The big issue emerging from Jen's therapy sessions, which she now has three times a week, is her difficulty trusting people. So her therapist, who introduces himself to Jack as Jen's friend, allows her to stalk him in the hope that it will demonstrate his trustworthiness. It works.

Girl Talk: Gretchen rails at Joey for lying to Dawson, tells her it's unfair on her, Dawson and Pacey and says that she should just sort herself out. Joey tells Gretchen she couldn't possibly understand how hard it's been for the love triangle.

Contempo Pop Music: 'Windows' by Amy Cook, 'Laughter' by Josh Rouse and 'In Metal' by Low.

The Big Issue: Gretchen: 'Trusting someone is like this gigantic act of faith. You know, you put it out there and you can never really be sure that you're gonna get it back.'

The Last Word: After **415**, 'Four Stories', anything would be a let-down. But this is not a bad episode, just feels a little samey, and is reminiscent of **413**, 'Hopeless', in that things don't seem to progress much. There are lots of nice scenes, and the juxtaposition of both couples' sexual situations is subtly done, but there's too little incident to carry an episode. The season is on a slow burn to a showdown – especially in the way Pacey is beating down his fears about college and his confusion about Joey's feelings for Dawson – but perhaps the slow burn is a bit too slow.

417
Admissions

1st US Transmission Date: 11 April 2001

Writer: Barb Siebertz
Director: Lev L Spiro
Guest Cast: Obi Ndefo (Bodie Wells),
Rob Nagel (Tom Frost)

Joey is accepted at Worthington College but Dawson is turned down by NYU Film School. However, Joey later discovers that Bessie has to contribute $15,000 to her tuition and they don't have that kind of money, so she can't go. Meanwhile, Dawson gets accepted to USC Film School. When Dawson discovers the money problem he offers Joey Mr Brooks's money, but she refuses. Dawson appeals to her to accept, and goes to Pacey to get him to work on her too. Joey, feeling guilty about her lie (**415**, 'Four Stories'), goes and confesses to Dawson and to Pacey. This clears the air but Dawson is hurt and Joey assumes the offer of money is rescinded. It isn't, and she accepts in the end.

Jack and Jen have decided to go to the same college and there are five by which they have both been accepted. Jack wants to go to NYU, and assumes that Jen will, too, since it is both her home and the place she's been raving about to everyone for years. But Jen is afraid to go back, and in therapy she realises it's because of unresolved issues with her parents. She can't remember what she and her father last spoke about and she asks Drue, who was there, to tell her what happened. Unfortunately, he can't recall much either.

The Ballad of Dawson and Joey: Joey says that when she met Dawson (in **415**, 'Four Stories') she felt for the first time in a while that things were finally OK between them, and Dawson agrees. She lied to him about her and Pacey because she didn't want to hurt him and didn't think he'd understand. Dawson's hurt by her lie, and by being told now. He can't quite figure out how he feels about it, but he tells Joey that she underestimates him, that things *are* right between them and will stay that way regardless: 'I'm certain about us and what we mean to each other, and I think you are too.'

The Ballad of Pacey and Joey: Pacey is ecstatic that Joey got into Worthington but when she finds she can't go he's ashamed to find that he's relieved. He admits this to her after she tells him she lied to Dawson, and he says it's because he feels for the first time that he's not the one holding her back. He tries to get her to promise to cut him loose if ever he does hold her back, but she refuses and tells him he has to stop thinking like that. They're still putting off talking about the future.

The Movie Brat: Dawson is gutted at being rejected by NYU and is convinced it means he won't get into USC, which is his first choice. He's overjoyed when he does get in, but that means he'll be going to California to study.

The Tomboy: Joey is outraged that she can't go to Worthington because of money, and has to accept that the system isn't fair. When Bessie throws her a celebration barbecue she's too proud to tell them all of her disappointment and refuses to let anyone feel sorry for her. She initially turns down Dawson's money because she's worried it'll ruin their friendship, and she'd feel obligated to pay it back.

The Delinquent: After her parents caught her in bed with Billy (first mentioned in **104**, 'Hurricane'), Jen knew she was going to be sent away. On her last night in New York she called Drue and invited him over to her house. She was wasted and made out with Drue on the sofa just before her parents arrived. Jen and her father started shouting at each other and Drue was thrown out. Drue was hurt because he liked Jen and she was just using him to provoke her folks. Jen apologises and Drue accepts her apology. She can't remember what it is she and her father were fighting about.

The Outsider: Although Jack wants to go to NYU he is willing to go somewhere else because it's more important for him to be with Jen. He and Jen have begun to bicker like an old married couple.

All Things Freud: Tom tells Jen that she's in therapy to learn to stop hating herself and blaming herself for whatever it was that drove her to drugs, drink and sex in a desperate search for affection at such a young age. He thinks it's related to something that happened with her parents, probably her father: 'You're doing it as a cry for love . . . because something robbed you of your childhood in a way that you'll be angry about for a long time . . . you blame yourself, that's why you don't want to remember.'

Guy Talk: Dawson goes to see Pacey to try to get him to talk to Joey about accepting the money and Pacey goes instantly on the defensive. First he insinuates that there will be strings attached to the gift; then, when Dawson says, 'Joey deserves better than . . .' Pacey interjects 'me' before Dawson can say 'Capeside', and Dawson has to calm Pacey down and make it clear that's not what he means.

Contempo Pop Music: 'Chemistry' by Semisonic, 'Bye Bye' by Marcy Playground, 'More Than This' by Anne McCue and 'The Sound of Fear' by Eels.

Backstage: Michelle Williams's wig, which first appeared in **410**, 'Self Reliance', has vanished in this episode – we're back to her own blonde hair.

The Last Word: As soon as Joey didn't get the financial aid it became obvious that Mr Brooks's will money was a set-up for this moment. It's all a bit contrived, seeming more like a nineteenth-century novel of inheritance, class and sacrifice than *Dawson's Creek*. If you can forgive the creakiness of it then at least everybody acts in a manner entirely consistent with their characters. Jen's storyline is worrying, and seems to be leading up to some repressed-memory, child-abuse revelation, which would be really hokey and not in keeping with the show at all; happily, the next episode resolves it rather better than that.

418
Eastern Standard Time

1st US Transmission Date: 18 April 2001

Writer: Jonathan Kasdan
Director: David Grossman
Guest Cast: Rob Nagel (Tom Frost),
Dylan Neal (Deputy Doug Witter),
Don McManus (Theo Lindley), Pat Hingle (Irv)

Jen and Joey are in New York, Joey to see the sights, Jen to meet the admissions guy at NYU. But Jen lied to Joey, and is really there to see her father and try to resolve the issues her therapy has raised. Joey goes with her, and they meet Theo Lindley, venture capitalist. He cancels all his appointments and takes Jen and Joey out to dinner to celebrate Jen's college acceptances, but then he bails out halfway and walks off as if it had merely been a business meeting. Jen follows him home and confronts him about the mysterious incident that set her on the road to self-destruction . . .

Gretchen and Dawson take a road trip, but their tyre bursts and they have no spare. They walk into a nearby town and get a lift back to their car with the local auto mechanic, Irv, who also has a spare tyre. Unfortunately, he dumps them by the road when he finds out they can't pay him. Dawson builds a fire on a nearby beach and they settle down for the night. It looks very like they're going to have sex until Gretchen calls a halt.

Pacey, stressed because of schoolwork, accepts Drue's invitation to go drinking at a local bar with a fake ID. They get very drunk, the bartender realises they're under-age, and then they get arrested by Doug for being drunk and disorderly.

The Ballad of Dawson and Gretchen: Dawson finally tells Gretchen he loves her, and it's clear she feels the same way about him.

The Movie Brat: This is the apotheosis of Zen Dawson. When the tyre blows, and he and Gretchen are stranded in the middle of nowhere, his entire response is 'well, this happened'. And when Irv dumps them back there his comment is 'well, that happened too' – expect him to ascend to Nirvana and join the Buddha any day now. He can build a fire on a deserted beach and light it with wet matches, something Gretchen finds very sexy. Irv thinks he'll make a grand car mechanic one day.

The Tomboy: Joey's mind is entirely blown, both by New York and by the Jen who emerges when she's back in her home town.

The Clown: The meltdown, so long in coming, has begun. It was inevitable: he's been avoiding the reality of his college prospects, working overtime to graduate high school, bottling up all his insecurity and fear. He gets drunk on tequila with Drue, of all people, after doing badly in a school test, which he hears other students saying they aced. When his fake ID is rumbled by the bartender he brazens it out and nearly starts a fight. When Doug sees Pacey arrested he asks him: 'You're not satisfied with being a moron and failure? You've got to add drunk to your list of credentials?' Pacey loses it, grabs Doug and screams, 'This is it for me! This is my whole life right here! This is all I get.' His inevitable failure to make college, and the likelihood of his failing to graduate and all that that would entail for him and Joey, is finally hitting home.

The Delinquent: Jen used to find Grams scary and hated coming to Capeside. One day, when she was twelve and her mother was taking her to Capeside, she complained so much that her mother left her at the station and told her to go home. Jen found her father having sex with Annie Sawyer, a seventeen-year-old girl from the apartment downstairs who was Jen's favourite person in the whole world. Jen ran out of the house, spent the first night in a parking lot, the second in a nightclub and the third drunkenly losing her virginity to a guy she met in a bar. From that point on her life went to hell and her father, who had seen her in the doorway, never acknowledged the problem. He pushed her away, made her feel ashamed and eventually sent her to live with Grams. She won't forgive him and she doesn't want an apology, but, when she tells him the story and makes him confront what he's done to her, she finally forgives herself.

The Dark Horse: Drue is a regular at the bar he takes Pacey to. The reason he takes him there is because it's next to the local community college, which seems a likely destination for Pacey, and he wants to show him there are good people around Capeside. And, bizarrely, he actually seems to be trying to do Pacey a genuine favour. Could Drue be trying to make friends?

Family Sucks!: At first Mr Lindley seems nice – he hugs Jen hello and seems proud at her college success. But at the restaurant, when he tells Joey why he loves New York, he's creepy. He focuses too intently on her, and, when his story finishes with him staring into Joey's eyes and saying, 'I'm madly in love with you', he's actually quite chilling. He tries to convince Jen she's making up the story about Annie and has the cheek to suggest she get help. He's a wreck by the time Jen finishes with him. When she says goodbye and leaves it seems clear that it's goodbye for ever.

School Sucks!: Pacey is snowed under with tests as he struggles to graduate.

That Three-Letter Word: Dawson tells Gretchen he no longer knows what they're waiting for and neither does she. Just as they're about to have sex she says she needs to know what's going on in his head, and the idiot actually tells her! He says that there's a part of him that thinks 'that everything should be perfect, and that Joey and I should have slept together for the first time'. Of course, by telling Gretchen that, he's saying that sleeping with her isn't perfect, and that's guaranteed to kill the mood. She tells him she wants to sleep with him a lot, but only when it's for the right reason, not because he has something to prove to himself about letting go of his past. So once again Dawson manages to scupper his chances of getting laid. After he's fallen asleep Gretchen bawls her eyes out.

Reality Bites: Dawson tells Gretchen that he still has reality issues, and views the road trip, with it's flat tyre and night spent under the stars, as 'a perfect example of how our visions for our lives conflict with realities. I still have my distortions and my delusions.'

All Things Spielberg: Dawson doesn't want to hitch a ride when they get a flat because he's freaked out by *The Hitcher* (Robert Harmon, 1986). When Pacey and Drue enter the bar Pacey quotes from *Star Wars* (George Lucas, 1977) and likens the bar to Mos Eisley on Tatooine.

All Things Freud: Jen feels that by confronting her father she has completed her process of therapy and decides she's done with it.

Guest Cast: Don McManus has appeared in numerous TV shows including *Northern Exposure*, *Party of Five* and *NYPD Blue*; on the big screen he's been in *The Shawshank Redemption*, *Hannibal* and *Air Force One* among others. Pat Hingle has a long and distinguished career ranging from an uncredited role in *On the Waterfront* to Commissioner Gordon in the Batman films.

Contempo Pop Music: 'Last Lament' by Susan James, 'I Can't Wait To Meetchu' by Macy Gray, 'Bring You Down' by Red Delicious, 'You Belong To Me' by Hypnogaja, 'Love In 2 Parts' by Erin McKeown, 'The Preacher' by Frostbit Blue, 'Sad Eyed Woman' by Tricky Woo, 'The World Is Crazy' by John Campbelljohn, 'Letters From the Wasteland' by Wallflowers, 'Show Me' by Vanessa Daou and 'Sweet Jane' by Cowboy Junkies.

The Last Word: The scenes with Jen and her father are unsettling and extremely powerful; thank heavens it wasn't a storyline about a repressed abuse memory. Instead, the reason for Jen's problems is far more unexpected, but no less shocking. Michelle Williams does her very best work on the show to date. Dawson and Gretchen's road trip is fun and shows the good rapport they have with each other, at least until Dawson puts his foot in it again. Pacey's meltdown begins and it's only going to get worse. Joshua Jackson is good at playing angry and resentful and he gets to let rip in this episode. But the abiding image is of Jen, in slow motion, leaving therapy having faced her demons and won.

419
Late

1st US Transmission Date: 25 April 2001

Writer: Jeffrey Stepakoff
Director: David Petrarca
Guest Cast: David Monahan (Tobey Barrett),
Deron Barnett (Will)

Gale, who finally decided to have the baby, is two weeks overdue and endures two false alarms before finally giving birth to a baby girl. Earlier she had a naming shower, where all the Capeside women gathered and suggested names. Gale chooses Lillian, after Joey's mother.

Joey is late and is worried that she is pregnant. She is totally unprepared for this, and fights with Bessie about it. Gretchen provides emotional support and tells Joey about her own pregnancy at college. Bessie and Joey make up before Joey takes a test and finds that she is not pregnant after all.

Gretchen has an interview for a magazine job in Boston and it really comes home to her and Dawson that they could soon be travelling to opposite sides of the continent. They eventually decide to live in the moment until the last possible second.

Tobey is beaten up on the way home from literacy class. He tells Jack he was mugged but in fact he was beaten up for being gay. Tobey doesn't want to report it but Jack intervenes, brings a policeman to Tobey's house and forces him to confront the issue.

The Ballad of Pacey and Joey: Pacey doesn't tell Joey about his arrest and his meltdown (**418**, 'Eastern Standard Time'), and when he phones her the long silences that fall and the looks on both their faces increase the sense of impending doom.

The Ballad of Dawson and Gretchen: Reality finally intrudes into their relationship and they have to face the fact that they're heading in different directions. They discuss the possibility of one of them joining the other, either in California or Boston, but both know that it's not going to happen. Gretchen suggests a long-distance relationship, but that's also a pipe dream. He asks her why she changed her mind about sleeping with him on the beach (**418**, 'Eastern Standard Time') and she tells him it's because, 'I can't take that next step, open myself up like that just to be left. I just can't do that . . . I've got to get on with my own life.' But she postpones her trip to Boston so she can see Dawson, and as they passionately make out they accept that they're just 'prolonging the inevitable, living in denial', but what the hell!

The Ballad of Jack and Tobey: They're getting on really well now, and their rapport at the literacy programme is obvious. Jack feels OK going to Tobey's house and now considers himself his friend.

The Clown: Doug got the charges against Pacey dropped (**418**, 'Eastern Standard Time') and has taken him camping to sort himself out. Pacey lied to Joey and told her he was going on a fishing trip, a lie he maintains when he phones to see if she's all right.

The Outsider: Jack finally confronts the political issues relating to his homosexuality. Tobey was always the activist, yet when he is beaten up he backs off and it's Jack

who forces the issue of reporting it because 'someday, I'm
going to want to walk through the park and I'm going to
want to hold some guy's hand and what if I forget to look
around first? What if the wrong people see me do that?' He
denies he's become a gay rights activist though. He says
he's a 'Tobey activist', which fits with his position that he's
not interested in the wider scheme of things, or changing
the world, just dealing with his own life and issues, and
those of his friends.

Family Sucks!: Dawson now has a baby sister, Lillian
Leery. Nice gesture naming her after Mrs Potter, but Lillian
Leery . . . it's an alliterative nightmare for the poor kid!

That Three-Letter Word: Joey to Dawson: 'Sex doesn't
necessarily bring people closer together. It's just a magnify-
ing glass . . . if there's a problem, it gets bigger, and if
there's closeness you get closer.'

All Things Spielberg: Mitch drags Dawson away from the
all-female naming shower 'before *The Vagina Monologues*
start'. This is a stage play formed of three monologues in
which women talk about their sexuality. They've been hugely
successful – and not a little controversial – and actresses such
as Calista Flockhart, Claire Danes, Alanis Morissette, Ricki
Lake and Gillian Anderson have performed them.

Grown-Up Stuff: The birth is not easy: it takes almost 24
hours and there are worries about complications because
of Gale's age. Happily, all is well.

Girl Talk: Joey can't think of any names for the shower so
she gives Gale the necklace Dawson gave her (**302**,
'Homecoming'). Gale tells the women how much she loved
and misses Lillian Potter, Joey's mother.

Joey's getting pregnant has always been Bessie's biggest
fear – that Joey would make the same mistakes she made
and end up stuck in Capeside when she should be going to
college and having a better life. Joey reacts badly to
Bessie's attempt at intervention and tells Bessie that she's
screwed up her life, but Joey's going to be better than that.

In the end she apologises to Bessie and tells her how much she respects what she's done by raising her and Alexander and building a good life for herself against the odds.

Gretchen and Joey have had a strained relationship since Gretchen lost her temper in **416**, 'Mind Games', so, when Joey asks her what's happening with Pacey, Gretchen tells Joey the truth because she's refused to lie for Pacey any more. Then she comes on really strong and has a go at Joey, telling her to back off and stop hassling Pacey about things. When Joey refuses to do that, Gretchen looks furious until she discovers the reason. After arguing with Bessie, Joey is surprised to find herself turning to Gretchen, but of course she's exactly the right person to talk to, and she tells Joey about her own pregnancy (**405**, 'A Family Way'). They discuss Dawson. Joey tells her that Dawson would 'lasso the moon' for Gretchen and they indulge in a little joint appreciation of his qualities: 'You cherish that big part of him that he always wants you to have. No matter what happens . . . you never forget him.' They also talk about Pacey as a possible father and Gretchen thinks 'Pacey would probably like the idea of a baby . . . he's great with kids, attentive to women. The problem with the scenario is that Pacey just can't deal with Pacey.'

Guy Talk: Mitch tells Dawson that guys don't love babies the way women do, they love the *idea* of them but the reality is 'pure hell'. It's only when a personality emerges that a father falls in love with his child.

Contempo Pop Music: 'Forever Young' by Joan Baez, 'Family Circus' by Micah Green and 'Walk When You Can Fly' by Karen Blake.

The Last Word: The stand-out storyline in this episode is the Jack–Tobey friendship and the way it's been maturing off screen between episodes. Lillian's birth is as expected, and Joey's having a pregnancy scare was too good a storyline to be passed up, so it was inevitable, too. In fact, the only problem with this episode is the lack of surprises. There were certain things that needed to happen for the story to move on and they all happen – heigh-ho! Pacey's absence is ominous, and leaves us wondering whether when he returns from his camping trip he will be mellower and sorted out, or whether his meltdown will go critical.

420
Promicide

1st US Transmission Date: 2 May 2001

Writer: Maggie Friedman
Director: Jason Moore
Guest Cast: David Monahan (Tobey Barrett)

The senior prom is held on a boat cruising around the creek. Gretchen and Dawson go, as do Pacey and Joey. Jen sets Jack up with Tobey against Jack's wishes, so he retaliates by setting Jen up with Drue and offering him $50 to follow Jen around all night. Pacey tries to organise the perfect evening for Joey but he rips her dress, ruins the corsage and rents a clapped-out nightmare of a limo. Joey pushes Pacey to tell her why he won't touch her any more and asks what's the matter with him, but he ends up losing his temper with her and dumping her at the top of his voice in the middle of the dance floor after he sees her dancing with Dawson. Joey tells him to go to hell.

Gretchen is freaked out by being at the prom, and feels old. She tells Dawson that she's going back to college and that it's over between them. Jen sets about getting drunk and Drue narrowly saves her from drowning by catching her when she falls off the boat. Jack and Tobey, despite initial reluctance from Jack, kiss and dance together at the prom.

The Ballad of Dawson and Joey: Dawson tells Joey he's stopped expecting ever to love anyone the way he loved her, because she was his first love and he knows it'll never be like that again; Joey feels the same. It's Dawson who spots how upset she is after her first discussion with Pacey, and it's he who runs to comfort her after the big fight. When Gretchen dumps Dawson she tells him he's still 'chasing after Joey, literally and metaphorically', and that he clearly has a lot of unresolved feelings.

The Ballad of Pacey and Joey: Joey tries to initiate sex but Pacey passes in favour of a turkey sandwich. He keeps his distance until she has to ask what's going on and then his resentment comes flooding out. He keeps trying to be what he thinks she wants him to be but all she wants him to be is himself and to tell her what's bothering him; he says that he doesn't think he has anything left to say. When Gretchen asks him what's up he says that ever since his camping trip he's been feeling angry at Joey for no reason, which makes him feel guilty, which in turn makes him angrier. He decides to try to talk it out with Joey, but when he finds her and Dawson, happy, laughing and dancing, he explodes and all the tension that's been building up in him for months pours out. He asks her why she's dating him, and says, 'I feel like I'm Josephine Potter's little charity project. I feel like I'm the designated loser . . . when I'm with you, I feel like I'm nothing . . . it's why I never touch you . . . it just reminds me that I'm not good enough.' Later, when he's calmed down he tries to explain properly. Pacey tells Joey he's become 'a man who hates himself' and he can't seem to stop himself taking it out on her. Last year he felt there were things he could give her but now he feels that there's nothing he can do for her, and since she is leaving town and he isn't he thinks they've reached the end of the road: 'You deserve better than this place, and you deserve better than me.' Joey has no response to that, other than to tell him he's broken her heart 'into a thousand pieces' and he should leave her alone.

The Ballad of Dawson and Gretchen: Being at the prom makes Gretchen feel old for the first time and she realises it's time for her to move on with her life, and that can't include Dawson. She knows it's an impossible situation, and although Dawson says he can handle that she tells him she can't. She's abrupt and decisive, and no matter how much Dawson protests he hasn't a chance of changing her mind.

The Ballad of Jack and Tobey: Tobey and Jack are now fast friends but Jen keeps pushing them together. Tobey wants Jack to ask him to the prom but Jen knows he never will, so she sets it up. When Tobey asks Jack to dance Jack tells him he's stepped over the line and it's just a platonic friendship. Tobey doesn't buy it all, tells Jack to sort himself out and walks off to brood. Jack comes clean and tells Tobey that he's no longer put off by how out or how gay Tobey is. In fact, he's attracted by how funny and handsome he is, and he's not afraid any more. So they kiss, and Jack asks Tobey to dance.

The Delinquent: Jen has been sad and screwed up since her confrontation with her father (**418**, 'Eastern Standard Time'). She's unhappy because all year she's planned to get back to New York but now she doesn't want to go there at all. She gets blind drunk and, but for Drue, would have suffered the same fate as poor Abby (**218**, 'The Perfect Wedding') and drowned in the creek.

The Big Sis: Gretchen did not get the job she applied for in Boston (**419**, 'Late') because she didn't have a college degree; so she decides to go back to college.

The Dark Horse: Drue refuses Jack's $50 at the end of the night, and actually takes good care of Jen when she's drunk, revealing that, no matter how much he might try to pretend otherwise, he does care. He's going to college in Boston.

Family Sucks!: Deputy Doug and Sheriff Witter make Pacey take a breathalyser test after the prom, so he can't drink.

School Sucks!: Pacey is officially still a junior and shouldn't be at the prom at all. In fact they're not allowed to sell tickets to him because of that, and he has to get Joey to pick them up for him.

That Three-Letter Word: Dawson buys condoms, hoping to sleep with Gretchen after the prom. Joey sees this and there's a moment of awkwardness, but she later says that if he is going to lose his virginity she's glad it's with Gretchen.

Kiss and Tell: The Tobey–Jack kiss broke new ground for American TV. Three quotes, taken from a variety of interviews given after the episode aired, illustrate various responses. Scott Seomin of the Gay and Lesbian Alliance: 'I timed it. It's like a 5½ second mouth-to-mouth kiss. We haven't seen anything like this before on network TV.' Heather Cirmo of the Family Research Council: 'The first kiss was disturbing enough' (Jack and Ethan, **323**, 'True Love'), but this one could influence 'impressionable teens who have questions about their sexuality, by promoting the myth that homosexuality is something you're born with.' Greg Berlanti, executive producer of *Dawson's Creek*: 'A lot of kids out there deserve to see positive images of who and what they are. I watched millions of teenagers kiss on TV growing up, and it didn't make me straight.'

Our Quips Are Wittier: Dawson tells Joey how glad he is they're still friends after all they've been through and she agrees, upon which he says, 'God, we're so healthy, it just makes me want to puke.'

Contempo Pop Music: 'You're An Ocean' by Fastball, 'I've Changed (Alternate Version)' by Josh Joplin Group, 'Ruby's Gone' by Eva Trout, 'Talk Show' by Dig Deeper, 'Sundrop' by Ego, 'Roses Around My Feet' by Tish Hinojosa, 'When We Collide' by KD Lang, 'Wonderful Thing' by Vagabond Lovers, 'Aftershocks' by Mary Beth, '20one' by Sid Six, 'Take My Hand' by Dido and 'Whadify' by Everett Bradley.

The Last Word: The single most melancholy episode of *Dawson's Creek* ever. Pacey's spectacular self-destruction is painful and heartbreaking to watch, and Joshua Jackson gives it his all to sell an anger that would have seemed impossible in Pacey only a few episodes ago. At least Jack got a happy ending.

421
Separation Anxiety

1st US Transmission Date: 9 May 2001

Writer: Rina Mimoun
Director: Krishna Rao
Guest Cast: Peter Jurasik (Mr Kubelik)

It's a week after the prom and neither Dawson nor Joey has spoken to their respective Witters.

Gretchen has signed up for some summer courses at college and plans to leave the day after tomorrow for a month's travelling. Gale tells Dawson to go and talk to Gretchen before she leaves, and he does, asking her to sign his yearbook. Inspired by Mr Brooks's tale of running away with Ellie (**409**, 'Kiss Kiss Bang Bang') and a conversation with Mitch about risk takers, Dawson persuades Gretchen to let him come with her. But, when Gretchen visits him that evening to see how his farewell letters are going, the spectre of Joey rises up between them and she changes her mind. When Dawson arrives to leave with her the next morning she has already gone and all that's left is his yearbook, with a farewell letter.

Mr Kubelik from Worthington College (**409**, 'Kiss Kiss Bang Bang') is having another party for freshman students in Capeside. He asks Joey to bring Pacey to meet the dean of admissions because they have an offer they want to make. Joey assumes they're going to offer Pacey a place at college. Unfortunately, the offer is to crew on the dean's boat that summer as a deck hand.

Grams is selling her house to pay for Jen's tuition. She plans to move into a retirement community. Jen refuses to let her do that and, after talking to Jack, she asks Grams to move to Boston with her instead.

The Ballad of Pacey and Joey: When Joey comes to ask him to the party, all Pacey can say is that he misses her, and she says she misses him too. They almost kiss when he collects her, and when she and he arrive and speak to Mr Kubelik there's a flash of the old Pacey and Joey. When he realises it's not an offer to come to college he tells Joey to stay at the party and enjoy her new life, but she replies, 'How can I enjoy it without you?' and drags him away. She asks if they can spend the night together, just to sleep, and Paccy agrees, but he sneaks out before dawn and watches the sun rise over the creek. Joey finds him and he apologises for his behaviour at the prom. He tells her how proud he is of what she's achieved and how ashamed he is that he 'decided to become a stereotypical guy who can't handle it when his girlfriend gets a better job than he does'. Although he says he hates that kind of guy he admits that at the party he was jealous of all the people who would get to spend time with Joey next year while he will probably be stuck back in Capeside. It's still over, but he tells her, 'At least we got a better ending this time. I am grateful for that.'

The Ballad of Dawson and Gretchen: Gretchen was trying all week to think of a way to say goodbye to Dawson, but had also considered just slipping away. When he persuades her to let him come with her, he says he wants to spend time with her away from all the pressures of Capeside – the college applications, job interviews, Joey – and just see if he and she could work out on their own. She thinks it's crazy, but he insists that it's their moment and they should grab it. She's convinced. But later, when she sees him with Lillian, and he mentions his fantasy that Lillian and Alexander will be *Dawson and Joey – The Next Generation*, Gretchen realises that he's still not let go of Joey, no matter how much he thinks he has. Her goodbye kiss with Dawson is obviously final, but he looks stunned when he finds her gone next day. In her letter she tells him to savour the last moments of this chapter of his life, that he belongs in Capeside for the summer and she finishes with, 'I don't need to spend a month in a car to fall in love with you – I already am in love with you, even more than you know.

Thank you for changing my life and opening my heart again . . . you'll never know how much it meant to me.' And that is that.

The Movie Brat: Dawson has applied for USC's summer programme, and sends his film on Mr Brooks to them by way of application. He's amazed at how attached he's become to Lilly already.

The Tomboy: At her first Worthington party Joey was a mess of awkwardness; now she glides through it with ease, totally in her environment and comfortable. It's a measure of how far she's come this season.

The Clown: Pacey went to the party hoping he could be Joey's knight in shining armour one last time, but she doesn't need him to be that any more and, as ever, he feels useless and insecure when he can't save someone.

The Delinquent: Perhaps following Drue's suggestion of Boston as a college destination (**420**, 'Promicide') Jen and Jack have decided to go to Boston Bay College, which puts them in the same town as Worthington College, and thus Joey. Jen admits that she's afraid to go to college, and even more so without Grams. Her request that Grams come with her is, she insists, selfishly motivated.

The Wicked Witch: Grams is willing to sacrifice both her house and, by moving into retirement community, her lifestyle, to send Jen to college. When Jen suggests Boston, Grams can't imagine what she'd do there, but compared with the retirement community it's an attractive offer, and Jen convinces her very easily by simply pouting and adopting her cute begging face.

Family Sucks!: The farewell scene between Pacey and Gretchen, when he tells her how glad he is that she came home this year and they both say how much they love each other, is really good. Especially touching is Gretchen's assertion that, aside from the bonds of family, she just plain likes Pacey.

Guy Talk: Mitch thinks that Mr Brooks reminds him of Dawson, because he was a dreamer and a risk taker.

Our Quips Are Wittier: Jen pushes Jack for a 'small juicy little morsel' of gossip about him and Tobey, to which Jack replies, 'When discussing my love life, try not to use the word juicy or morsel, OK? It cheapens me.'

Blooper: Jen says she's eighteen, but the official website establishes that her eighteenth birthday is on 22 May, after graduation.

Contempo Pop Music: 'Dead Yet' by Mud'l Head, 'Show Me Heaven' by Jessica Andrews, 'Write Me a Song' by Edwin McCain, 'Windows' by Amy Cook, 'One Small Year' by Shawn Colvin, 'Around and Around' by Mark Kozelek and 'Waiting For My Real Life To Begin' by Colin Hay.

The Last Word: Can this season get any more melancholy? Just when Pacey seems about to get a break the writers kick him when he's down by raising his hopes of college and then cruelly snatching them away again. Dawson gets left holding the baby, literally, and Gretchen departs the series, perhaps never to return. Joey and Pacey break up for the second episode in a row, and this time it's even sadder than at the prom. On the happier side, Grams is manoeuvred into coming to Boston very nicely, thus keeping her in the series when it shifts location next season. Another tear-jerker episode and, though I'm loving this season, I'm also crying out for some smiles and escapades to lighten the load. Please?

422
The Graduate

1st US Transmission Date: 16 May 2001

Writer: Alan Cross
Director: Harry Winer
Guest Cast: Dylan Neal (Deputy Doug Witter),
David Monahan (Tobey Barrett),
Harry Shearer (Principal Peskin),
David Downes (Mr Kasdan)

It's graduation time and Joey has a speech to write for the ceremony, but her concerns about Pacey leave her too preoccupied to write it. Bessie gives Joey a letter written by their mother just before she died. Joey can't bring herself to read it, so she gets Dawson to read it for her, and it helps her write a speech about those people who are missing from her life.

Pacey is refused admission to the graduation rehearsal because his grades are borderline. When a throwaway line from Mr Kasdan infuriates Pacey he storms out of his final exam, the one he needs to pass in order to graduate. Mr Kasdan comes to Pacey's house, apologises and allows him to retake it. Pacey passes the exam and graduates, but he doesn't tell anyone except Andie. He tells Joey he needs to go off and live his own life for a while and, without saying goodbye to anyone, he leaves to take the summer job he was offered by the Dean of Worthington (**421**, 'Separation Anxiety').

Jen and Drue set the sprinklers to come on during the graduation ceremony, but are caught in the act by Principal Peskin. He takes them to his home and makes them listen to three hours of his dismal cello playing as punishment.

Andie returns for graduation and tells Jack that she has decided to defer Harvard for a year and stay in Italy.

The Ballad of Dawson and Joey: Joey's mother's letter reads, 'Keep close those who shared your childhood. They will always love you in a way no one else can and they will always be with you.' It seems clear she was talking about Dawson.

The Ballad of Pacey and Joey: Joey wants to find a way for her and Pacey to remain friends but in the real world that's a lot harder to do than to say. Pacey tells her he's still in love with her, will be for some time, and needs to be on his own in order to get over her. When he sees her at the graduation party he says that he didn't want their relationship to end this way and asks her, 'If I were lucky enough one day to find myself owning a sailboat again, and I were to ask the woman that I love to go sailing with me, would she?' Joey replies that he wouldn't even have to ask, so there's hope for the future after all.

The Ballad of Jack and Tobey: Tobey is concerned that Jack will not acknowledge him as his boyfriend and Jack says he will when the time's right. Sure enough, when Andie meets Tobey at the airport, Jack introduces him to her as his boyfriend.

The Movie Brat: Andie talks to Dawson about Gretchen and he tells her he's over it. He's accepted it as a great time in his life and his 'first mature relationship', but now he's ready to move on. Andie is surprised he's not overanalysing it to death and angsting himself into speechlessness, and she tells him how much he's changed – she has seen the new face of Zen Dawson.

The Tomboy: Joey has won something called the Capeside Pinnacle Award, presumably for academic achievement, and she sits on the stage at the ceremony with honours robes on. Her speech seems to be about both her mother and Pacey, and it's touching in spite of the obvious mawkishness of the moment: there are 'people in my life who are gone now, people I miss very much and people who I am haunted by in different ways, but whether we're separated by death or merely distance, I know that they're still with me because I keep them in my heart.' Her mother's letter also manages to be moving even though it's a sentimental device.

The Clown: Dawson, Joey and Doug all offer to help Pacey study at various times and he rejects and resents all their efforts. Being excluded from the graduation rehearsal in front of the whole senior year is a crushing humiliation and he begs Mitch not to do it, but the principal has given specific orders. When he has graduated he tells Andie that he finally feels he can be proud of himself and that he's sure he can 'overcome anything'. He doesn't tell the others because he doesn't feel the need to compare himself to them any more. His achievement is his own and was done only for him, not to prove anything to anyone else. The last time we see him he's on a plane to Miami to meet the dean of Worthington's boat.

The Basket Case: Andie is happy and carefree for the first time since her elder brother died. So Jack doesn't mind when she says she's going to stay in Italy for another year and defer Harvard.

The Dark Horse: Drue's father refuses to come to his graduation, which in turn leads to a fight between Drue and his mother. He comes and begs Jen to let him crash at her place. She takes pity on him and even allows herself to be roped into his sprinkler scheme, which works in the end despite their being caught red-handed. Grams realises that Drue is a 'duplicitous, smooth-talking butt-kisser', but she lets him stay another night at the house so he can help her pack.

Family Sucks!: After Pacey graduates Doug comes to tell him how proud he is of him and Pacey responds by telling Doug how much he's always looked up to him. He even grudgingly accepts that Doug is straight, which is a first. It's a great scene between the two of them and if, as seems likely, this is the last time we see Doug on the show, it's a fitting resolution to a relationship that's added a lot to the series.

Bessie also gets a possible farewell scene, with Joey telling her how wonderfully she's brought her up, how she considers her a second mother, and how much she loves her.

School Sucks!: When Pacey's pencil breaks before his final exam Mr Kasdan makes a crack about Pacey always being unprepared, and Pacey just explodes: 'I've been busting my ass in your class for the last five months, just to keep my head above water . . . none of the teachers here care . . . for the honour students, you're willing to bend over back- wards, but for me, a student who could actually use that help, you can't wait to get rid of me!' When he storms out it really looks like Pacey's blown his final chance. But Mr Kasdan proves himself Capeside High's best ever teacher and later he tells Pacey, 'You're not an idiot or a punch line, you are why I teach. Those honour students that turn your stomach, they don't need me. But you . . .' Pacey rightly realises this is a story that he's going to be telling for years to come.

Bloopers: It may seem like a blooper but it's really an in-joke – Jack calls Andie his little sister, she calls him her little brother, and they can't both be right (see **Backstage** for episode **404**, 'Future Tense'). Meredith Monroe returns for one episode and is credited as a special guest star, even though she has remained in the main credits throughout the season.

Contempo Pop Music: 'Pinch Me' by Barenaked Ladies, 'If It's Hurting You' by Robbie Williams, 'Dream Too Small' by Amy Dalley, 'If' by Dragmatic and 'Fields Of Gold' by Eva Cassidy. Bessie puts lipstick on Joey to the sound of 'Good Mother' by Jann Arden, which is a direct reference to when the same thing happened in the first ever episode.

Ker-THUNK!: Andie's deferment of Harvard is pretty convenient because Harvard is not that far from Boston and since the show will be set in Boston next year if Andie were at Harvard there would have to be reasons why she wasn't featured regularly.

The Big Issue: As Joey says in her speech, 'In time, that's all that we're going to be to each other anyway, this population of memories, some wonderful and endearing, some less so. But taken together those memories help make us who we are and who we will be.'

The Last Word: The melancholy lifts at last as Pacey comes good, Andie returns and we have a graduation ceremony to give a real sense of closure to Capeside High. Katie Holmes is especially good in this episode, playing her sadness at the state of her relationship with Pacey. Drue also comes across as wholly likable for perhaps the first time as well, which augurs well for his role in the next season. The mawkishness of Joey's mother's letter and the final speech is easy to forgive because both are handled well and kept just this side of oversentimentality.

423
Coda

1st US Transmission Date: 23 May 2001

Writers: Gina Fattore and Tom Kapinos
Director: Greg Prange

Everyone says goodbye to Dawson as he gets ready to leave for the USC summer programme.

The Ballad of Dawson and Joey: Since graduation, Dawson and Joey have been spending a lot of time together. We open with them both in Dawson's bedroom watching the horror movie that Dawson was shooting back in 100, 'Pilot', and musing on how far they've come since then. Dawson admits to Jack that he's thought about staying in Capeside so he can spend the whole summer with Joey, and that he can't get her off his mind. Joey admits to Jen that she feels the same way. Their first attempt at goodbye, on the porch of Joey's house, is stilted, awkward and tearful. They meet later that night on Dawson's lawn – he going to say goodbye to her, she coming to say goodbye to him. Joey tells Dawson how incredible he is and assures him he'll get a beautiful LA girlfriend in no time. She drops a bombshell when she tells him she wants him to stay for the summer. She knows he has to leave, but she just wants him to know she's been thinking about it. She's worried he'll hate her for telling him and he replies, 'I could never hate you, Joey, and not for lack of trying, either.' He tells her that it's time for him to get out of his bedroom, and for her to find herself without him around. She says that he's 'proof that someone out there is thinking of me, my friend who was with me always. It's pure magic. I'm gonna miss you, Dawson.' And then, at last, a kiss . . .

The Ballad of Pacey and Joey: Pacey hasn't called Joey at all since his departure. He's keeping busy to keep his mind off her, and Dawson says to Pacey that Joey's doing the same, although he's sure she thinks about him all the time.

The Movie Brat: Dawson calls his second movie, *Creek Daze*, a 'self-indulgent piece of crap'. Dawson is on the Apple side of the endless Mac-versus-PC debate and he would rather not have a laptop at all if he can't have a Mac (could Apple possibly have some sort of sponsorship deal with the show? I wonder). He's massively in denial and hugely stressed about leaving. His parents are going to bring Lilly to LA for Thanksgiving, so Dawson won't be back in Capeside till Christmas. Jen and Jack buy him a mobile phone so he can keep in touch. Dawson won't promise Mitch that he won't try drugs at some point: he promises only not to become a total junkie. His favourite movie is *Jaws* (Steven Spielberg, 1975, see **104**, 'Hurricane'); his most embarrassing moment is kissing Eve in front of the whole school (**302**, 'Homecoming'); his greatest regret is rejecting Joey's offer to sleep with him (**301**, 'Like a Virgin').

The Tomboy: Joey will be spending the summer working at the Yacht Club. Her most embarrassing moment is offering to sleep with Dawson (**301**, 'Like a Virgin'); her most life-altering moment was when Dawson kissed her (**112**, 'Decisions').

The Delinquent: Jen and Dawson say an emotional farewell, friends for ever. She jokingly tells him never to call her again, like all the men in her life. Then she corrects herself – he can't fulfil her stereotypical image of men because she and Dawson never slept together. He asks if she's got five minutes and she replies, with a smile, 'For you? Always!'

The Wicked Witch: Grams is very unsentimental about moving out of her old house. When she was younger she and her husband first lived with his parents and then in a flat above his law office. Joey, Pacey and Dawson lived in terror of Grams and her house when they were little. Pacey once offered Joey a dollar to touch the front door, but she was too scared. Grams's final pronouncement on the gang is that they go on about things too much and are too 'dour and depressed'.

That Three-Letter Word: Dawson laughs when he realises that he's the only one to graduate high school still a virgin – it definitely wasn't his plan!

Metatextuality: The poster on Dawson's wall for Mr Brooks's film, *Turn Away My Sweet*, credits Greg Prange, *Dawson's Creek*'s executive producer and the director of this episode, as producer.

All Things Spielberg: The gang go to see *American Graffiti* (George Lucas, 1973), which is about a group of friends on their last night together before college. Joey asks Dawson what he would say if he ever met Spielberg and all he can think of is 'Thanks'. Joey and he end up watching *E.T.* in Dawson's room and afterwards she asks if it got the Oscar, and Dawson corrects her: it was *Gandhi* – a total replication of the first ever scene of *Dawson's Creek* (**100**, 'Pilot').

Grown-Up Stuff: Mitch doesn't handle Dawson's imminent departure well. He takes a pointless stand on the type of computer Dawson should have and then starts a fight with him about whether or not he can go out with the gang on his last night in Capeside – he calls Dawson 'insensitive'; Dawson calls him 'overbearing'. Gale tells Mitch off for expressing his fears about the future in such a silly way so Mitch swaps the PC for a Mac and admits to Dawson that he almost doesn't want him to leave. 'Son or not . . . you are one of my favourite people.' His farewell speech covers all the bases – no sex without a condom, don't take drugs, don't join a frat house. But his final nugget of wisdom is 'it ain't over till it's over', which he admits is more than a little lame.

Girl Talk: Joey asks Jen why she thinks Joey wants Dawson to stay and Jen says, 'It's this little voice in my head that says, "I like your hair colour. What number is that?" ' This is a direct quote of the first really bitchy comment Joey threw Jen's way in **100**, 'Pilot'. Between them they rip Dawson lovingly to shreds with his annoying habits and his 'crushing self-analysis'.

Guy Talk: Pacey calls Dawson from the Caribbean to say that he still thinks about when they were friends, that being Dawson's friend used to be all that mattered to him, and that he regrets not saying goodbye to him before leaving. Dawson gets a chance to tell Pacey how proud he is of him.

Kiss and Tell: The final shot of the season exactly replicates the final shot of Season One – Joey and Dawson silhouetted against the window kissing.

Our Quips Are Wittier: When Jen says she is like Boo Radley (the reclusive neighbour in *To Kill a Mockingbird*), Dawson replies 'except beautiful and with breasts'. Jen's reply – 'wit, we like that around here' – is exactly what Dawson said to her when she first entered his bedroom in **100**, 'Pilot'.

Contempo Pop Music: 'Packing Blankets' by Eels, 'Rock Me To Sleep' by Jill Sobule, 'How You've Grown' by Natalie Merchant and 'Daydream Believer' by Mary Beth.

The Big Issue: As Dawson says, 'This chapter is over'.

The Last Word: A perfect end to the best season of *Dawson's Creek* so far. With Pacey away we're back where we started: Dawson and Joey watching movies in his room, sharing their feelings and kissing as if nothing had happened in the last two years. Their characters have changed so much, especially Dawson's, but they've found their way back to each other at last, if only for one brief moment. Full of nods back to the pilot episode, this clearly signals the end of *Dawson's Creek* as we know it. Next year will be set in a new town and it will be a wholly different show, especially considering that Dawson will be 3,000 miles away from the rest of the characters. It's easy to think of Seasons One to Four as a whole, and the next two years – the show is set to run for six years at least – as a sort of sequel or spin-off show. All the issues raised in the pilot and beyond are addressed and resolved beautifully by this point and there's a sense of completion and closure to everybody's story that's very satisfying.

Books

	The Beginning Of Everything Else	by	Jennifer Baker
#1	Long Hot Summer	by	KS Rodriguez
#2	Calm Before The Storm	by	Jennifer Baker
#3	Shifting Into Overdrive	by	CJ Anders
#4	Major Meltdown	by	KS Rodriguez
#5	Double Exposure	by	CJ Anders
#6	Trouble In Paradise	by	CJ Anders
#7	Too Hot To Handle	by	CJ Anders
#8	Don't Scream	by	CJ Anders
#9	Tough Enough	by	CJ Anders
#10	Playing For Keeps	by	CJ Anders
#11	Running On Empty	by	CJ Anders
#12	A Capeside Christmas	by	CJ Anders

The first book is an adaptation of the pilot episode, whereas the other twelve are original novels featuring the regular Capeside cast. CJ Anders is especially good at capturing the movie-riffing, angsty feel of Seasons One and Two. The characters feel right, the dialogue sparkles and the books are actually a lot of fun. The only problem is trying to work out where they fit in the run of episodes. For example, take *A Capeside Christmas*: if this is Christmas Season Three, after Dawson and Joey have broken up, and before Pacey and Joey get together, then it's fine. Unfortunately a couple of throwaway references throw that right off: Jen says that Henry has already left, and Dawson refers to Joey's relationship with Pacey, which puts this squarely *after* Season Three, when Dawson and Pacey weren't speaking and Joey was dating Pacey. Even more awkward are the books set during summer breaks which directly contradict the events referred to on the TV show. For example, *Playing For Keeps* sees the whole gang, all still best friends, working at a summer camp, when in fact Pacey and Joey were on the *True Love*. These books are published by Pocket Pulse books in the US and by Channel Four books in the UK.

A second series of books started in 2001 – the *Dawson's Creek Suspense* books. At the time of writing only one had been published: *Lighthouse Legend* by Holly Henderson and Liz Tigelaar, who have written for the series (**321**, 'Show Me Love'). As a supernatural mystery thriller for younger readers this is entirely adequate – like the Three Investigators or the Famous Five – but having the Capeside gang play Scooby-Doo doesn't work at all. This book actually features real ghosts! Also, the relationships are as they were Season One or Two and bear no resemblance to the period of the series in which the book purports to be set – the summer after Season Three. Announced at the time of going to press were:

#1 Lighthouse Legend   by   Holly Henderson and Liz Tigelaar
#2 Bayou Blues   by   Anne Fricke, Barbara Siebert and
                             Barbara Siebertz
#3 Mysterious Boarder by   Holly Henderson and Liz Tigelaar

Music

To date there have been two soundtrack CDs released featuring music from the series.

Songs From Dawson's Creek
This CD has surfaced in a number of variations. The US, Canada and Australia had a limited run of five collectable covers, a group shot and one cover each for Jen, Pacey, Dawson and Joey. There was also an enhanced version which contained some screensavers and wallpapers for computers. International versions featured a number of bonus tracks, none of which appeared on the show, so your guess is as good as mine as to why they're on the CD at all, but the track listing for the US and Canadian version ran:

Kiss Me	Sixpence None The Richer (**206, 218**)
Lose Your Way	Sophie B Hawkins (**219**)
Feels Like Home	Chantal Kreviazuk (**218**)
Life's A Bitch	Shooter (**211, 219**)
Ready For A Fall	PJ Olssen (**220**)
Stay You	Wood (**309**)
Any Lucky Penny	Nikki Hassman (**218**)
Shimmer	Shawn Mullins (**218**)
London Rain (Nothing Heals Me Like You Do)	Heather Nova (**201, 221, 322**)
To Be Loved	Curtis Stigers (**219**)
Letting Go	Sozzi (**222**)
Cry Ophelia	Adam Cohen (**221**)
Did You Ever Love Somebody	Jessica Simpson (**206**)
I Don't Want To Wait	Paula Cole (theme song)

Songs From Dawson's Creek Volume II

I Think I'm In Love With You	Jessica Simpson
Crazy For This Girl	Evan & Jaron (**408**)
Respect	Train (**404**)
I'm Gonna Make You Love Me	The Jayhawks (**403**)
Givin' Up On You	Lara Fabian

Superman	Five For Fighting (**402**)
If I Am	Nine Days (**411**)
Never Saw Blue Like That	Shawn Colvin (**403**)
I Think God Can Explain	Splender (**411**)
Teenage Dirtbag	Wheatus (**409**)
Broken Boy	Michal (**411**)
Just Another	Pete Yorn (**405**)
Show Me Heaven	Jessica Andrews (**421**)
Daydream Believer	Mary Beth Maziarz (**319, 423**)

'Teenage Dirtbag' was not included on most international versions, but loads of bonus tracks were, none of which featured in the show. At the time of writing a soundtrack CD featuring Adam Fields' superb scores for Seasons One and Four was being planned but had not yet been confirmed.

Web

Official Sites

The *Dawson's Creek* web presence, which is centred on www.dawsonscreek.com, is one of the very best TV show websites around and it takes quite some time to find all the goodies hidden inside. It has a complete episode guide, clips and stills from each episode, it sometimes contains scenes which were cut from episodes (two scenes that were cut from **423**, Coda, were especially interesting), preview clips for upcoming stuff, polls, chatrooms and all the usual stuff.

In addition surfers can poke their noses into the computers of each of the six main characters (Andie's site is closed now) and read their emails, instant message chats, journals, homework assignments and so forth at www.dawsonsdesktop.com. All the material ties in closely with the episodes and adds depth and follow-ups on characters and storylines that may appear to have ended too abruptly on the show. For example, you could find out that Tom, Jen's psychiatrist, secretly attended her graduation ceremony but only told her that later by email, or, you could read Andie's postcard to the gang when she was away in Italy. It is a superb expansion of the Capeside world. If you're going cold turkey in between seasons you can read the characters' summer diaries and find out what they're doing while they're not on screen.

But it doesn't end there. Other extras are hidden away on www.capeside.net, such as the Potter B&B site, and in the Virtual Eyes section (www.capeside.net/virtualeyes/) you can read a less sympathetic view of the gang's activities, as well as Abby's Diary. Capeside High also has a site of its own at www.capesidehigh.com and here you can read regular rants from Pacey about whatever's getting his goat this week. Finally you can view the online version of the Capeside High yearbook at dynamic.dawsonscreek.com/yearbook/main.cfm. With the gang leaving both High School and Capeside at the end of Season Four, a lot of these sites might be mothballed now, but with luck they'll remain online as an archive of older material, and they're well worth a visit.

For behind the scenes info check out www.dawsonscreek.com/
newsletter where all your questions can be answered by those in
the know, and there's an archive of interviews with the team that
make the show. Finally there's the superb music guide at
www.dawsonscreekmusic.com, which details every song in every
episode, where in the episode it was heard, when that song or
artist has appeared in other episodes, and contains sound clips
and links to the sites of all the artists.

Unofficial Sites
For a while the best *Creek* fan site was the mighty 'I Hate Jen!'
but it's gone now and for obvious reasons fan sites and
commentary sites are more open to change than the official ones,
so don't blame me if they're not there by the time you read this.
I'll just point out a few of the best and you can find your way
from there . . .
  www.paceyspond.com is a good all round site
  members.netscapeonline.co.uk/accessdcreek/ has good tran-
scripts of episodes
  www.mightybigtv.com/show.cgi?show = 3 is the place to go if
you don't mind the show being ripped mercilessly, but often
hilariously, to shreds. It used to be a *Creek* only site, but now
there are loads of shows covered here.
  For behind the scenes news updated regularly hit
dcd.fanforum.com

http://www.sixesandsevens.net/troubledwaters
If you liked or hated this book, agreed or disagreed with any of
my reviews or, God forbid, found any errors, please let me know
by visiting my website.

People

Kevin Williamson

Scream (1996), *Scream 2* (1997), *Scream 3* (2000): All three self-aware horror films were directed by Wes Craven, but Williamson wrote the first two.

I Know What You Did Last Summer (1997): Another knowing horror film. Williamson wrote the screenplay.

The Faculty (1998): Williamson wrote this excellent horror movie version of *The Breakfast Club* (see **106**, 'Detention').

Halloween H20 – Twenty Years Later (1998): Michelle Williams featured, the *Creek*'s Steve Miner directed, Williamson co-produced. Too short and not really very good.

Teaching Mrs Tingle (1999): Katie Holmes starred in the first film Williamson both wrote and directed. Not as good as it should have been.

Her Leading Man (2001): Williamson's second attempt at directing, from a script he co-wrote with current *Dawson's Creek* executive producer Greg Berlanti.

Cursed (2001): Another Williamson script.

Williamson has created two TV shows: *The Wasteland* (see the intro page to Season Three) and the forthcoming *Glory Days*. He has an official web site at www.kevinwilliamson.com.

James Van Der Beek

Laputa: Castle in the Sky (1986): A young James provided the voice of the hero for the US release of this Japanese animated movie.

Angus (1995): The film that was supposed to make James a star, but didn't. He plays a bully.

I Love You, I Love You Not (1996): Another flop, this time James had a small role alongside Claire Danes.

Harvest (1999): Filmed before *Dawson's Creek* but released after, this independent film features James as a 'preppy pothead'.

Varsity Blues (1999): James plays the anti-Dawson in this by-the-numbers, yet surprisingly enjoyable, football movie from MTV. The film was big hit.

Scary Movie (2001): A brief cameo as himself.

Storytelling (2001): James featured as a college student who at one point has a gay sex scene. His entire role was apparently cut from the film by the producers.

Jay And Silent Bob Strike Back (2001): Another brief cameo, again as himself.

Texas Rangers (2001): A western, directed by Steve Miner which should, with luck, propel James into the higher reaches of big screen stardom.

On TV: *Clarissa Explain It All* (1991)

Aliens In The Family (1996)

The Panel (1998)

Saturday Night Live (1999)

There are numerous fan sites devoted to him, a list of them is available here: www.bomis.com/rings/vanderbeek.

Katie Holmes

The Ice Storm (1997): Superb film from Ang Lee with a small role for pre-*Creek* Holmes.

Disturbing Behaviour (1998): High school version of *The Stepford Wives*, in which Holmes looks moody, pouts a lot, and runs away from things.

Go (1999): Excellent episodic film. Holmes has little to do but gets some good scenes at the end.

Muppets From Space (1999): Cameo in which Joshua Jackson and Holmes (as Joey and Pacey) hang out with the Muppets and wish that Dawson were around.

Teaching Mrs Tingle (1999): Holmes kidnaps a teacher in Kevin Williamson's directorial debut.

Wonder Boys (2000): Holmes appears as a red cowboy boot-wearing college student who has a crush on Michael Douglas.

The Gift (2000): Holmes goes topless and develops a southern accent in a short scene as a murder victim.

Phone Booth (2001): Joel Schumacher thriller.

Abandon (2002): Psychic thriller with Holmes as lead.

The two best Katie Holmes fan sites are www.katie-holmes.com and www.kateside.com.

Joshua Jackson

Crooked Hearts (1991)

The Mighty Ducks (1992), *D2: The Mighty Ducks* (1994), *D3: The Mighty Ducks* (1996): Trilogy of Disney films about an ice hockey team, starring Emilio Estevez.

Digger (1993)

Andre (1994)

Magic In The Water (1995): *Free Willie*-a-like whale film.

Robin Of Locksley (1996): Younger version of Robin Hood.

Scream 2 (1997): Cameo as a film class student.

Apt Pupil (1998): Bryan Singer's adaptation of a Stephen King novella starring Ian McKellen.

Urban Legend (1998): Post-Scream horror flick with Josh as a bleached-blond college student who hates the theme to *Dawson's Creek*.

Cruel Intentions (1999): Bleached blond Josh as gay conspirator in brief but very amusing cameo.

Muppets From Space (1999): See Katie Holmes.

The Skulls (2000): Josh's first leading role in a thriller about a secret society at an Ivy League college. By-the-numbers but actually very good, and Josh is excellent.

Gossip (2000): Small role as an accused rapist in an excellent psychological thriller. Another in Josh's long line of well-performed cameo roles.

The Safety of Objects (2001)

Lone Star State Of Mind (2001): Josh is the lead in a film directed by the *Creek*'s David Semel.

He has also done some television movies:

Ronnie and Julie (1996): High School version of Romeo and Juliet with Josh as Ronnie.

On The Edge Of Innocence (1997): Teen movie about escapees from a psychiatric hospital. Josh's character apparently believes he's engaged to an alien.

The Laramie Project (2001).

While, on TV:

The Outer Limits: Episode: 'Music Of the Spheres' (1997)

The Simpsons: In 'Lisa the Tree Hugger' Josh voices Jesse Grass (2000)

Fan site: www.joshua-jackson.net

Michelle Williams

Lassie (1994): Revamp of evergreen collie dog movie.

Species (1995): Michelle played the young alien that grew up into Natasha Henstridge.

Timemaster (1995): Kiddie sci-fi.

A Thousand Acres (1997): A modern update of King Lear starring Michelle Pfeiffer and Jessica Lange.

Halloween H20 – Twenty Years Later (1998): See Kevin Williamson.

Dick (1999): Comedy about Watergate that works really well if you've an encyclopaedic knowledge of Nixon's downfall.

But I'm A Cheerleader (1999)

Prozac Nation (2000): Adaptation of Elizabeth's Wurtzel's best-selling book, also starring Anne Heche and Christina Ricci.

Perfume (2001): Film of Patrick Susskind's disturbing historical blockbuster.

Me Without You (2001): Williams effortlessly masters an English accent and gives a superb performance in this terrific Britflick.

Beatrice (2001): Williams stars as the eponymous Beatrice.

Her TV movies are:

My Son Is Innocent (1996)

Killing Mr Griffin (1997): Kevin Williamson's film *Teaching Mrs Tingle* was originally called *Killing Mrs Tingle*, this is a similar idea.

If These Walls Could Talk 2 (2000): Multi-award-winning episodic movie in which Williams has a lesbian affair with Chloë Sevigny.

And on TV *Step By Step* (1991)

Home Improvement: Episode: 'Wilson's Girlfriend' (1993)

Baywatch: Episode: 'Race Against Time – Part One' (1995)

The best fan site is at www.michellefan.com

Kerr Smith

Lucid Days In Hell (1999)

Hit And Runway (1999): Smith is a gay actor in this comedy about film making.

The Broken Hearts Club (2000): See **409**, 'Kiss Kiss Bang Bang'.

Final Destination (2000): Horror flick about Death hunting down plane crash survivors. Smith gets a good role.

The Forsaken (2001): Smith picks up a hitcher and then has to help him kill a powerful vampire.

Pressure (2001)

On TV, in *As The World Turns*: Smith did a year as Ryder Hughes in this long running supersoap.

Baywatch: Episode: 'The Natural' (1998)

Official site: www.celebrityblvd.com/kerrsmith/

Best fan sites: www.kerrsmith.com and home.hiwaay.net/ ~emedia/kv/kerr.html

Meredith Monroe

Strong Island Boys (1997)

Fallen Arches (1998)

Mary Jane's Last Dance (2001)

Full Ride (2001)

G-S.P.O.T. (2001): Meredith is co-producing this film as well as appearing in it.

Movies on TV include:

Beyond the Prairie: The True Story of Laura Ingalls Wilder (2000), *Beyond the Prairie 2: The True Story of Laura Ingalls Wilder* (2001): Meredith plays the eponymous Laura in this continuation of *The Little House On The Prairie*.

And her TV shows: *Hang Time* (1997)

Dangerous Minds: Meredith was a regular as Tracey Daiken.

Jenny: Episode: 'A Girl's Gotta Pierce' (1997)

Promised Land: Episode: 'Crushed' (1997)

Sunset Beach (1998)

Night Man: Episode: 'You Are Too Beautiful' (1998)

The Magnificent Seven: Episode: 'Manhunt' (1998)

Players: Episode: 'Con-undrum' (1998)

Cracker (the American version, otherwise known as *Fitz*): Episode: 'Faustian Fitz' (1999).

Meredith has also done a number of high profile TV commercials for 7-up, Mentos and Ford amongst others, as well as photographic magazine ads. She also was the photo model for the covers of *Nancy Drew* books for a while.

Best fan site: <u>meredith.almilli.com</u>

If You Like This, You May Also Like . . .

The 80s' teen flicks of John Hughes were a huge influence on the early years of the *Creek* – and the show is littered with references to both Hughes films in general and some in particular. The most significant references are listed alongside the films:

Sixteen Candles (1984) – **202**, 'Crossroads'
The Breakfast Club (1985) – **106**, 'Detention'
Weird Science (1985)
Pretty In Pink (1986) – **316**, 'To Green With Love'
Ferris Bueller's Day Off (1986) – **404**, 'Future Tense'

Cameron Crowe is a favourite of the *Dawson's Creek* writers and his films are referenced constantly, especially in Seasons Three and Four:

Fast Times At Ridgemont High (1982)
Say Anything (1989) – referenced too many times to count, but especially in **309**, 'Four To Tango'; **314**, 'The Valentine's Day Massacre'; **411**, 'The Tao Of Dawson'.
Singles (1992) - **411**, 'The Tao Of Dawson'
Jerry Maguire (1996) – **215**, ' . . . That Is The Question'
Almost Famous (200) – **411**, 'The Tao Of Dawson'

Other 80s' teen flicks, both cutesy and dark, include:

The Sure Thing (1985) – **304**, 'Home Movies'
Better Off Dead (1985) and *One Crazy Summer* (1986), starring John Cusack, written and directed by Savage Steve Holland.
Heathers (1989) and *Pump Up The Volume* (1990), both starring Christian Slater.

On television the most significant precursor to *Dawson's Creek* was the series *My So-Called Life*, which starred Claire Danes. Like the *Creek* it paid close attention to the lives of the lead character's parents and it featured a gang of kids in high school who had angst coming out of their ears: including an alcoholic delinquent, a gay kid and a self-aware, conflict-addled lead, albeit female. It only ran for a season but if you ever get the chance to see it, don't pass it up, it's excellent.